SERGEANT KENNEDY'S WORLD WAR II DIARY

An account of his three years overseas
in the Army Air Force

by

William M. Kennedy

Order this book online at www.trafford.com
or email orders@trafford.com

Most Trafford titles are also available at major online book retailers.

Note for Librarians: A cataloguing record for this book is available from Library
and Archives Canada at www.collectionscanada.ca/amicus/index-e.html

Printed in Victoria, BC, Canada.

ISBN: 978-1-4269-0438-7

*Our mission is to efficiently provide the world's finest, most comprehensive book publishing
service, enabling every author to experience success. To find out how to publish your
book, your way, and have it available worldwide, visit us online at www.trafford.com*

Trafford rev. 5/27/10

www.trafford.com

North America & international
toll-free: 1 888 232 4444 (USA & Canada)
phone: 250 383 6864 ♦ fax: 812 355 4082

PROLOGUE

It was July 30, 1942 when I entered the service. I had a bad attitude about war and the military. One of the reasons was that I was leaving my bride of two months; another was that, at 24, I felt a little long-in-the-tooth for soldiering. It had been five years and four months from the time I was graduated from High School until I got out of college with an economics major and no marketable skill.

During that time I had failed several courses in two years of chemical engineering at Penn State, transferred to Allegheny College for my junior year, dropped out for a year to work in a steel mill, finally was graduated with the class of 1941.

I was angry at myself because I was unable to master the subjects in science that were required to get a good job in industry. I decided that I would learn accounting (easier than the tough science courses) and moved to Cleveland where I could go to night school and would be near the girl I hoped to marry.

The machine shops in Cleveland were busy in July, 1941. I was able to get a job in one of them as a timekeeper on the four to twelve shift. I took a course in cost accounting that met in the morning at Cleveland College. It was going to require several years of accounting courses but this program would have to be put on hold.

My feelings about the war were mixed – from the time that Germany marched into Poland in 1939 I believed that we would be in the war. What was happening in Europe was over there. I wanted England to win but not enough to go over there and fight. Then, on December 7th suddenly after Pearl Harbor, we were in it. I did not talk about it but I thought if it were not for my family, I would have been a conscientious objector. As I reviewed my life up to the point when I entered the service, it seemed to me that I had not made many smart moves. I loved life, did not have a death wish, and hoped to come through the war alive. I would settle for a tour of duty, undistinguished but honorable. I told Barbara that I would probably be gone for a year and a half.

We boarded the train at the railroad station under the Terminal Tower after kissing our loved ones goodbye. The first stop was Camp Perry where in two days we got shots that made our arms sore, were issued uniforms and mailed our civilian clothes back home.

From Camp Perry most of us went to Camp Croft in South Carolina for basic training. This lasted four-and-a-half weeks during which time we learned to make beds, shoot rifles and talk in obscenities, the language of soldiers. We were not allowed to leave the base and the exercising, regular hours of sleeping, eating and absence of alcohol soon made even the office workers and winebibbers as healthy as horses. It had been my custom in civilian life to begin the day in a serene manner with a breakfast of orange juice, toast and coffee. Breakfasts in basic training were full-course meals of oatmeal, meat, eggs, fried potatoes and gravy which I picked at briefly at first. In a few days I ate a hardy meal along with the others.

Afterwards, some of us were sent to a camp up in Little Falls, Minnesota for Army Aviation Military Police training. This was our permanent assignment and we learned who our commissioned and non-commissioned officers were. We reviewed what we had learned in basic training, marched, hiked and learned the names of the other members of our company. Except for the non-commissioned officers we were all new to the army and did not know each other. There were about a hundred of us in the company. September was cold in northern Minnesota – it snowed enough on September 29th for us to have a snowball fight.

When we moved to Lockbourne Air Field near Columbus, Ohio on October 7th, we were sure that it would be warmer and for some of us it was closer to home. We were there for only three weeks.

The next move was to Camp Kilmer, New Jersey – rumored to be the last stop before going overseas. We arrived on Thursday, October 29th, were issued our bedding, ate our evening meal, and made plans to go to New York City over the weekend. At four o'clock the next morning, the first sergeant woke us up and told us to pack for embarkation. I had been in the army three months when our company was shipped overseas.

ABOARD THE TROOP SHIP WEST POINT

My first ocean voyage – We were on this ship thirty days from New York City to Bombay, India.

We heard that there were 15,000 troops on the ship.

William M. Kennedy

1942

WORLD WAR II – MY STORY

It was Friday October 30, 1942 when we quick-marched aboard
the West Point in the New York harbor. From the time when
I trotted up the gangplank of that ship until I walked down it
thirty days later, I was hungry. We were encouraged to move
quickly by the guards stationed at fifty-foot intervals on the
dock. I followed at a quick trot the man in front of me to our
quarters which turned out to be a compartment on U deck.

Oct. 30, 1942 Friday – Came on board at 5:00 P.M. Found
Quarters and were fed. I could see that the mess hall on the ship
was designed to reduce the time required to feed the troops.
The men eat while standing at four-foot-high counters which
extend the entire width of the mess hall. The ship was the former America built in 1940—renamed the West Point.

Oct. 31, Saturday – Went on guard duty today from 5 P.M.
to 9 P.M. Many more soldiers came on board – lots of officers.

Nov. 1, Sunday – When I woke up we were at sea. We left
about 2:30 last night. Our course seems to be southwest, from
what I can see. We have an escort of four other ships; don't
know whether there are any other troop ships or if they are all
cruisers.

Nov. 2, Monday – Up at 4:30 to go on guard duty. Our
company will have guard duty for the entire trip. When we
roll out in the morning it is completely dark except for the
few red lights at every fifty paces in the corridors. Our water
is rationed. Salt water is turned on in the faucets for one hour
a day. We use this to wash and do our laundry. Drinking water is available at the various fountains, but there is always a
line of men filling their canteens. Chow is terrible with lines
of men crowding, sweating, pushing, swearing all over the
ship. Food is good when the end of the line is reached. Two
meals are served each day. It takes four hours for each meal

to be served.. Our compartment is in U Deck. There are seventeen of us arranged like this:

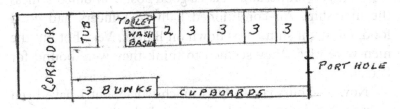

Our Compartment – West Point

Our quarters are comfortable compared to those of the men on the main deck where there are no facilities for washing etc. Some men sleep in the mess hall and some on the steel floor of the promenade deck . Troops are allowed on the main deck (front of the ship) and on the promenade deck (rear of the ship).

This morning we are about 300 miles off the coast of Florida. It is quite warm, even on deck. Our course seems to be northeast. An airplane flew quite low beside our ship at about eleven o'clock this morning. It was a large Navy plane. We seem to have left the convoy as I could see no ships this morning. The guesses of the men as to where we are going:

1- Cairo, Egypt (around the tip of Africa),

2- Africa, Dakar

3- South America

4- Carribean Islands—this sounds the most logical to me.

5- Capetown—rumor is that there is a new base there. November 3 – Tuesday—The sea became choppy today and a few men were seasick. We have been told to set our watches one hour ahead tomorrow afternoon at 2 P. M. Got a cold last night. Took a bath today in salt water that was so cold that I could only keep one foot in the water at a time. Felt cleaner. Mess has improved so that the entire ship eats in an hour and a half. We hear that the senior officers called the warrant officers together and told them to solve the problem and bring order out of chaos. It appears that our first stop will be Rio as this rumor persists.

Nov. 4—Wednesday—Had a good post near officers' mess the first shift. Air-conditioned hallway. Officers had good food. On night shift I was down on B deck. Very hot but the men were nice. They seemed to think they were bound for Persia.

Nov. 5—Thursday. Cold is much worse, but I have been eating and keeping out of bed as I think this is the best way to fight off a cold and grippe. Had a nice post Thursday night. All I did was sit behind a counter in an office (with an electric fan on) and guard a safe. Found out that one of the men smuggled aboard a little puppy. When their captain found out he had the dog examined and deflead. The men said that the captain talked to the ship's captain as he did not want the puppy destroyed because the men had become attached to it. They said that the ship's captain had the puppy. Last night our time advanced one-half hour. When we were in our bunks before we fell asleep the man in the bunk below me and the man in the bunk above me had the following conversation:

First soldier, "The way I look at it, when your time comes, it comes and you ain't gonna live ten minutes more."
Second soldier, "Personally, I don't think the Lord made this United States ship to go down."
F.S. "Yeah, you got so much happiness and so much bad times and I'm gonna use up all them moments of pleasure to the best advantage."
S.S. "I don't know whether to have my mother put my money in government bonds or not. The government's not gonna be able to pay off. Look at the money they're spending.
F.S. "Yeah, but look at the taxes."
S.S. "That's right too. I want them to put what the family doesn't need in bonds."

F.S. "You just let your mother do what she thinks is best, she'll do what's right. Boy, before I come in the army, I had life easy. I'd work a month, make a little money, not too much, cause every time I made a pile, my wife would haul me into court for non-support. Then I'd get government security for a while, then I'd work a while, and work it that way."

S.S. "Yeah, when your time comes, you don't think you're goin' to heaven, do you?"

F.S. "Damn right, I don't do nuthin."

S.S. "You swear, don't you?"

F.S. "Uh huh."

S.S. "You run around with women, don't you?"

F.S. "A little."

S.S. "That's the greatest sin there is"-cordin to the Bible."

F.S. "Everybody that's married is sinnin."

S.S. "Yeah, but there's legal sinnin' and illegal sinnin."

F.S. "What the hell do you know about the Bible?"

S.S. "By God, I know as much about the Bible as any bastard in the United States. When I was twelve, thirteen, four-teen, I used to read the Bible all the time."

F.S. "Yeah, how long did David live?"

S.S. "He was an old son-of-a-bitch, he lived a couple of hun-dred years."

F.S. "Nine hundred years."

S.S. "You're goin' straight to hell when you die."

F.S. "When my time comes, I'm going' to heaven. By gees, I remember when I used to see me goil, she never used to send me out when she wanted anything. She would put on her glad rags and go down and get it. I remem-ber one time we was in her apartment and in walks her husband."

S.S. "Was he mad?"

F.S. "They was separated. After a while we each bought a pint of whiskey and drank them , then I put on my hat

to go and she says, 'Where are you goin', you stay here.'
and she left her husband go home."
S.S. "There's a lot of queers around New York, huh?"
F.S. "You said it."

Nov. 9, Monday. My cold is much better. I have had a post
on the sun deck for the last two days. My shift was at such a
time that I could see the sunset and the sunrise. All four of
them were beautiful. From the sun deck the night skies are won-
drous, full of a million stars. I finished War and Peace. Now, I
have to decide what my next book will be. Guess I should wait
to see what is available.

Nov. 10. Tuesday. An uneventful day. We expected to reach
Rio today, but I guess we were premature. All sorts of rumors
around about men leaving the ship at Rio. Personally, I don't
think anyone will .

Nov. 11. Wednesday. At last we sighted land. Only one who
has been at sea for a long time can realize what a very welcome
sight it is. We are not allowed on deck so we all crowded around
the port holes (one to a cabin) to see the harbor. The view is
beautiful. The houses have red-tiled roofs and the mountains
seem to rise directly out of the sea. We were a half day coming
into the harbor from the time we first sighted land. My guard
post was outside on the promenade deck. From here the view
of the city was excellent.

The ship was anchored at the prow only and it revolved
slowly counter-clockwise so that I was able to see the entire
harbor side of the city in the four hours that I was on guard.
We seem to be in the middle of the harbor about a half mile
east of the city. The first impression that I had was that we
were on a lake. The harbor seems to be surrounded by mountains, even at the entrance. The mountains rise up out of the
sea on all sides of the harbor and the city of Rio seems built
on the sea with successive ranges of mountains rising behind
it like a backdrop. It appears to be a clean, modern, busy, liv-

able city, differing from an American city only in the color added by its red-tiled roofs on some of the buildings. To the left of the city Sugar Loaf Mountain bulges up like a great gumdrop. We could see the cable car suspended on a thin thread between the top of the mountain and the level ground of the shore at an angle of about thirty degrees. What a trip that must be! The western shore of the harbor—that part directly opposite the business district—appears to be the factory district. I noticed some oil refineries too. Ferries chug to this district from the business district and back again, carrying early-morning commuters. A seaplane made several trips at fifteen minute intervals from the business district to a point almost out to Sugar Loaf. I wondered if this was a commuting service for the wealthy. Now to get back to the western shore—the mountains in the background loom up in successive ridges just as on the other side of the harbor. The foreground is something out of a Disney pastoral: several small islands, each one seemingly complete in itself, guard the shore. These islands are green, smooth knolls on which can be seen cattle, houses, docks, and even people.

Nov. 12. Thursday. This morning of the second day in the harbor at Rio, the Shell Oil tanker steamed out to our ship , and the long business of refueling began. I was on guard on the outside deck and was able to see the men on the tanker. They wore open sandals that looked comfortable and spoke only Portuguese. That night I was again outside and when the full yellow moon came up from behind the mountains, I could only wish that Barbara were here.

Nov. 13. Friday. The sailors had hoped to get shore leave in Rio, but no one was allowed on shore except the captain, who got his orders and came back on ship. We left Rio at 4 PM today. As I took my post at 5 PM , I was able to see the harbor. We passed very close to Sugar Loaf Mountain which looked more awesome than it had when seen from a distance. The sides of the mountain are steep, furrowed rock of a dark brown color with here and there a patch of green foliage. The mountain rises out of the sea which lapps its sides continuously. Further on we passed a small rocky island off our port side. On this island the only sign of habitation was a light house. I watched the light house until it became a tiny speak on the horizon.

Nov. 16, Monday. Nothing eventful has happened except that the weather has become colder, the sea rougher. We are heading southeast. Our next stop will be Bombay. We were told this Saturday night on fairly good authority. When we reach Bombay we will be separated according to our shipping numbers and sent to various destinations. Things in general look good. Willie Hoefling has been in the hospital with grippe for the last three days.

Nov. 18, Wednesday. Morning : "Come on, roll out, evah bodie, roll out". the first sergeant shook me and continued on down the tiers and rows of bunks, shaking each body in each bunk and repeating over and over, "Come on, roll out, time to git up, evah bodie, roll out." The first sergeant was a tough old army man – a firm practitioner in early rising (4:30 A.M.) He was not old in years as he was strong enough to flatten anyone in the company.

The next sound that I hear emanates from the larynx of the soldier in the bunk over mine as he clears his throat and spits across the aisle right in the middle of the bathroom floor. I think he must derive some feeling of power from this; possibly because of the greater distance from the top bunk to the floor. I jump out of my bunk, the middle one, and feel around for my shoes. There are no lights. It is black-out time, and except for the infrequent red lights in the hallway outside of our cabin, everything is in darkness. After I find my shoes, I stumble into the corridor and put them on feeling for each eyelit and threading the shoestring into the same. After I have my shoes laced, I stumble back into the room. By this time the stateroom is bedlam and since my bunk is located in the entrance opposite the bathroom door, the area in which I am dressing is like Times

Square at 5:30 P.M. on a Friday night. Men from the back of the stateroom are crowding into the bathroom and out into the corridor – then back into the stateroom to collect forgotten life belts, or pistol belts or hats.

After I have felt my way into my pants and shirt, I unhook my pistol belt from the bunk, take out my canteen, dash across the three-feet of space between me and the bathroom door, wash my face in canteen water. My face feels greasy but it's better than nothing. I dash back to my bunk, put the canteen back in the holder, fasten my pistol belt on, and realize that my hat is somewhere in my barracks bag, which is somewhere under the bottom bunk. I drag out the barracks bag, untie the ropes, and feel around for my hat. No luck! I rush out into the hall and thread my way through other soldiers, swaying with the listing of the ship, bumping and swearing, being sworn at, and finally locate the first sergeant who has the only black-out flashlight in the company. I find my way through the same maze back to the stateroom, drag out my barracks bag again and with the help of the black-out flashlight, find my hat which I put on immediately.

I grab my steel helmet, realize that I have forgotten my glasses, delve into the pocket of my jacket which is hanging on the inside edge of my bunk, and locate them. I put on my glasses, grab my life belt, rush out into the hall, and try to find my sergeant of the guard. I wish I had a glass of orange juice to start off the morning but, hell, you can't have everything.

Our MP company occupied six staterooms on U deck. These were good quarters for enlisted men, probably because we had guard duty for the entire trip. The whole ship was crowded – we heard that there were 15,000 of us – the staterooms were crowded and hot. Most of us showered about once a week. Some of the troops had to be reminded to shower.

Lloyd Bowman who was in one of the other staterooms told us about their problem. Homsey was a big 250 pound, six-foot-three Oklahoma boy who sweated all the time. After three weeks their whole stateroom began to stink of Homsey. It was generally agreed that someone should tell Homsey to take a shower, but as Bowman said, there were no volunteers. The feeling among the intelligentsia in their stateroom was that anyone who volunteered to tell Homsey to do something would volunteer to be the point man in a combat infantry squad (the point man's job was to draw enemy fire to determine the location of the enemy). In addition to his size, Homsey had the muscles and mind of a Clydesdale draft horse, was naturally illtempered, quick to take offense and had no sense of humor. The concerned men of their stateroom concluded that the problem required the resolute, steadfast leadership of an officer; accordingly, they went to the lieutenant for the solution. The lieutenant sent word to Homsey to report to the orderly room. Sergeant Butler, the company clerk, reported the conversation:

Lieutenant:	"Homsey, how are the showers on the ship?"
Homsey:	"Pretty good, I guess sir."
Lt.:	"Do you use them, Homsey?"
Homsey:	"Yes, sir."
Lt.:	"When did you use them, Homsey?"
Homsey:	"Why, I don't rightly remember, Lieutenant."
Lt.:	"Well, Homsey I think you ought to take a shower today."
Homsey:	"Yes, sir."
	As far as we know, that's the only shower that Homsey took on the West Point.

Nov. 24, Tuesday. We have been at sea for 24 days and the officers who were so immaculate in their dark brown uniforms at the start of the trip have begun to look more like the enlisted men in their dress. We all look pretty bad. Ship life has settled down to a daily routine and we have accepted the cold weather around the cape and the warm weather of the Indian Ocean as a matter of course. The sunrise has been beautiful for the past several days and the moon, which has been full, lights up the ocean like a beacon. War news has been very favorable according to ship news and it seems to us that the war may be shorter than we expected. Today I wrote Barbara a V letter and I understand it is the only one that she will receive before Christmas. I wrote regular letters to Barbara and Mother yesterday. After our night shift Willie Hoefling and I talk about life at home. Willie is from Chicago. He talks about his brother-in-law, who is a commercial artist and a good guy. I talk about Barbara's sister Jean and her husband, Al who are both good guys. We talk about the places that we will see when we visit each other.

When we had been at sea for about a week whispers were heard about coffee being served in the mess hall at nine o'clock every night. Willie Hoefling and I investigated, found truth in the whispered rumors, and made a habit of drinking coffee in the mess hall every evening after we had finished our four hour tour of guard duty. Presently, the whispers became louder until finally it had been shouted all over the ship. When we went down for coffee one night the mess hall was packed with soldiers rattling canteen cups and conversing and cursing loudly. It should be explained here that the lights aboard ship were turned out at nine, except in the mess hall where the kitchen night shift held forth. After the soldiers had filled their canteen cups they would wonder through the corridors (still rattling canteen cups, still cursing, still shouting) until the wee hours of the morning – waking up officers and men. Grumbles were heard and action was taken.

One night when Willie and I had walked down the narrow steel stairway to the kitchen, we were met by a big fat M.P. who informed us that there was no more coffee. We went up to him and whispered confidentially in his ear that we were guard and had just come off guard duty. He let us in and we had coffee. The next day a bulletin announced that coffee was to be served for the guards at ten o'clock every night; thus, the mob of outsiders was kept out.

Willie and I began to drink this nectar of the gods with one Paul Prosser, a former WPA recreational leader from a little village in Pennsylvania. This soldier would entertain us with his true tales of famous gangsters. He had been an avid reader of TrueDetective. He knew who every gangsters' true sweetheart was, how each met his downfall, where each had operated, and many other interesting little sidelights about anyone who was notorious.

After nine o'clock when lights were out, no smoking was permitted anywhere on the ship. In the kitchen, however, this rule was winked at for some time, and when we came down for coffee after guard duty, we smoked until one of the MPs on duty told us to put out our cigarettes. Finally, a lieutenant was stationed in the mess hall and he ruled with an iron hand. There was no more smoking and we drank our coffee in the dark as the lieutenant decided that enough light filtered into the mess hall from the kitchen.

This coffee is watery, faintly colored with canned milk, flavored with sugar and tasting like dishwater. Yet we drank it and waited until ten o'clock to stand in line for more. Since we were served only two meals a day, we were so hungry that we thought a crust of bread to eat with the coffee was a delicacy.

One night Willie, Paul Prosser and I were having our coffee and pretending to be ordering our dinners at an eating establishment—a little game we played. The conversation went like this: Pvt. Kennedy "What will you have, gentleman, Oh waitress."

Pvt. Prosser,	in that expressionless monotone, dead-pan manner of his, "I'll just have hamburger with french fries and onions."
Pvt. Hoefling,	"Two of the same, relish on the hamburger and a double portion of coconut custard pie."
Pvt. K.	"I'll take two of your foot-in-diameter hamburgers with relish and a fresh peach pie with a quart of your home-made ice cream on top and hurry, waitress." (Simulates patting waitress on the fanny)
Pvt. H.	"Well, I'm full, how about you fellows?"
Pvts. P & K.	"yep"
Pvt. H.	"How about lighting a cigarette, Prosser?". Willie said this jokingly as the place is dark and there are lieutenants and MPs about fifteen feet from us.
P. Prosser.	"Say, I wonder if I could?"
Pvt. K.	"I don't see why not."
Pvt. H.	"Just step behind the post, no one will see you."

With that P. Prosser stepped behind a post and struck a match that seemed to glow for an eternity with a flash that lit up the entire mess hall and lit his cigarette. Willie H. And I stifled our laughter as the fat MP and the lieutenant looked around with their mouths open and the MP looked at the lieutenant and asked,

"Did somebody light a cigarette?"

in a tone that implied that he did not expect an answer as no damn fool would be lighting a cigarette in the dark when the guard is around. They picked up the threads of their broken

conversation and wove on. P. Prosser had outwitted the law of
the army.

P. Prosser,	noticing our nervous behavior, "What's the matter, somethin' wrong?"
Willie H.	"My God, that light looked like the Lindberg Beacon in Chicago."
Pvt. K.	"My God, Prosser, You're crazy."
P. Prosser:	"All famous criminals weren't afraid to take chances, John Dillinger –"
Willie H.	"Gimmie a light."

An added element of suspense to this comedy occurred every time P. Prosser took a drag on his cigarette. To do this he held his canteen cup over his mouth as though he were drinking and held the cigarette in his other hand in the cup. The reflection from the glow of the cigarette was cast over a radius of ten feet every time he took a drag. Willie and I were nervous wrecks, but we laughed and listened to P. Prosser's account of John Dillinger's betrayal by his "true girl friend".

The next night P. Prosser tried again. The MP barked,
"Put out that cigarette, you."

P. Prosser. "Cigarette? Me? Put out? Not allowed to smoke here?" All of this in that expressionless, monotone, dead-pan manner of his.

It looks as if there will be no more smoking in the mess hall at coffee time.

Wed. Nov. 25. The weather is hot. We know we really are in the Torrid Zone. The latest rumor is that we may be getting off at Bombay. We are having turkey tomorrow – I saw the crates of "Fine Turkeys" in the pantry. It may be a little like Thanksgiving; we can talk about having turkey, but most of us will be thinking about what it would be like at home.

Thursday Nov. 26. Thanksgiving. This is my first Thanksgiving away from home. Had a good post on the morning shift, outside on the top deck. Talked to a marine who had been to Black Mountain College near Asheville, North Carolina. Washed my suntans and other laundry and took a shower. We had a wonderful turkey dinner, with a menu. The dinner took a long time to serve and the last ones to eat were served vienna sausages instead of turkey. The day was terribly hot. We crossed the equator at 2:30 PM. What a different Thanksgiving!

Nov. 27, Friday. We expect to reach Bombay about Sunday and it would appear that all units are to leave the ship. I hope we do as Bombay sounds fascinating and India – that's adventure. The sea was choppy today, reminding me of Lake Erie and Cleveland and Mrs. K. My post was just outside the mess hall, very hot from the steam baths in which the men wash their mess kits. I washed my clothes in salt water (cold) yesterday and I'm afraid there is going to be an unpleasant aroma of soap about them. They look clean but the salt water won't wash out the soap. The orders are that we are to have clean khaki uniforms to debark in. When you take a bath in salt water your eyes burn, special soap must be used to get a lather, and if you wash your hair, it dries stiff and sticky.

One of the rules of the ship is that we must carry our life jackets with us at all times when we are out of our compartments, and our helmets with us when we go on deck or are on guard. It is 7:30 PM here, 11:30 AM at home. I wonder what Barbara is doing.

Nov. 28, Saturday. We have been ordered to be ready to debark tomorrow. It is not certain what units will leave the ship, but our company will not have any more guard duty on ship. It is a little cooler today. Last night Willie Hoefling, Paul Prossser and I went on deck after coffee time and talked under a million stars and a big silver moon. There was a cool breeze, a calm sea, and good talk of food and philosophy. Prosser is a good, honest, solid citizen, as harmless and well-meaning as any man

I have ever known. Romanovich, our company clerk, tells me that this diary will be worth a thousand dollars if I keep it up. He quotes Mark Twain about the value of a diary. Could be!

Nov. 29. Sunday. My post was outside from five to nine in the morning. Finally found the big dipper among the stars, for the first time since we left the U.S.A.

Strained my eyes looking for land—nothing until two o'clock in the afternoon. Then we saw it! That first feeling when you see land after seeing nothing but ocean for eighteen days. It's enough to convert a heathen. I was able to go on deck for a very short while after dark to see Bombay. It seems to me that the skyline of Bombay is a series of curves, not like New York and Rio which are angular. While we were coming into the harbor at Bombay, we passed any number of small native sail boats. After we had anchored, we could see that the harbor was full of them, large and small, with one, two, or three sails. One large rowboat came quite close to the ship. It was a native with his family. The male members wore fezzes of dark blue feathers on their heads.

In the evening Willie H. and I went on deck to watch the moon come up over the mountains. It came up at about midnight slowly and haltingly as though someone were hoisting it up on a pulley—raise it a little, stop, up a little more, stop, then, suddenly it is entirely visible over the mountain. Thought about one of the poets "she's a copper maiden dressed in a wisp of clouds". Stayed up too late.

Nov. 30, Monday. Today our ship took on water from a ship flying the French tricolor. We were allowed up on the promenade deck in the afternoon and from the deck we could see much of what was going on. Several native craft hung about the ship begging and trying to sell their wares. Native men wear shorts and shirts with long tails hanging out. Our C.O. told us that we were going to debark here and that we might get shore leave. Men with money had it changed to rupees. Sailors were given shore leave from five to eleven tonight. My post was at the stern on the port side and I was able to see the sunset. After I was off duty Willie H. and I had coffee and wieners (left over from supper) and good talk under the stars on deck.

Dec. 1, Tuesday. This is the hottest December first in my life – up to now. Sunrise was beautiful this morning. We took on oil today. The powerful little tugs took us to the dock right beside the Bombay Refreshment Center where "fresh water showers, dressing rooms, and light refreshments may be had".

On dock besides the host of natives of all casts in their native costumes, were English, Australian, and Scots officers. Those aboard ship with money have begun the complicated process of converting dollars into rupees and annas. Willie and I have been trying to figure a means of obtaining rupees without American dollars.

INDIA

5 ½ hours to see Bombay

8 days in a British rest camp in Deolali

Dec. 2, Wednesday. Well, Willie and I managed to borrow some rupees and this morning after guard we all set off for town. We started at nine o'clock and were told that we had to be back on the dock at 2;30. We started by walking down the dock, crossed the railroad track and began walking up the street which runs parallel to the dock. A native in a carriage began shouting at us giving us to understand that he wanted us to hire his carriage. We bargained with him and agreed on a rupee and a half (fifty cents) and a pack of American cigarettes for one hour. He drove us through the modern part of the city and into the native quarter. He stopped the carriage while the horse drank from a trough in the middle of a crossroad where I gave a native a cigarette. It seems that American cigarettes are considered special in India. Our driver couldn't understand English well enough to know exactly where we wanted to go, so we went where he wanted to take us.. Every time we stopped there were natives begging for annas—tiny black dirty mothers with their babies begging for them, toothless old men with rheumy eyes, withered shrunken faces and legs that looked too thin to support their frail bodies. It was a surprise to me that there were so many more natives than English in Bombay. I had always imagined that these cities of India were English cities with a large native population; instead, they are entirely native with a sprinkling of English people.

Our driver pointed out the post office, cinema, custom house, American market, and stopped the carriage at a little shop in the native section. He motioned for us to follow him into the shop which was a curio shop. The native proprietor took us to the back of the shop where we found several officers bargaining with the clerks for carved ivory, metalwork, silks, and sandalwood articles. We looked around and walked out followed by our driver who wanted to know what was wrong. We told him "No payday". We rode around a little longer until our hour was up, paid our driver and set off on foot. We walked through the English quarter of that section of the city and then set off to see the native quarter.

We turned down one of the little side streets in the native section and were alone with the natives. It is hard to describe the poverty and squalor. All of the people were dressed in rags, except the youngest children who wore nothing. Children played in the street, left their games to follow us and beg, "Anna, sahib, one anna, sahib", finally gave up and returned to their play. Native shops dealing in pices instead of annas (twelve pices equal one anna) occupied the corners. Natives walked here and there carrying their packages, baskets, and jars on their heads. In the windows, hallways, and doors of all the buildings we could see people. Every available inch of space seemed to be used. Oxen and cows stood at intervals along the street.

As we walked down one of the streets we saw an ox pulling a two-wheeled oxcart carrying a small tank of Shell kerosene. The tank was bright yellow with the red shell emblem, reminding us of the other civilization. We had walked so far into the winding maze of streets that we were lost. We were the only whites in the area. Native women with naked babies and native children followed us with their incessant chant of "Anna, sahib, anna"—always accompanied with that gesture with the right hand held palm outward to the forhead. Goats wondered at will all through the native dwellings, and the smell of the native quarter was comparable to that of decaying flesh. It seems to me that the natives must be immune to disease or they could never survive in the midst of such filth. We turned a corner and there at the end of the street we saw civilization.

We walked down one of the main streets, stopped at a clean little shop which sold "french coffee and cakes". This was not very filling, although it tasted good after the army food. When we came out of this shop we ran into Fabiz from our outfit. The three of us walked through the business section visiting shops and comparing prices with those in the USA. Willie wondered if the Bank of England would cash one of his checks. We told him that he would be wasting his time to ask. We went into a British Canteen near the business section and had tea, buttered toast and cakes. This was the best place to eat that we found in Bombay, though they served nothing but light lunches. The women who worked there seemed to be volunteers, like our U.S.O. Our waitress had been to New York City. She said she liked to shop there. When we left there we walked through the Army and Navy Department Store. It was quite modern with golf clubs, stationery, leather goods and candy for sale.

Another store in the business section sold alcoholic beverages and Willie thought we ought to buy some whiskey. I tried to discourage him as it was past noon and we were due back at the ship by 2:30. We made it past that store but we couldn't persuade Willie to pass by the next one that sold spirits. Willie went in and bought a pint of "Okay Whiskey". Fabiz and Willie began to sip the whiskey and Willie soon decided that he could write a check and ask the Bank of England branch to cash it. The Okay Whiskey and the heat soon had Willie and Fabiz very unsociable. It became a matter of me pulling and pushing and dragging them (finally!) back to the dock. Neither one of them was in shape to do guard duty, but I ended up at the post on the gang plank – an interesting experience.

No one was allowed to bring any alcoholic beverage aboard ship, so anyone who had any with him finished it, with a little help from his friends, before coming up the gangplank. There were some fights which we broke up. It took four of us to bring one man aboard. Another soldier had rented a car to see Bombay. He drove it down the busy road that ran parallel to the dock, parked it, and began to walk across the road with the cars driving in both directions. He passes out cold in the middle of the road. All of the traffic avoided him. Four of us stopped the automobiles, picked him up, and carried him to his bunk on the ship. It was some day.

Dec. 3. Thursday. (Six months ago Barbara and I were married). When I was on guard in the early morning shift on the promenade deck, I had a clean view of the dock. It was deserted except for a native who slept curled up on one corner. Around seven o'clock he woke up, took off his clothes and his turban and washed under a stream of water that came out of a pipe that stood about six feet high and was apparently intended for public use. He dried himself with his hands, put on his clothes, wound his turban on his head, and was ready to begin his day.

We moved off the ship at noon and waited on the station platform for two hours until the train appeared. It was a funny military train on the European model separated into open compartments (eight men to a compartment) with the aisle on the right side of the car. The car was made of wood and had only four wheels, as did most of the Indian railroad cars that I saw. The first part of our journey was through Bombay. I can't say the slums, it was simply the native quarter. As we road slowly through this section, the natives held up two fingers in the V-for-Victory sign and the children ran after the train fighting over the annas that the soldiers tossed from the train. At the frequent stops, entire families would come up to beg, sell knives and candy, and gaze at the train. Soon we passed out of the city and saw date palms, rice fields, cows (not fat like our American cows), and water buffalo wallowing in ponds and streams. We passed several refractories where the natives were shaping bricks by hand and several quite modern-looking apartment houses. After about two hours the terrain became hilly and in the distance we could see mountains. These mountains were not in one continuous range, but were comparable to the bad lands of Texas; that is, the surrounding country appeared level or gently sloping and each individual mountain seemed set down in the middle of this level ground. At a distance they appeared red, deep purple, and yellow when the setting sun shone on them. When our train passed close by we saw that they were very steep. Some rose up from the plateau like sheer cliffs and were russet brown in color.

Several passenger trains passed us going in the same direction as our train. I was amazed at the way the natives hung out of the doors and stood on the edge of the open doors of the moving train. When one passed us moving just a little faster than our train, the passengers waved and little boys shouted. I noticed that there were separate cars for "Ladies", but most of these were empty since most of the women were with their families. The coaches had only four wheels and seemed fragile compared to our heavy steel American coaches.

The major crop in the district that we were passing through was rice and the land was divided up into little patches about thirty feet square. Each patch was surrounded by a dirt ridge about six inches high to hold water over the rice sprouts when the monsoon season sets in. Monsoon comes in May and lasts until August.

We arrived at our destination at nine o'clock, detrained by crawling out through the windows of our compartment. We found our individual packs and barracks bags, which we had thrown out the windows, and waited for what the future held. I was detailed to load barracks bags on to a British truck so I rode to our area. We were disappointed when we found that we had to sleep in tents. After turning in our fire arms (we were told that this was a precaution to prevent them from falling into the hands of the Indians) we had our first Indian meal. It was a stew of some sort with tea for the beverage. Not many of the men ate tonight. The future does not look promising.

Dec. 4, Friday. Today we were told that we are in Camp Deolali, built in 1863 and virtually unchanged, it seems to us. All of the hard work is done by the natives. Most of the men are in camp for a rest. There are British, Scots, Irish, Australian, Native, and with our arrival, American troops here. The village about three miles from here is called Deolali. We will have guard duty in town and , aside from calisthenics, close-order drill, and a short road march in the morning will have nothing to do. We will be served four meals a day , counting tea at four in the afternoon.

In the daylight the camp looks much nicer. Up on the hill about an eighth of a mile from our tents we can see a native temple which reminds me of a grain elevator with five minarets on top. The plot of ground in front of the temple is fenced in and we have been warned that all temples are out of bounds for troops. The natives don't care to have unbelievers investigating their holy buildings. At the end of the road in front of our area we can look over a plateau to a range of mountains which reminds me of the pictures of the Grand Canyon. A road winds up the plateau about midway between the end of our road and the mountain range. In the evening we saw ox carts plodding their way to and from the village. Now and then an ancient truck would pass, stirring up clouds of dust. It hasn't rained here since August, so every wind stirs up the dust.

We have been told that we are not to buy anything edible sold by the natives and not to drink out of any bottle in town. The only water that is safe to drink is that which comes out of the taps in the camp. There are very few cobras (! ! !) near the camp and the other precaution was about the mosquitoes which our C.O. told us carried malaria; therefore, we sleep under mosquito nets. The beds are more comfortable than the beds on the ship. They have rope mattresses. We sleep over one blanket with three blankets over us. The nights are cold but as soon as the sun comes up at 7:45 it becomes warm and by ten o'clock it is actually hot. At four o'clock it becomes cooler and the temperature gradually decreases.

The barracks have a brick foundation which serve as a wall for a height of about three feet. Attached to this foundation and extending up to that place where the tiled roof overhung, was the woven matting which made up the major portion of the building. The matting was cut out to form the windows and doors. The porch extended along the entire front of the building. The floor of the porch was stone blocks fourteen inches square and set in concrete. Large hawks and ravens flew over the camp living on refuse that the natives had discarded. Most of the trees are small and scrubby except for a few ancient knarled ones of an unknown specie.

If you walk down the dusty dirt and asphalt roads at night, you need to walk carefully to keep from being run down by the old two-wheeled horse carriages. These jingle noisily up and down the road in total darkness except for the dim light from the lamp on each carriage.

Dec. 5, Saturday. Rested up today. Have done nothing but sleep and try to eat since I got here. At five o 'clock we went on guard. I was paired with Willie H. and our duty was at the bazaar in town. We were on from five to eleven in the evening. We enjoyed it as we had to walk all over town in the shops and up the alleys to make sure that none of our boys got into trouble. No danger of that. It seems there is no liquor to be had in town. Even if there were, our soldiers couldn't buy any as they haven't been paid for a couple of months. Willie and I agreed that the town is like something out of Arabian Nights. All of the natives wear native dress, goats and cattle wonder over the dirt streets and into the houses. There is the sound of the chattering of merchants calling their wares, haggling of buyers and sellers, crying of the children begging. There is some electricity in the town, but the chief means of light is the oil lamp.

I talked to a British soldier who had been at Dunkirk, Norway and Africa. He lost the sight of one eye at Dunkirk, but said, "Oh, that's not so bad, I still have me other eye. A man needs only one eye to carry on". Another British soldier said he had stayed at Durban, south Africa for five weeks and had tasted "American style" hot dogs, ice cream and pie. Had an altogether interesting day.

December 6, Sunday. Rested in the morning. Had guard duty in the afternoon from two to six. The town seemed different in the afternoon. The smells were terrible and the dust covered the entire village. Willie H. and I discovered the native grain mill, several bookshops, a Chinese cloth merchant (the cleanest store in town), and a fairly good café patronized by British troops. I talked to a young British soldier whom I met in the bookstore on the ground floor of the café, and heard his story. He had been at Dunkirk with the Royal Artillery. I'll try to quote him:

"The last news I had was last Thursday (I had asked about war news) and the Russians were advancing on Rostov, your boys are doing a good job in the Solomons, and we've got Jerry cornered in Africa. He'll have his own Dunkirk."

I asked him if he had been at Dunkirk.

"Yes, that's where I got these feet. A Jerry bomber, shrapnel, scars keep opening up. Haven't done a thing for the past twelve months. It was uncanny the way their air force spotted us. No matter where you'd go, he'd be there and whoosh, you couldn't do anything about it. I remember one time we had a wonderful bivouac, perfect camouflage and concealment, and he found us there. We found that the farmer in a field nearby had cut the grain in the shape of an arrow pointing directly at our camp. It was that way all the way through." I asked him again about Dunkirk.

"It lasted six days. I was scheduled to go out on the last day. I was on an ack-ack gun. On the third day the Jerry bomber knocked out our gun, so I became a casualty and left on the fourth day with the wounded. I was flat on my face when the bomb came, just got me on the feet. Not as bad as a lot of them. I wish we had the air force then that we have now." After he got back to England, he was sent along with many of the wounded to South Africa, then later to Deolali. The British expected the Germans to invade England after Dunkirk.

I notice that most of the men who have been in the fighting won't guess how long the war will last. The war has become a part of their daily life and when I tell them I think it will be over in a year and a half, their eyes get the faraway look and they say with infinite patience, "Oh, there's no way to say. It'll be over soon now."

An Irishman who said he was one of nine remaining men in his battalion told me that he had talked to German and Italian prisoners, "They don't want the war", he said. Soldiers are the same everywhere.

Dec. 7, Monday. This morning we had calesthentics, close order drill, and a short road march. In the afternoon I shaved and showered (very cold water). Felt much better. Fresh water is a luxury after the salt water on the ship. We were on guard duty from five to eleven. Sergeant Bill Thomas couldn't go on guard as his leg which he had hurt the first day we arrived, had become infected. He was sent to the hospital. Willie H. and I talked to a storekeeper named Jals who is the most intelligent of the natives that I have met. He told us that the weather became cold in February, "Ooo, forty at night." and that once it had gone to freezing and "All the trees turned black."

If I'm still here when we have a payday, I'm going to Jal's shop to buy something. Bill Hart bought us some soda pop at a place that British men and officers patronize. Tasted good. I saw a bracelet of pice coins which I want to get for Barbara, if I'm paid here. We made the rounds of all the native shops. The vegetable and fruit market had all of the fruits and vegetables that we have at home. Potatoes are about an inch in diameter but taste the same. Smells of the town are not so bad a night. We walked back to our area, lit our lanterns, and Willie and I talked and smoked for about an hour. I told him about my third year at college.

All he could say was "What a life." I agreed with him.

Dec. 8, Tuesday. I got up before the last notes of the bugle playing British reveille (it's long and really beautiful echoing over the hills in this strange land) had ended. I dressed, took down my mosquito net, and made my bed. After reveille we had calisthentics, close order drill, and instructions in dissembling the M-1 rifle. Willie and I went to the post exchange and had tea and cakes. Natives wait on us and we try to appear casual. This is my last half-anna that I'm spending. The British officers in India all carry swagger sticks so that the natives can distinguish the ruling class from the other ranks in the British Army. Naturally, when the American soldiers realized that it was possible to buy swagger sticks, they bought them.

For those who could afford them, the swagger stick did wonders for the American soldier's self-image—that of the Hollywood-type of overlord in India. This may have confused, if not impressed some of the natives of the lower classes. In the short time that we had been in India we had not met many British officers. Those we had seen appeared to us to be clean looking, stern-faced, humorless individuals. Certainly they were not amused at the thought of America G.I.s walking around the streets of India carrying swagger sticks. In fact, they tended to regard this as a bold attempt on the part of the enlisted men of the U.S. Army to raise their position in the pecking order of the universe. They communicated this feeling to our American officers who announced to us that it was against army regulations for anyone except an officer to carry a swagger stick. This whole affair left us with the impression that our own officers were on the side of the British officers who are still mad because they lost the Revolutionary War.

In the afternoon I had Shovan cut my hair on credit and went to tea. In the evening Turner, Salasky, Willie and I had good talk of home and food. After the war is over, Turner will go back to his farm in Illinois, Salasky wants to go back to his job as a rubber moulder in a factory in Chicago, Willie wants to get a job as an usher in Music Hall until he has enough to open a bookstore. I want to go back to my old job as a timekeeper and continue to go to night school in accounting, get an apartment and live with Barbara in the USA for the rest of my life.

We all turned in, Turner blew out the lantern, and talk drifted to pictures, movie actors and actresses. Willie and I were agreed that Mickey Rooney was our favorite, that Shirley Temple had a great future. We decided that we would visit each other when we get back to see whether Willie's sister or my sister-in-law was the best cook. Fell asleep looking at the stars and thinking of home.

Dec. 9, Wednesday. Today I had guard duty in the morning and thus didn't have to stand the Colonel's inspection. Had a post on the road to an area restricted to American troops. We sat on the stone bench in front of the great gate of the New Sanitarium. Across the road was the Sheth Bhagwandas Narotamdas Sanitarium. I don't know what sort of asylums these are but the grounds about each are beautiful with many shade trees, trimmed shrubs and flowers. Each asylum is enclosed by a wall. Inside the wall there appears to be a neat, almost modern section of a town.

In the afternoon I showered, had tea and more tea. Willie sold his $1.50 American watch to a native buyer for $2.00. It kept fairly good time. We went to Lumley's Canteen and had little tomato sandwiches and tea. We went with Gilbert who apparently enjoyed our company as he said he hadn't laughed so much in a long time. Reason: I have just been made a Private First Class and they ribbed me about polishing apples and wanted to know if I would take them to PFC mess. The British army has different messes –one for sergeants, one for OR's (other ranks). I don't know how fine a breakdown in messes they have, but it seems undemocratic to us. Came back to camp and slept soundly.

Dec. 10, Thursday. Today we move again. I'll miss the ancient mess hall with the natives outside the door to collect our left-overs. They stand with two containers, one for tea, one for food. In our country these would go in the garbage container. In India it is food for the natives. Sometimes, they eat it right there. I did my laundry in a hurry, hoping that it would have time to dry. It did.

We left camp at 8:30 in the evening. As the long column of marching men wound up the dusty road an old British officer rode his bicycle past the column and said in a voice that told us that he knew what war was, "Goodby boys and good luck to you all" He repeated this several times as he rode past us. We marched the two miles to the railroad station and waited, and waited. Patience is something that you learn in the army. At 11:45 we boarded the train and got in our compartments, six soldiers to each compartment on this Indian military car. The seats are like park benches; the seat is one bunk; the back of the seat pulls up to form the second bunk, and the luggage rack is the top bunk. There are three bunks on each side of the compartment. I slept on the top bunk fairly well. The slats did not bother me.

What I remember about Deolali: Dust, dust everywhere. The red spittle in the dust on the main street that we thought was blood, until we found out that it was from the betelnut that the natives chew. The smell of incense in the various shops to mask the more unpleasant odors that are present where people don't enjoy the advantages of soap and water. The old-fashioned horse carriages with their little side lanterns and jingle-jangling bells winding up the dark roads. The starry skies at night. The sky is the one thing a soldier feels that he has in common with the people at home. Great filthy birds, little jackasses, oxcarts and oxen.

ABOARD THE DUNERA

With a monkey for company

Dec. 11, Friday. Our train arrived in Bombay at 10:30 A.M. We bought bananas and carbonated water from vendors who came up to the train. The colored water tasted like hair tonic. It was in Japanese bottles which are sealed with a glass marble and opened by forcing the glass marble down into the bottle. The neck is made narrow to form a trap for the ball which rolls around and stops up the bottle if one tips the bottle too much while he drinks. We had a breakfast of creamed chipped ham, bread, butter, and tea on the dock, then boarded the ship. It is the Dunera out of London and was built for a troop ship. It is much smaller than the West Point. We sleep in hammocks and eat at tables (16 to a table) in the same section that we sleep in. We have Bombay, a monkey that Clemens and Colvin bought, in our section. They made a little coat with corporal's stripes for him. He has his bed in a box under the table. I decided to quit smoking today, at least for a while. Willie Hoefling is going to quit after New Years.

Dec. 12, Saturday. Slept so-so in the hammock last night. We sailed at about eight o'clock and will be nearer home wherever we go. We have three meals a day and the chow is good. Much better than the native chow at Deolali. It appears that we aren't to do guard duty which will make the trip more enjoyable. We gain an hour's time tonight. Willie and I went up on the sun deck and talked with Corporal Hale (newly won stripes) who wants to save enough to build a house on some property that he and his wife have in Maryland. Amused us by telling us all about his in-laws. Hale is a good solid citizen. Decided not to quit smoking just yet.

Dec. 13, Sunday. Today, I lost my Eversharp pencil that Jean and Al gave me. Made me feel like hell as it was a good pencil and a gift to boot. Willie and I had tea and cakes through the courtesy of Gilbert and Eagen. Talked about how different from Sunday at home; then about the cultural advantages of living in cities like Cleveland and Chicago. Willie thinks that everyone could be made to appreciate good music. I think that some people are incapable of appreciating music. It seems I'm becoming less idealistic but it's not time for introspection yet.

Dec. 14, Monday. Stood guard duty in the company area from four to eight in the morning and at night. Paul Prosser's joke: "There are only two kinds of pie that I like, warm and cold".

ABOARD THE DUNERA –We are in Lower Troop Deck No. 2 which corresponds to B Deck on an American Ship. On either side of the ship tables extend out from the wall. These tables are about twelve feet long and three feet wide with a bench on each side. At the end of each table toward the wall there are cupboards for plates, silverware, and canteen cups. Under the opposite end of the table are the dish pans and buckets and pans used for washing, and carrying water and food. Two orderlies go to the kitchen each meal and get the food for their table. After the meal is over, a man goes up to the main deck and brings down a pan of hot salt water for washing dishes.

Under the end of our table which is connected to the wall (starboard side of the ship) in a box which serves as his barracks, lives Bombay, the monkey. From the time we sit down to eat until we have finished washing the dishes the pet squeals and chatters and jumps up on the bench, putting his front paws on the table begging food. At first this annoyed Willie and me since we sat directly over his box and were continually knocking over Bombay's water can and worried when we put our feet down lest we tread where Bombay had done his natural duty; however, despite this inconvenience, we soon learned to eat our meals with pleasure. When Bombay was caught with his face in the butter jar we scraped the top off the butter and ate it.

Every morning at ten o'clock when we had ship inspection, the monkey's box had to be cleaned and the dishpan set on top to conceal him from the British Navy. Strange as it seems, the monkey was quiet during these inspections.

On one of our beer days Corporals Clemens and Colvin (joint owners of Bombay) conceived the idea of getting the monkey drunk. His drinking pan was filled with beer and the monkey drank it as if it were water. When he had finished he lifted his head and his face was covered with foam. He lay down and absolutely refused to play, then fell into a drunken slumber. Clemens and Colvin think it may stunt his growth. We'll see. Paul Prosser says, "I'm tough, I eat brick ice cream and marble cake".

Dec. 15, Tuesday. Sea quite rough today. Felt seasick three different times, but managed to hold down what I had eaten.

Dec. 16, Wednesday. Today we were paid for the first time in two and a half months. I got one hundred and thirty-two rupees or forty dollars. Feels good to have money in my pocket.

Dec. 17, Thursday. Last night Willie H. and I slept on deck, fell asleep looking at the stars. Willie suggested that when I build my house, I build a sleeping porch where he can sleep when he comes to visit us. Sighted land today at nine o'clock. At first we could not decide whether it was a cloud or land. At three o'clock we put in at the harbor at Aden. The town is at the base of a mountain that is totally devoid of vegetation. It seems small compared to Bombay. We sailed out of Aden at 6 PM. I stood guard at our quarters from four to eight in the evening. I slept on the floor as I had to get up early. I think when the war is over I'll be able to sleep on any kind of bed.

Dec. 18, Friday. Got up at five AM as the old guard forgot to wake me. We passed some rocky land at nine this morning. One of the attachments we have had on the Dunera is a barrage balloon fastened to the stern of the ship by a cable. This is to entangle any attacking airplanes, and reminds us that we are not on a pleasure cruise. Slept on the sport deck.

Dec. 19, Saturday. Bad night for sleeping. My cold is worse. I hope I can get rid of it by Christmas. Climate is getting hotter. Paul Prosser says that "Apple pie with cheese is not to be snickered at." Went on sick call for my cold. The doctor excused me from duty for two days and ordered me to come to the hospital for cough medicine at three and seven o'clock. This is one of my bad days when I feel as if the war will last forever. I'm thinking of how far we must drive back Germany, and when that is finished there is still Japan – tears the hell out of me. Monday, we begin to wear our helmets at all times. We have had air raid alarm drill and gas mask inspection and drill. We'll soon be entering the theater of operations. Today is probably the first day of Barbara's Christmas vacation and if we were back in Columbus she would already be there – tough luck.

Dec. 20, Sunday. Up late last night talking to Sergeant Butler, the company clerk. He had studied five years for the priesthood and gave it up. Was immediately inducted into the army. Told me about the various kinds of monks and monasteries. In the afternoon Willie and I went aft on the sun deck and listened to a soldier playing the piano. The tunes that he played, Mary, Would You, Alice Blue Gown, and many others reminded us of faraway places and times past.

Have guard duty from four to eight, an easy job watching quarters. Bought my first English cigarettes, Needlepoint, made in South Africa, not too bad. The toothpaste that I bought smells and tastes of ether. Hope I can finish this tube before I put myself to sleep. One of the boys bought some hair oil, manufactured in South Africa and the stuff smelled like a blend of alcohol, linseed oil, garlic, and spoiled food. I can't believe that these products are representative of what the South Africans would buy.

Dec. 21, Monday. This morning we passed several islands which were rocky and reminded me of the Rocky Mountains in Colorado, red in color. Later the formation of the land changed and instead of mountains rising directly out of the sea, there is a sandy beach which stretches for a half-mile inland at which point the mountains begin. It is like a stage setting.

At one o'clock in the afternoon we disembarked from the Dunera on the docks near Suez. I missed my breakfast as I had guard duty on deck. We lined up in company formation on the dock and waited. Finally, we marched over to our train and found our car. Egyptian trains, we found, were even more uncomfortable than those in India. The coaches are odd little four-wheeled frame cars with seats like our park benches, every two facing each other. The windows had shutters instead of glass. We waited in the cars for two hours before the little Egyptian engine began to huff and puff and slowly move us forward.

SUEZ , EGYPT

We are in Africa, It's a 5 hour train ride to Heliopolis Depot where we spend one week, receive a lot of mail. We are here for Christmas.

TOBRUK, LIBYA

55 members of the 981st MP company travel by C-47 transport plane to a landing ground east of Tobruk. We begin guard duty.

William M. Kennedy

During the two-hour wait on the train, we watched the laborers on the dock. The overseer had a club and a long whip which he used to hurry the recalcitrant workers. While they worked, these descendants of one of the world's oldest civilizations sang to the rhythm of their work, the loading of long steel pipes onto a ship. The pipes were stacked in layers and rolled down a wooden board ramp to the paved dock. As one of the pipes was rolled down from the top of the stack, it would jangle and clatter when it slipped from the board runway onto the stone pavement of the dock. This clattering was the high point in the song of the laborers when the chanting suddenly increased in tempo and intensity and was accompanied by hand clapping.

At three o'clock when the train began to move, we all had our heads out of the windows to see Egypt. We passed through level desert land and in fifteen minutes were in Suez where we stopped for about ten minutes. The station platform was filled with grinning natives who waved at us. Little boys ran up and shouted excitedly, "Americaine, Americaine". Our train puffed out of the station amid the waving of the natives from the platform and from windows of apartment houses along the way. Here, as in India, the show of friendship by the people as our train passed did wonders for our morale. The country became flat and sandy and just as night was falling we came into the desert. We saw several camels nibbling at the few clumps of grass. The camels stopped eating and ran when our train passed by. A big moon came up over the sand dunes and it became cold. We put up our shutters and sat in the dark. It was seven o'clock and we were very hungry. Some of us hadn't eaten since breakfast as we were on guard duty on deck and missed the noon meal on the ship. We talked of food as we remembered it at home and speculated about what we would get at the next camp. We thought it would be like the food at Deolali.

At eight o'clock we arrived at our destination, Heliopolis Depot. We detrained, formed as companies, and marched for what seemed a half hour to our section of the camp. We stopped in front of a brick building while our sergeant talked to the camp sergeant for several minutes. We were told to get our mess kits ready, drop our packs, and come in to eat. We walked into the mess hall and couldn't believe our eyes. Here was a clean, new American mess hall in Egypt. The meal consisted of corned beef hash, green beans, spinich, white bread and jelly, pineapple, and coffee with cream (canned). It was the best meal that I ever ate. Everything was American, even the soap that was used to wash our mess kits.

After dinner we were shown to our barracks. These were large new brick buildings with one end walled up and containing the shower and wash room. The windows had specially treated screens to keep out the mosquitoes. We slept on native rope cots with wooden frames and had four blankets which we needed. We slept soundly.

Dec. 22. Tuesday. We have been told that the camp was built by American engineers in about six weeks, that mail takes fifteen days from home, that transportation is good to Cairo which is fourteen miles away. We also learn that we are not to leave the camp area. I am sleeping beside Turner and Willie Hoefling. All we do is sleep, eat, and wash clothes.

Dec. 23, Wednesday. Captain Hinote, our C.O. tells us that we may be living in a hotel in Cairo, doing police duty and getting four dollars a day for meals. Today, we got mail from home. It was wonderful. I had 32 letters, 19 from Barbara who is very worried. Her last letter was written November 27th. The mail was not without its sad news too. Blackburn learned that his father had died and Sergeant Shaw learned that his little girl, an only child, had died.

Dec. 24, Thursday. Fifty of us have been selected to go to Cairo to be a headquarters guard company. We have been given Sam Browne belts and told to polish them well as we will need to make an impression. We will be living in a hotel. This will mean that I can cable Barbara every week. I would like to send her a Christmas cable, but I can't change my money to Egyptian currency or borrow from anyone.

Dec. 25, Friday, Christmas. For breakfast we had hot cakes, syrup, and bacon for the first time in three months. We had a wonderful turkey dinner and everyone ate too much. In the evening I had to do guard duty at the warehouse from six to ten o'clock. It was a good Christmas but I couldn't help thinking of last Christmas when I was at home with Barbara.

Dec. 26, Saturday. Went to the show (free) with Willie H. to see a war picture which was too realistic to be enjoyable.

Dec. 27, Sunday. The latest rumor is that we may not go to Cairo after all. You never know.

Dec. 28, Monday. today the company was called together and we were told that some of us would be moving up near the front. Fifty-five of us (supposedly select) men are to go. In the evening we were issued our battle dress, two additional blankets, and ammunition. All privates and pfc's were issued rifles instead of pistols and we were told that we would be leaving by plane from Heliopolis in the morning. We are to take one barracks bag and carry only essentials.

Dec. 29, Tuesday. Up at four-thirty, breakfast, piled into the trucks at six. We were cheered by the rest of our company as we set out for Heliopolis. Willie Hoefling, Paul Prosser, and Turner were left behind. We arrive at the airport at seven and wait around the trucks until eight o'clock when the trucks drive out to four C-47 transport planes, fourteen men to each plane. The pilots are buck-sergeants. They tell us that they will be flying low to discourage strafing by enemy aircraft. This is my first airplane ride and I'm not excited at the prospect. Our plane takes off with a roar flying very low.

In fifteen minutes we pass the pyramids which look small to me. Suddenly, the desert land stops at a sharp line of demarcation, and green fields begin. This, we learn is the beginning of the Nile valley with its network of irrigation ditches. Towns are compact little dots with high buildings, yet small enough that we can see three or four of the towns at the same time. After an hour we have crossed the Nile valley and are over the desert. In a half hour we pass over that part of the desert where British and German armies fought last November. Tank tracks tell the story of many a skirmish and battle. There are burned tanks, trucks, wrecked airplanes, abandoned fox holes. These could still be used (I hope not!!) if the pattern of advance and retreat continues as it has in the last year. Finally, we land at an airport near Tobruk. All around us are tents, dust, and more tents and dust. A truck drives up as we get off the plane. We crawl on and are driven to the mess tent where the food is good for field rations. After chow we go back to our barracks bags and are told that we are at the wrong field. The trucks drive us to another field seven miles away. On the way we see wrecked trucks, airplanes and tanks with the Italian cross and the German swastica on them. I was surprised to see the amount of German and Italian equipment that we were using. The water wagon was German, two tanks marked "Trink Wasser". All about us are German auxiliary trucks and motorcycles. We arrive at the other airport, round up huge tents, pitch them, go to mess, see many RAF boys in their blue-gray uniforms and smartly cocked hats. We go back to our tents to bed. One long full day.

Dec. 30, Wednesday. Today we were given new tents which we pitched. Somebody's elbow bumped my glasses which broke, while we were pitching the tent. When I went to the HQ tent to see if I could send them to Cairo with someone our CO was helpful, "Jesus Christ Kennedy, why'd you break your glasses." I was unable to respond intelligently to his question, but it helped me to realize that the problem of the broken glasses was my own.

In the evening I was detailed with two other men to guard a big American bomber. We took along our shelter-halves and blankets, pitched the tent beside the plane. Two slept while one guarded.

Dec. 31, Thursday. Well, we learn that we were right the first time and must move back to the other field. After breakfast we take down the large tents, pack up, and wait for the trucks to come. Finally, at six in the evening they come. The ride takes an hour since it is over a winding desert road. We are hungry. We arrive at our destination, unload tents and equipment, march over to the mess for another good meal, return and pitch our tents. We slept well on the good earth.

1943

Jan. 1, 1943, Friday. Today we finished pitching the tent and leveled the ground inside the tent. These are British tents; the inner tent has walls about three feet high, then there is an outer tent fly that provides added protection from the sun, rain and sand. In the afternoon we had just finished digging the drainage ditches around the tents, and digging our fox holes and trenches (for protection in the event of a visit by Jerry planes) when the first sergeant blew his whistle calling us to the orderly tent. He informed us that the entire company would begin guard duty at six o'clock. There would be two men to each plane. We will take our shelter halves and each pair of men will pitch their tent beside the plane which they guard. One man will sleep in the tent for two hours while the other man guards. At the end of two hours, the man on guard will be relieved by the man in the tent.

At six o'clock we met outside the orderly tent ready to go on duty. Two trucks drove up . These were canvas-hooped six-by-sixes that held twenty men on two side benches. We all crawled into the back on the side benches and the long job of posting the guard was begun. My partner was Private First Class Andy Reese. We were the second pair on the truck and sat far back at the end of the bench. The ride was rough. We were all nervous and unsure of ourselves. We tried to make jokes to ease the tension. VanDuyne groused as was his habit and we heaped coals of fire on his grievances as was our habit. At intervals the truck would come to a lurching stop and two soldiers would jump off to be posted. Finally, we were the last pair on the truck. We hopped down when the truck stopped at our post, carrying our rifles and blankets wrapped in our shelter halves. The lieutenant pointed out the huge bomber which we were to guard. It was rather obvious which plane we were to guard as there was no other plane within a quarter of a mile of us. The truck rumbled off into the night and we were left alone with the huge bomber, a B-24 Liberator.

We decided to use the shelter halves as a sleeping bag instead of a tent. We chose a spot about fifty feet from the plane and I made up the bed while Reese guarded the plane. We used two double blankets over one shelter half to sleep on and spread the other three on top. As I was to take the first shift, Reese was the first to sleep. He lay on the three top blankets, rolled himself up in them and spread the second shelter half over him. I haven't mentioned our clothes , but I think I should as the average person thinks of the desert as being warm at all times. As soon as the sun sets, the desert becomes as cold as our North Central States in the winter. We wore long underwear, our regular winter woolen uniform and our battle dress. The latter consisted of a heavy woolen two-piece uniform-the jacket buttoned onto the pants-the pants buttoned around the ankles and the heavy canvas leggings were much shorter than our American leggings-covering about six inches of the calves above the ankles. The idea of the British battle dress was to make for uniformity in dress for the army in the western desert. About midnight, always, we were obliged to put on our American overcoats over the two other uniforms. So much for our habiliments.

I walked around the plane, noted the name, was careful not to bump the two bombs laying on the ground beside her, and noticed that the sky which had been clear and starry on other nights, was tonight cloudy and black. In another climate I would have expected it to rain. In a little while raindrops began to fall and Reese called to me to ask if he really felt raindrops. We moved the sleeping bag under the wing of the plane and Reese went back to sleep. At nine o'clock I wakened Reese and slid into the warm bed while he put on his overcoat and cartridge belt and took over the guard duty. I remember thinking of how nice my bed at home was, of how Barbara looked when she smiled, of what it would be like when I came home. Then I fell asleep.

"Kennedy, Kennedy, wake up. It's an air raid". Reese shook me till my teeth chattered. I heard anti-aircraft guns and looked in the direction that Reese pointed. Tracer bullets were shooting across the sky like a fireworks display, then we heard the plane.

"Let's make for the fox hole", Reese said, "I don't want to be around when those bombs on the other side of the plane go off." We started but I turned back sleepily to get my helmet, rifle, and cartridge belt. We started for the fox hole again but it seemed pointless as the enemy plane had passed over the field by now. We watched for about five minutes, but it didn't come back. "I heard it when it first came over, no lights on it and it zoomed down trying to land, I think," Reese explained, "then the ack-ack guns went into action, and it dropped a couple of flares, and left."

By this time it was eleven o'clock and my turn to do the guard trick. It was very cold and windy and though I looked and listened for more planes, none showed up. At one o'clock I woke Reese for his trick and went to bed, but not to sleep. The wind roared around and in our sleeping bag so that I had to keep pulling down and tucking in the outside canvas. I dozed a little and at three when Reese came to get me I was already awake.

From three to five, I spent the most uncomfortable two hours of my life. The wind was blowing sand so that I couldn't see ten feet in front of me. In a short time the sand was in my eyes and ears, down my throat, in and through my clothes, under my fingernails –everywhere. This was to be my first sandstorm. No matter how often I spit, when I closed my mouth I could feel the gritty sand in my teeth. When I tried to rub the sand out of my eyes it was like trying to brush flour off of your face with hands that are already covered with flour. I tried my handkerchief, but it did little good. At five I wakened Reese and went to bed where the sand merely filtered in. I slept a little. At six-thirty Reese woke me up as the guard truck had come to take us back to camp. When we got off the truck in our camp area, we nearly lost our way trying to find our tent. The sandstorm seemed to be worse. In a short time the mess sergeant blew the breakfast whistle. We went over to the chow tent where the cooks had prepared a good breakfast of oatmeal, hot cakes, syrup, and sausage. We walked outside the tent to eat and our meal was immediately covered with sand. It seemed strange eating red oatmeal, but it tasted good anyway. I would have gone up for a second helping if the sand hadn't burned my eyes so badly. We went back to our tents and slept. The wind blew continually and the sand filtered through the tent and covered our equipment and the blankets under which we slept. When we got up to eat lunch a cloud of dust rose up from each man's bed as he unrolled himself from his blankets. We went over to the cook's tent, got our meal in our mess kits, covered the mess kit with its top, and came back to the tent to eat. When we had eaten we went back to sleep. At three-thirty in the afternoon the wind subsided and the sandstorm was over. One other discomfort of this desert duty is that we get only one canteen of water a day for everything, drinking, washing and shaving. The heavy drinkers have long beards. This has been some New Year's Day.

Jan. 2, Saturday. The airport here is a huge thing, built by the Italians. In the hills all around the airport we hear the engineers setting off the enemy mines. There are many wrecked enemy planes in our camp area. Most of them were caught on the ground by our bombs. The Germans and Italians passed this way about two months ago. The retreat was more like a rout. I talked to the British soldiers who man the anti-aircraft guns on the field. They are with the Royal Artillery and were so close to the German Army that at one camp they came upon a German mess where the dishes filled with warm macaroni were set around a table. They filled their pockets with chocolates, flints for cigarette lighters, shirts, shorts, stockings, blouses from the supply store. The post office had mail and packages ready to be sent to the fatherland. Some of the soldiers were sending rations of beef (the Britishers called it "bully beef") back home and from this assumed that conditions were bad in Germany.

Jan. 3, Sunday. Guard duty today. Just another day. Cigarettes are very scarce. The only kind available are Marvels at thirty cents a pack, five packs to a man, every ten days when the Traveling Canteen Truck comes around. There is a rumor that eventually we will be issued cigarettes. I asked Lt. Svella to take my glasses with him when he goes to Cairo. Lt. Svella was a corporal in the regular army and, as a Second Lieutenant, is the lowest ranking of the three officers in our company. Up to this Point he has kept a very low profile. I'll send the broken glasses to Willie Hoefling and ask him to take them to an optician. The next time I'm near a big town, I'm going to have a pair of sturdy glasses made. The other men in the outfit have GI steel-rimmed glasses which they got at basic training camp. I guess my basic training period was too stepped up.

Jan. 14, Thursday. Lt. Freeman, the officer who is in charge of the contingent In Cairo, arrived today. He brought out money piasters with him. We had left our Indian rupees in Heliopolis to be converted into Egyptian piasters. I bought some tobacco from the stock he brought with him from Cairo. We learn that the boys who were left behind at Heliopolis are now doing guard duty at headquarters, living in a hotel and getting four dollars a day to live on; they eat together and save at least two dollars a day. Some life.

Jan. 15. Friday. Received a letter from Barbara dated December 14th. She was worried and wanted me to send a cablegram. I wrote a letter to Willie Hoefling enclosing money and asked him to send the cablegram. I gave the letter to Lt. Freeman who is going back to Cairo today. I hope she gets the cablegram this weekend.

Jan. 17, Sunday. Jim Morrow, the sergeant in charge of our tent, was sent back to the hospital in Cairo today. He has been suffering with intestinal flu for some time but has accepted it as one of the hazards of war. He is forty-five years old and it has been hard for him sleeping on the ground. He was a peace officer in Texas and the day after Pearl Harbor he and his son both enlisted. In our tent conversations he has said that he hoped to walk down the streets of Berlin with a machine gun. Life is not complicated to Jim; he is a law-and-order man. The only people who have problems or cause trouble are those who don't obey the law.

When our company was at Lockbourne Army Air Base near Columbus, Ohio Jim's wife came all the way from Texas to see him. Barbara came down from Cleveland to see me and we met briefly on the base as a foursome. Jim assured Barbara that he would look out for me. After we were in the desert Jim talked about how the officers and sergeants met to decide who would go out to the desert and who would be left behind at Heliopolis. He said that no one knew who I was; he told them that I was a good boy and so I was included in the select group to go out to the western desert. I thanked him for looking out for me, but I could not help feeling that I might have been able to manage on my own in Ninth Air Force Headquarters back in Cairo.

That's life. My glasses came back today.

Jan. 18, Monday. Four of the boys have bought motorcycles from the British soldiers in the area. They are vehicles abandoned by the Germans and Italians in their last retreat and overhauled by the British. The prices ranged from two pounds ($8.00) to four pounds ($16.00). They run all right but have only an immediate value as the men have been told they cannot take them with them when we move.

Jan. 22, Friday. Yesterday, several of our bombers left on a mission at 4:30 AM and returned at 11:00 AM. Immediately after they returned we heard that the Allies had taken Tripoli. We have reached another milestone. For the past several days it has rained intermittently. I wonder if it is the beginning of the rainy season. The British on the ack-ack guns say that summer begins in March. We may not be here to see summer.

Last Saturday night Reese and I were on guard when we saw anti-aircraft fire over El Adem. It was the first time that we saw a plane shot down. At first it appeared to be a flare or a star; gradually, it increased in size and soon the entire plane was burning., a flaming red rocket against the black sky. The plane gyrated crazily into a tailspin, tracing a parabola to the horizon, breaking into several smaller flames. It disappeared below the horizon which glowed red a moment later as the plane crashed to earth and exploded. The next night we were warned to be on the lookout for two German aviators who had parachuted from the bomber. Two days later one of them was in the hospital tent here. He had been wounded by the flak, made his way to a native village. The natives turned him over to the military.

Jan. 23. Saturday. As soon as we had finished breakfast of hot cakes and sausage we got permission from the first sergeant to go to Tobruk, sixty miles from our camp. There were five of us, Zilk, Krieger, Quinlan, Clemens, and I. We walked down the road beside the airfield and were picked up by a soldier in a command car. Zilk, Krieger and I got in and, as there were two other soldiers in the front seat, Quinlan and Clemens agreed to meet us in Tobruk. The rugged little command car bounded and leaped over the rocky road, while those of us inside were bounced and jolted. The road wound down from the plateau on which the airfield was situated to the level ground that extends to the Mediterranean six miles away. The rocky road straightened out and about two miles further joined the solid tar and gravel road that led to Tobruk. The driver of the command car said that he was an orderly assigned to a colonel and was on his way to Benghazi to meet the colonel.

At intervals, on both sides of the road we passed British and Free French camps, motor pools, wrecked cars of every description, crashed German and Italian airplanes. All of the allied airplanes had been hauled away for salvage. The traffic was very heavy. We passed convoy after convoy traveling in both directions. At one point we saw a herd of camels grazing around wrecked axis tanks.

When we had been traveling for an hour we came to an intersection where the traffic was directed by a British MP. He came over to the car looking smart in his red-topped garrison cap, white gauntlets, and Sam Browne belt, and asked the driver if he was going to Tobruk. When he learned that his destination was Benghazi he said, "You'll have to use the Axis By-pass." This is the road that the Axis had constructed in their first invasion of Africa when they by-passed Tobruk.

We got out of the command car and waited for our next ride. In five minutes we were on an English truck which took us to within six miles of Tobruk. Our next ride was on top of some boxes in the back of an open truck driven by a native soldier. We had an excellent view from our position on top of the boxes. As we approached Tobruk, the camps became more numerous and the wreckage and wrecks of war were everywhere: German planes, gliders, field artillery, anti-aircraft, German Ford V-8 trucks, minefields enclosed by barbed wire. We passed a demolished church, and two great concrete pillars used by the enemy for a road block; on either side of the pillars barbed wire entanglements ten feet deep extending for a hundred yards on either side of the road. Then the trenches began where the Germans must have dug in. Within an area three miles east of Tobruk you could not go a hundred yards without seeing a foxhole or a trench. The ground is covered with small rocks which push through the sparse green grass and occasional purple flowers. There are too, the Axis cemeteries –compact plots a hundred yards on a side with hundreds and hundreds of little wooden crosses and a large obelisk monument shared by all.

Soon the road wound down a hill and we saw the bay and harbor of Tobruk and on the other hillside the city itself. In the harbor we saw wrecked ships of every size, many were sunk so that only the masts were visible. A German glider lay half-submerged at the edge of the bay. The road rounded the tip of the long narrow bay and ended in another highway running perpendicular to it. Our driver stopped and indicated to us that he would turn left toward Derna at the intersection. We jumped down, walked to the intersection, and turned right toward Tobruk. The road bordered the bay which was on our right. On our left were the bombed ruins of what had been a large beautiful modern building. Further on , the ground on the left of the road sloped steeply up to a high stone wall at the top of the hill. The wall had been bombed away in places but the round building which formed a part of the wall and may have been used to store powder, remained intact. We walked down the road staying on the edge (which was a slew of mud) to avoid traffic. We left the main road to walk up the hill to the city and down a mud road to the docks. We passed groups of South African negro soldiers who were repairing the docks, walked along the edge of the docks and looked in the water. We were amazed to learn that we could look through ten to fifteen feet of water and see the bottom of the harbor covered with wreckage. A British MP came up to us and told us that we had no business there and to "Get out before I get me bloody head in a jam". We turned up another road away from the docks and were in the town. A modern building with marble floors, high ceilings, built around an open court had been bombed out. The open court and fountain was covered with bricks and mortar. Almost all of the buildings in Tobruk were built of stone, covered with a smooth stucco of pastel colors.

We turned the corner and walked toward the square, stopping at a large building that looked like a bank and was only partially demolished. A British soldier was working inside and he volunteered to show us the air raid shelter for the bank. He removed a slab of the marble floor behind one of the counters and led the way down a ladder into the earth. We followed him to the bottom of the shelter which was thirty feet below the floor of the bank and into a passageway. The passageway extended for a distance of about thirty feet, turned at a ninety degree angle to the left, extended for another twenty feet to the bottom of an old well. We climbed another ladder to the top of the well. The shelter, he told us, had been dug by the Germans who must have labored hard to complete it. We agreed , knowing that in addition to the job of digging through practically solid rock, they had the job of hauling it up and away. The British soldier told us that the city had not had an air raid since Christmas Eve when one bomber came over killing five soldiers and wounding twenty-seven. He told us to look inside the church on the square and wished us "Best of luck".

In the street outside of the bank a car drove up and a handsome young British Lieutenant got out and came over to us. He warned us that "many of the buildings have been boobied" and that we should enter all buildings through a window, not tread on any planks, and to be very careful if we picked up anything. We thanked him, saluted, and walked down the street to the city square to see the church. The church had received no direct hits, but the greater part of the roof had been blown off, and there were holes in all the walls. The floor was of inlaid marble. We waded through a half-foot of water up to the altar, undamaged except for two four-foot high marble statues on either side of the altar. The faces of each of these had been pock-marked by shrapnel. The end of the church behind the altar had been blown away and a pile of rocks lay there. We walked out of the great wooden doors at the front of the church and looked at the exterior once more. Above the main entrance were the letters D.O.M. I must find out what they stand for. The most significant feature of the church is the high bell tower to the rear of the church on the left-hand corner of the building. The bell still hung in the tower, the whole untouched by bombs. We walked down the street beside the church away from the square. Many of the white soldiers were quartered here.

I was surprised at the amount of marble used in the houses of the city. Wood is scarce, but every cafe, theater, night club, and large house had floors and even walls of beautiful inlaid marble. The street numbers of the buildings were of marble. We walked down a side street, ate our canned rations on the porch of one of the best hotels, then walked through the buildings of what had been an Italian motor pool. These garages had been used by the English and when Rommel came they were forced to leave. One stouthearted Britisher had daubed a message to the axis with green paint on the inside wall of a large garage: "We'll be back again, you square-headed obscenities". He had the date there too, but I can 't remember it. We all hoped that he came back.

We walked down to the square again and investigated the other side of town. The square had a modernistic fountain and must have been beautiful at a time when the shrubbery had been trimmed. The buildings in this side of town were in the same condition as those in the other side – a shambles. A bombed building loses its character and it is often impossible to distinguish a theater from a restaurant, or a hotel from a public building. We went down a street toward the highway and passed a lone Wog swathed in his white cloak and turban. He was the only native that we saw. Tobruk is a city with no inhabitants except the military.

We came to the highway which wound down a hill over-looking the harbor and joined the road to Derna. Halfway down the hill the road passed the Scuola Benito Muscolinni, a beautiful modern structure now occupied by RAF officers. We went through the rooms that weren't used for quarters. The floors were of marble. The doors opening onto the corridor were of a composition wood with shiny chromium handles. One end of the building had been bombed and piles of sand and rocks lay in the corridor there. We walked down the road toward Gambut and our camp.

Two days later I went back to Tobruk to see the buildings formerly occupied by the Italian garrison for the city and to visit the Italian and German warehouses for souvenirs. The town was no longer interesting to me – there was too much destruction. I saw South African troops in formation on the square, heard the metallic beating of their cleated shoes on the cobblestones as they marched; heard a member of the RAF praise them for mopping up the city – killing and capturing German soldiers – but my mind wasn't on all this. I was think-ing of what a beautiful modern gay colorful peaceful city To-bruk must have been before war came to leave it an ugly un-happy colorless pile of rocks where not a soul dwells – save the military.

January 18, Thursday. Rain has been with us spasmodically – many holes all around – weather cold – nothing eventful ex-cept that the rumor that we were to return to Cairo has been squelched. I hope I see Cairo before I leave the area. Today Zilk and I found that we could buy cartons of cigarettes at the of-ficers' PX for forty piasters – got a carton of Luckies, matches and a cigar. Am saving the cigar. Also discovered that we have a day room – three tents with electric lights, a stove, library and radio – all the comforts of home.

January 29, Friday. Went to the traveling canteen and bought cigarettes, beer and matches. As I started back to my tent I met Howard Crissman from Butler. We recognized each other at the same time. He is a gunner on one of the planes, Jerks Natural. He told me that he is married to a girl in Colorado. He came here from England and hasn't heard from home for six weeks. Must look him up later. More rain.

January 30, Saturday. Still cold and rainy. Reese and I had a long talk with Sergeant Maines, crew chief of our regular plane," Hot Freight". He is from a little town in Pennsylvania – doesn't like the desert. He is generous with his candy, cigarettes and liquor. At first he kept us in cigarettes when we had none. He has been here six weeks – came from England. The sergeant had an original expression to describe something he couldn't explain, "Beats the shit out of me." Reese and I thought this was pretty profound.

February 15th -- I am not sure the exact date when this Liberator crashed. At about ten o'clock on that February morning six of us were in the bed of the half-ton truck riding along the road on the east side of the field bound for the water hole. We had reached a point directly opposite the dirt runway and parallel to it at the point where the planes landed, when we saw the "Red Avenger" coming down for a landing. It appeared to be coming down at an angle of forty-five degrees – too fast for safety. It hit on its front wheels and shivered from nose to tail. The right tail fin snapped off and flew up in the air and the right front wheel assembly collapsed. She skidded along for about a hundred yards and slid around in an arc which the left wheel traced using the motor on the right side of the plane as a center. Sellers said, "I'll bet she's a salvage job," but I thought the damage would be slight as the only things that seemed to be wrecked were the tail fin and the landing wheel.

We continued on to the water hole, filled our cans and barrels and started back. A crowd had gathered around the wrecked plane and we stopped. and walked out to see it. The ship was a complete wreck – the body was bent in the middle, the tail gunner's turret was wrecked, and the nose was smashed. What had caused the damage was the full load of bombs the

Red Avenger was carrying when it landed. No one was hurt and the bombs, which must have been jarred terrifically, had failed to go off. Ordinance men were dragging the bombs off when we came up to the plane. In a little while the salvage crew dragged the plane off the field.

February 24, Wednesday. The long gap in this journal represents what I consider the nadir of my fortune. I have been depressed to the point where letters from home failed to cheer me up and I haven't written home more than four times since I would have written a cheerless letter. We will be moving from here in the next few days and that breaks the monotony somewhat. I don't think I'll get to see Cairo—only a few of the men have been there – sergeants and cooks. Everytime they come back they tell such glowing stories of the life that the other half of our company is leading that we feel worse. They live in a hotel with hot and cold running water, have servant "wogs" to make all beds, shine shoes, and do any errands. They are on guard at headquarters – on four hours—off thirty-six hours. Many of them are drinking heavily and spending money. They are paid four dollars a day for meals, eat in a group for $1.32. They save $80.40 in a thirty day month in addition to their regular pay – a PFC would make $145.69 a month—clear. And we don't even get to see Cairo. What a life. Sometimes I think that I was too good a soldier. I hope that we get home before they do.

SOLUCH, LIBYA

February 25 to April 5, 1943

February 25, Thursday. We were roused out of bed at 2:30 A.M and got ready to move. The full moon made it much easier to take down and pack our tents. We ate our breakfast (hotcakes and bacon) at 3:00 A.M. and went back to our packing. When we had finished Sergeant Morrow called to the driver of our truck. He drove up to our tent and we loaded our tents, cots and packs and climbed in the truck. When the others were loaded there were twelve of us in the back of the truck, sitting on tents, cots and packs with rifles and helmets stuck in every corner. It was five o 'clock when our convoy of five trucks, each dragging a little covered trailer, started off from Landing Ground 139. I was in the last truck and we kidded one another about being the first ones to be strafed if the Jerrys should find us.

We took the Tobruk road and turned left at the entrance of that city in the direction of Barce. When we had left Tobruk behind us the terrain became hilly and we saw palms and little patches of grass. Soon the ground was a beautiful green with purple, white and brilliant red flowers covering the meadows. The smell of the flowers and the green grass reminded me of spring at home. It was wonderful to be rid of the desert. At 11;30 our trucks stopped in a little valley and we had a lunch of spam and pineapple sandwiches and a huge Palestinian orange. Our truck driver told me that he had been overseas since last September and that he hadn't seen any fighting. He is the one man who has answered me truthfully when I asked that question. Most of the Americans that I have talked to have tried to impress me with their answer without admitting that they have never seen action. The fighting fascinates me and I want to talk to someone who can tell me exactly how he felt when the bullets were flying around him. An English soldier in India told me that he thought over his life from childhood on when he was about to see action at Dunkick. He was wounded by shrapnel. I think I would be too weak to run if I were in the middle of the fighting. There are too many impersonal things – like bombs, artillery and grenades in modern warfare.

We started again at twelve o'clock. At intervals we passed stucco buildings, Italian style. All of these were built in the same pattern, three arches and two pillars in the front flanked by two double-doored entrances. We wondered what they could be and decided that they were Italian government buildings.

The road from Tobruk on was hard-surfaced tar and gravel. The battle for Africa had taken place along the entire route and the land was strewn with wrecked tanks, automobiles, guns and airplanes. Occasionally we would see the wreckage scattered over a wide area where one army had dug in and the fighting had been hard. Near these places would be the graves of the dead – an unpainted wooden cross marking each. At six-thirty our convoy stopped at one of the buildings which I have described – located in a green valley. We climbed off the truck, unloaded our packs and cots and went into the building to investigate.

It had been unoccupied except for troops for some time – there were writings on the walls. One of the truck drivers told me that they were model farms built by Mussolini who planned to colonize Libya. The Italian dictator meant for the farms to be occupied by Italian immigrants who would multiply and build a second Italy, but as I recall few Italians were lured from their native homes. The buildings were constructed in a U shape about an open court (in which was a fountain) with the open part of the U to the back and a lattice work gate closing the U. The exterior was of a deep pink color and the side wall bore the huge crudely painted "DUCE" in black letters four feet high. It had been occupied by Italian, German and British troops. We were the first American troops to use it. The floors were of tile and the rooms were surprisingly clean. The C.O. told us that we were not to sleep on the ground so we decided to sleep in the building. Zilk, VanDuyne, Yorkston, Young and I picked a room with a door and shutters (to keep out the wildcats), set up our cots, unrolled our blanket rolls, and carried our packs in. Our room opened on to the entrance hall on the right side of the building. Colvin and Hale had built a big fire in the great fireplace in the hall and we stood around the warm fire listening to the captain in charge of the convoy spin yarns – waiting for dinner.

Our mess sergeant had set up the kitchen in a room on the other side of the house and at eight-thirty chow was ready. We ate green beans, corned beef, graham crackers, an orange and coffee – it was delicious. We ate sitting in front of the fire in the hall on our side, washed our messkits, and climbed into bed. Van Duyne and Zilk were too full of elan vital, or maybe youth to go to sleep so we sang loud and long for an hour. Finally, a sergeant kicked on our door and informed us that "Other guys are tryn' to sleep." It was a long day and it was wonderful to sleep under a roof again, albeit an Italian roof in Libya. I wondered if any little Italians had ever slept in my bedroom of the evening as I fell asleep.

February 26, Friday. The topkick woke us up at seven. We dressed, rolled our bedrolls, unfolded our cots and went to breakfast – rolled oats, prunes and coffee. When we had finished packing we piled into our trucks and the convoy moved on. The country was beautiful in the early morning with dew sparkling on the pine trees and the green grass and the smell of the flowers. We came into Barce at about ten o'clock. It is a beautiful little town – the streets are bordered with date palms, lemon and orange trees and we saw several automobiles (Italian-made). We stopped at the British petrol depot in Barce. The depot had been the home of a rich Italian farmer. It was surrounded by lemon and orange groves. When we had our gasolene tanks full we rolled on to Barce Pass. The road down one side of the mountain pass reminded me of the road up Pike's Peak – zig-zagging down an almost-vertical mountain onto the plain. Coming down the mountain we could see the Mediterranean about a mile away. On the plain the grass was green and we saw cattle and sheep grazing. We passed several settlements which were, I think, native, i.e. Arabic. These were surrounded by high stucco walls inside of which were many tall palm trees and beautiful buildings of smooth stucco in pastel colors. These settlements were off the main highway but as we rode by we could see sheiks riding camels or talking to one another and many donkeys and sheep. I wish that I could have stopped at one of these settlements.

At noon we came into Benghazi. It had been bombed but not as badly as Tobruk and people were living there. We passed through the town and stopped at an airport about two miles from Benghazi. We ate corned beef sandwiches and after an hour's time started back to Benghazi. We rode for three quarters of an hour and came to a little town called Benina. At the airport we were told that our camp was outside the village. Once more our convoy moved on. A major rode in the command car at the head of the convoy to direct us. We back-tracked on the Benina road for about two miles and then crossed a level stretch of ground to a spot a half mile from the highway. We unloaded our equipment, emptied the trailers and pitched our tents. We were the first outfit on the site and heard rumors to the effect that the airport was not yet finished. We unfolded our cots and settled ourselves; had dinner at seven and went to sleep.

Feb. 27, Saturday. Worked on our tent in the morning and in the afternoon were told that we could go to Benghazi. Zilk, Yorkston, Brooks and I set out for the town at one o'clock. We got into town at two and went to the Jewish market. It is situated on a side street that runs off from the old public square. The market is actually an arcade, the street in the middle being about twenty feet wide. Most of the vendors were Jewish although some were Arabic.

On the iron doors that folded over the front of many shops whose owners had not yet returned were scribbled invectives—relics of the nazi progroms. Most of the goods were cheap. Prices are controlled by the British military but there are many violators of the fixed price list. We bought souvenir handkerchiefs and walked back toward the center of town. We stopped in a coffee shop "in bounds" for British troops, had coffee which tasted terrible—eight cents (two piastras) a cup. The shop is run by Arabs. We looked in a few more shops trying to find something good but there doesn't seem to be anything good for sale. Always where there are natives living, there is that sweet pungent odor that I first noticed in India. I think it must be some kind of incense. At any rate it will always be associated with the East for me. We came back to the old public square and saw two Italian girls and an Italian man walking toward one side of the street (out of bounds for troops since civilians lived there). The girls had that way about them and I remarked to the boys that I thought all Italians had evacuated. One of the boys said a British MP told him that the Italian ladies were doing a hustling business all over town until the MP's came in. They are not allowed on the streets during certain hours now. One of the boys from our outfit told me that he got into the good graces of an Italian girl by paying for her dinner. He said that it wasn't possible to buy a female companion. This is another of the horrors of war—no pun intended. The fear of starvation is greater than that of possible ostracism. We walked back through the town and thumbed a ride back to camp. Had cold tomatoes and corned beef for supper.

Sunday Feb. 28—Worked on the tent again. Jim Morrow made a table from two Italian ammunition boxes.

Monday March 1—Got paid today. Guess I can send Barbara some more money for an Easter present this time. Weather has been cool lately. The tar and gravel runway is nearing completion. The negroes from British South Africa corps are certainly fast workers. They are as happy-go-lucky as our own American negroes.

Tuesday March 2—Our idleness was too good to last. Today we had rifle inspection. I passed but a lot of the guys got "gigged" and were told that they couldn't go to town until they passed. Played poker in the afternoon.

Wednesday March 3—Today is my ninth wedding anniversary. Nine months ago Barbara Flick became Barbara Kennedy. She is now Mrs. PFC Kennedy. At ten o'clock Jim Morrow and I left with Sergeant Ford for Benghasi. We got into town at 11:00 o'clock and went to the cathedral immediately. The cathedral's two domes are the one distinguishing feature of the skyline of Benghasi—visible for about eight miles. We walked up the driveway on one side of the large rectangle that fronts the cathedral and up the steps to the entrance. The guard on duty was Arabic and when we asked him if we were allowed in he signalled that we could. At first the interior of the church seemed undamaged except for broken windows but a closer examination revealed that the tile floor had been cracked in many places and a large hole near the entrance where dirt had been used to patch the floor testified to the damage done when a part of the shallow heavy marble balcony had fallen. Many of the marble images and statues had been damaged slightly and here and there a jewel from one of the altars was missing. On the whole there had been little thievery by German and Allied soldiers. I have never been in a church that impressed me more. The two domes were covered with black marble except for the tiny circle window at the very top of each which serve as skylights. The marble is laid in a pattern that lends height to the very high domes, and depth to the nave which is formed by the second dome—that is, the one toward the back of the church. When one looks up into the first great dome he feels insignificant—this feeling never left me as I walked toward the nave. I have never been in a building where there was so much marble. The only plaster visible in the church is that used on the side walls between the marble strips. All of the woodwork is mahogany as are the benches. The church is still being used for devotional purposes and is in fact marked out of bounds to troops except for that purpose. While we were admiring the church we were startled to hear gunfire. At first I thought it was the ack-ack guns shooting at a Jerry plane but then I remembered that the British South African troops practiced street fighting with live ammunition in that section of Benghasi. The area is barricaded. They use machine guns, hand grenades, mortars and rifles—firing at fixed targets.

We left the church and walked down to a native coffee shop off the old public square and had coffee (terrible) and native pastries resembling doughnuts and cream puffs (edible). We went once more to the native market where I bought an end table cover for sixty piastres, a toothbrush holder and toothbrush. Don't think I'll use it to brush my teeth. I talked to a British soldier in one of the shops who said that he had lived in Benghasi before the war—that he was Jewish and when the pogroms started had escaped to Palestine. From there he traveled to Egypt and joined the British army. His mother had been sent to a concentration camp in the interior of Libya by the Germans (he said) and when he came back to Benghasi with the British, the camp had been transformed into a refugee camp by the Allies. He said that his mother was still alive and that he had seen her. He seemed happy and said of Hitler "The time come for him now".

We left the market and walked about five blocks to the American canteen where we paid five piastres (twenty cents) for a bottle of Canada Dry Fizz Water. Each of us drank about one-third of the bottle. We walked to the road to Benina and thumbed a ride home.

Thursady, Mar. 4- Today the bombers started to come in to our field and we knew that our days of rest were done. In the morning I rode to the airport on the other side of Benghasi to get my rifle fixed – part of my rear sight was missing. We went to the post office where I sent Barbara a cablegram for fifty cents (like Western Union numbered greetings—you pick out three numbers). I also took out a money order for forty dollars. In the evening I went on guard from six to twelve-thirty.

It certainly is an experience guarding in this country. At night you hear jackals whine, birds screech, rats digging underfoot. Some of the boys saw a wildcat. At L.G. 139 Sergeant Stout was walking guard when something jumped up a him clawing holes in his field jacket. He shot at the animal several times with his forty-five but missed. From the size of the claw marks, it was decided that a wildcat which had been seen around the caves near the plane Stout was guarding had done the dirty work. Moody set a trap for the cat but didn't catch it as we had to move a day later. The cat was about the size of an average dog. The mess sergeant says that Libya is full of wildcats – that they won't attack a man but will tear up a bundle of clothes while a man looks on from his bed. I don't know if I believe that or not.

Friday Mar. 5—Wrote Barbara an airmail letter and tried to tell her where I was. Key words—Ben cause he—I hope it wasn't too obscure. In the afternoon I slept as I had to go on guard on the last shift. Wrote some of my journal in the evening and slept from ten to twelve. Had a long cold night.

Saturday Mar 6—Ate breakfast and went to bed and slept until four o'clock. The fellows said I snored so I must have slept soundly. When I woke up I went to the orderly tent to see if the guard roster was up and had a pleasant surprise—a letter from Barbara. It was written on Valentine's Day. Went on guard from six to twelve-thirty—pretty cold as the wind started to blow at ten o'clock. Was glad that I could climb into my warm cot for the rest of the night.

Sunday Mar 7—After breakfast I decided to make a stove as it was cold and the wind was still blowing. I walked up to the runway, got a fifty gallon drum and carried it back to the tent. Next I went out to the old Italian ammunition dump and got tin and wire for my stove pipe. Cut a hole near the bottom of the drum with a cold chisel and hammer, formed the stove pipe and quietly set it up in the tent. When I woke up Zilk and Young for chow the stove was finished even to the mud plaster. In the afternoon I moved back the tent pole in the back of the tent to make more room for the stove, wired the upright part of my stove pipe and started the fire. Washed my hair (an inch long now) and face. Tonight is my night off and am I glad! The wind is howling. Our tent is standing up better than most of the others as we have anchored ours around the edges and banked up dirt. Sergeant Morrow is forty-five years old today. He celebrated by taking fifteen pounds from the poker sharpies this afternoon. It's been a long day—wrote Mrs. K—think I'll turn in.

Monday Mar 8—After breakfast got my laundry together and went with Zilk, VanDuyne and Sgt. Blossom in the company truck to Benina. Lt. Koppel, special service officer of the 344th Squadron—good friend of VanDuyne's—went with us. We stopped at a trash heap outside of Benina and there the lieutenant picked up long steel poles, camouflage netting (to be used for a backstop on the softball diamond), an old settee and anything he thought he could use. We loaded all of this on the truck and drove over to HQ of the 98th Bomb Group where Blossom and Koppel had business. Next stop was the wog laundry where we left our clothes and bought some wafers at the shop near there. The native who ran the shop had had chocolate two days ago when VanDuyne and Zilk discovered it but he was sold out and wouldn't have any more until next week. We just got back to camp in time for chow. After chow Zilk put up our clothes line using the two steel barbed-wire posts that we had confiscated from the dump in Benina. I heated water for a bath. I used an old steel ammunition box (Italian) for a tub and took a good bath. It felt wonderful—the best bath I've had in two months even if the tub was twenty-four by twelve inches. Put on clean clothes and shaved—cleaned my battle dress in gasoline. Bought soap, towel, shaving cream and one bottle of beer from the canteen.

After supper we were told that another MP company was to go on duty tonight and that we would have the night off.

From here on we will alternate with the 975th—having one night off out of two. Captain Hinote also told us that we could go into Cairo in groups of five and that we should apply to him for leave. I can't apply until next month as I don't have the money but I hope I get there. After dark Zilk and I went down to the gasoline storage area and rolled a fifty-five gallon drum of 100 octane gas up to our tent. We need it for cleaning our clothes and for the stove. Played casino with Zilk and then a little poker with Zilk and Young. It has been a long day.

Tuesday Mar 9—This morning we had a tent inspection at ten o'clock. The C. O. informed us that we might do well to change the location of our clothes line as it was between our foxholes and the tent. Zilk demonstrated how he could run in a crouch under the line and I jumped over it after the C.O. had gone, but Sergeant Morrow thinks we ought to move it. Zilk and Young made three winding paths (bordered with small rocks) emenating from our tent entrance and transplanted two plants to the front lawn. I had to admit that his work made the front of the tent look better.

In the afternoon Young, Zilk and I went to Benghasi. Everytime I go into the city I notice a few more shops have opened and more Italians have moved in. I bought a ring for 35 piastres which fits me but which I hope can be made to fit Barbara. It has a camel and two palm trees on it and would be nice costume jewelry for a woman. I also bought a table cover for 35 piastre – it is very bright and typical. We went to the American canteen but could get nothing. A boy there told me that a ship was in the harbor with supplies on board but didn't know when the canteen would get them. We came back to camp, ate salmon patties and rice and bread. I am going to bed now as I must get up to be on guard at 11:30.

Wednesday Mar 10—Last night was windy. If we were at LG 139 we would be having the worst dust storm yet, but here the dust doesn't blow in our tents. The wind is from the south and is warm for a change—it may be the beginning of summer. After breakfast I slept until two o'clock, got up and began to wash when the truck drove up with the boys who had been to Cairo to attend Blecker's trial. Blecker fell asleep while guarding one of the planes at LG 139. He was taken to Cairo for court-martial. He was sentenced to one year in prison with a dishonorable discharge. There have been many others who have been caught falling asleep on guard but Blecker fell asleep right after one of the officers had warned the company that the next man to fall asleep would be court-martialed. It is characteristic of the garbled thinking of some (of those in authority) to let a thing go too far then crack down without allowing a sufficient time to elapse for new sterner policy to be impressed on the men. Since this was not done, Blecker seems in the minds of the men in the company to have been the victim of an unjust authority. I can't see how any soldier could allow himself to fall asleep on guard. I was surprised to hear that different men had been caught asleep by the sergeant of the guard and escaped with a gentle admonition. Well, the boys returning from Cairo brought mail and a few packages. I got a package from Aunt Alm—two books, See Here, Private Hargrove and Private Purkey, in Love and War. It was wonderful to get the books and I got eleven letters—three from Barbara, three from home, three from Mary Louise, one from Aunt Alm and one from Eleanor at Oster's, where I worked as a timekeeper before the army called. After chow we were told that the other MP's had left and we would be on guard. I was on the first shift and it was windy, but warm. The latest rumor is that the part of our company in Cairo is coming here after the best men have been picked out for MP duty in Cairo. One company is being made by consolidating the best men from the three companies in Cairo. Harry Hibbs is on the investigating staff. Anyway, for a while I thought I was an investigator. Came off guard at 12:45 and went to sleep.

Thursday March 11 – This morning I washed my winter underwear, aired my blankets on our clothesline (still not moved), talked to a little Arabian vendor on a donkey about three feet high. He comes around trading eggs for V cigarettes – one egg for one package of ten. V cigarettes are those that are issued free to Allied Armed Forces in the field. They are made in India and taste like hell unless you haven't had a cigarette for a couple of weeks. They bite your tongue and differ from American cigarettes in that you can't taste them in your throat. Almost everyone whom I have talked to (English, French, Indian, Arab and plain "wog") prefers American cigarettes to any other. Often when a group of American soldiers is passing some of the British South African negroes, one of the negroes will salute and say "Cigarette, sahib?" When one of the Americans gives him a Lucky or a Phillip Morris (the only two brands available overseas at the present time) he will click his heels loudly and give his best salute. American soldiers are the best paid in the world and pay generously for services. The native laundry at Benina refuses, as of today, to accept any more American laundry. The laundry was organized to wash the clothes of the RAF. Americans paid more for their laundry and theirs was done fast; accordingly, the RAF laundry was late. The British then go to the wogs and tell them if they want to remain in Libya they had better stop fooling around and get out the RAF laundry. It looks as if we do our own laundry for a while.

In the afternoon Bass, formerly of the Cairo group arrived. He weighs 235 pounds and is funny. The boys decided to kid him about air raids etc. Every night at five o'clock the British shoot off about sixty tons of Italian ammunition in a field about a mile from here. The noise and reverberation is terrific, even when you expect it. Bass was moved into the same tent as Van-Duyne who started at four o'clock to talk about the air raid we had every evening around five. He had his helmet on and had Bass do the same. They were looking in the direction of the field when the smoke and fire rose up.

Van said "Here it is, run for the fox hole." Bass beat him to the fox hole and when they were both in he turned to say something to VanDuyne when the explosion came. Bass got down so low that he was one with the earth. He was in a daze for the next half hour, thinking about what he had gotten into. Homsey finally told him what it was about. It wouldn't seem so funny to me if somebody pulled a trick like that. I was on guard duty on the night shift so I slept until midnight, went over and drank coffee and went on duty.

FRIDAY March 12 – Slept until noon today and in the afternoon wrote letters to Barbara, Jim Gettemy and Bob Vought. Last night was warm but the wind is coming from the north again and it is cooler. Went on guard on the first shift. Ordinarily guard duty is a dull tiresome task but here in the Libyan desert the one thing we have not suffered from is ennui. One hears the weirdest cries from a strange bird—not only at dawn or dusk—but all through the night. Wildcats prowl around to add to their occasional yowling to the other sounds. Then, too, one never knows what sort of strange bug or smaller animal he may be tramping on when he walks his post in the darkness. The ground here is teeming with scorpions, moles, snails and huge black beetle-like bugs about an inch-and-a-half in diameter. When we were gathering rocks to weigh down the edges of our tent we found a scorpion under almost every rock. The first night that I spent here I was squeamish when I thought how easily one of the scorpions could crawl between my blankets but I haven't thought of them since then. I think the little insect (some are three inches long) minds his own business which is under the surface of the ground.

We were relieved at 12:30 and were in a gay mood as we were provided material for a joke. From 11:00 o'clock on Bass had kept shouting to the guard on the plane beside him, "What time do we get relieved?" He had been used to shorter hours in Cairo. He had also committed the outstanding faus pas to date when he hung his overcoat on the nose gun of his plane and forgot it. Later, when he ambled around the side of the plane he halted his overcoat. This was attested to by the guard on the plane beside Basses'.

Saturday –March 13 –So we come to another weekend. This morning we dug the floor of our tent down about a foot to make more headroom. In the afternoon I went with Sellers to clean up the baseball diamond and had to do more digging. Was pleasantly surprised to learn that I had the night off. Some of our B bags arrived today. Mine was not in this load but I understand there is another load coming. I hope nothing had happened to it as I have things in it that are not replaceable – my journal number one for instance.

Sunday March 14—Last night when I went to bed I heard a hollow grinding sound, then dirt falling to the floor; along with the sound something was bumping the legs of my cot. After I had been in bed for an hour I got up, lit the light and looked. There were about ten shovelsful of dirt in mounds on the ground between my cot and the earth wall. We had disturbed the moles when we dug the floor of our tent and they were busy making more tunnels. As I watched I could see them shove dirt out of the holes but couldn't see the moles themselves. I scraped away the dirt from the entrance to the tunnels with a board and waited for a mole to appear, but none came. The light, I think warned him. I wedged the board between the earth wall and the legs of my cot so that the holes were blocked and crawled back into bed. In a little while I heard them again—scraping loudly against the board but I think they finally gave up trying to get through. Then I fell asleep.

This morning I was on a detail helping Sergeant Blossom unpack a box of sundries shipped from Cairo and cleaning shot guns. In the afternoon I borrowed the December Reader's Digest from Carroll. We had mail call and I had two letters from Barbara, one from Eleanor at Oster's and one from Pa Kennedy. I am on the last shift tonight, so I guess I'll get to bed.

Monday March 15 – Last Saturday when the B Bags arrive from Cairo where we had left them when we came into the desert, some of us didn't get our bags. At first we thought that they would arrive shortly on another plane. There were rumors to the effect that the men who had not received their B bags were those who would be transferred into a new company being formed in Cairo of men selected from three other companies. I am not counting on getting into Cairo as anything can happen, but I won't regret leaving the field for a place where I can have a warm bath every day. Slept until noon today then read Reader's Digest. Went on guard on the first shift. Several of the boys have motorcycles now; they have paid from two to ten pounds for them and they all seem to run.

Tuesday March 16 – Slept long today as I was tired. Got up at one o'clock, washed some clothes in gasoline, wrote a letter to Barbara using my new APO number and read Reader's Digest for October '42. The war picture doesn't look as rosy as it did a month ago. Sometimes I think I'll be an old man by the time I get home. Slept until midnight then went on guard. Wrote a letter to Pa Kennedy before I went to bed.

Wednesday March 17 – St. Patrick's Day. Slept until 11:30, ate lunch, took a bath and shaved in the afternoon. We take bathes in little Italian ammunition boxes about 24 by 12 inches – 6 inches deep. Washed some clothes in gasoline. The latest rumor from the orderly room is that we are to move again about 35 miles from here – just when we get settled – some fun. I have tonight off if no more planes come in.

Thursday March 18 – After breakfast I pegged the back flaps of our tent down. We had left them up when we dug out the floor of the tent. Last night the wind blew and it became cold. Was certainly glad that I had the night off as I heard the wind between five layers of blankets. Lt. Svella came back from Cairo and brought mail and chocolate candy – no cigarettes. I got a letter from Mary Louise and one from Mother. This was ordinary mail so I didn't get one from Barbara. Cigarette shortage is acute.

Friday March 19 – It rained all day today. This morning we were informed that we would be moving to a field about thirty-five miles away. We are to leave tomorrow morning at ten o'clock. Sergeant Morrow has had rheumatism since the day we dug out the floor of the tent. It began to rain about noon and the ground became muddy. In the evening Reese, Brown, Butler, York, Zilk, Young and I played blackjack and I lost my last pound. We were issued five packets of V cigarettes which alleviated the shortage. Went to bed at nine thirty and the rains came.

Saturday March 20 – It has been a long day. We got up at five-thirty. Outside it was clear but the rain had come down in torrents last night and the company area was a slew of mud that stuck to our galoshes and weighted our feet down. After breakfast we took down our tent and gathered our equipment in one pile, then helped the captain take down his tent. Other men helped take down the mess tents and load the mess truck. Our truck drove up at eight o'clock and we loaded our equipment, Gregorin's equipment, and climbed on the truck. We drove up to the point where the dirt road from the camp area meets the asphalt highway that runs from Benina to Lete to Benghazi and waited for the other trucks.

While we waited we watched the British South African negro soldiers drill. They like drilling and would put many an American or British outfit to shame. In a little while another troop came marching down the highway, led by a colored sergeant. They were singing one of their native songs – it seemed to us that it needed the accompaniment of tom-toms. Soon we were joined by the five other trucks and our convoy was on its way – eight trucks in all. We turned right on the highway toward Benghazi. Before we got there the rains came. Two of our trucks were uncovered and the boys in them were soaked. We were glad that our truck was a covered one. In about an hour the rain stopped and the sun came out. The road became very rough. A sign at the side of the road read "Danger. This road is

bombed. Convoys travel 100 yards between trucks." We could
see that the road had been bombed relentlessly. Further on a
sign painted on the side of a native building read "You will not
laugh if Jerry strafes" and the first warning was repeated. We
saw no airplanes while we passed over this posted road which
was about ten miles long. We went through a pleasant little native village named Ghemine – all of these native villages have
one thing in common – the Mohammedan church built in the
same pattern. The tower with the conical roof tipped with the
crescent is the dominant characteristic of the village skyline.

At two o'clock our convoy stopped at the side of the road.
We had been riding for forty-five miles and apparently missed
our destination. Lt. Svella went back to check and returned
an hour later. We turned around and rode to a point about
seven miles from where we had parked and turned right on
a mud road. From the signs we deduced that our army had
passed through making the road – for when an army moves
over ground a permanent road is made. The grass and sage had
been worn away in an area about a hundred yards wide and
deep ruts and mud holes from the recent rains made the road
rough. Wrecked tanks, guns, automobiles, empty five-gallon
gasoline tins and German water cans testified to the past pres-
ence of the armies. We traveled on this army road for an hour,
then came on to a hard rock road. On both sides of the road
we saw camels grazing as far as we could see. We passed several small villages and soon came to Soluch, our destination.
Soluch is on the Benghazi railroad and seems to have been a
pleasant little Italian-Arabian village before the war came. We
were escorted to our tent area and were pleasantly surprised to
learn that the MP company which was moving from Soluch to
Lete (to take our place) was willing to exchange tents so that
we had tents already up and in most cases dug in to a depth of
three feet and sand-bagged. We moved our equipment in and
went to chow. Jim Morrow's back was bothering him so much

that he was taken to the hospital in the evening. I slept until three o'clock when I went on guard.

Sunday March 21 – We learned that we are to move again – this time to another area of this camp – nearer the field. We picked out sites for our tents in the old irrigation plot. This project extends over an area a half mile square. The large square is divided into sixteen smaller squares.

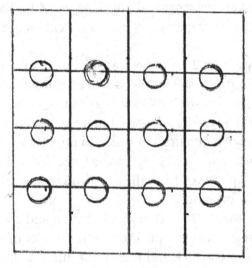

Irrigation Plot

In the diagram the circles represent the deep wells from which the water was drawn to irrigate the barren soil. The cross sections in the crude (modesty is in order) diagram represent piles of rocks about six feet high. Each of these smaller squares is divided into smaller squares about twelve feet on a side. From the well the water was poured (I don't know exactly how) into tiles to the right and left in the direction of the arrows and then ran down other tiles into each square, then into the smaller squares. I don't know what crop was raised here but the irrigation must have meant a lot to the Arabs in the area. I imagine that the project was sponsored by the Italian government. The winch used to raise the water in the wells was turned by a donkey walking around the well. It must have been a droll sight in the nineteen-thirties to see the twelve little donkeys walking in circles around the wells. The Germans poured tar into the wells so that they are useless as a source of drinking water. They may have been poisoned too as it is a favorite trick of the Nazis.

After we had picked out our tent sites we took down the five unoccupied tents left by the other MP Company, hauled them up to our new area and put them up. Zilk, Young and I came over after supper and put up ours. Went on guard at three AM.

Monday March 22 – Today we took down our tents – those we were living in – emptied the sandbags around the tents, and moved to our new area. We ate lunch at our company mess (a relief not to stand in line for an hour as we did at the camp mess) and moved into the tent and slept until we went on guard at nine o'clock. The guard duty is to be three shifts, the first shift being made up of men from the squadron who work from five to nine in the evening.

Tuesday March 23 – Today Zilk, Young and I worked like slaves digging out our tent. We dug out rocks of all sizes. I finished at three o'clock and then went into the village of Soluch (about the distance of a city block from our area) to buy American cigarettes for the first time in a month – four packs per man, but we went through the line twice. The offices of the squadron are in a beautiful Italian building on one side of the town square and it was here that the cigarettes were sold. I borrowed money from Reese to buy mine.

Wednesday March 24 -- This morning we finished our tent, filled sandbags and built up the sides and tightened up the ropes. After lunch the company store opened for the first time in a month. We were allowed one Imperial quart of Black Horse Ale, seven packs of cigarettes, a chocolate bar (Palestinian milk chocolate), Bull Durham (I got this to smoke in my pipe), toothpaste and matches. We felt like a lot of happy kids on Christmas. After we had bought our allotment, Ries, Koester, Zilk, Young and I sat around the table in our tent and had a party. We sang and talked of home, smoked and talked of drinking bouts – had a wonderful time except that we should have had more ale. In the evening I wrote Barbara and Mother. Went on guard until three AM.

Thursday March 25 -- After breakfast I slept until noon. After lunch we had gas mask and helmet inspection. All of us except Gregorin were gigged on our helmets so I had to wash mine. Something I haven't written as yet is that the ground around here is teeming with lizards of all sizes up to eight inches. They scamper from one clump of mesquite (it looks like mesquite) brush to another. At the end of our section of the irrigation project the few tiles remaining are virtually full of these lizards. If one walks along the tiled main aqueduct leading from the well, they scamper before him, their clawed feet making scraping noises on the tiles, and disappear into the side adits. From these side water pipes, t hey peer up at the intruder with their dull reptilian eyes.

In the afternoon at four o'clock the boys who were visiting Cairo came back and brought my B bag with them. I was glad to get pipe cleaners, pictures of Barbara and my field jacket. In the evening Yorkston came over to our tent and brought a quart of Old Tradition Bourbon which the boys had brought him from Cairo. It was enough to make us feel mellow. Some of the boys were nearly drunk – nobody knows how much liquor was brought in from Cairo but it was appreciated. I slept until one o'clock at which time I went on guard.

Friday March 26 – Since we have been at this field we have had three air raid alarms – all around five o'clock in the evening – and we haven't seen a single plane. I hope we are always so lucky. I haven't mentioned anything about the town of Soluch yet. It is a typical Libyan village, part native and part Italian. It is at the termination of the railway to Benghazi. The railway is a little narrow gauge affair and was bombed by both armies.

The beautiful modern (though small) station is destroyed and a train of cars on the siding was reduced to steel skeletons by the incendiaries. The town itself is not greatly damaged. The streets are lined with shade trees of an unknown variety and there is the ubiquitous Mohammedan church dominating the skyline. I haven't had time to explore the town yet but I want to now that we are settled. It must have been a beautiful sleepy little town full of sunshine and peace – before war came.

Bob Yorkston has moved in our tent. From all the information that we can get, Jim Morrow will not be back. He has been sent to Heliopolis Depot to be reclassified. This life is too rigorous for a man forty-five years old. He'll probably be given an office job over here or at home. Yorkston is a T corporal from Zilk's home town, Nielsville, Wisconsin. He is small, nice looking, twenty-one years old and a good boy. He will be a good non-com tent leader, I think.

Saturday March 27 – This morning we had rifle inspection and when the C.O. threatened to break any non-coms who were gigged, every one of us except Bass passed. In the afternoon I slept for an hour then borrowed a half pound from Ries and went in to Soluch to the canteen. It was a beautiful afternoon and as I entered the streets of the village, the sunshine on the street, the smell of the bright yellow blossoms on the olive trees that line the streets, the green grass in the courtyards of the Italian homes, the native adobe houses, the little donkeys, the silent Arabs suddenly inspired me. I was glad to be alive and Spring gave me new hope.

I bought 7 packs of cigarettes, an Imperial quart of beer, matches and candy and came back to the tent area. After chow in the evening we went into Soluch again where "Big Broadcast of 1943", a program of orchestra music, singing and pantomime was given by the 376th Bomb Group. The show did not begin until Colonel Compton, the Group commander (24 years old and a full colonel) had taken his seat in the middle of the front row. It was a very good program and relieved the monotony.

Sunday March 28 – Here we are at the beginning of another week. Slept most of the day. In the evening I played volleyball, washed, ate some fruit cocktail which somebody got from somewhere and hard-boiled eggs. While we were talking in the tent Brown, who was boiling eggs on our fireplace suddenly caught himself on fire; he threw a can of gasoline on the fire and his pants caught on fire. He ran into the mesquite shrubs and rolled around until the fire was smothered. He came into our tent and I gave him some burn ointment for the pain. The burns weren't serious, but Brown will be more careful the next time he throws gasoline on an open fire.

I just learned that the large black bugs we have been seeing around here are the scarabaeus or scarabs – regarded by the ancient Egyptians as symbollic of resurrection and immortality. The scarab is watermarked in the Egyptian half-pound note.

Monday March 29 – Today I took a sponge bath since we had a physical exam today and were given typhus and cholera shots. We had mail call in which I received two letters from Barbara, one from Dad (postmarked Jan. 7 and sent to the wrong APO), one from Jean and Al and a letter from Mary Louise with a lot of clippings from home. Dale Byers is a statistician with the Air Corps, Bill Sutton is teaching in finance school – everybody else is a sergeant. Guess I'm not the type.

Something a little out of the ordinary happened today when three of the boys were able to get drunk on lemon extract. The boys started to shoot their rifles and pistols from their tents and were warned by the captain. I don't know what their punishment will be, but it is possible to court martial them for wasting ammunition. The lemon extract came from a freight train which they were guarding. Somebody (ingeniously) thought of the high alcoholic content of lemon extract and pilfered several bottles of same.

Tuesday March 30 – Last night Bass and Golish were caught sleeping on guard. They have been placed in the "guardhouse", a tent on the opposite side of our camp area. This means that we have yet another post to guard.

About three weeks ago five of our boys went to Cairo. They were fellows who had bad teeth, needed glasses etc. Red Weidle was one of those who needed glasses. He was given money by a lot of the fellows and instructed to bring back liquor (most important), camera film and other sundries. The big city proved too much of a temptation and Weidle spent all of the money on wine and women – with the women claiming the greater portion. The gay French, Greek and Arabian ladies of Cairo are certainly hustlers. Weidle spent over two hundred dollars in two weeks and he had no hotel bill for the first week as he stayed at the Red Cross Service Club. The boys were mad at Weidle but he is a little guy, was repentant so nothing was done to him physically. He figures that in three months he can call his pay his own. I played volleyball in the evening and went on guard. It was a nice warm starry night.

Wednesday March 31 – This morning after breakfast we had mail call but there were only a few letters and I got none. The company PX opened and I borrowed a pound from Salzer to get ale, cigarettes, candy, shaving cream, English wafers and chocolate-covered peanuts. Today is my fifth month of foreign service which I understand is counted from the day a man embarks. I hope that I am home before another five months passes. Wrote Barbara and Uncle George and slept until guard time. At midnight the clocks were set ahead one hour. The first shift were the gainers and stood one hours less guard.

Thursday April 1 – We were paid today and after I paid off my creditors I played poker – won forty piastres in about five hours – good for me. The only April Fool prank was played by Zilk and me on Ray Young, the gullible one. We forged an official looking document ordering Young to report to the C. O. Immediately in reference to a medical discharge. Young was excited and went to the orderly room where Butler, the company clerk, announced "April Fool". Young was speechless.

Young had been writing to a girl back home and when he got her picture, Anderson asked Young for her address. Young gave Andy the address and the young lady in question wrote Andy a sweet letter and seemed interested. Soon Andy had her picture too and the boys have their hands full trying to determine who has the inside track. Andy and Young read each other's mail from the young lady and neither one knows where he stands.

Friday April 2 – Received a letter from Barbara today. It was dated March 8 and she had received my cablegram of March 4. Washed some clothes in the afternoon. We have been ordered not to send clothes to natives as there are several cases of leprosy among them. In the evening played blackjack and won fifty piastres. Went to bed and slept until 1:30 when Sergeant Johnson came in and said "Rommel is evacuating". It seems that the planes had returned from their mission with the news. I am not too optimistic. Latest rumor is that we go to Turkey when the African campaign is completed. Time will tell.

Saturday April 3 – Last night the mechanics were working on the planes all night getting them ready for an early morning mission. The weather was bad so they didn't go up. I hope they get up in time to make it hot for Rommel. Went into Soluch after breakfast to get my allowance of beer, cigarettes and candy. I have more cigarettes now than I've ever had at one time – nineteen packs of Luckies. Went to bed and lay for an hour without sleeping – thinking of home. After chow I shaved, shined my shoes for the first time in over three months and got ready for retreat. At four o'clock the first sergeant blew his whistle and announced that there would be no retreat. We were glad as it was raining. Zilk got two more packages from home. One of them contained a dozen candy bars. He has had nine packages from home. Van Duyne came over and told us what he and Miller did today: they were riding their motorcycles over the desert when they saw a grey fox. They ran the fox down and Van Duyne kicked it on the head knocking it out. They killed it by driving over it with the motorcycle. A funny thing, the left front foot was off at the first joint. Van said he must have been caught in a trap at one time and escaped by tearing off his leg. He also said that the fox ran fast for having only three legs. Van brought the fox into the camp area. He was a beautiful looking specimen. I went on guard duty at nine o'clock. It was cold and windy.

Sunday April 4 – Got up for breakfast and went to Soluch to the canteen where I bought another can of "Africaner" tobacco. Came back and slept until four-thirty. Played volleyball and poker – lost all of my money and a pound of Yorkston's. I am giving up the game. The Middle East News for April 2nd was very optimistic. I'm going to bed as I go on guard duty at one-thirty.

Monday April 5 – Slept until noon today. Got up for chow and learned that we are to move tomorrow to Berca No. 2 – nearer Benghazi than we were at Lete. We were glad that we would be near a city again and sorry to be moving as we had worked hard digging in our tent. We did a little packing in the afternoon and went on guard from nine to two o'clock.

BENGHAZI, LIBYA

April 6 to September 18

William M. Kennedy

Tuesday April 6 – Had breakfast of hotcakes and bacon at six-thirty and we began packing and taking down our tents. We had a truck with Clemens and Colvin and hauled a lot of kitchen equipment with us. We had seven trucks in our company which left for Benghazi at ten o'clock. The first two hours were over the dirt road made by Allied and Axis armies. Just as we came to the main highway we had a rest stop and looked at each other. We were covered with dust – our faces looked tan with yellow spots. Those of us with glasses reminded me of the proverbial colored preacher. We arrived at Berca No 2 at about two o'clock. An officer in a jeep led our convoy to our new camp site. We crossed the landing field and traveled over a ridge and into the white sand of the sea shore. Our camp site was in a slight depression beside the Mediterranean and under palm trees. It was just like the spot you might choose to build a cottage at the seashore. The land sloped gradually up and away from our camp site, leveled into a plateau on which, at the further end lay the landing field. At the top of the slope where the plateau begins, a native Arabian village sets surrounded by palms. The natives graze their donkeys on the grassy slope and cultivate their little patches of garden which they irrigate from wells.

Our tent is the nearest one to the mess tent. Our crowning achievement is our tile block floor which cost us about five hours of hard work to lay. We found the tiles near the spot we had picked for our tent. The blocks are about six inches square and about a half inch thick. The floor is laid in red and white checkerboard designs. When Zilk and I went searching for more tiles to complete the floor we met an old Arab working in his onion patch. We gave him two cigarettes and asked him where we could find more. He pointed to the shore with a sweeping gesture and said "Americano" – pushing an imaginary something with his hands to indicate "came", "chug-chug-chug" with gestures for steering a car, then a sweep of his hand away from the shore. By this we understood that there had been a lot of tiles but the on-the-ball Americanos had driven down to the shore, loaded them on their trucks, and carted them back to their tents on the other side of the field.

After evening chow we finished our tent, watched the great crimson ball of sun set into the Mediterranean through the palm trees. What a wonderful place for a honeymoon. I hope Barbara and I can come back here someday as I want her to see this – to sleep with the quiet rumble of the sea as a lullaby – when the roar of an airplane won't drown out the susurration of the Mediterranean.

Wednesday April 7 – Spent the day filling five-gallon cans with sand. We lined these around the outside of the tent, then raised the tent so that it rested on the tops of the cans; this gave us about twelve inches more headroom. We filled sandbags and anchored the bottom edge of the tent onto the tops of the cans with the sandbags. It was a windy day and we had a hell of a time with our tent.

In the morning we walked up to the shore – up the ridge that runs along the edge of the shore and down to the sloping beach. The beach is wide and extends as far as the eye can see on either side. The sand is white and very fine. On the ridge that runs about a hundred yards from the water line are the palm trees, very old and therefore very tall. Some of the boys have their tents under the palms and have a wire clothes line strung from tree to tree.

In the evening our tent was full of men, smoking and talking – mostly about the merits of various automobiles. A "new" model means a 1942 model.

I went on guard at 10:30. Phelps and I were guards at the main gate. We have little business. As we watched the giant searchlights play their beams in the sky over Benghazi Phelps told me about the women that he almost married. He is thirty-five and still can't see the advantages of being married. Came in at three-thirty and went to bed.

Thursday April 8 – Got up for breakfast and then went back to bed until noon. In the afternoon the company store sold candy and cigarettes. I didn't buy any as I had squandered my money in poker at Soluch. I hope I learned a lesson: gambling doesn't pay. Yesterday while Zilk was rambling around the area he discovered an enameled sign which he brought back to the tent. It turned out to be a sign which formerly hung in front of the Belgian consulate in Benghazi. It is about three feet high in bright green, red and yellow colors. It has the Belgian coat of arms and motto, "Union Makes Strength". We have it hung on a frame (made from an old steel bed) in front of our tent.

I think that one of the nomadic Arabian tribes camped in this area at one time as there are torn shreds of tents like the Arabs used, native dishware, native shoes (baby shoes) and bones of many donkeys. They must have been caught in one of the many bombings that the city suffered.

Since we have been attached to the heavy bomb groups it seems to me that there have been a comparatively small number of casualties. As a civilian I had imagined that bombers were shot down on every mission and that the crews of these were fatalities. I am glad to learn that I had a mistaken impression. Most missions are carried out without fatalities and when a bomber is shot down the chances of the crew bailing out and becoming prisoners of war are pretty good. Often the bomber is able to fly to our own territory before the crew abandons it. Another mistaken impression I had was about the effectiveness of ack-ack fire. Flak is more of a hazard to our bombers than the fighting planes of the enemy. Every bomber has patches over holes made by flak. Moody and I counted two hundreds and some patches in a ship that we once guarded. Went on guard duty from six to one-thirty.

Friday April 9 – Slept this morning. After the noon meal we banked sand up against the five-gallon cans which make our foundation. Butler, Young and I went down to the shore and went swimming. We bucked the big waves for about twenty minutes, then came out and lay in the sun for about an hour. Later in the afternoon we had mail call. I got five letters and not one from Barbara.

Saturday April 10 – I am to be gunner on our armored car for the next two days. The two men in the armored car guard the entrance to the field. In mail call I got the January issue of Reader's Digest and two letters from Mary Louise – still none from Mrs. K. Went on guard from six to twelve.

Sunday April 11 – Slept all morning today. Felt pretty disgusted. Read my Reader's Digest and another book. Went to Ries' tent and he gave me some Bond Street which he had received from home. Got two letters from Barbara. Slept until twelve and then went on guard.

Monday April 12 – This morning on guard duty before I was relieved I talked to a young Austrian Jew who is a member of a company of engineers in the British Army. He said he had been living in Palestine for five years before he came into the army. He was born in Vienna and lived there until 1936 – avoided speaking of the pogroms. He is an intellectual, only twenty-two, but seemed ancient with the years that come to the young through suffering. He was not bitter. His mind had enabled him to accept his fate philosophically. His English is very good, better I told him, than the English that soldiers use. He said he didn't think it proper for a foreigner to use the slang of a language. I asked him if he had wanted to go to college. "That is hard to say. One goes to college because one's parents have enough money to send one."

"But what of your hopes, your ambitions?" I asked. He shrugged his shoulders.

"I must do something with the hands, but let's win the war first."

I felt only pity for this grown up yet so young little jew who wanted to do something with his hands because (I suppose) he felt that a trade could not be taken away from one. He must have been a brilliant student in the Vienna before Nazi-ism. I would like to see him again but I doubt if I will – things are so uncertain.

After breakfast I slept until noon. In the afternoon we bought a little gasoline stove from an Arab peddler for one pound and a pack of Lucky Strikes. Got two letters from Barbara and everything is fine. I have tonight off. Blossom and Ries came in out tent and we talked of school. Blossom explained the operation of the linotype press – he had three years of advertising at a small college in New York State. Went to bed at 11:00.

Tuesday April 13 – Zilk, Young, Carrol, Ries and I went to Benghazi today. The town has been cleaned up considerably since we were here last. Civilian automobiles and trucks are beginning to appear and many more shops are open. The ghetto is a madhouse with Arabs, Jews and Greeks haggling with one another and with soldiers. Nubians from the south peddle bracelets – not to soldiers, but to merchants. They are the wholesalers and the currency which they demand for their wares is strange to me. It is, I suppose, a more common currency for trade among the North African coast than the Egyptian money. There were old Arabs from Tripoli with their withered faces turned away from their customers as if it were no matter to them whether the deal was done or not. We had native doughnuts and tea at one of the Greek shops. Talked to a Jewish MP (U.S.A.) who interpreted to me a conversation that he carried on with a native shopkeeper. We came back at two o'clock after stopping at the British Nafi store where we ordered pies. We thought they were fruit pies but they were meat pies – and fatty. Wrote Barbara and went on guard from six to twelve-thirty.

Wednesday, April 14 – Got up for breakfast then went back to bed until 10:30 – went in swimming and sun-bathed until noon. The day was hot and the Mediterranean was calm. Swimming was wonderful. After chow I went swimming again.

I have tonight off again so the boys are accusing me of using suction. I go to work tomorrow at six in the morning on the armored car. Wrote Barbara two letters and went to bed.

Thursday, April 15 – I'm writing this with my new Eversharp which is one of the gifts in the package from Barbara. Others are a pipe kit with a new pipe, two books, Topper and Strategy of Terror, a snapshot folder and Xmas snaps, apron for toilet articles, steel mirror, baby powder, shave cream, toothpaste and caramels. It was mailed January 19th so I am hoping for the other package from Mrs. K. Kawalec and I were on the armored car from six to twelve this morning.

This afternoon I read and smoked my new pipe. After chow this evening we had visitors. Wrote Barbara and went to bed.

Friday April 16 – This morning I straightened up my barracks bags and put them on the side of my cot nearest the tent. At noon went on guard at the main gate with Alabama. When I came back at six I had received the Oster Dopster and a carton of Camels from Dad mailed in December. Went to bed early as I didn't feel well – think I ate too much candy yesterday.

Saturday April 17 – Rifle, tent and mess kit inspection this morning. Got gigged for having rust in the chamber of my rifle. Cleaned it after chow. Tomorrow I stand another rifle inspection with the seven others who were gigged. Wrote letters in the afternoon, played volleyball in the evening, and went to see a real movie at the other camp area across the road. I don't know what the name of the show was but it was a murder mystery with Milton Berle and Martha Scott. We all enjoyed it as it was the first we had seen in three and a half months. Went on guard at midnight.

Sunday April 18 – After rifle inspection I went to bed and slept until two o'clock when Zilk, Van Duyn and Ries woke up Yorkston, Young and me. They had returned from church in the cathedral in Benghazi. They were heating cans of pork and beans on our gasoline stove. We joined them in the meal of beans and pineapple. I read until chow. After chow we had a volleyball game. Read and slept until time for guard. The other evening I talked to some of the English boys on the ack-ack guns. We don't have any American ack-ack crews on this side of Tripoli from what I can gather. We talked about mail. Their ordinary mail reaches them about three and a half months after it is mailed in England. Air mail takes nine weeks. Compare this with our V-mail which takes twelve to fifteen days or our ordinary mail which takes a month at the most. I guess they are too interested in fighting to think about mail but I should think that the salutary effect on morale would justify efficient mail service.

Monday April 19 – Slept this morning. In the afternoon we were issued our sun helmets which look very smart. We were driven into Benghazi to see a show "Adam Had Four Sons", but when we got there we were told that the show had been cancelled since the generator to operate the projector had not arrived. We walked around the ghetto, ate native pastry and drank tea at one of the little tea and confectionary stores, then came back to camp. In the evening after volleyball, heard the news – it was good.

Wednesday April 21 – Went in swimming this afternoon – wonderful. In the evening we saw a movie. Sleepytime Gal. It seemed good to us but was, I suppose, considered second-rate back home.

Thursday – April 22 –Last night my post was the mess hall and I ate cinnamon rolls (one dozen) until two o'clock when the bakers left. In the morning I had hot cakes and coffee. Came back to our area and slept until four o'clock. In the evening I sent Barbara and Mother and Dad cablegrams. Blossom came in and we heated oxtail soup and spaghetti on our stove. Had a good snack finishing with Young's pineapple. We decided that after payday we will do this more often. Zilk and Yorkston tried to tell us about how much better Wisconsin is than any other state. Young and I upheld the negative. I have tonight off and am about ready to go to bed. Night noises: loud braying of the little native donkeys and raucous barking of the many native dogs. Barbara's package of November 14th arrived today. My moccasins finally came – with four pairs of socks and the snap-shots taken when I went home one October weekend. It took five months for the package to arrive. Guess I'll get to bed. The sand fleas are calling.

Sunday April 25 – Today was the queerest Easter I have ever known. I kept thinking it was Thanksgiving. Guess it was on account of the day being cooler. In the evening we played chinese checkers and had a snack of crackers with cheese and oxtongue – cookies for dessert. Went on guard in the evening.

Monday April 26 – Two letters from Barbara in which she called me down for writing a gripe letter to Mother instead of to her. Guess I deserved that. Barbara also told me that Dad is to be operated on for a hernia and then take a month off. The month off will certainly do him good.

Sunday May 2 – It has been hot for the past few days. The heat is different here – there's no place to keep cool. When I drink water from my canteen it's warm and makes me more thirsty. The Khamsin (fifty) winds have come blowing sand and the flies, beetles and night insects swarm everywhere. The wind is hot and the flies are terrible. They seem to be attracted to us like iron filings are to a magnet, and are almost as thick. When we go down to the beach our bodies are covered with them. Last Saturday we went up the road to the day room to see King's Row. Show was late in starting as we had an air raid alarm – the first in a long time for us. The Jerries came over to bomb an incoming convoy. We downed several of their planes. I don't know if they got any of the ships but the water tasted of oil Sunday when we went in swimming.

Went on guard from ten until two tonight. Something must be up as the guard has been doubled. Had a letter from Barbara today in which she said that she knows I'm in Libya – good girl.

Monday May 3 – The hot sirocco wind blows yet – water is warm and makes you thirsty – you aren't hungry and you go from one tent to another trying to find the coolest tent. All are hot. We open the back of our tent so the wind can blow through the tent. It helps a little. When the sun goes down the heat is enough to keep the flies moving for a couple of hours. When the flies hibernate, the locusts come – large tan-spotted with brown insects five inches long – large editions of our American grass-hopper except that they don't spit "tobacco juice". There is a kind of black beetle, longer and smaller than the scarab that has appeared. He is fast on his feet and amuses himself by crawling over any object extending up from the ground – thence on to the guard who leans against that object, for example an airplane wheel. Then there are those insects attracted by light; of these there are all of the American types and many indigenous to Africa – some with long-jointed, hard-shelled bodies that look like a tomato bug with wings. I think, on the whole, that I'll take America.

In the evening Blossom, Yorkston, Butler, Keller, Bowman and I played Cavalcade, a horse racing game. We didn't play for money as I learned my lesson last payday. I intend to derive some material enjoyment out of this pay. I want to buy a lantern for one thing.

Kreiger and I were on guard together and he spent three hours telling me of his two wives and many conquests. When I hear stories like his I try to look for a reason: is it that he was caught in the whirlwind of adolescent surprises and never got out. He isn't over-sexed, he's simply a phylogynist (who of us isn't) who is incapable of experiencing deeply and therefore unable to love any woman ; so, he chases from one woman to another, marries and divorces on occasion and is apparently satisfied with life. What is his trouble? I think that in general there is a direct relation between intelligence and conventionality. I think that Krieger's case may be regarded as general.

Sunday, May 9 – Mother's Day and I hope that the cablegrams I sent three days ago arrived on time. Yesterday we learned that Tunis and Bizerte have fallen and the end of the African campaign is in sight. We are beginning to wonder where we go next. Benghazi is becoming more of a city with many Italian, Greek and French families coming back. I haven't been in the city for about three weeks but the boys who have been say that you can buy "eggs and chips" which means "fried eggs and french-fried potatoes". Liquor is going to be sold by the town merchants in about ten days. The Arabian and Italian people of the town knew that Tunis and Bizerte had fallen before we in the army did. They had a celebration two night's ago and Paul Koester told me one of his wog friends said "Tunis and Bizerte no more – pretty soon no more war – vive l'Americano". I hope he's right.

Yesterday I went swimming and got a bad case of sun burn on my legs. It pains me to walk. Last night I saw "A tale of Two Cities". Was on the last shift. We have been seeing movies regularly now. I think they are fine for morale. The best morale builder, of course, is mail. Lately, we have been receiving mail regularly. Barbara sent me her slipper size in inches so that I can have a pair of slippers made for her. Aunt Lynn wrote me that she has taken out a $500 War Bond for Barbara and me – to start housekeeping. I hope we'll be able to use it someday. Aunt Alm sent me an Easter Greeting card and El at Oster's sent me mail. Slept all day today and am going to rest until it is time to go on guard as my legs don't feel so good.

Monday May 10 – Wrote letters to Barbara and Mother in the morning and went swimming in the afternoon. We put the volleyball net down on the beach and played between swims. The sea was rough today and we had a wonderful time bucking the waves.

William M. Kennedy

Went on guard the first shift. My post was the mess hall and commisary – had a very pleasant night. The mess sergeant and cooks decided to make pork sausage and onion sandwiches and brought me a big one. Later they invited me in for some hot chocolate; first, they insisted that I finish a bottle of beer explaining that "It's pretty flat, but you're welcome to it". I tipped the bottle up and started to gurgle it down my throat before I realized that it was funny beer. Then they told me that it was rum. I drank two big cups of hot chocolate and talked to the boys about the war, army of occupation and home. Was relieved at ten by Koester. Came back to the tent area – bull session with Walter Butler and to bed. Slept wonderfully on the rum.

Wednesday May 12 – Last night I saw Vivacious Lady with Ginger Rogers and James Stewart. I had seen it before but it was good. Came back and had lunch (midnight) with Yorkston and Blossom – spaghetti, spam and hot cocoa. Went on guard on the last shift. Slept all day. There is a rumor that we will be leaving for Tripoli shortly – and I haven't seen Cairo. VanDuyne, Mulree, Cave and Snyder are going into Cairo for a week. I gave VanDuyne a pound to buy a necklace of scarabs for Barbara. I hope he buys the right kind. I don't know if I'll ever see Cairo. Some of the boys think we may be going to Palestine. I don't think so. Played softball this evening. The war doesn't seem any nearer to being over.

Thursday May 13 -- This morning we learn from authentic sources that hostilities in North Africa ceased at 11:15 last night. The war doesn't seem any nearer to being over but of course it is. Went in swimming with Zilk this morning – water nice but wind cold. In the afternoon I went with Blossom into Benghazi. It is cleaned up considerably and there are many civilians about. Little Italian girls (as cute as any) who have seen a lot for their five years play in the Piazza Municipio – some ask for chewing gun: "American, gum?". The shops have many new articles and are cleaner than they were at first. We ate in a new Greek restaurant in the Piazza Municipio called the Metropoli

96

– had french fried potatoes and sponge cake. Tables actually
had white cloths and a menu – "10% for service" printed at
the bottom. Four of us ate there: Sergeant Johnson, McManus,
Blossom and I. Tasted good. Blossom made eyes at the cashier
who was a woman old enough to be his grandmother , but
white, and therefore interesting. We stopped at the quartermaster's for supplies and came back to our camp. I had bought
a photo-folder and some postcard photos of the city at one of
the native shops. The vendor attracts the shopper's attention
to the photo-folder by having two very nude ladies in ancient
Egyptian headress for pictures in the show window. The postcards have the titles in Italian and German and cost too much
(three for twenty cents, i.e. three for five piastres) but I'm glad
that I got them. I put Mother and Dad's pictures in the folder –
they don't quite fit. No mail from Barbara yet.

Friday May 14 – Last night was my night off and this morning I was awakened by Paul Koester, Sergeant of the Guard and
told that I was to go on duty from seven to twelve in the morning as Young was sick. I had to guard the 513th Squadron mess
hall and ate breakfast there. Sergeant Pete Peterson was on the
area guard and he stopped to talk a little while every hour. He
is from Wisconsin, likes golf, has a brother who is a painter
(artist) but runs a lathe for a living since he hasn't as yet made
a name for himself. Came off guard and swam and played volleyball until two-thirty. After evening chow we played softball.
Three V-mails today – all Easter letters – two from Barbara and
one from Jean and Al.

Saturday May 15 – Inspection all morning. On guard from
two to six this afternoon. For the present I am one of the "sunshine boys" since I don't work at night. Played softball and then
went to the show put on by the 376th Bomb Group. They had
an orchestra and a take-off on Dr. I. Q. . Officers and men were
asked questions. If the questions were answered correctly the
man received three packs of cigarettes; if an incorrect answer
was given the man had to take the consequences. Most of the

consequences involved making a fool of oneself on the stage. Colonels all answered correctly but one captain didn't know his seventh general order and was laughed down. A colored quartet (Engineers) sang spirituals and a little English soldier with a lot of courage came to the front and sang, "Ma, I Miss Your Apple Pie", and "Goodnight, Sergeant Major". The chaplain (Captain Flinn, a swell guy) announced that the new schedule called for a movie every three days (a new picture) and that sounded like good news. Came back to camp, made cocoa and read. Slept soundly.

Sunday, May 16 – Got up for breakfast at seven. The morning was beautiful – palm trees silhouetted against a sky of purple and pink – native mud houses silhouetted against the same background. It would have been inspiring under other conditions – would look romantic in a movie. At breakfast talked baseball and football. Went on guard from ten to two. Played softball in the evening and then went to see The Hunchback of Notre Dame. It is necessary to have a pass now if you want to go into town. This may mean simply that things are being organized or it may mean that we are getting ready to move and close tab must be kept on all the men. Had three letters from Barbara, one from Dad, and one from Mary Louise. Slept soundly.

Monday, May 17 – Wrote six letters this morning, three to Barbara, one to Dad, one to Mother and one to Pa. Went on guard from one to six. Went to the movies to see Ida Lupino in The Hard Way. It was very good. While the show was going, the ack-ack and shore batteries started and the sky was lined with red and white tracers. For a minute I thought we were being bombed but it lasted only fifteen minutes. I think it was only practice. Came back and went to bed but not to sleep. All four of us argued about the merits of Wisconsin as opposed to those of Pennsylvania. It started when Yorkston and Zilk talked about Dennis Morgan (The Hard Way) being from Wisconsin. Young and I talked about actors and actresses from Pennsylvania (Jimmie Stewart) but we had to invent a lot. We shouted at each other for an hour and finally dozed off. We all felt good inside.

Tuesday, May 18 – Up at six this morning and went on guard until ten. In the afternoon went to town with Butler and Sellars in the armored car. Went through the market (ghetto) and Butler and Sellers ate eggs and tomatoes at Metropoli. I watched. Went to the Naafi but it was closed. Talked to some Italian prisoners who were working inside some of the buildings. They seemed happy. I found out using my meager German that they had been taken at El Alemaine last November. We got a ride with a couple of English boys. One of them told us (we stopped at their quartermaster's for a while) that he had been in Africa three years. He came here when the British first took Benghazi, went to Greece, thence to Crete ("Lovely there for three weeks until all hell broke loose. Plenty of Hurricane fighters but they were new and the guns were coming by trucks. Germans beat the trucks. Hurricanes went up with out guns to molest the German planes and the Germans shot them down. It was bloody murder. Then back to Alexandria"). We asked him if he thought he would be going home soon and he said with a shake of his head, "I don't even give a damn any more". I think we'll soon be moving but I don't know where. We may see Italy yet. Wanted to write letters tonight but Bass came over and told me his life story – took all evening but I could write a book about the man. Finally to sleep thinking about Barbara.

Wednesday, May 19 – Read The Rasp this morning and went swimming in the afternoon. Went on guard from ten to two at night. My post was the tech supply and one of the guards from a nearby plane came over and talked to me. He said he was a member of a combat team of one of the bombers, hurt his back and was grounded. Later, he was broken from a technical sergeant. He had been in the army five years and in peacetime had served in Panama and Hawaii. Said that Hawaii was the best place he had been for having a good time and saving money. Didn't amount to much.

Thursday, May 20 – Slept until noon today. When I awoke it was raining for the first time in a month. In the afternoon the sun came out and it was hot enough to go swimming; however, the water had a film of oil over it so we didn't go in.

Friday, May 21 – Saw the movie Casablanca. It was very good.

Monday, May 24 – Was on the first shift last night so I had a good night's sleep – too good as I slept through breakfast. This afternoon I went in swimming. The water is still a little oily. We have been given our orders for defending the camp area in the event of a beach landing or paratrooper attack. Hope we beat the Axis to the punch in this. I wish we could get the invasion started. Saw Wake Island in the evening. It made us all want to fight the Japs. While we waited for the show I talked to an English soldier who had been in Africa three years; he had been married two weeks before he left for Africa and hadn't seen his wife since. He had been at the siege of Tobruk which lasted three months when the Germans had the British bottled up in the city. The Germans bombed and strafed the city continually from the airport four miles outside the city. I told him I had seen the airport and could imagine how hot it must have been in the city. He told me how the British sneaked out of the city one dark night and escaped by the sea in small boats to Alexandria. He knew the air raid shelter in the bank at Tobruk and was near Helfaya Pass when the Australians went in and liquidated the Jerries trapped there. He said "The Aussies don't take prisoners". He said most of the damage to Benghazi had been done by Allied bombers.

Tuesday, May 25 – This morning Zilk, Young and I went with Butler and Blossom to the G.I. laundry at Benina. It was a beautiful morning and we enjoyed the ride. In the afternoon we went into town to see a movie; the British have renovated the Italian theater cater-cornered to the Banca di Roma. The picture was English and fair. We had trouble following the sound as the English talk so fast.

The town was full of troops as the Eighth Army is moving back to Cairo. They look big, tough and healthy. I didn't know the English boys grew so big although many of the boys were New Zealanders and Aussies. Two New Zealanders stopped us and asked if we wanted to buy a biretta (Italian pistol). We looked at it and asked the owner what he wanted for it. He said he wanted to trade it for a watch. We didn't have any money and Zilk didn't want to part with his Elgin.

Wednesday, May 26 – This evening I heard Captain John Craig lecture on his experiences in the Phillipines with Japs. After 1935 when we were giving Manuel Quezon and his followers a loose rein in governing the islands, the Japs made headway. According to Craig there was a Japanese colony in the Phillipines, worshiping the emperor, schooling their children in emperor worship, teaching them the Japanese language in schools owned and subsidized by the United States Government. He visited the schools and found it to be true. He maintained that if we did not chase the Japs out of the islands in the next year, they would have a strangle hold on world markets because of the slave labor. Captain Craig exhibited a Japanese pen marked "Parker Vacuumatic Pen – made in USA". USA is a town in Japan. He said it worked exactly like a Parker. He had taken the pen to Parker to be examined and the Parker people told him the only thing about the pen that was theirs was the nib. He had paid twenty-five cents for the pen in Panama eight years ago. It was a copy of a pen selling for $7.50. Eight million of them had been smuggled into the U.S. and sold to American school children. My experience with Jap articles has been that they look like our American products but function very differently.

Thursday, May 27 – This morning I was on guard at the main gate with Jack Salzer. We talked about Cleveland and his father's laundry business. He owns three laundries and the family lead a nice life with automobiles and motor boats. They belong to the Yacht Club. In the afternoon Butler, Carrol, Salzer and I went into Benghazi to the show. We walked through the native market, bought candy and went to see She Knew All the Answers with Joan Bennett and Franchot Tone. It was good. Came back, played softball and went up to hear Lt. Col. Wittridge of G-2 talk on "What Tunisian Campaign Means". I heard this man before on the Dunera when he told us about what our behavior should be if we were taken prisoner. He said he thought it plausible that Italy would fall without invasion. He said that seven of the finest divisions of the German army had been annihilated at Tunis and that the reason for this sudden crumbling of resistence had been the failure of their transport planes to bring in supplies because they had been shot down. Asked why they didn't try to evacuate some of the troops as the British had at Dunkirk, he said he assumed that the Italians thought the ships would be of more use to them around the peace table or that they were saving them for something else.

Col. Wittridge said that if Turkey should enter the war it would simplify the invasion since we could go through Greece, a friendly country, rather than through Italy. I think his talk made us realize that we have an excellent Intelligence Division and that we are not going to be caught napping. After the lecture the Sky Blazers, a traveling entertainment group from the Ninth Air Force put on a skit for about an hour and a half. The rain came as the show was ending. More rain fell in fifteen minutes than I have ever know. When I got back to my tent I was soaked from the skin out. Took off my clothes, dried myself and crawled into warm underwear and a warm bed.

Friday, May 28 – Today dawned bright and clear after yesterday's or rather last night's rain. The sun beat down hotly but the wind was much cooler. I don't think that this nice cool weather will last. I've heard too many stories about the heat. This morning Phelps came in our tent bringing his diary for me to read. It is short, humorous (rather satirical, I think) and more sensational than factual. Phelps wants to write for the pulps someday.

This afternoon I wrote Mother Flick and Barbara. Was on guard from six to ten tonight. Talked to Lloyd Bowman about letters, home etc. He says he can't think of anything to write home about so he writes his fiance every other day. Came back from guard duty and heard Zilk and Young acclaim the Sky Blazers. The king of Greece was here today on a sort of inspection tour. He didn't get down around our end of the camp but some of the boys saw him.

Saturday, May 29 – This afternoon Koester, Cave, Sneider, Mulree and VanDuyne returned from Cairo. They drove back in a Jeep and truck which belong to the company now. Among other things, they brought an energizer, so there will be electric lights in the captain's tent now, I guess. VanDuyne spent the pound I gave him. He said he couldn't get any jewelry. I might have known that I couldn't trust him but I wanted something nice to send Barbara. Koester brought back a lot of books and magazines to read.

Sunday, May 30 – Slept this morning. After lunch Butler came into our tent to tell us that the sea had washed up the body of an English sailor. We went down to have a look. It turned out that Sergeant Shaw and Sellars had seen the body floating about a hundred feet from shore. They swam out and pulled it into the shore. I couldn't tell how long the man had been dead, but the only decomposed part was the head which looked almost like a skull with the hair completely gone. He wore no clothes except his shoes and stockings and had his emergency kit around his neck. The kit contained a raincoat, clothes, jack knife and English whistle and pistol. His body was chalk-white except for the purple veins and red sores which the rocks had scraped. The shoulders were draped with heavy black seaweed – seemed symbolic. He was very small – little more than five feet tall – could have been a boy. Oh yes, another thing in the kit – a card from the Seaman's Protective

Association. The sergeant covered the body with the oilskin raincoat from the pack and sent Sellars for the medics. They came and carried the body away on a stretcher. I think that he was on one of the ships in the convoy that was bombed coming into Benghazi about a month ago. The heavy rain last Thursday night probably washed him in toward shore. Anyway, his worries are over.

Monday, May 31 – Today is the day set for the trial of Golish. Bass will be tried tomorrow. Rumors kept coming down in the camp from the court-martial which was held here instead in Cairo. The trial lasted all day and when it was over Golish was sentenced to serve a year and get a dishonorable discharge, known as a "DD".

I was on the first shift and my post was the second mess hall. One of the sergeants from Officers' Mess told me about how the MP's in town had called him down for being out of bounds. He said that he had been taking his laundry (as had a lot of others in his outfit) to an Italian laundry which was out of bounds. The women, he said, "were not too busy to stop washing long enough to go upstairs"; hence, I imagine, the unusual popularity of the laundry. The sergeant talked as if the laundry was the Italian ladies' main source of income. I doubt it. The MP's told the sergeant that he was to stay in bounds in the future but did not suggest another laundry.

Today was payday and for the first time in three months I had money left from last payday. Came home at midnight and went to bed.

Tuesday, June 1 – This evening our softball team played another outfit and won 9 to 8. We were lucky. After the game we were all gathered around Homsey, VanDuyne and one of the natives who has a garden in our area. Homsey was acting as interpreter and was trying to smooth over a difficulty that VanDuyne and the Arab had. It seems that when VanDuyne first thought he was going to Cairo, the Arab gave him money to buy him a pair of clippers. Later, when Van thought he was not going, he gave the money back to the Arab. Van did go to Cairo and never bought the clippers. The Arab doesn't even speak to VanDuyne now. He wanted to know why Van hadn't used his own money. The Arab is explaining his feelings to Homsey who is interpreting for Van and all of us listening. Van explains to Homsey that he spent all of his own money (and incidentally a pound of mine too). Then why hadn't Van asked Sergeant Koester for money to buy clippers? Van didn't think of that. In spite of Homsey's intervention and pleadings in Arabic, the wiley native refused to accept Van back as his friend. His was the unforgiveable sin of ignoring the considerations of friendship. I think in this respect for friends, the Arabs are one-up on the Christians.

Sent a cablegram to Barbara today. I should have sent it yesterday.

Wednesday, June 2 – Slept until two o'clock today, then went in swimming. The day was warm and the water was wonderful. Came in at three to buy canteen supplies – no beer or cigarettes. Had six letters today, two from Barbara, one from Jean and Al, one from Dad, one from Aunt Alm and Unk, and one from Pa. Made me feel good. There is going to be a change in our guard duty – don't know quite what it is.

Thursday, June 3 – The change in guard is to Airbase Security. We will have charge of fifty-calibre machine guns placed around the field and will have three smacking new patrol cars right from the states. We are on duty twenty-four hours a day with an alert at dawn and dusk. During the alert we take our posts and prepare for action. It's a change from straight guard duty and we all enjoyed it.

Today is our anniversary – one year married. Received a telegram from the folks at home (in Butler), two letters from Barbara, one from Mother Flick. It has been a pretty good anniversary.

Friday, June 4 – This morning after breakfast, at eight o'clock Hale, Wiedle and I went in swimming. The Mediterranean was as calm as an indoor pool and the sun was warm. Stayed in the water all morning. In the afternoon had to clean the big guns – a hell of a job. Came back, ate spaghetti with Butler, Zilk and Yorkston and went to bed.

Saturday, June 5 – Inspection this morning and then pick and shovel work all afternoon. Some grind. It has been a lot cooler today. Every morning just as dawn is breaking, an Arab on his little donkey moves slowly out of the native village, bound for Benghazi two miles away. The donkey trail runs along the highest part of the ridge which runs parallel to the sea shore and about a quarter of a mile from the sea. Thus, whether one is along the sea shore or up on the plateau, the traffic on the trail is silhouetted against the skyline. At a distance this native on the donkey (all natives ride side-saddle) looks philosophical with his head bowed in preoccupation – returning to this world to urge on the little donkey with his whip – by fits and starts; and that is exactly the way the little donkey travels – at a leisurely walk until he is accelerated by the whip into a sudden burst of speed – gradual regression to a leisurely walk – whip, whip, another sudden burst of speed, etcetera. Sometimes the first Arab to appear on the skyline between the palm trees in the background is driving his two-wheeled cart loaded with un-threshed grain to the market in Benghazi.

In the evening the Arab drives his few sheep (mostly black) across the field down over the rocky slope toward the village enclosure. A barefoot native girl patters behind, stooping here and there to pick up something. We wonder if she is gleaning grain or picking up grasshoppers.

It's a cold night and as we drive by the village a fire blazes in one of the roofless rooms (bombs dropped here) of a mud-brick house. It looks cheery and makes us homesick – for here is family life and these people are almost as happy as they have ever been with their sheep, grain, tomatoes, onions, donkeys, dates, wives and kids.

Thursday, June 15 – Much has happened in the last ten days. I hope I can remember it all. First, we have our machine gun placements dug and our work with them has settled into a routine of stand-to very early in the morning and evening, clean guns in the late morning, swim and sleep in the afternoon. We have had one air raid since we set them up and that a false alarm. Rumor had it that we were to expect a parachute attack, air raid or possibly beach landing. Our intelligence is certainly on the job.

Yesterday morning Yorkston came into our tent (right after the victory parade in Benghazi where General Alexander had reviewed our armored cars) with the news that parachutists had landed ten miles from here. We laughed at him and I crawled into bed. Ten minutes later Sergeant Shaw called all sergeants and corporals in the armored cars to the orderly tent and they went out on a field patrol. Walter Butler told me what Headquarters had told him: that 120 parachutists had landed in the vacinity and that most of them had been killed or captured by the British. We were all told to stand by and rumors were rife.

I didn't go on duty until early in the evening and Red Miller and I were told that we would be on our emplacement all night. We had eight riflemen from the squadrons to help us. In the meantime, machine gun nests and patrols had sprung up all over the camp and we felt more secure. After a hectic night in which nothing happened I went on one of the armored cars after breakfast. Jack Salzer and I patrolled until noon. We had searched the native villages and had orders to stop and frisk all natives on sight. Note: no wog ladies appeared. Rumor had it that the parachutists had been dressed as wogs. Read two letters from Barbara which made me feel swell. She has guessed that I am in Benghazi.

This evening before chow a bulletin from headquarters stated the facts: One hundred and twenty Italian parachutists had landed. They are the pick of the Italian Army parachutists and are reputed to be ardent Fascists. All but twenty of these have been killed or captured but the remaining twenty constitute a threat of sabotage since they are armed with time bombs and apparently mean to damage our heavy bombers. We are told that they may be a suicide sabotage squadron or this may be the preliminary to an all-out invasion by parachutists, beach landings or both. Also, there may be air raids accompanying these. We work all night again tonight. I'm tired but a little of the tension of the last thirty hours has lifted – and we are determined now.

Sergeant Blossom, acting Sergeant of the Guard this afternoon stopped five slugs from his own Tommy gun at five o'clock today. It had jammed and he pressed the wrong lever. The Tommy gun is the captain's but as he is away at gas school at Tel Aviv, Blossom commandered the gun when the parachutists landed. I hope Bloss doesn't lose his arm. Five slugs is a lot. They were all in the upper part of the arm near the bicep and the medics didn't know if his arm was broken. He did not lose consciousness. Must get ready to go on guard again.

Wednesday, June 16 – Last night was pretty tough on us physically, although nothing eventful happened. We didn't have the eight riflemen to help us so we had to work two hours and sleep two hours alternately. Only thing of any consequence was a bullet whizzing by over my head at about three o'clock. I think it was from one of our own guns. The amazing thing to me is that more of our own men aren't casualties – with the bursts of gunfire all over the place. I suppose they're firing at shadows. Came in this morning after being relieved and went to bed.

Woke up at two o'clock when Yorkston and Young left to patrol in the armored cars again. The latest bulletin says that all but two of the parachutists have been accounted for. Since two English uniforms have been stolen from the shops in town, we are to stop and demand identification cards from all suspicious looking characters in English army dress.

Since the first night of the alerts when we slept on the ground, I have had a fever and chills – perspiring when I slept. At first I thought it was nervousness but after I had adjusted myself to conditions I doubted that this was the cause. Lt. Svella has been in the hospital for four days with the same symptoms – as is Bob Cumberworth. In the lieutenant's case the doctor wasn't sure whether it was malaria or fever caused by sand fleas. Since Captain Hinote is in Tel Aviv at the gas school, we have no officers in the company. Blossom's condition is good. The five bullets made only flesh wounds. We go on guard again tonight at six o'clock.

Thursday, June 17 – Conditions have become quite normal again, although Captain Green told Miller and me last night that there were still two parachutists on the loose. One of the others is in the hospital with an ugly wound through the hip. The bullet entered on one side, castrated the Italian, and bored through the other leg. Yorkston and I went over to the hospital to see Blossom who is doing fine. Incidentally, the parachutist mentioned above is in a tent nearby. He doesn't speak English.

In today's bulletin we learn that our ack-ack guns are firing at enemy reconnaissance planes – that's good news. I never did like the idea of them fooling around up there. Went to the show after our stand-to – saw Stage Door Canteen and thought it was swell.

Friday, June 18 – Lat night the two slippery chutists destroyed three planes. They know enough to keep away from our field. It seems that a master sergeant (crew chief) found a time bomb in his plane, took it out, searched many other planes on the field and discovered three or four other bombs. He did the searching himself. He should have a medal.

Zilk, Hammon and I went to town today. Many new shops have opened. At a really nice stationery store (bomb-scarred) I bought a pen, pencil, letter-opener and sealer for Barbara. Afterwards, I thought it was a foolish purchase but when Barbara uses them she can think of where they were bought. We ate at the Cafe Metropoli – spaghetti and chicken. The chicken was just too tough, but the spaghetti was edible. We went to the Garrison Theater and saw Holiday Inn with Bing Crosby and Fred Astaire. It was good – made us homesick. When we came back we were told that there had been an alert and that all of our men had to stand by their guns. Went to bed and slept like a log.

Saturday, June 19, 1943 – No inspection today. The lieutenant told us that we would clean up our equipment instead. The bulletin this morning is not too encouraging. We are told to expect a low bombing attack, beach landing and paratrooper attack simultaneously, and to go armed at all times until further notice. Also, this morning at 9:30 Lt. Bixby of 323rd Service Group Finance Detachment called and asked me to stop in to see Major Olson about my transfer. I had stopped there last Sunday while waiting for Walter Butler to get the payroll checked. One of the boys took me in to talk to the lieutenant and he had me leave my name, qualifications and location. I wrote my request for a transfer and now I wait for Ninth Air Force Headquarters in Cairo to act. It will probably be a long time, though the major seemed to want me to start work immediately. I hope it goes through as I'm afraid I'll get stale if I don't have something to think on – even a little. Yesterday I got six V-mail letters – three from Barbara and three from home. They were anniversary letters and cheered me up a lot.

Ten of our bombers at Benina had time bombs in them; we lost three but it could have been a lot worse. Captain Green informed us tonight that the two chutists who were responsible for the sabotage at Benina had been caught but there were sixteen still at large. These were from the second group that landed the day before yesterday. I wonder when we'll have them all wiped out. Wrote Mother and Barbara today. Guess I'll get to bed as I'm pretty tired.

Sunday, June 20 – This morning at dawn, two of the plane guards at Benina were killed. It would be called murder if it weren't an act of war. One was shot in the forehead, the other in the back. I've just been thinking about that bullet that whizzed over my head the other night – it might not have come from one of our own guns. It seems that we are in for these commando tactics by the Italians from now on – just as are the Nazi guards on the west coast of Europe. I guess all we can do is keep our eyes open and our guns ready. We are ordered to go armed at all times now and tonight, after Stand-to, I felt like a Pilgrim when I went to the show with my rifle, although there were a lot of others in the crowd. The show was "Love Finds Andy Hardy" with Mickey Rooney. This afternoon Yorkston, Young, Reis and I went swimming. The waves were so big that they bowled us over – the seaweed wrapped around our legs so that it was impossible to swim. Slept well.

Monday, June 21 – The first day of summer. This morning we shot our machine guns in the salt flats in our camp area. I hadn't realized the noise that the fifty-caliber machine gun makes when it goes off. We had to put cotton in our ears. I have tonight off, the first day off for over a month. I remember how tough I used to think the seven-day workweek was. Went swimming again this afternoon – waves still high – it's certainly some sport when they're so big.

Thursday, June 24 – Since no more acts of sabotage by the parachutists have been reported, life has once more become routine. Five percent of any one company will be permitted to go into Benghazi now. The latest rumor, confirmed by headquarters is that the rest of our company is coming from Cairo to join us. They are to be here sometime this weekend. I wonder how they will like it. Mail has been pouring in these last few days and today I tried to answer some of my back mail. Walter Butler heard from his fiance – she did receive the diamond ring that he sent; he has been a different man since he no longer has that worry on his mind. Today, we were able to buy seven packs of Camels and a cigar; that alleviates the cigarette shortage somewhat. No word about my transfer as yet.

Friday, June 25 – Spent the day down on the beach. The big news of the day is that the rest of the company has arrived. Saw Willie Hoefling and tried to get him oriented. He says he likes it here and I think it will be a good thing for him. They look soft and pale compared to us desert rats. Got a letter from Barbara today and one from Phyllis Flick. Mail is coming through fine. Guess I'll go to bed.

Saturday, June 26 – After inspection this morning I went in swimming. This afternoon I went swimming again. Willie Hoefling couldn't get over how tan and healthy I looked. He said, "Your wife should see you now." Yesterday, (while I'm throwing roses at myself) Mulree told me that he and Bowman had decided that I had improved more than any other man in the company since we've been in the desert – and added that my wife should see me now. I've been thinking that if my transfer goes through I'll probably leave the army in the same condition that I entered it. It would grieve me a little and yet I don't want to forget my accounting. Some English troops (an armored car unit) have camped below us in the salt flats. They were sent here because of the parachutists. They have had no leave for eighteen months, but have had very little action. One of the boys told me that one of their men was wounded and an officer killed by a strafing Jerry.

Sunday, June 27 – Went swimming today. Talked to Willie Hoefling about life in Cairo. The boys who didn't drink or run around saved from seven hundred to a thousand dollars for the six months that they were there. They have money-order receipts to prove it. This was made possible through the generous per diem allowance ($4 per day) paid by the government. I can't help thinking how much Mrs. K and I could have used that money. Went to the show tonight and saw "Mrs. Miniver" again. We got back at midnight and the boys on duty were just leaving to take up gun positions when the alert sounded. We got our helmets and equipment and stood by. Next order was to go to our tents and wait until we were ordered to come out.

Zilk and I had hardly laid down with our clothes on when we heard three pistol shots – the signal for an invasion. We got our equipment on and a couple of seconds later the whistle blew. We stood by in our company area until headquarters sent word that it was a false alarm. We went to bed all wilted. It seems to me that we have been going through the same nervous tension these last few weeks that the boys at the front go through. Every time we hear the alert we get all keyed up, our hearts begin to pound, and our knees feel weak. I always think of my dog tags and insurance policy. It's been a quiet Sunday.

Monday, June 28 – So far, it's been a long, hard day: calisthenics, rifle drill and swimming this morning – putting up the big pyramidal tents and swimming this afternoon. Then, to top it off, we were informed that G-2 had inside information that tonight was THE NIGHT for the low bombing and straffing raid. Nothing has happened yet, but we expect to be called out tonight. Yesterday a big convoy came into Benghazi and we expected the raid to come then, but it didn't. The last two days have been terrifically hot but the wind is coming off of the sea; early this morning it shifted and came in from the desert. We are getting lots of sun.

Thursday, July 1 – Not much eventful has happened – yesterday a recon plane was sighted and fired at but I don't know if the two pursuit planes that took up the chase were able to force it down. Today Zilk, Young and I went into Benghazi and saw Rhythm on the River with Bing Crosby and Mary Martin. We bought watermelons and brought them back with us. After stand-in went to see Sweater Girl and then Yorkston and I ate half a watermelon. It was delicious, just like an American one.

This morning most of us went in swimming from ten to eleven. The water was wonderful. Reis and I towed back (from about a quarter of a mile out) an Italian aluminum emergency boat. Sellers and VanDuyne had paddled it out and we intended to paddle it in, but the wind was against us and after fifteen minutes we were no nearer the beach. We got out and swam – towing the boat – plenty of exercize.

981ˢᵗ M.P. Company—Our Tent in the Desert.
Left to right: Zilk, Young, Yorskston, Kennedy

THE FINANCE DETACHMENT

323rd Service Group

On July 5, 1943 I leave the 981st MP Company

and begin work as a member of the finance detachment.

Sunday, July 11 – Much has happened in the last ten days. First, on Monday of this week I came into town to work for the Finance Office on detached service until my transfer comes through. We live in what was formerly an Italian apartment building. The floors are of terrazzo marble and the rooms are cool on the hottest days. We live on the second floor where a roof terrace opens off two of the rooms at the side of the building. From this terrace (actually a second story open porch) we can look down on the solid mass of one-story Arabian huts, with here and there an opening for the chickens to scratch and the children to play. The whole section reminds me of an ant hill, but in appearance it's more like a one-story version of our Indian pueblos; these urban homes of the Arabs are built solidly into the more modern Italian buildings. At intervals we can see an Arabian woman scurry across one of the little open squares and vanish in the darkness of a doorway. The roofs of these huts are covered with dirt (insulation?) on which the grass grows sparsely, as grass grows in this country. Our office building is separated from the apartment building where we live by a narrow alley. It is about the size of the other building, but the construction is not quite as ornate, although it has the same marble floors. The roof, or third floor of our living quarters is a large porch from which we can see the entire harbor. It's a wonderful view.

Today we had the afternoon off and we went swimming. I'm afraid I'll lose my tan working inside. This evening Tim Benitz and I went down town and I bought Barbara a pair of slippers like those worn by the Arabian women. Don't think I'll send them until I find out if she can get an extra shoe coupon. I bought a pair of shorts and was measured by a tailor who is making me another pair. Tim and I went to the show to see "Suspicion". I enjoyed it again. We got a ride home which saved us a long walk. My room-mate is Slonim, a tech-sergeant who is friendly and on the ball. I certainly enjoy working with the men in this office.

Wednesday, July 14 – My transfer finally came through and I'm now in finance. Walter Butler brought my records in this morning. He told me a tragic story. When the men over thirty-seven were sent home, Gilbert was to be one of them. He was a quiet, mild-mannered little man who had been an accountant before he came into the army. He was married just nine months before he was drafted and he talked about his wife and thought about home-life too much. When we were at Camp Ripley in Minnesota I remember how the cold bothered him and how he read and re-read his wife's letters. Both Gilbert and his wife were middle-aged, but as much in love as two kids. In Minnesota, he and I had a conversation just after our overseas' exam. He remarked casually that one doctor thought he had a heart murmer, but a second doctor assured him that he was "plenty sound". We laughed, not because Gilbert might have a heart ailment, but because of the farce the doctors made of the overseas' examination.

Gilbert was in Cairo with our detachment there, and after all the red tape had been untied, seven of our company were ready to go home. The day of embarkation came and the seven were loaded with their barracks bags onto a truck. At the dock they jumped off the truck, each one carrying his two barracks bags over the worn cobblestones to the gangplank, and up the gangplank into the ship. As Gilbert was walking up the gangplank he dropped dead.

Last night Tim Benitz and I walked down town to get our tailor-made shorts and a pair of sandals which Tim had ordered. The shorts weren't ready – the tailor finally was able to explain that his wife was ironing them. The sandals weren't finished yet. We stopped in the Cafe Metropole and had very weak lemonade and cookies. The theater was crowded (SRO) so we walked across the street to the park, sat on a stone bench and talked.

We stopped in the Naafi and had lemonade and rissoles ; these are an English cake fried in deep grease like a doughnut.

They are bullet-shaped, made with ground vegetables and meat mixed into the dough. They are almost tasteless. We sat at the tables in the semi-darkness, smoked and listened to a British soldier play the piano. The favorite tunes of the British soldier are tunes that were popular in America two years ago. These are also the favorites of our soldiers. They are the reminders of home, girls and peace. Most of the soldiers sang as the pianist played – sang with a faraway look in their eyes. I think I'll remember that scene always. We left the Naafi as it was closing time and walked down the Via Vittoria toward home. I talked with Tim for a while before going to bed.

Thursday, July 15 – Today I got a letter from Jim Gettemy – the first I have had from him since I've been in the army. He told me what he knew of the boys of Alpha Chi Rho; made me feel good to read his letter. Guess I should get mail from Barbara tomorrow. I get my mail a day late as Butler or Branen brings it in from Berca the next day. I suppose it will be a month before my mail comes here. I wonder what Barbara's reaction to my transfer will be. She'll be glad that I'm using my head instead of my brawn !!!. The men and officers in this outfit are tops. Tonight we played volley ball. Took a fresh-water shower at the British "Bath Unit" and put on clean clothes. Guess I'll go to bed.

Friday, July 16 – Went to the show tonight. It was a poor show, but I talked to some British boys there who were nice. They hung on to every word I said about America and said they wanted to see our country. Got a cold playing volley ball. Ironical that I should go through a winter like last without getting a cold and then catch one when I'm working in an office in the summer.

Saturday, July 17 – My cold is no better. Tonight I went up on the roof of our building to see how the city looked in the moonlight. It is beautiful. The white buildings reflect the moonlight to such a degree that it is hard to describe. The Arab quarters are a study in light and shadows and the Moslem cemetery is bathed in moonlight. The water in the harbor looks black.

Sunday, July 18 – Today I had my first lesson in Arabic from the little boys that play on the Via El Rook. This afternoon I went out to Benina to see the boys in the 981st MP Company. Went swimming and had my hair cut. I got the folder for Mother and Dad's pictures while I was there as it came in the afternoon mail. Also got a letter from Mother. Came home in time for chow.

Monday, July 19 – Today, after the evening meal I had another lesson in Arabic from my native friends. Later, Tim Benitz and I went down to the South African YMCA to attend a class in Italian. It was a little deep for us, but we decided to go again. When we came back we talked until quite late. Tim's father was a professor at Notre Dame. His parents are both dead. Tim is thirty-five , has made money at times ($7,000 a year in 1938 and 1939 in the wholesale candy business). When he came into the army in the first draft he sold his business to a firm for a down-payment of $2,000 and $1,000 a month for two years. He received a total of $3,000 and the firm went under. He is philosophical about it and says he was happiest when he was earning the least. When the finance office moved into Tripoli, it was nine days after the Germans had left and they were ahead of some of the British infantry units. They had several bombings while they were there, but liked it as they were quartered in a beautiful Italian home with a piano and lots of wine. Tim and Irv Slonim vouch for the truth of the following: One headquarters group attached to a fighter squadron moved into a camp just as the Germans were leaving. The Germans looked at the Americans; the Americans (all clerical personnel) looked at the Germans; the Germans hopped on their trucks and high-tailed to the west and the Americans began to pitch their tents. Funny things happen in a war. Talked to a British paratrooper who said that the Germans were good fighters, but the Italians were treacherous. He blamed the Eyeties for placing bombs under our wounded so that when the medics went to move them they were blown up.

Tuesday, July 20 – Yesterday's raid on Rome seems to have been very effective according to the radio. I am CQ today and must stay close to the office. Tonight I sleep here with a gun on the table beside me.

Wednesday, July 21 – Everyday a Jewess from Benghazi comes to clean out our living quarters. She probably understands three words of English and when we give her our laundry she chatters at us in Italian. When she brings the laundry back she lays it down piece-by-piece and indicates by holding up her fingers, the price in piastres of each article. She is a big-bosomed girl in her mid twenties I'd guess. It is hard to judge anybody's age around here as the war has accelerated the age-ing process for some.

Karmilowitz and Bergland came up to their room about noon today while Julia was cleaning. I heard "Chum" Karmilow-itz say, "How are they hangin' Julia? Are they hangin' all right?" Bergland then asked,

"Are they hangin' low, Julia?" Poor Julia just looked at them with an enigmatic look on her face and countered with,

"Uh? Uh?" She probably thought they were asking about their laundry.

Tonight Tim Benitz and I went to our Italian class at the South African YMCA. The charming little Italian who teaches the class speaks excellent English, but uses Italian exclusively in class. We are not learning much.

Rumors are rife about our going home, but I don't think we'll go home until the war is over. If we should go home we would be sent to another theater, and I'm satisfied with this one. Our troops seem to be moving well in Sicily and that would be my bet for a move.

Friday, July 23 – Tonight Bergland and I went down town to a show. We saw "Big Street" with Henry Fonda and Lucille Ball. It's a Damon Runyan story which I liked. Bergland didn't like it very well. We rode home with the MP's in their truck. These are town MP's and not from my former outfit.

This last month has shattered my record as far as looking at white women is concerned. I had seen only about five white women in seven months until I moved to the finance office. The Red Cross now has a couple of women in town and nurses are seen often. I remember the first white woman I saw during this long time was a British girl – she was thin and looked sexless, but I wanted to talk to her just to hear a woman's voice – only I didn't and she kept walking.

Monday, July 26 – The big news today is that Mussolini has resigned. Most of us felt that we were perhaps a step closer to victory and home. I suppose the people of the United States are thinking that the fighting is practically over. Tonight we saw a good movie – Diana Barrymore, Robert Cummings, Kay Francis in "Between Us Girls". It was opening night at the new open-air theatre just a couple of blocks from our quarters. Things are getting settled here, so we expect to move.

Tuesday, July 17 -- Today, Branon, mess-sergeant of my old outfit brought in two letters and the Oster Dopster – one letter from Barbara and one from Mary Louise.

Monday, August 2 – Yesterday the bombers raided the Rumanian oil fields in a raid that made the headlines. Most of the boys who went on the raid figured that it would be their last ride. Casualties were high, but it seems that the raid was a success.

After work yesterday Tim Benitz and I went down town. He took about six pictures of me which I hope to send to Barbara soon. He has a good German camera which he bought in Cairo. It has a gadget for taking your own picture. We set the camera on a bench in the park and took a picture of both of us. We stopped in the Naafi on the way down town and had a lemonade. After Tim had his hair trimmed we had cakes and another lemonade. Came home and went to a show.

Wednesday, August 4 – This morning Captain Hinote stopped in the office and mentioned that Paul Prosser was outside in the jeep and that he was on his way home. I went down and bid him goodby. I'll always remember the fun that he and Willie Hoefling and I had coming over on the boat. He seemed excited and happy about going home to Neuville, Pennsylvania. I told him that I missed the hills. He said that he hoped he would be seeing me soon and I told him "in another year". He is over thirty-eight and just a kindhearted, harmless old man. While he was in Cairo he got mixed up with one of the cafe dancers (Arabic) and spent all that he earned on the lady. Willie Hoefling thinks that Paul got nothing in return though Paul said that he did.

After chow tonight I had a hot shower at the British Bath Unit a couple of blocks down from our quarters. Another record of mine was broken – it was the first hot shower I had since I left the states nine months ago – also the first time I have felt really clean in all that time. I have decided to let my hair grow – most of the boys here have theirs long and I can't always keep my hat on when I have a snapshot taken for Barbara. Tonight I worked in the office studying regulations, etc. I almost forgot: Zilk has made corporal. It begins to look as if I really did give up a corporal's rating when I came into finance, but I'll never regret it. Oddity: somebody signed the 981st MP Company payroll for me. When we checked it the boys immediately accused me of trying to draw two pays by working from the inside. I think Walter Butler thought he was doing me a good turn by signing for me. I was on detached service when the payroll was made up.

Sunday, August 8 – Today for dinner we had chicken, mashed potatoes, peas and cherry pie. Each man contributed fifteen piastres toward the chicken. The past few weeks our chow has been of a lower calibre than formerly – we have heard rumors of a scarcity – that this will last until the fall harvest, etc.

Sergeant Kennedy's World War II Diary

There is an English soldier who eats regularly at our mess hall. He is known to us only as Jack. He is likeable and above average intelligence. The boys like to get into arguments with him about the lower standards of living in the British Army. In most of the arguments three or four Yanks will take one side, and Jack will uphold the British side. Here's a sample:

Yank 1: "The trouble with England is your aristocracy. Lady this and Lord that – they're no better 'n you are – they don't work – just collect money while you commoners work".

Jack: "Who doesn't work? The aristocracy is the backbone of England".

Yank 2: "Yeah, you don't see them in the front lines fighting. You guys are doing the fighting to save their necks".

Yank 3: "Yeah, so they can go back to their castles, and have you 'Sir' them".

Jack: "Listen, that doesn't mean a thing. I'm just as good as they are – they don't think they're any better than I am. It all goes to make up that place called little old England – the greatest place in the world".

Yank 1: "Look at your clothes. Why can't you eat the way we eat. Why do your officers eat so much better'n you do. Look at their clothes. They're shit'en on you, Jack".

Yank 2: "Sure, they eat the gravy and give you the slop – they're shit'en on you, Jack". Here the argument reaches it highest pitch with the Yanks firing argument after argument at poor Jack. His face is red, and the red reaches halfway over his head, for he is partly bald.

Jack: "Nobody shitzon me. Listen, nobody shitzon me".

Then they all laugh – Jack along with them. The Yanks laugh because they think that they have won the argument and

123

Jack laughs because three years of war in the desert have made him older and wiser. He has come up against the barrier of misunderstanding that divides one nation from another. That wall will be there always – until people on earth live as one people – eons from now.

Today I got three letters from Barbara, one from Mother Flick and the film that Barbara sent last May. Wrote Barbara this afternoon and went to see "Panama Hattie" tonight. It was good. Bergland and Duino are on furlough now and I go next. It will be swell to see Cairo – hope I can send Barbara something nice.

Thursday, August 26 – Tomorrow I go on furlough to Cairo, Alexandria and Tel Aviv. Since this is an occasion I decided to use my bound leather diary book. Places that I want to see are the pyramids, Jerusalem, Bethlehem, the cities of Cairo and Alexandria. Places to eat – vouched for by the boys are the American Red Cross in all three cities and ice cream bars.

CAIRO, EGYPT, PALESTINE

I am given a ten day furlough

Friday, August 27 – This morning I finished packing, took a shower, collected money from the boys who wanted me to do errands and rode to Benina with Lt. Bender of the M.P.'s who had business in Cairo. We waited an hour and finally got on the plane. The passengers were all majors, captains, tech-sergeants, and two privates, Couch and me. I enjoyed the ride to Cairo more than I did the ride to Tobruk back in December – we passed directly over the towns in the Nile Valley instead to the side of them. They looked like toy cities. The irrigation canal looked like a little ditch, but we could distinguish camels, donkeys, and men walking on the road beside the canal. We landed at Heliopolis airport at a quarter to five, boarded the bus which took us to where we could get the "tram" (streetcar in U.S.) for Cairo. We rode to the end of the line and walked two blocks to the Grand Hotel.

This is run by the American Red Cross – rooms are entirely free except for tips – the only absolute charge is a 25 piastre deposit for towel and soap. Meals are wonderful – ten piastres for dinner. Our room has three beds with mattresses, a balcony – it is a corner room on the sixth floor. Tonight I had a hot bath in a bathtub for the first time since last October 30th – ten months ago. From the balcony I watched the city move. The streets are partly blacked out – street lamps are blue – taxi lights are green, purple, pink or yellow – it makes for a colorful picture. Sounds are not quite American – the clang of the streetcar bells sounds old-fashioned as does the honk of the taxi horns and the click of the hoofs of gharri-horses, the crack of the drivers' whips, the wail of the street vendors – panderers at this time of night, I guess ("Hey Yank, wanna woman?"). The only modern sound is the band, very American, playing on the roof. Cairo is the one place I have been, to date, where there is no dearth of women. Tonight at dinner I met a man who is on the staff of Stars and Stripes, the Army newspaper. We talked for about an hour with some sailors who were in from Suez. One boy who seemed intelligent had been on some of the tours. He advised me what to see and what not to see. Tomorrow I'll get my glasses fixed and my errands done, then go sight-seeing on Sunday. One of my errands is to deliver our Eyetie calculator to Major Doddridge and try to get an American calculator. Just killed A bug of some kind, hope it isn't a bed bug. I seem to be the only one in at this time -- Couch went to look up a lady whom he knew the last time he was here. Couch is only a private—first class, but he is an operator. When he unpacked to get dressed for his date he put on a blouse with master-sergeant's stripes. He explained, "Well, last time I was here I wore sergeant's stripes so I thought I ought to give myself a promotion." The U.S. Army Air Force may consider Couch a private first class, but when he is on furlough, he wants people to think of him as a master sergeant. I don't have his chutzpah, but I like his attitude.

My other room-mate is a stranger to me. I haven't seen him yet. It seems queer to have cold water to drink with your meals, ice cream – I had some tonight (not quite American} – someone to wait on you hand and foot. The Arabs are a wily race – we think them naïve and they are willing to oblige us by being naïve – and raking in the piastres. The man who carries his own bag, shines his own shoes, and does his own errands is looked down on by them and made to feel inferior. The Arab is a wily fellow and we Americans are his meat. Think I'll get to bed as I want to get up early tomorrow.

Saturday, August 28 – This morning I got up at a quarter to seven, had breakfast, got my glasses fixed, and took a taxi to the finance office where I delivered the old Eyetie calculator to Lt. Glass. Couldn't see Major Doddridge as he was out, but talked to his secretary, a sergeant who was formerly with the 323rd Finance Office. He told me that he thought I could get a new American calculator when I come back on the fifth of September. Hope I can swing the deal as the boys really need it. I walked back from the Finance Office – it's about an hour's walk – stopped at an ice cream bar (American Bar) and had a dish of ice cream. Looked through some book stores, tried a few words of French which were understood. French is understood by most of the business places in Cairo. Normally, Cairo has a population of one and a half million, but refugees and soldiers have swelled its population to three million. On the streets one sees Arabs in their white robes, red fezzes and sandals, soldiers of every description, and civilians of every nationality. Vendors sell magazines, "Feelthy pictures, Yankee." The pictures are concealed inside of the magazines. From the balcony of room 606 of the Grand Hotel I can see the Hotel Claridge and Smuts House flanking Shari Sherif Pasha. Cairo taxis are dark blue with white fenders – this makes them easily recognizable. My fare from the Grand Hotel to the American Embassy (the Finance Office is near there) was seven piastres – I paid ten. Everyone expects a 10% tip. To the left from my balcony I can see (to the southeast) across the city to the Citidel and a bare mountain range beyond. The mountains are entirely devoid of any sign of vegetation. To the southwest the city stretches out. Further down to my right is the Hotel Exmorandi. The girls of Cairo (must be careful here) seem to me to be divided into these classes – the business girls, professionals, and the husband-seekers. The business girls consist of those who have left their hearts at home and sell their bodies to the soldier who shows them the best time. They pick fairly clean soldiers and will bleed them of their last piastres if they can. They are not averse to lifting the inside of a soldier's wallet. These girls usually have other jobs – sometimes clerking in the bazaars or waiting tables in some of the better bars; they look on their night work as just a little extra income. Some of them may enjoy it as some are outrageously young – though pretty thoroughly skilled in the art of persuading the soldier to part with his pounds. The professional prostitutes in Cairo work in conjunction with the gherri drivers at night. The driver picks up the soldier or soldiers – they talk business; the gherri driver takes a route down a dark alley – pauses for a moment while the lady hops in – drives at a slow pace through the byways while the lovemaking is in progress. Afterwards, the lady is paid and dropped off at the spot where she was picked up. The husband-seekers are the British A. T. S. girls in khaki, Red Cross girls, WAACS, and many; of the higher type of refugees. These girls, the refugees, date soldiers, but since they are always accompanied by their mothers, it discourages a certain type. I think the A. T. S. girls have been very successful in getting husbands out of the eighth army. They pick nice clean boys and the girls are nice looking in an English sort of way. There is something wrong with their legs, though, according to American standards.

This afternoon I took the non-expense tour to the Citadel, Mosque and Bazaar. We had a guide, taxi and tips – all furnished by the Red Cross. I'm getting a return for my investment. There were only nine of us in our party – six Canadian RAF boys only ten days out of New York, two boys from the U.S. Merchant Marine and myself. The Citadel looks like a huge medieval castle except that there is no moat. The fortification was erected in 1183, I believe, by Saladin, sultan of Egypt who captured Jerusalem and opposed the Crusades. The Citadel Mosque, or Alabaster Mosque was built in 1805 by Mohammed Ali to commemorate his victory over the Mamelukes, rulers of Egypt, in the name of the Caliph in Turkey. The Caliph was the secular and religious head of Islam. It is built entirely of alabaster and is modeled after the church of Constantine, Sante Sophia in Constantinople. Before we were allowed to enter the court, all of us had to have leather slippers tied over our shoes – it being holy ground. Arabs who come there to worship remove their shoes at the entrance to the court, go to the Fountain of Desecration in the middle of the court and wash their feet, face, and hands up to the elbow; then they enter the interior of the Mosque of Mohammed Ali. It is a huge building with great rock crystal chandeliers and thousands of lights hung from the dome. The entire ceiling is covered with enameled designs. Mohammedans pray five times a day – once before the sun is up, again at 1:30, 4:30,

6:30, and 9:30. I asked the guide if this schedule was rigidly adhered to. He said, "It is like all religions, fifty-fifty. There are good ones and indifferent ones." Two priests perform the ceremony during prayer time; one reads from the Koran while the second explains to the assembly the meaning of the words of the Koran. One of the pulpits, the small one, was given by King Farouk and the priest uses this instead of the big one when the King comes to worship. Mohammedan women may come into the mosque, but not during the prayer hour. The floor of the mosque is carpeted. On the right , as one enters, is the tomb of Mohammed Ali, founder of the mosque. Through the grilled windows of the wall about the court we could look far down and see the city spread out in an expanse below us. It is restful around the mosque. I wish Barbara could have been with me. From the Mohammed Ali Mosque we rode back down the winding road to the bottom of the Citadel and through the city to the Bazaar.

The Bazaar district is the same throughout the Middle East – a narrow lane just wide enough for one vehicle at a time to move through – flanked by narrow stalls in which the goods are sold. There are coppersmiths, gold vendors, tobacco vendors, cloth vendors, leather shops, grain shops, watchmakers, photographers, jewelers and antique shops. Our shop was of a type that would interest an American soldier tourist and now listen to the craftiness of the Arab at work. Our guide, who draws a commission from the shop's owner for each article sold, has won our confidence by cautioning us to hold on to our pocketbooks. He tells us that his shop is vouched for by the Red Cross (it is not as the tour was advertised as including only the Mosque and Citadel) and that it sells genuine Arabic perfume, not diluted – that anyone who makes a purchase which he finds unsatisfactory can return the same and get his money back. This, I believe is the way the scheme works: Guide #1 is in charge of assembling the party, that is, those who have signed for the tour at the Red Cross desk. He introduces us to Guide

#2, who is old and apparently wise, sees that we are all bundled into taxis along with Guide #2. We are taken to see the Citadel and the mosque. While we are viewing the mosque, guide #2 tells us that the bazaar is included in the tour, but that if we have seen the bazaar we may not want to go. "Have you gentlemen seen the bazaar?" he asks.

"Well", we say taking the bait, "if it's in the Red Cross tour, we might as well see it", and thinking that the guide may have been trying to get out of part of his job that the Red Cross is paying him for. Guide #2 had previously impressed us by tipping the Arabs who strapped the slippers on over our shoes and saying,

"Everything at the expense of the Red Cross, Gentlemen". We come out of the mosque and are whisked away to the bazaar; there, low-and-behold, is Guide #1 apparently visiting with the proprietor. He greets us joyfully and bids us make ourselves welcome. The clerks turn out to be very shapely young ladies who lean over the counter, pat your hand or your cheek, wriggle their hips slightly and look at the prospective buyers with smiles and expressions that say, "Oh you Yankee, you and I could have a lot of fun, just the two of us." To add to the hominess of the shop, these little cuddle girls tell you the price of an article in "bucks". A leather purse is "eighteen bucks" or "eighteen fish". The ladies show perfume to the boys and must put some on their arms, a different kind on each arm. When we had finished looking and buying, our old guide calls the two taxis and we rode back to the Grand Hotel. It was a lovely tour and it cost me nothing.

At dinner tonight a boy sat down at my table and said, "It's a wonderful world".

"Why?" I asked.

"I'm going back to God's country." He had been in Persia for a year. He is a radio man and has been with the Russian supply line in Persia. He said there was absolutely nothing in Persia – just a desolate hell. He had several Russian friends.

One of them had fought at Stalingrad and gave him his cap insignia which he showed to me. It was a red star with the hammer and sickle insignia in it. He had conversed with his friend in French and had gone to parties and drunk vodka with him. We are shipping a tremendous volume of supplies into Russia and the Russian soldier is very grateful. This American soldier told me that the Russian soldier is the finest fellow on the face of the earth, that he looks on us American soldiers as a kind of god and will do anything for us. He said that the boys who had flown to Moscow told him that the city was a veritable hell – people starving and homeless with nothing to eat. The reason: we are shipping plenty of food to Russia, but the Russians allow it to sit on the Persian border while they take planes, tanks and guns instead of food. The current Russian drive is the thing which must take precedence over a little thing like sustenance. I can't help admiring the Russian spirit. This American boy told me that the Russian soldier realizes that the USA is winning the war for the USSR, no matter what Stalin says. I wished him luck in his trip home.

Wrote a letter to Barbara and came up to my room, but stopped to talk to a couple of sailors. They told me about their tour which was much like mine; also told me of another interesting place which they visited. It's about two blocks from the Grand Hotel. You walk up a flight of stairs – at the moment you reach the top, about ten young ladies rush out and fall all over you feeling all over you with their hands. Naturally, you are not one to be backward, so you let your hands wonder over them. In a minute or two the lady in question says, "No more, Yankee. First buy me a drink, then you can play some more." Each drink costs fifteen piastres, so you spend quite a little. After each round of drinks the young lady zips down her dress, you look and feel and begin to get excited. Up she zips her dress again. "No more until I have another drink." Plunk, down goes fifteen more piastres and so ad infinitum. The boys who told me this didn't know if a man finally got satisfaction after buying so many drinks. They didn't stay to find out. It would be interesting to know.

Sunday, August 29, 1943 – Lat night before I went to bed I listened to Frazier, my room-mate tell me about his experiences in the war to date. He came over with me and is in the Medics of the ground crew of a fighter squadron. Today has been a very full day. At eight o'clock after breakfast I started on the tour of the pyramids and the sphinx with the same boys that I went with yesterday. This tour was to cost us just twenty-one piastres each, with the pictures and camel ride being extra. We rode out in a taxi down the Shari Fuad El Awal, left on the Shari Malika Nazli, left again on Shari Mariette Pasha past the Egyptian Museum, right on Shari Khedive and crossed the bridge that spans the Nile. I think this scene from the time one crosses the Nile bridge all along the Nile valley is the most picturesque that I have ever seen. The black sod must be the richest in the world – three crops a year are harvested by the land owners. As we passed outside the city, we could see miles on either side of the road – the land is level and as far as one can see, cultivated – green with corn, sugar cane and thousands of tall palms laden with ripe pendants of dates. The asphalt highway is in two sections with the tram tracks separating the traffic. It is possible to take the streetcar out to the pyramids. As we rode out toward the pyramids we passed beautiful private homes at intervals of perhaps a mile. The land is divided into squares by the irrigation ditches – on both sides of the road are the deep ditches which hold water. At the edge of the Nile Valley there is a sharp line which marks the end of the irrigated land and the beginning of the desert; the pyramids and sphinx are at the edge of the desert. We got out of our taxi and mounted the camels which were to take us up the hill to the pyramids and sphinx. The camel ride was bumpy – the pyramids were what I expected. We had our pictures taken sitting on the camels, went into the temple of the sphinx which is constructed entirely of granite. We went into the tombs of the high priests, our guide leading the way with a candle into the dark caverns. The size of the stones in this building was remarkable, but I couldn't get excited over such achievements of the ancients as dragging a boulder six hundred miles. They hadn't the airplane and the radio of our age. The sphinx is smaller than I had imagined it and is somewhat disfigured by the sand bags that hold up the chin as well as by the cannon ball that Napoleon had fired at it so that he could leave his mark for posterity. The sphinx is situated on lower ground than the pyramids, and is in a hollow. Sphinx represents a king (our guide said), i.e. strong as a lion and intelligent as a human. The men who guide these camels have their own private little graft – they bother you for a tip from the time you get on until you get off. Many families had come to the pyramids for a Sunday outing and some were eating their lunches on the steps of the big pyramid, Cheops. In the shadow of the pyramids (they are in a settlement called Giza) on the irrigated Nile Valley is a golf course, Mena Golf Club. I wish I could have played there. We got in our taxis and came back to the hotel, went over to the Red Cross Snack Bar – cata-cornered to the Grand Hotel on the corner of Shari Sloiman Pasha and Shari Fuad El Awal. We had limeade (synthetic) and doughnuts. This bar is just a corner of America with a juke box and all the trimmings. We had lunch and left at one-thirty for the non-expense tour to Memphis and Sakkara. We rode in a government truck and followed the same route we had taken in the morning until we had crossed the Nile River Bridge. We turned left off the road to the pyramids and passed through an old native quarter of the city and up the Nile Valley, instead of directly across it, as we did in the morning. The air smelled earthy – except in those places where the water buffalo were numerous. The dirt road was bordered by trees (cyprus, I think) and the canal ditches. Natives lay in the shade of the tall sugar cane beyond the ditches, or turned a wooden cylinder (Archimedes' screw) to sluice water from the canal up to the ditches perpendicular to the canal and running into the fields. Water buffalo wallowed in the canal. Native villages constructed of black mud bricks are situated at numerous places along the canal. Men and women waved at us from the side of the road – we passed two-wheeled ox carts loaded with sugar cane. Snowy white egrets flew over the fields or waded in the water of the canal. The ancient city of Memphis is now about sixty feet under the earth. The Egyptian government intends (so our guide informed us) to buy the land and date palms from the owners to excavate the ruins of that city. The only things of interest at Memphis are the statues of Ramses the Great. These are huge monuments – both are laying down – one outside on a hill, and the other is in a building constructed with a platform around the statue so that the tourists may view the old king better. These statues of Ramses were interesting to me because I had studied about them in my Art Course. The natives living in the vacinity bothered us by continually asking us for "bucksheesh" or trying to sell us little mud statues, scarabs and pottery. We also saw the alabaster sphinx which is a small replica of the large sphinx.

From Memphis we drove on to Sakkara which, unlike Memphis, is on the edge of the desert. Here, we were urged to hire a donkey for five piastres, but we decided to walk. First we viewed the tomb of Ti, called the Mastaba of Ti. I enjoyed this because it was something that you have read about and seen only in photographs. From the Mastaba we walked to the Tombs of the Sacred Bulls. It was cool in this cavern where the twenty-four bulls were buried. The ancient Egyptians worshipped the bulls (to be sacred a bull had to have certain markings) until it was forbidden by one of their conquerors. We piled into the truck after this and arrived back in Cairo tired and dusty. Took a bath, after which Jim Wickware of the RCAF came up to meet me for dinner. We ate and then went to the Strand, an open-air theater. The show was The Talk of the Town with Cary Grant, Jean Arthur and Ronald Colman. We came out of the show at ten-thirty and Jim and I talked for a while. He is twenty, good boy from Ottawa, went to Magill for two years. He got my address and promised to write me. Went to bed, very tired.

Monday, August 30 – Got up late this morning so I ate at the Snack Bar and then set out to find the Standard Hotel to deliver the films for Lt. Tippet. While I was looking for the hotel I heard someone say "Kennedy". I looked around to see Emil Krantz, late of the 981st, but now supply-sergeant of the 781st. I walked with him around the corner while he left his khakis to be cleaned; then we started back to the Standard Hotel. While we were passing a barber shop a little Egyptian girl of about eighteen ran out, threw her arms about Krantz, and amused herself by playing with his hair. He patted her a little and then was ready to go on to the hotel. I asked him if the little olive-skinned girl was his girl friend and he said "one of them". We came to the hotel in a little while and I delivered the films to Lt. William's sergeant. I talked with Krantz for a while. He told me that if I was going to Tel Aviv I would have to make arrangements with Captain Miller of Special Service who might fix me up with a second-class ticket on the train. He drove me down in the company jeep and the Captain told me to be at the station at one o'clock – he would see what he could do. We drove around town a little more and returned to the Standard Hotel. Leodas was in by this time and he and I chatted for a half hour about old times and other business. I forgot to mention that Emil Krantz and I went to see Cordero (Sergeant now) and Hibbs of censorship. Hibbs gave me his address and I told him I would look him up when next I got to Cairo. Came back from the Standard Hotel, ate, and met Romanovich and Dick Coe of Stars and Stripes – we talked over old times again. Had to leave in time to get to the station – took a cab (five piastres) and walked in where Captain Miller was waiting. He got me a second-class ticket for one pound thirty-two and a half piastres. There were five of us American soldiers and an old Frenchman

(I would say he was forty, but his face was lined and scarred) who was a Flight-sergeant in the RAF – more about him later. The ride to Tel Aviv is a sixteen hour one and, as one sleeps during the trip, the third-class passage (this is the only way that a soldier is allowed to ride, unless he pulls wires) is a grueling experience. Seats in the third-class coaches of the Egyptian State Railway are like wooden park benches at home.

Second-class coaches have leather cushioned seats – there are no beds on any passage, from what I can learn. Well, anyway I got my second-class passage without having to bribe the ticket agent as Tew of our Finance Detachment did. The coaches are in the conventional European design, i.e. divided into compartments with the aisle being on one side of the coach. Six men sit in a compartment. I sat opposite the Frenchman and by using a French word here and there, giving him a pack of American cigarettes, smoking his Egyptian fags, reading his newspapers, and asking him questions, I got his story.

Mr. K: "Are you a Palestinian?"

Frenchman: "Nooo, I am Free-French, I'm going to Jerusa-
    lem. Do any of you gentlemen speak French?"

Mr. K: "Ma Francais est pauvre."

Frenchman: "I am with DeGaul and against Germany and
    Petain." He first tried to tell me the above in his own
    language, but when I looked at him with bewilderment
    he repeated it in English. His English, incidentally, was
    inversely proportional to my French, that is cultured
    and correct. He continued, "When France fall, fell, I
    escaped to England to fight the Germans. I think all
    good Frenchmen fight with DeGaul. The people of my
    country can not be blamed for taking orders from the
    Germans – there is nothing else they can do now."

Mr. K: "Are you married?"

Frenchman: "Fifteen days ago I learn that my wife is dead
    last March. My brother was killed in the last war. My

wife was a nurses aid and she was too much tired, so
she died."

Mr. K: "Did you have children?"

Frenchman: "I don't know. I was married just two weeks
before France fell – so I don't know if I had a child or
not. My mother write me that my wife died last March.
If I had a child I suppose she would mention it, but she
did not."

"What did you do before you came into the army?"

"I was general manager of a society, a corporation. There
were six factories and I was general manager."

"What did the factories make?"

"Ah, that is bad, that is very bad. Munitions. It was formed
six months before France Fall – fell."

This Frenchman was the first Free-Frenchman that I have
talked to and I found him charming, sensitive, patriotic and a
good man. He told me that his father-in-law was a general in
the army and that his father had been a Vice-president of the
Chamber of Deputies. His home was in Paris and when I mentioned that I had read of the Germans talking about tearing
down the Eifle Tower for the iron it contained, he said, "They
will do it." When I said I thought it a mere threat, he replied,
"Oh, they will do it, those Germans." He lit one cigarette after
another and when we were trying to sleep, he stood in the aisle
looking out into the night thinking – and smoking.

Tuesday, August 31 – We arrived at Lydda, which is the
station for Tel Aviv, at six-thirty in the morning and boarded
a G.I. bus which took us to Tel Awinskya, the Army camp. We
ate breakfast there and then set off for Tel Aviv via the thumb
route. Arrived in town at the Red Cross Hotel and found out
that my furlough papers had to be signed by the MP there.
Had the papers stamped and came back to the hotel, found
my room, and walked to a place where they served ice cream.
While Dorsch, a corporal who came up with me and I were

eating ice cream, Red Miller of the old 981ˢᵗ walked in. He said that he and Ellsworth had been on furlough for the past seven days and were due to go back today. They had been drinking almost every day and had had a good time. There were several girls around the store and he and Ellsworth seemed to know them quite well. In the afternoon I found out why.

Dorsch and I came back to our hotel room, registered for the three-day tour of the Holy Land, etc. After dinner we went back to the place where we had the ice cream and the boys started to drink. I drank one bottle of something like orange crush but the other boys were on wine. Each bottle seemed to cost more than the last and the little ladies did their job well. At three o'clock we left the tavern and went back to the hotel. After dinner in the evening I talked to Red Miller for a while and then went back up to the hotel library where I read until bedtime.

Wednesday, Sept. 1 – The first thing that happened in this long and eventful day was that Dorsch woke me at four AM and asked me if I had taken his wallet to check it. I told him that I hadn't and it seems that his wallet with fifteen pounds together with his cigarette lighter had been lifted. The MP's came up to investigate this morning. It seems to be a regular occurence for things to be stolen there.

We all got into the bus at 8:30 AM and left for our three-day tour – fifteen men and the Red Cross hostess and a guide. From Tel Aviv we set out for Jerusalem on the same road which had been used by traders for centuries. It is an asphalt highway now. The terrain at first is level or slightly rolling. Cattle and shaggy black goats blocked the road frequently. Some of the fields were ploughed and some were filled with orchards of orange trees. The edges of some of these fields were bounded by a cactus hedge. The river beds were dry, for this is the dry season. Far off, to our left we could see the mountains of Judea. Soon, we came to a town that had been inhabited by Christians until the invasion of Saladin in the twelfth century. At that time Saladin, the sultan of Egypt who opposed the Crusaders, conquered Palestine and the Arabs took over. Most of the Christian churches were destroyed or converted into mosques, since the Mohammedans recognize most of our prophets. When the Crusaders came (11th to 13th centuries) to recover the Holy Land from the Moslems, many of these churches were restored. This history is necessary to an understanding of the architecture of the Holy Land. The Crusaders built castles on the high hills overlooking the trade routes running through Palestine. The purpose of these castles was to provide protection through the garrison in the castle for the traders on the road. These were plundered and robbed by the nomadic tribes who lived on their loot taken from the caravans. We crossed a valley called Valley of Thieves (the real name is unpronounceable Hebrew) and came into the Jordan mountains. These are rocky and barren – fit only for grazing cattle or sheep. We passed two more towns and came to Jerusalem. The old city of Jerusalem is bounded by a wall and is set apart from the modern city of that name. The houses of the modern city have red-tiled roofs. It is situated on a hill and is high enough above sea-level (2400 feet) to be quite cool, even in August. The finest hotel in town is the King David. Another fine building is the YMCA which is, in fact, a hotel. From Jerusalem we set out for Bethlahem over the old route. On the way we saw the Well of the Magi where the Three Wise Men are reputed to have seen the reflection of the star in the east, an old Greek monastary which dates from the 11th century, and Rachel's tomb. Bethlehem means house of bread. the population is 7, 500 – one hundred Arabs and 7, 400 Christians. There is not a single Jew living in the city, our guide assured us. We went first to the Church of the Nativity, which was interesting to me from an architectural standpoint. The entrance is now a rectangular door five feet high by four feet wide; above this doorway can be seen the architecture of two other epochs – the stones forming an arch above an arch.

The first arch had been filled in to form a smaller arch which in turn had been filled in to form the present entrance. The idea of the smaller entrance was to form better protection. We passed through the interior of the Church of the Nativity into the grotto where Jesus was born. This is a cave which has been fitted up with shrines, holy water, lamps, rugs, paintings and the smell of incense. It is very impressive when one enters – even if he is an agnostic. Two nuns who were silently praying made it more impressive still. The manger where Jesus was laid is in the same grotto directly opposite his birthplace but is about three feet deeper. We came out of this grotto and through the Church of St. Catherine into another grotto where the mothers of Palestine are supposed to have hidden their children when Herod ordered them slain. The Church of St. Catherine is the only Roman Catholic churh that is near the birthplace of Jesus. All of the other architecture is owned by the Greek Catholics. We came back to the Church of the Nativity and examined the interior. This is really impressive. The present church dates back to the time of the Crusades and is an interesting study in Greek architecture. Originally, Helena, the mother of Constantine, had built a church on the same spot. This church was destroyed by Saladin. In 1927 Palestine suffered a severe earthquake and the foundations of all religious edifices were excavated to determine if they had been weakened. Three feet under the floor of the present Church of the Nativity was discovered a section of mosaic. This was part of the original floor in the first church – the one that Helena built.

We came back to Jerusalem, ate at the Jewish Service Club and then set out to see the Mount of the Ascension. This spot is reputed to be where Jesus ascended to Heaven and his footprint is in the rock in the mosque – for it is a mosque, having been converted when Saladin took over. As we rode away from this spot the little Arab children spit on us and threw stones because we had failed to give them anything. I wonder what the preachers do when they come here. From the Mount of

Ascension we set out for Jericho. This is a long ride, and hot, through the wilderness of Judea – a descent of 3600 feet to the Dead Sea (Biblically the Salt Sea) which is 1200 feet below sea level. The mountains here are white, rocky and barren. There is a certain rugged beauty in them. Camels and goats grazed in the valleys; trenches and gun emplacements had been dug by the British to defend this land. Soon the terrain became rocky cliffs and then we passed into the Plains of Judea. Crossing the plain we came to the city of Jericho – green with vegetation. Palm trees, banana trees and orange trees were everywhere. We passed through the city and stopped outside. Here, our guide told us, had stood the ancient city of Jericho whose walls came tumbling down; Joshua had placed a curse on this spot and the old city had never been rebuilt. The city of Jericho is fertile because of one spring which supplies water for the area around the city. The present inhabitants of Jericho are darker than other Palestinians and believed by sociologists to be decendents of the ancient Moabites. Our guide showed us Mount Quarantania where Jesus is supposed to have been tempted by the devil. From Jericho we rode down to the Dead Sea. The guide told us that chemists are now obtaining many minerals from the Dead Sea. We saw many chemical factories around it. The sea is fifty miles long and ten miles wide. It is 29.2% salt – nothing can live in it. We stopped, got out and were told that we were to swim in the Dead Sea. We were warned not to get water in our eyes or to swallow any. Our bathing suits and towels were already paid for. We had a wonderful time in the water which was uncomfortably warm and of a gray color. You can't see the bottom even in shallow water. It is almost impossible to swim in the water. Your feet move either in front of you or in back of you. It was the most unusual swim I have ever had. I had heard stories about the buoyancy of a person in the Dead Sea but I never believed them. I suppose no one will believe me when I say it is impossible to sink in the Dead Sea. I went out as far as I could go – it is supposed to be nine hundred feet deep – and tried to sink. I relaxed – my feet just came bobbing up in front or behind. We took a fresh water shower, drank a cold glass of grapefruit juice and started back to Jerusalem. We are staying at the San Remo Hotel. It is a clean modern building. The hotel is operated by Jewish refugees who speak German among themselves. Most of the people of Palestine today are victims of the Jewish pogroms. The meal tonight was very good. It has been a very full day and as tomorrow will be another, I think I'll go to bed. Wish Mrs. K were with me on this trip.

Thursday, Sept. 2 – We woke up at seven this morning, had breakfast and were on our way to see the Garden of Gethsemane. There are eight olive trees in the garden. These still bear fruit and are believed to be the original trees – the ones that were in the garden at the time of Jesus. They are gnarled. Morning glories bloom about the walls of the garden. Beside the garden is the Church of Gethsemane or Church of All Nations, so called because parts of the mosaics in the ceiling have been contributed by different nations. The church contains the Rock of Agony which is directly in front of the alter. Under the present floor, mosaic work from the 4th century has been uncovered. The windows of this church have alabaster frames with many circular panes of blue glass; this gives an effect more impressive (it seems to me) than the vari-colored windows of some churches. From the Church of All Nations we went to the Garden Tomb – recognized by the Protestants as being that place where Jesus was buried. Our guide showed us what Protestants believe was Golgotha (Place of the Skull). The face of the cliff bears a remarkable resemblance to a skull. It is almost uncanny. We walked into the tomb where Jesus was buried and our guide explained that the custom of the ancients was to lay the body on a slab in the tomb; when the next member of the family died the body (now decayed) on the slab was dumped in the space under the slab and the second body was laid on top of the slab. In this garden we were also shown the ancient wine press.

Next, we went to the old city of Jerusalem. There were three main gates in the old city which is entirely surrounded by a high wall with machicolations and battlement towers. The Golden Gate, which is the one that Jesus passed through on his way to Calvary has been closed by walling in the arches. The other two main gates were the Damascus Gate and the Jaffa Gate. The first church that we visited inside the walls was St. Anne which is Greek Catholic. Anne was the mother of the Virgin Mary. In the courtyard around the church we walked deep down into a grotto to see the Pool of Bethesda. The reason for the descent is that the present city is about sixty feet higher than the ancient city. All of these shrines have been destroyed and rebuilt a number of times as the country changed from Moslem to Christian.

The Mosque of Omar is a beautiful example of the Byzantine architecture of the 12th century. The building is surrounded by a huge courtyard. We put slippers over our shoes and went inside the mosque. In the very center of the interior is a huge boulder where Mohamed is believed by Moslems to have ascended to Heaven, and where Christians believe Jacob offered to sacrifice Isaac. In the center of this boulder is a hole where blood from the early sacrificial alter ran down into a grotto and thence over the side of a hill which is opposite the hill of the Garden of Gethsemane. We went down into the grotto and were shown the sites where King David and King Solomon prayed – small altars are built in these little niches. Behind the Mosque of Omar is another mosque which stands on the site where King Solomon had his palace. Underneath the palace we saw the stables of King Solomon. We went down a narrow stairway into these underground stables. These were rebuilt by the Crusaders and only a part of the original stables remain, but they cover an immense area. The ceilings are high vaulted with arches. From Solomon's stables we came to the Wailing Wall, where Jews come on certain hours to wail for their lost glory and their temple. This wall was part of the original Jewish temple built by Herod and is a section of the original western wall of the old city. We saw the Jews wailing, women on the left, men on the right – facing the wall as they read from their holy books in a sort of chant or cry to God in their prayers. One old woman was swaying back and forth, hands clenched in front of her, crying in agony, tears on her cheeks. These Jews leave a little slip of paper in the chinks of the wall when they depart. Their request written on the paper will be granted if it is found favorable by Jehovah. In 1927 the Jews wanted to build a temple on this site, but as the wall actually is part of a Mohammedan mosque, the Arabs refused to allow it. Riots flared up and the British moved to establish military control. We left the Wailing Wall and moved toward the Via Doloroso – passing on the way the Tower of Antonis – that general's monument to Cleopatra. The Via Doloroso (Way of Sorrow) is a narrow street containing the seven stations of the Cross; these are the seven places where Jesus fell while carrying the Cross. Each one of these is marked. Some are controlled by the Mohammedans.

The seven stations procede to the Church of the Holy Sepulcher, where the Catholics believe that Jesus was buried. This church is in many sections – each section owned by a different denomination. The huge iron scaffolding made necessary by the earthquake of 1927 mars the beauty of the building. Under this church is a grotto where the original cross was found in an old well by Saint Helena, the mother of Constantine. On the walls, the very old stone walls, are cut tiny Greek crosses – the marks of the Crusaders – used in lieu of their initials. In the upper part of the church is the Statue of the Holy Virgin, a thing of priceless gems worth twenty million dollars, our guide said. From the Church of the Holy Sepulcher we passed again through the Via Doloroso – this street is one of the most colorful of any native street that I have seen. The first impression on the senses is the mixture of unpleasant odors emenating from the little stalls of the shop keepers; vomit, decaying meat, exotic incense, native foods, manure, smells that come from too many humans being together in a confined place. Flies are thick and are on everything. The narrow little street teems with people coming and going, donkeys carrying wares that their owners are selling or delivering to buyers – buyers haggling with the vendors. Men and women with running sores covered with flies – babies – filthy little babies crying, combing the rubbish on the edge of the street – for what? Beggars, palms outstretched, covered with filthy rags. In the shops – leather goods, meat, calico, bread, cakes, basket weavers, iron ware, laces, jewelry, grain, spices and drugs. A coffee vendor passes with his brass urn carried over his shoulder as if it were a bagpipe. This is a tired world – very, very old.

We went to the Oriental Bazaar store and there a lieutenant and I bought our wives Crusader Jackets for five pounds. These were originally seven and a half pounds but we were firm and in an hour had them at our price; our hostess Kay had told us to hold out for the five pound price.

After lunch Mike Logan and I went with Charley Zaimes to the Oriental Bazaar again. Charley was going to make some big purchases, so the owners and clerks started the bargaining by bringing us Turkish coffee – it was very good. It is served in demitasse cups, black, very thick, very hot, very sweet. Our guide showed me how to drink it: first, the glass of cold water is drunk, then with a loud noise one takes a sip of coffee – the noise is almost impossible to avoid since one must take in air in order to cool the coffee. I enjoyed the coffee and the bargaining that followed. Zaimes bought a white sheepskin coat, crusader jacket, black onyx and pearl locket and some other jewelry which came to about a hundred and twenty-five dollars. He made out a Red Cross check for the amount plus an additional pound as the owner claimed that a Mr. Cohen charged him that for accepting checks. We left the Oriental Bazaar Shop and set out for Haifa in the clubmobile. The country was beautiful as we were passing through the mountains. At one point we stopped and Charley took pictures of Mike Logan and me talk-

ing to an Arab on a horse – mountains in the background. We
caught up to the bus about forty miles outside of Haifa and arrived in Haifa about a half hour ahead of it. In Haifa we stayed
at the Savoy Hotel. After a shower I had quite a long talk with
Charley Zaimes. He is twenty-three, the youngest War corre-
spondent to be accredited by the U.S. government in this war.
His wife is a photographer for the Red Cross in England. He
thinks a lot of his wife and plans to fly to England in November. He has been a newspaper man since he was fifteen and has
been in every state in the union. He has had articles in many of
the leading magazines and wants to write a book on the Zionist
movement. He was in the National Guard when it was first mo-
bilized, but was discharged after ten months because of his eye-
sight – he wears very thick glasses. He was on one of the Lib-
erators that took part in the Rome raid – enjoyed it. He and his
wife had a hard time when they first went to Washington, but
together their income climbed to six hundred a month in eight
month's time. He has interviewed and photographed Cordell
Hull, knows Quentin Reynolds, Frank Gervasi, Pearson and
Allen – all the big newspaper men. He gave Mike Logan and
me a drink of gin and we then went down to dinner.

After dinner we were invited to two private homes. I went
with Zaimes, Kay Dull (our Red Cross hostess for the trip),
Meisner, Logan, Dorsch and Lt. Otten to the home of Mr. and
Mrs. Haddeus. They are Jewish – the nicest people of their race
that I have ever known. They came to Palestine twelve years
ago – not because Mr. Haddeus didn't do well in Chicago (he
is a CPA – two partners, offices in New York and Chicago), but
because he thought he might be able to help solve the Jewish
problem. His wife is a botanist with a Masters degree and a
Ph.D. except for her thesis. His theory is that the reason that
the Jews have not been assimilated into other nations is that,
unlike other peoples, they have no nation to be from. If there
were a country recognized as Jewish, people of the various nations would think of a Jewish person as being one of them since

other Jews lived in the Jewish state and spoke Hebrew. They have a little boy of nine who is mature for his age. After the war they plan to go back to the states. Mr. Haddeus wants his boy to grow up in America – he says he has no way of learning team play in Haifa. We had scotch and sodas (Haig and Haig!), took one picture, came back to the hotel and bed.

Friday, September 3 – We got up at seven this morning and after breakfast set out for Mount Carmel. The Carmelite monastery there offers a beautiful view of Haifa and the harbor. The monastery is a stronghold and the present building is the fifth church to be built on the same spot – the present church dates from 1631. We were shown the cave where Elijah, the prophet is believed to have lived – vestments which were the gifts of ancient rulers; these are beautiful, hand-worked gold embroidery – mother-of-pearl mosaic in some cases. Again, we had our picture taken before one of the pictures painted by one of the brothers. Two of the brothers acted as our guides. After we viewed the city and bay from the roof we were taken to the shop where souvenirs were sold. I didn't buy anything. We drove back through the city of Haifa from Mount Carmel and drove toward Tiberias. I haven't mentioned anything about the city of Haifa, but all that need be said is that it is as modern as any American city and almost as clean.

On the road to Tiberias we visited a collective farm, called a kibbutz. This farm is five years old and in that time they have reclaimed much of the original wasteland which was given to the group of the Zionist movement. We were shown cows that are being developed through cross-breeding, sheep, the orchard, fields, homes of the workers, the nursery and finally were given fresh milk, coffee, and apples. Women do the same type of work as the men and the babies are all reared in the one nursery where they are cared for by certain women. Mothers may have their children only at certain hours of the day. There are a hundred and sixty people in the settlement – forty of them are babies or very young children. The people seemed happy –

they are hard workers, all of them. Something I noticed when we were touring the fields was the stone watch-towers at intervals. I asked one of the men why they had these. "For defense", he said, "against the Arabs". One of the things that we don't know about life in this part of the world. From the collective farm we drove to Nazareth, took some pictures and then drove to Tiberias on the Sea of Galilee. We ate at the Hotel Atara Tiberias, drank french coffee, and then went swimming in the Sea of Galilee. This was fresh water and we found it hard to swim in it after the Dead Sea and the Mediterranean. We took some more pictures and then started for Tel-Aviv. We stopped at Hadera for orange juice and arrived in Tel-Aviv at six-thirty in the evening. I got my laundry, which I had left before starting the tour, took a shower and had dinner with Mike Logan. At noon today we heard that the British Eighth Army with Canadians had invaded Italy – haven't heard anything else. Logan told me at dinner that Charley Zaimes had been called back to Cairo and would be leaving sometime in the evening. At the information desk the girl told me that he was staying at the Yarkon so I walked there. It took me about an hour to get to that hotel and they informed me that Zaimes was staying at the Bristol. I called up and left word that I would be going with him. We had made previous arrangements to leave the next day at five. Came back to the Palatin and found out that Zaimes would be leaving at midnight, so I stayed in the lobby reading.

Around eleven o'clock the MP's came into the lobby bringing four young civilians and three soldiers. The soldiers were all drunk and one Polish soldier's face was a mass of blood. It seems that there is a movement among the young men of the town designed to intimidate the soldiers into neglecting the young girls of Tel-Aviv. No one could identify the boys as being those involved in the fight. The MP officer came into the lobby and talked to the Jewish boys (civilians). He said, "There is some sort of a movement going on among the young people of this town – you take this message to your young people from me: 'If you people want war, you're going to get it – and some of your young people are going to be killed, understand?'. It seemed to me that his statement was a little strong.

Saturday, September 4 – Charley stopped by at midnight and we left for Cairo with Tom, his chauffeur, and Charley in the front seat, and me in the back on a mattress – sleeping the first shift. We stopped at Tel Awinsky for petrol and had meat loaf sandwiches and grapefruit juice at government expense. After a while Tom got in the back and Charley drove. We stopped at a Naffi at three-thirty for petrol and waited until the doughnuts were ready at four. We each ate eight doughnuts, had a cup of tea and were on our way. At five I got in the back again and when I awoke we were in the middle of the Sinai desert. We came to the Suez canal at about nine o'clock, were ferried across and arrived in Cairo at 11:30. I didn't have any trouble getting my room, number 309 – decided not to have lunch as the doughnuts were heavy in my stomach. One of my room mates was a boy named Al Lubin who had his clothes in two little wicker waste baskets. I noticed that they were all civilian clothes and when I asked him if he was in the Merchant Marine he said that he had been interned in a neutral country and couldn't talk about it. His legs and chest were full of shrapnel wounds and his nerves were shot. He had been in one of the bombers from England that flew on the low-level Ploesti raid. He is a radio man and had been a successful interior decorator in New York City before the war. We both slept in the afternoon and our other room-mate, who was a little the worse for drink, woke me for chow. I had asked Lubin to wake me as he had an appointment with a New York Times reporter at five-thirty, but he left early and told our other room-mate to wake me. He wouldn't let me fall asleep again and when I was dressed I discovered that it was only 4:30. Wrote a little, ate, came back to the room and listened to Al Lubin's amazing story. Here it is:

"We had been practicing a long time for the raid in England and when we got to our base in Africa we did some more flying at two hundred feet. On July 30th at briefing we learned that our target was to be the Ploesti oil field in Rumania. The colonel told us what to expect and we knew that it would be the last ride for a lot of us. It's funny, when you go on a mission you always think of the possibility of the other boys being hit, but you can't consider yourself as a possible casualty. I guess it's a good thing. The armorers were nervous when they found out what kind of bombs they had to load – acid bombs for delayed action – they were to be set to go off an hour after we dropped them. They had to be delayed that long because we would be flying so low that a bomb bursting under us would blow us to kingdom come. These acid bombs are funny things to work with. In England the Fortresses used them once and two of them blew up on take-off. That's why we were on edge as soon as we climbed into the plane for the take-off. As we taxied over to the runway my heart jumped up in my throat every time we hit a bump. As we roared down the runway my legs felt weak, but we were soon in the air and I felt better. We circled the field and moved to the other planes in our position in the vee of vees. One of the planes had just taken off below us. It flew low for about a quarter of a mile, then we saw it disintegrate in a belch of flame. We tried not to think of it because we knew there would probably be worse accidents before the mission was over."

"When we were in the middle of the Mediterranean the leading plane in one of the other outfits blew up and disappeared in the sea. That gave us a funny feeling. After we got over land we still had a lot of flying to do. Moony, our pilot and captain kept giving us a pep talk at intervals. When we were about a half-hour's ride from the target, I got out the first-aid equipment and sulfanilamide powder. I have a sheet of armor plating that protects the radio of the ship, so I always act as nurse as I don't expect to get hurt. Then we saw Ploesti – black smoke and flames were shooting up into the sky – Jerry pursuit jobs swarmed all over hell, diving at our planes and missing them and crashing into the ground. I stuck my head up between Moony and Hank, our co-pilot. We were at two hundred feet now and could see the faces of the men who were shooting at us below. The noise was terrific. I saw a little girl running across the field and suddenly she was blown in two pieces – the twenty millimeter canon on the Jerry pursuit ship had missed us and cut that little girl in two. A second later that pursuit job was smashed in a million pieces on the ground; he had dived too low and couldn't pull out. We were almost over our target now and flying through walls of flames. The flames must have gone up to a thousand feet. I heard a clunk and then I felt sick – one of the twenty millimeters had bashed Mooney's face and head in – he never knew what hit him. Hank took over from the co-pilot's seat, but I felt sure we were going to crash right on the target. I turned around to pull the emergency bomb release and saw that Jake, our bombardier had just released the bombs – right in the middle of the refinery. I turned toward Hank and felt a sharp blow on my chest that knocked the wind right out of me. My heart felt like it stopped and I thought 'I guess my chest is smashed – I guess it's all over for Alex Lubin'. I sat down and started to cry because I wanted to live. I just took living for granted and now I'm going to die. The waist gunners came through the bomb bay passage – looked at Mooney and then at me. They didn't do anything. Afterwards, they told me they thought I was dead. Pretty soon I discovered that I could breathe, although my chest ached, and I could move my arms – my legs hurt too. I opened the box of sulfa pills and emptied them in my hand. I took one and looked at the clock above the radio. I thought 'I've got to take one of these every ten minutes'. I was bleeding like a stuck pig. Blood was running down my left arm on to my hand and all over the sulfa pills. I was afraid to put them down for fear I'd lose them. Pretty soon there was so much blood in my cupped hand that the pills were floating. Every ten minutes I'd pick one out of the pool and eat it. It sounds funny now, but I couldn't see the humor in it then. One of the waist guners came back up and cut my pants off above the knee, dusted sulfa powder on my legs and on my chest and arms. He told me that our gas tank had been hit and the gasoline was pouring out. We were going to try to get out of Rumania into Turkey to land – if our gasoline held out. We made it into turkey and crash-landed in a big field. I can't talk about all the things that happened in Turkey, but I just about signed my life away. I signed a paper saying that I would never fight again if I escaped. At the hospital there was a Greek Baroness who had been at Ploesti after the raid. She said that the damage was terrific. I also got a package of Lucky Strikes inside of which was a new American ten-dollar bill. I can't talk about all the things that went on there, but I escaped. Before all of this happened, I used to be a quiet sort of guy, but since this happened, I just can't seem to stop talking. Pictures keep coming into my mind and I can't sleep. I hope my fighting days are over, but I don't know."

Al had just arrived in Cairo this morning and had been at a ceremony where other heroes were awarded the Distinguished Flying Cross. He said that Generals and Colonels were shaking hands with them. They told him that his DFC hadn't arrived yet as he was reported missing in action. One of the captains recognized him or he would have been out of luck – he had no means of identification. From what I could gather his escape was surrounded with intrigue in which a lot of the higher-ups had been linked. I wish I knew the whole story, but he said that he is sworn to secrecy as to the method of his escape. I'll bet it's an interesting story. Guess it's not for me. Tonight I missed Barbara. I felt lonesome and an aching longing for her. I guess it may be the city that does it. I hope I can get the crusader jacket in the mail in time to reach her for her birthday. I hope she likes the jacket too – even if it is a sort of trinket and will probably have to be remodeled.

William M. Kennedy

Sunday, September 5 – After breakfast I went to see Major Dodderidge about the calculator. We are getting two new calculators and two new adding machines, but they won't be in for a while as they are on the docks at Suez. I won't have to worry about carrying them back anyway. I walked back from the finance office, stopped to have ice cream, and buy a little book on Arabic for ten piastres. This afternoon I signed up to take the non-expense tour on the Nile tomorrow. I was afraid that I wouldn't get to take this, but it looks like I will now. Wish I could have gone to Alexandria as I wanted to get those shirts for Berglund, but my bank account said "no".

Monday, September 6 – After breakfast, this morning, I got a haircut and a shoeshine and at ten o'clock was on hand in the lobby for the Nile trip. We rode in government trucks through the city and down to the river where we boarded the motor launch that was to take us to the Delta Barrages. Our guide explained that the Barrages were actually dams to raise the level of the Nile for irrigation purposes. They were named for the engineer who built them, a Frenchman named Barrage. Mohammed Ali, who conquered the country for Turkey in 1805, discovered that the income of the peasants (called Fellahs) was not enough to bring needed taxes for his army. When the dam was completed it added two million acres to the fertile soil of Egypt, making a total of four million acres of agricultural land. I guess that this eventually increased the income of the peasants and their ability to pay more taxes. We started downstream at ten-thirty.

The Nile is high at this time of year and while in the city of Cairo the river bank rises ten feet to the level of the surrounding land, further downstream the bank was just a foot high and in some cases even with the surface of the water. While we were still in the city we saw women and children bathing at the water's edge – I guess their modesty does not extend beyond their own race. The water of the Nile is as dirty and muddy as any I have seen. People living along the Nile use it as their bath-

154

tub, sewer, and drinking reservoir. Every evening the women come down to the water's edge to fill their vessels. They carry the vessels to the cisterns near their home and dump the water in. Of course, the water that is used is taken from the top of the cistern (a large clay vessel) so that some of the impurities have settled, but the water is far from pure.

As we rode downstream we passed under a low bridge – our launch cleared it by three feet. The river became very wide, a mile, I would guess, and we passed many sail boats of all sizes, but of a peculiar pattern. The boats were carrying stone blocks, bales of cotton, grain, pottery, and flax. The land on either side of the river was either a corn field. banana grove, palm trees, or at intervals, a native village. Occasionally we passed single mud huts where a native family (all except mother) would be lolling in the shade of the tall corn field close by. Sometimes we passed a native turning a tombola, a cylindrical affair to convey water from the river up two feet or more to the level of the irrigation ditch that ran into the field behind. The two other methods used to accomplish this are the motor-driven pump which is used on a few fields by the wealthy land owners, and the ox-wheel.

This is as colorful an apparatus as the old mill or the Mississippi steamers used to be. Usually the native sprawls in a spot of shade nearby and the dull ox is blindfolded and allowed to walk in his circular journey hour after hour.

Ox (F) spends his days going round and round turning horizontal wheel (A) which has a serrated edge as does (B). Wheel (B) turns and turns axle (E) which turns wheel (C) Bottom of (C) is under water. To the edges of (C) are fastened tin cans which fill as the wheel revolves under the water and empty the water into a trough (D) as they move to the top of the wheel (C). Water in the trough (D) flows into the irrigation ditch.

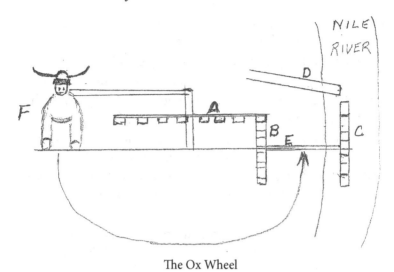

The Ox Wheel

The water in the Nile is as smooth as glass; occasionally we come to an area where ripples would appear – similar to the ripples on a little creek. We arrived at the barrages at noon and walked through the park area to a little railway line. The tracks are narrow gauge and are used for little push carts. Four people sit on each cart and a native pushes it. We rode a distance of about three city blocks and got off to see the Barrage Museum. In it we saw miniature scale models of the dams, tombolas, and the Nile locks. We rode out to see the two dams which have been superceded by two new ones, then back to our boat. As always, the natives bothered us for baksheesh, but we stood off their challenge this time. The park on the island between the barrages is a beautiful spot with grass and trees . It is used as a picnic ground. The trip back was uneventful except for a short stop during which one of our boatmen took off his clothes, dived down, and cleared the rudder of some weeds that had become entangled in it. While we were stopped near the edge of the river a naked boy of about twelve ran up to the boat and asked for baksheesh. The nurse who was with some hospital patients had her back turned toward the boy, but she reached in her purse and held a coin out behind her. The boy took it and scampered away. All of the men laughed at the nurse, but she was a good sport.

Got back to the hotel at four o'clock and found that I had a couple of new room-mates. They were nice boys. One was named MacCauley and the other was Herb somebody. We talked a long time, then went down and had some ice cream. After dinner we went to the show. They had bought some White Horse scotch and we had a big shot – they became garrulous. Mac taught music in a little High School in upstate New York. He has written a symphony which he hopes to have published; is at present a corporal and chaplain's assistant. Herb is a farm boy from Oregon – wants to go back to marry his sweetheart. He is twenty-five. Mac is thirty.

Tuesday, September 7 – Couch and I got up early this morning (5:30 A.M.) and rode out to the airport in the car that the motor pool sent over for us. We got to Benina at one o'clock after an uneventful flight and called the office. Wood came out and brought us back to Benghazi. I had a lot of mail and felt guilty about not writing to Barbara.

The first thing that Klahn said when I came in was, "Did you hear about Sergeant Johnson of the 981st?" He had been shot by Whitmire last Saturday. Later, from Walter Butler, I learned the details of the affair. Here is the story: Whitmire is from Georgia, twenty-four years old – has done time in a Georgia Chain Gang – has a twisted outlook on life. He has been in several fights since he has been in the army and always draws a knife. He had tried to transfer out of the company, but could not because of his bad record. He is unprincipled, naive and unmoral – these qualities make him dangerous and we all knew that he was dangerous.

Johnson was twenty-four, a staff sergeant, hot-tempered, quick to forgive – good at heart. He wanted only to get back to his pretty wife in South Carolina. He had served three years in the army during peace time and was called back in after Pearl Harbor. At first I hated him, but as I got to know him, I liked him. He was straight forward and would give a private a break. I played poker with him, went to shows with him, and talked about our personal post-war problems. He hadn't gone to school after the fifth grade and admitted that he was ignorant, but was cocky at times. He was nice looking and true to his wife.

Saturday evening at six o 'clock Johnson was sitting in his tent writing a letter to his wife. He heard someone come in, looked up into the soft, steady, big brown eyes of Whitmire who had his pistol leveled at Johnson's chest. Whitmire shot into Johnson's heart. Johnson cried, "Don't shoot me again Whitmire" – not very famous last words. He died almost instantly.

Whitmire came out of the tent – saw Sergeant Brannon running up the hill, aimed at him and shot twice, but Brannon had begun to zig-zag back and forth and took refuge in an old German fox-hole. The captain ran out of his tent and Whitmire aimed at him – the gun jammed. He ran back to his own tent to get Hammon's gun. Corporal Sellars, one of Whitmire's tent-mates knew what was up by this time. When Whirmire came back into the tent and grabbed Hammon's gun. Sellars took it from him and held him until he could be turned over to the MP's in town.

Johnson was beyond help. The amazing thing was how he was able to live long enough to say anything. When he shouted, "Don't shoot me again, Whitmire", it served as a warning to the other boys and probably saved other lives; if he hadn't cried out, Whitmire could have gone from tent to tent – until he had killed his enemies. A mere rifle shot is so common-place that we always laughed when we heard one and joked about having to clean the rifle. Johnson probably saved somebody's life.

When Whitmire was questioned he gave as his reason something that Johnson had done to him back at Lockbourne Field in Ohio last October. After Whitmire had cut LaBear slightly in a fight over a girl at one of the dances, both men had been held by the post MP's. No one had seen Whitmire pull the knife and LaBear wouldn't squeal – everyone knew he had used a knife, but he was released. When he came back to the barracks in the morning, Johnson told him to get out because he didn't want any so-and-so who would pull a knife on one of his own buddies.

Whitmire remembered this. He was child-like and easily hurt. He has large soft brown eyes that remind me of the eyes of a fawn. Yet, he is a killer. I've heard him talk of having killed men and I've heard him speak of killing others "Whenever I get the chance" – this, with that steady unflinching gaze. He is in the custody of the Benghazi MP's – waiting to be tried.

Wednesday, September 8 – This evening while we were waiting for the show to begin at the 1140th, the news of the surrender of Italy was announced. We were happy and thought of how it may shorten our time in the army by some months. We may get back by next summer.

Thursday, September 9 – This afternoon Blossom and Carroll stopped in to see me. I was glad to see them. Bloss has completely recovered from his arm wounds where the tommy gun damaged it. The doctors grafted skin from his hip over the bad places on his wrist. They came to tell me that Andy Ries, Lloyd Bowman, and Grover Kellar were on their way back to the USA by plane. They are to report to Kessler Field in Mississippi for pre-flight training. I am glad to see them get a break. Things happened so fast that they couldn't believe their good luck. Ries will see his wife, Bowman will marry Marge, and Kellar will see his girl friend. They will collect seven dollars a day per diem when they get back to the states. It's sure nice for them.

Saturday, September 11 -- This was to be my day off as we've had a lull just before October payrolls come in. Walter Butler drove in this morning to take Whitmire some cigarettes. After he came back from the guard house he asked me to ride out with him, so I decided to spend the day with the

981st. I had just started my round of visits when Butler called to me from the orderly room (tent) to say that I was wanted in town immediately to start packing. It came as a surprise to me as I hadn't expected to move for a month or so. When I got in the boys said that Major Olson would not be going with us – Lt. Jessup and a new lieutenant from Cairo will be our officers. It turns out that the new lieutenant is Lt. Glass whom I met on my furlough in Cairo. I'll sure hate to see Major Olson leave us. He's the best officer I've had since basic training. The rumor is that we're heading for Tunis – from there, nobody knows.

Through the courtesy of Special Service on the first floor of our building we saw Idaho with Roy Rogers tonight – it was a horse opera. For the past month we've been seeing all of the pictures that come into this area as soon as they arrive. We have a very select audience – about twenty of us – and have a good time. We're getting a little tired of movies, though. We're all packed and ready to move – all we do now is wait for the "go" signal.

Monday, September 13 – A lazy day – I read Hemingway's The Green Hills of Africa which wasn't so bad – the book is a true record of a month of big game hunting. Hemingway's dialogue gets a little tiresome. Played ping-pong with Berglund and Slonim, took a shower and then wrote a while in the evening. Most of the boys from the 43rd and our outfit had a party on our second-story porch. They waxed sentimental after a while and sang loud and threw empty bottles down into the Arab quarters. The MP came up to warn them to act with a little more discretion and not to throw bottles as the wogs were getting mad. They persuaded Couch to sing "Moonlight Becomes You So". Couch has a voice that is below average and he is kidded about his singing. He doesn't seem to realize that they are kidding him and so he obliged the boys by singing. When he had finished, the hooting, whistling, and applause and laughter was so loud that he was persuaded to sing another song. The boys had a wonderful time. I can't go this wog whisky – bought some for the trip but I'll mix it with water and use it for medicine.

Finance Detachment July 1943. Sitting (LtoR) Lt. Jessup, Willner, Maj. Olson. Standing (Lto R) Slonim, Dutton, Kennedy, Johnson, Couch, Tew, Karmilow-itz, Riccardi, Klahn, Wood, Zabowa, Berglund. Taken in the office in Benghazi.

William M. Kennedy

Kennedy in Benghazi.

Finance Detachment Billet and Office, Via Mafluga, Benghazi.

Finance Detachment, just before we left Benghazi.

ENFIDAVILLE, TUNISIA

Sept. 10 – Nov. 23, 1943

Major Olson does not come with us.

Saturday, September 18 – Today we learned that we were moving by airplane. We loaded all our equipment onto trucks and took it out to Berka Two and on the transports. At first we were going to leave at noon, but as one of our two transports was to have a hundred-hour inspection, we were told that we would leave tomorrow morning. We slept under the plane on our cots tonight. It's the first time I've slept under the stars for a long time. Before dark we read and played Chinese checkers. Our new lieutenant is nice – both lieutenants are like enlisted men, unassuming.

Sunday, September 19 –Had an early breakfast at one of our nearby QM outfits and took off at eight o'clock. Arrived at the airport at Tripoli at 11:30, ate at the NAAFI there and landed in Tunisia near Enfidaville at 3:30. Slonim went with an officer who met us to see about trucks to haul our equipment to the 323rd area. The second plane landed twenty minutes after we did. After we unloaded the second plane a sergeant drove up in a weapons carrier and took us to where the 323rd Group Headquarters was camped on the other side of Enfidaville. After chow we stopped in the village to see about getting a building for our office. We learned that the only one available had been bombed, but could be fixed. We slept under the stars again tonight. The 323rd is camped in an olive grove – the hills are covered with olive trees – almost as far as one can see. The fields are fenced with tall prickly-pear cactus. This is beautiful country. Enfidaville seems like a nice little town of probably three thousand. West and south of the village are high mountains. Sheep, cattle and camels graze in the fields, but most of the terrain is covered with olive groves.

Monday, September 20 – After breakfast we moved our equipment into the town in our future front yard. The building to which we have been assigned must have been beautiful before the bombings. It was owned by the Society (corporation) which owns all of the olive groves in this district. There is a central building with a high dome and a right and left wing.

The central portion is used by the Society for offices and the Director and Assistant Director had residences in the left and right wings. There is a beautiful big garden in the rear of the building and a concrete tennis court. The garden is formal with palm trees, pine trees, cactus and flowered shrubs. We are to have the right wing. The Assistant Director and his family live in the left wing. We had about twenty Italian prisoners of war to help us repair the place. They are friendly, cheerful, hard-working men and enjoyed helping us. I talked to several of them – they want to go to America when the war is over. One, braver than the rest, asked Riccardi who speaks Italian, if he could join the American Army. War is pretty ironic at times. If the American Army would agree to allow every German who deserted his own army to join ours, we could probably end the thing in a hurry.

Tuesday, September 21 – Today, we talked to the oldest son of the Assistant Director. He is sixteen and a half, very intelligent and speaks excellent English. He says that in a few weeks he will be going to school in Tunis. We asked him if we could put our ping-pong table on the long porch in the rear of the building and told him that he and his friends could use it during the day. He said "Of course". Later, we played ping-pong with him and his brother and two little sisters – they are about twelve and fourteen. The family is very nice. All are educated. I am getting a lot of practice speaking French.

Paul told me that the Germans had been in Enfidaville from the middle of November until about the middle of May. They had used the right wing (where we are now located) for their headquarters, and had moved the Assistant Director and his family across the street in one of the buildings. He said they had treated the people with courtesy – until later when they knew they would have to move out of the area. They had burned doors, benches and chairs for fire wood last winter. All of the benches from the little church in town were chopped up and burned.

Wednesday, September 22 – Today, Walter Butler stopped in – my old company is about five miles outside of town. He thought we had a nice set-up here. I told him he should have seen the building before we worked on it. We have a running water faucet in what used to be the bath room and a shower at the side of the house – all the comforts of home. From the roof of our building we get a nice view of the town and surrounding hills. After supper tonight (we ate with the 1140th which is stationed just outside of town) Johnson and I played tennis with Paul and George. The only balls available are very dead but we had a good time.

Thursday, September 23 – Talked to a Free-Frenchman today. He told me an interesting story. He had been in the French infantry in 1939 and was taken prisoner between the Siegfried and Maginot lines. After the fall of France he was shipped to North Africa with French-collaborationist officers. When the Americans landed on November 8th, DeGaul broadcast to all French troops in Africa telling them to arrest their officers and not to resist when the Americans landed. He was in Algiers and he, with three hundred comrades, did arrest their officers and allowed the Americans to enter their area without a fight.

We have had quite a lot of wine since we have been in Enfidaville. It's pretty good, but there isn't much sweet wine. I guess the Germans drank it up. Wrote Mother, Jean and Al and Barbara today. Wish I'd get a letter from Barbara. Mail simply hasn't come through yet.

Friday, September 24 – This afternoon Berglund and I went with Lt. Glass to Soose. It took us about an hour in the jeep. The road is straight and hilly – there are a few reminders of the war – wrecks of trucks and ambulances – enemy ammunition stacked in the olive groves near Soose. We had made the trip to exchange some large franc notes for smaller ones. As I was the only one who spoke French (??) I had to act as the translator. The first bank that we went to was not open, but the cashier lived in the same building; he told us to go to the Bank d'Algerie as they had the money there. As the bank did not open until three o'clock, we rode around town. It must have been a town of about fifty thousand; the business section seems to have been near the docks and hence is a wreck as are the docks. We stopped at a cafe and met a truck full of boys from the 981st. Paul Koester is a staff-sergeant now – replacing Johnson who was killed. We didn't get anything at the cafe as we didn't want wine and there was no lemonade. The architecture of the town is quite modern. It's a railroad center. We did our business with the cashier at the little bank and came home to Enfidaville.

Saturday, September 25 – Tonight, I went with Berglund down to the Arab quarter to get a bottle of wine. After we came out of the Arab's courtyard some of the Fighting French across the street hailed us. They were eating their evening meal on a table on the sidewalk outside their quarters. They insisted that we have some of their wine which they said was from Algiers. It was good wine. I talked to them for about a half hour – about the war. "Paris by Christmas" is their slogan. They had nothing but praise for American bombing, planes, clothes and supplies as they tried to show their gratitude. Berglund and I drank quite a bit of their wine which was stronger than we thought, as we felt a little light-headed when we left. Later, we went out to the 323rd Headquarters and saw "In Old Chicago", which I had seen in High School. The Assistant Director and his family, our neighbors, were guests of the colonel at the picture.

Tuesday, September 28 – Today our mail arrived – five letters from my best girl, Mrs. K. I wrote her a double V letter by candle light. Felt more like writing after hearing how things are at home. Also, got a lot of birthday V-mails from Mother, Dad, Mary Louise, Don, aunt Nell and Uncle Har and Harriett – also a nice note from Unk.

Wednesday, September 29 – Today I am 26 years old – more than half-way to thirty and I haven't accomplished anything. This morning I got the second half of a V-letter from Don. He wrote it just after he arrived at Gainsville, University of Florida. He seems to like it.

Last night was wonderful for sleeping – cooler than it has been in five months. Since we set the clocks back an hour it gets dark an hour after chow.

A couple of days ago Walter Butler stopped in and told me that the 981st was moving up to Tunis – they may be attached to a fighter squadron. Van Dyne and Zilk rode in on their motor cycles the day before yesterday and we talked a while. I miss the old gang, even if I am glad to get out of the outfit – can't have everything. Lt. Glass left this morning. He has been transferred to another finance outfit. Lt. Seitzer out of the office in Tunis is now our Finance Officer. He has been with us for about a week. He is small, quiet, nice-looking, a good officer – a first lieutenant. I am reading The Yearling – wish I could write like that. It's been a pretty good birthday – considering.

Sunday, October 3 – This morning after breakfast five of us went to Tunis in the weapons carrier. It took us two hours to arrive in the city. On the way we picked up four British soldiers from the Irish Guards. I was surprised at the size of the city. It has a population of 180, 000 and has suffered very little as a result of bombing, except in the area around the docks. Things are quite normal. There are several large theaters which show very recent American movies.

We parked our car in the parking lot provided for government vehicles and walked to the Red Cross Center. The main street in Tunis is really two streets with a parkway about twenty-five yards wide dividing them. Down the parkway is a wide promenade bordered by huge shade trees. It is here that the French families stroll in the twilight and early evening, while thousands of birds that roost in the great trees overhead clamor noisily. The American Red Cross has taken over two buildings in the city – one, a hotel; the other, recreation rooms and the snack bar. We arrived in the city at about 11:30 and went to the Red Cross Recreation Center. When we learned that they had only the snack bar and that we would have to find a place to eat, we separated and decided to meet at 8:00 PM at the Red Cross. Tim Benitz and I tried to find a place to eat, but there were lines everywhere – in front of the movies, in front of every restaurant. I never knew there were so many American soldiers in Africa. We met an MP (one who had been in Tripoli) who recommended a place to eat. We had spaghetti, onion and tomato salad with egg soufle – not a very satisfactory meal. Food is terribly scarce in Tunis – for civilians.

After lunch we got on the street car and rode to Carthage. The ride took us a half hour, but we enjoyed it – even if we did have to stand. We talked to a French soldier who had escaped from the Germans. He said that he and his comrades had slit the throat of a sentry and gotten away in the night. They fought with DeGaul. The train line crossed a body of water after we were out of the city. We made several stops at clean little suburban towns of white, smooth stucco houses with tiled roofs or flat roofs in the Italian style. When we arrived in Carthage we were met by guides and gherri drivers who bothered us. Tim and I teamed up with two other soldiers to hire a gherri for fifty francs a piece. We told the guides that we didn't need a guide. One young boy of fourteen followed us and offered to be our guide for 100 francs, then 50. We offered him ten francs a piece and he accepted. The first place that we visited was the ruins near the shore. The view was beautiful, but I was uninspired by the ruins, floors with patches of ancient mosaic, cisterns, a wine basin, ruins of the bath. I think I was not in the mood. We saw the huge Roman theater, fairly well preserved. It is an amphitheater with the seats rising in steps up the hillside; in the center of the semi-circle is the stage. We took some pictures here. Next, we rode to the huge amphitheater and saw the prison where Christians were kept until they were released to be eaten by the lions. We also saw the den where the lions were held. The Roman Catholics have built a shrine in the amphitheater for one of the early Christian martyrs. We took pictures in the amphitheater and had our guide, Louis (who was born in Malta) sing us German and Italian songs. We went to the Cathedral of Notre Dame de Carthage. This is a beautiful church , supposed to be the largest church in Africa. It is about eighty years old. It is built on the highest hill around Carthage and the large Norman tower can be seen for miles around. It is always peaceful inside a Catholic church. There is an atmosphere that is not present in the churches of other faiths. Their images, statues, beautiful paintings, confession booths and heavy drapes are symbols of mans' suffering – past, present and future. Somehow, it is comforting to me – the fact that the church acknowledges that this is the way life is. Inside a Catholic church I am consciously aware of human suffering; and then, when I have been there a while, I feel dull and despondent and want to get out of the place because there's no answer to the question there.

We rode back to Tunis arriving at five o'clock. We ate at the snack bar and I read a little in the recreation room. At 8:00 PM Wood came into the building and said that the car was parked just outside. We went out and found two British sergeants from the Scotch Grenadiers. Wood had met them in a bar and they offered to take us to their Sergeants' Club on the way home. It seems they were located in an area about halfway between Tunis and Enfidaville. We started out for home – lost our way a couple of times in the dark maze of streets – stopped to pick up one soldier who was hitch hiking and caught thirteen. They ran from the block which we had just passed and kept climbing in. There were seventeen of us in the back of that little truck – Grenadiers, Free-French and Yanks. One of the French had passed out on the floor – there were five of them and they didn't know a word of English. As we rode along in the dark, the Frenchmen jabbered among themselves, the English talked by twos and some of us sang "Take Me Out to the Ball Game", "Tangerine", and "The Marine Song". In about a half hour the French got off, then we rode for another half hour in the truck

– comfortably empty. The English boys were Grenadiers. They had fought at Mejaz-El-Bab – two months in the front lines. One of the boys told us that he had a nice girl friend in Tunis who was a school teacher and that it was just like home for him. We arrived at the camp of the Grenadiers and Sergeant Button led us up the road on foot, through an olive grove, across a deep ditch and into the big tent where the Sergeants of the Grenadiers did their eating and drinking. It was eleven o'clock and they were about to close up – Sergeant Button bought us each a stiff drink of cognac. It tasted just right as we were tired and pretty much on edge. The sergeant guided us back over the deep ditch, through the olive grove, and down the hill to where we had parked the car. We rode for the next hour in silence and arrived at Enfidaville at twelve-thirty – ready for bed. It has been a long day.

Tuesday, October 5 – Played tennis at noon and after dinner tonight. After dark we played rum and tried to get the World Series on the radio – there is five hours' difference in time between Enfidaville and New York City.

Tuesday, October 12 – Last Friday morning I went to the post office around the corner to deliver our mail. I met Bob Cumberworth as I was walking out the door. He looked at me and said, "Well, Jesus Christ, what the hell are you doing here."

"Well I'll be damned", I said, "I thought you guys were in Italy by now", and then I remembered that he had been at the hospital in Cairo and said, "Oh, are you just coming back from Cairo?"

He said, "Yeah, I'm all messed up, I've been chasing the company all over the country. I don't know where I'm going to stay or what the hell I'm going to do. I'm all messed up. I suppose you heard about it."

"Yeah", I said. While I was in Cairo on furlough Emil Krantz had told me about the doctor removing one of Bob's testicles. He had been in the hospital for a bad rupture. He was nice looking, big and healthy looking, married to a pretty college girl who had presented him with a little daughter after Bob was overseas. When Bob said, "I suppose you heard about it", I said,

"Yeah, when did you get in and where are you staying". I thought he wouldn't want to talk about the operation and that I could cheer him up a little. He seemed depressed, but I didn't think much of it at the time as he had been unhappy since we had left the states. He said,

"I flew in yesterday and stayed at the Bomb Squadron last night. There's a guy here who's going to take me out to headquarters now". I said, "The company was up here, but they moved up to Cape Bon. They're going to Italy, I think. They'll take care of you at headquarters."

The truck driver who had driven him in from the bomb group came over to us. He had stopped in the Post Office to ask the direction to 323rd Headquarters. The truck driver said, "There's a guy here who'll take you on out".

Cumberworth said, "Well, I've got to get out to the truck now." I walked with him to the truck, shook hands with him and asked him if he had enough cigarettes.

He said, "Yeah, I got enough, thanks, Kennedy." He climbed into the cab beside the driver and I walked up the road. As the truck passed me he called out, "Don't take any wooden nickels." I never saw him alive again.

This is what happened after he left me: He went out to the 323rd Group Headquarters where they told him that he could ride into Tunis on the truck the next day and that Headquarters in Tunis would help him to find his company. They would put him up for the night. For some reason he felt that he wasn't welcome and decided to go back to the bomb group to spend the night (this is conjecture). This is factual: At about five o'clock one of the British MP's saw him get out of a truck on the edge of Enfidaville near the bridge. The truck driver said, "This is as far as I go, bud", and Bob walked up to the MP and asked him if he could sleep in their quarters for the night. He told him that his own army didn't want him. The little MP told him that he was welcome and could eat with them. He said that Bob ate a good meal and refused to come with them to the movies. He was given blankets and a cot, talked a little while with the corporal and then went up to his room. At eight o'clock they heard a rifle shot, ran up to the room, and found his body. He had sat on the cot, placed the muzzle of the British rifle that was in the room under his chin, and pressed the trigger. The MP's said that the shot destroyed his head. The floor, walls and ceiling were covered with blood. He had finished himself quickly. I'm thinking of how his young wife and his mother and father (he was very close to them) are going to feel. Who knows what must have gone through his mind that day, I think that coming from the hospital after an operation of the kind he had, he was psychologically unbalanced. Then, to feel simply lost in an Army was too much. Things we can't control.

Lieutenant Tippet stopped in to see me the day before yesterday and I told him what I knew about Bob Cumberworth in the form of a statement. I was the only person from the 981st who had seen him alive after he left the hospital. He was buried in the military cemetery at Kirawauna. I also saw Willie Hoefling and Paul Koester who were with Lt. Tippet. Willie said that he had gallstones and was worried about his mother as his brother had been drafted.

Tonight when I went to get water at the water point across the street, I got into a conversation with a young English soldier who was with the combat engineers called "sappers" – nice work. They clear mines, anti-tank, anti-personnel, and boobytraps. He had been with the Eighth Army and when they reached Tripoli his unit was transferred to the Fighting French who came up from the south over the Libyan desert. They were attached to a small force of about three thousand soldiers – every man had a rifle, but they had two twenty-five pound field guns, three Bofors guns and a couple of other items that constituted their heavy weapons. In addition they had a thousand American trucks and some captured Italian machine guns. They held a small desert outpost and the enemy had a similar outpost about ten miles to the north. The only activity consisted of laying mines to harass the enemy and sending out scouting parties. The Jerries apparently didn't like the idea of having them so close , so they sent an armored column and some Stukas down to wipe them out The Jerries arrived at eight one morning and spread out in a semi-circle, shelling the garrison with their field guns, strafing and bombing it with their ME 109's. From eight in the morning until two in the afternoon the French held off the Jerries at 1000 yards. They expected to be wiped out to a man. About two o'clock they sighted a squadron of Stukas coming toward them and figured it was the end. From their rear the RAF Hurricanes came. They swooped low and played havoc with the German armored column – almost wiped them out completely, engaged in dog fights with the ME 109's and Stukas who turned tail and ran. The Fighting French and their English sappers blessed the RAF that day. They knew they were living because of it.

Friday, October 15 – Today I went to Tunis again. This time we went by the Zaghuah route. It's a beautiful drive through the foothills of the Atlas mountains. We passed through villages of Arab sheepherders. Their huts are constructed of mud bricks with thatch roofs and are quite indistinguishable at a distance since they are the same color as the surrounding terrain. We saw sheep and camels grazing on the slopes of the hills and passed many of the two-wheeled carts (the wheels are six feet in diameter) hauling rocks – the horses barely moving and the Arabs bundled up in his cloak, not seeming to care. Zaghuan is situated at the foot of a mountain. The houses are clean and white with red-tiled roofs. The town seems to be set down in the middle of an orchard and the shade provided by the trees makes it cool. After we passed through Zaghuan we passed the Roman aqueduct – it follows the road for about two miles and is about thirty-five feet high in some places. The water came from the mountain above Zaghuan and flowed over the aqueduct to Roman Carthage. This remarkable engineering achievement must be seen to be appreciated. I was more impressed by the aqueduct than I was by the Sphinx and the Pyramids. The water flowed about ten miles (at least that, it's a pretty rough estimate) through a conduit approximately three feet in diameter. To maintain a gradual drop in the water level from the mountain to the city of Carthage it was necessary to elevate the conduit over the valleys and tunnel underground through some of the hills. It is in the valleys that the high Roman arches used to elevate the conduit stand as a monument to the builders – the fine-thinking engineers of ancient Rome.

We got to Carthage at noon, went to the Red Cross Recreation Center and asked about a place to eat; they suggested the Maison Dorei or Golden House. It is located on a little side street called the Rue de Lorraine. The French prefer to eat in semi-privacy; their restaurants are all located on little side streets or far at the back of a bar. Their salads are hot, greens (almost grass), lots of onions and garlic. Spaghetti takes the place of potatoes (this may be a war measure). We had tomatoes and sardines for our first course. Another thing, they eat with the fork only – there is a spoon to serve, but no knife. We asked for a knife. We didn't take wine. The waiter thought we were crazy – "Pas vin?"

"L'eau", we said. Dessert was dates served in a straw basket. They tasted good.

We next went to the train that was to take us to Carthage and as I went up to the window to buy tickets I heard someone say,

"Kennedy, Bill Kennedy". I turned around and saw no one. Then I heard the person call again and there, already on the tram was Howard Bolam of Butler. I went over to him and he asked if I was going to Carthage. We were and we all got on and introduced each other. He was with Bill Ballard, another T/5.

Howard and I had gone through High School together and
spent our first night at Armco hauling bricks in a wheelbarrow
in June, 1937. He had been with the first wave of troops that
stormed Sicily and had been placed on a non-combatant status
a month ago because of foot trouble. He told us about climbing
down over the side of the boat onto a landing barge, landing
with machine-gun fire on one side and artillary shells busting
on the other. He said that he was certainly glad to get out of
combat. He said that the Sicilian campaign went like clockwork
– just like maneuvers. He said that he had met Jack Sutton who
is a dentist's assistant around Constantine and gave me Jack's
address. We went out to Carthage, hired a gherri again and
toured the ruins. I enjoyed it as much as the first time.

After we had seen the ruins we stopped at the French Red
Cross refreshment center which consists of a bench and two tables under a tree in front of a little house operated by a French
woman and her daughter. We had sandwiches (two kinds: tomato and date jam) and lemonade and caught the train leaving
at 4:30 for Tunis. We arrived in Tunis at five o'clock, bid Howard and Bill goodbye and went to the Red Cross Recreation
Center. Al Klahn and Howard Couch signed the state book and
Vince Riccardi and I went up to the third floor to the reading
room.

We met an Italian who was sweeping the floor and I asked
him in my best (?) French what they were serving at the snack
bar. He looked at me blankly and said "Toilet", pointing to our
left. I said,

"Comprenez-vous Francais?" and he said,

"No, Italian", so Rick took over since he is our Italian interpreter. They talked for about fifteen minutes and Rick explained what the Italian said. He was a civilian prisoner and
thought Mussolini was sick in the head. He said that the ardent
Fascists of Italy had been the college students – they had wanted the war and since the invasion had been emigrating to Germany since they had no other place to go. He talked about their

Fascist commentators who told the Italian people that America had no guns, no airplanes, no rubber for tires. He looked at our uniforms and laughed – he talked about how often American planes had bombed the Italian cities.

We read for a while in the reading room and then went downstairs to pick up Klahn and Couch. We decided that we wanted a good meal and not a snack and met a boy who was from the 1140th who knew a good place to eat. We followed him down the darkened street – Tunis is blacked out. As we came around a corner we noticed an Arab slumped over in a doorway in a pool of what we thought was blood. We stopped and a crowd quickly collected. An Englishman lifted his head up and asked him what happened. The Arab said "Vin". He was not hurt, but drunk, the "blood" was wine.

The restaurant was far at the back of a bar in a little room. The meal was good, the wine excellent. There were seven of us, the cost was thirty-five francs each – seventy cents in American currency. We ate and drank and walked down the dark streets of the city to the finance office where Lieutenant Seitzer was to meet us. When the lieutenant came in I went with him in the weapons carrier to an Italian friend of his. I stayed in the car while he went up to see his friend. We were parked in a dark alley and I watched the people pass in the dark – thinking that it was one of those moments that I'll always remember – like recovering from the flue, or finding a tootsie roll, or Buffalo Bill's grave, or riding the Standard Oil launch over Kil von Kull, or walking down the campus at night, climbing Nittany Mountain at midnight, working in a steel mill in the very early morning. A girl walks down the alley, a British soldier follows her, comes back – it's a mistake – voices chattering in French behind shutter-darkened windows – Tunis at night with the stars overhead. The lieutenant comes back with a skillet, sauce pan and a two-hundred watt bulb. We go back to the finance office and pick up the others. We arrived home at ten o'clock.

One thing, I forgot to mention – at the Maison Dorei while we were eating a Frenchman came over to our table and asked us if we had any cigarettes to sell. He said, "Name your own price". We told him that we had none but one of the Americans at the table beside us asked him how much he would give. Again, he said "Name your price". The G.I. said

"Two hundred francs".

"Done", said the Frenchman and bought two cartons for four hundred francs – that's eight dollars. The soldier told us that he had sold three cartons earlier in the morning at the same price. Five cartons for twenty dollars – some business. The five cartons cost the soldier two dollars and a half.

Saturday, October 17 – Today three men from one of our ordnance companies went out the Zaghuan road to salvage some parts from one of the wrecked trucks in a field near the road. They had the wrecker and lifted the truck on the hoist to get at the underside of the truck. The chain on the hoist was twisted; they lowered the hoist again and the truck came to rest on a different patch of ground. Thee was an explosion – either a mine or a booby trap. One of the men was killed outright, the other two were badly injured. One of the injured men crawled over to the dead man, felt his pulse and knew that he was dead. He then crawled over to the third boy who said, "I'm done for, take care of yourself". His friend forced him into the cab of the wrecker and drove thirty miles in a truck which had four tires nearly flat into Enfidaville to the medical detachment and collapsed as he crawled out of the truck. The medics took care of both men who were riddled with shrapnel. As they pulled the mosquito boot from the one boy's foot, the blood poured out. The medics guessed that the driver has a 75% chance of recovering, the other boy a 30% chance. If he does recover, he will owe his life to his buddy who wouldn't let him die in peace. The third boy has been buried.

Sunday, October 18 – Today I played tennis in the afternoon, took a shower and ate. For supper we had chocolate cake and pineapple ice cream – it was delicious. Yesterday I washed my blankets – two of them. I hope I boiled out all of the bed bugs and sand fleas. Last night we heard a short wave broadcast of the Penn State-Navy football game. It was 7 to 6 Navy at the end of the third quarter when it faded and we never knew who won – some fun. I should have written a letter tonight, but I've spent most of my time on my diary. Also must get to work on my novel.

Saturday, October 30 – A week ago we were given our shots; since I had not received the last set of shots I was due to have four shots, two in each arm – typhus, typhoid, tetanus and small pox (vaccination). I felt all right in the evening but when I went to bed I had chills and a fever. I spent the next two days in bed with a fever and ate almost nothing. When I got up I was weak and couldn't enjoy a cigarette. I decided to try to quit smoking and haven't had a cigarette in four days, but I'm smoking my pipe. I hope I can cure myself.

The big news is that when we pay off tomorrow it will be in American gold-seal currency. It's wonderful to work with dollars and cents exclusively and not have to bother with the business of converting into francs. What it means we can only guess – I think we're going to Italy in the near future. It's the policy to pay units embarking for Italy in gold-seal and then having personnel convert to occupational lire upon arrival in Italy. We may know soon.

Last Thursday I had my eyes examined. Tuesday I go back for my final exam and then I hope I'll get a pair of strong GI glasses.

Friday we saw Bette Davis and Paul Henreid in "Now Voyager". It was a wonderful picture, one of the best that I have seen. We've had a lot of rain recently and the wadi between Enfidaville and the field where the 1140th is camped has been overflowing with water from the Atlas Mountains to the south. This made it necessary for us to use the bridge instead of the ford (which was dry) when we walked to chow. Speaking of chow, we've had fresh meat and fresh butter quite often recently. The Red Cross has taken over the Hotel d'Enfidaville and will open up in the next few days. We're hoping that they will have doughnuts as they did in Benghazi.

We have a new man, a private, Bob Palmer (nickname, "Dagwood") from Columbus, Ohio. He arrived in Africa on the 13th of September. He is short, blond, easy-going and likable. He has been to Finance School and has all of the latest texts – which I hope to read.

It has been cold lately – too cold to take a shower and we have begun to think about getting shutters and doors up and some sort of heat. We haven't done anything about it as yet.

Sunday, October 31 – Just a year ago I started this journal when we boarded the West Point in New York harbor – that ought to be a record of some kind. We had an easy day today – played tennis in the morning and took a shower in the afternoon – it was pretty cold, but worth it as I felt like a new man. I've been talking to Dagwood Palmer about his trip over here. He landed at Casablanca and stayed there for two weeks. They didn't do any work, just got passes into Casablanca every day and back to their camp each night at ten o'clock. He said that it's a nice town and told us about a place that was very similar to "Ricks" in the picture "Casablanca". This was in response to Chum's question, "How is Ricks and how is Humphry Bogart?" Palmer said that in this restaurant there is an orchestra and a colored man who plays the piano and tries to imitate the negro in the picture signing As Time Goes By. We laughed and asked him about Ingrid Bergman. He said they met a charming American girl in the restaurant who was apparantly married to a French officer. I hope that I can see Casablanca and Algiers before I go home. From Casablanca Dagwood flew to Oran. They saw Algiers from the air. Oran is much smaller than Casablanca but is a large port.

There are so many places in the world that I want to see and the little part of the world that I have seen has whetted my appetite. My nature is such that I can think back to places that I have seen and remember only the quaint, pleasant and the bizarre – and forget the filth except the terrible poverty which it symbolizes. I want to have a lot of these memories. I want to remember those nights on the West Point drinking coffee with Paul Prosser and Willie Hoefling, sitting on the deck with the stars and moon and ocean all around; riding the funny little Indian train through the mountains to Deolali – those cool nights in the tent with Hoefling, Slasky, Turner and Thomas – lying in my cot looking at the stars through my mosquito net and finally listening to the beautiful, poignant notes of the bugle sounding British taps – walking through the crooked blacked-out lanes with Gilbert and Hoefling to the British canteen to eat little tomato sandwiches and tea. Gilbert is dead now, but I'll always remember how he kidded me on that night because I had just made P.F.C. He was a charming little man who loved his wife – not made of the stuff of soldiers. I'll always remember the old, old mess hall at Camp Deolali and the ancient canteen with its worn stone floor where Hoefling and I drank tea, ate tastless cookies and talked about what we would do after the war was over. Guess that's enough reminiscing – wish I could get something done on my novel. I just procrastinate and think up excuses for not getting on with it. We expect to move soon, and I've missed getting to Kairouan to get the rug. It feels good to have gold-seal American money in my pocket again. We are going to the show at 8:30 tonight. It is Margin for Error – it should be very good. No writing tonight, I guess.

Monday, November 1 – The picture last night was good although it was somewhat different from the play which I had read.

This afternoon I went with Lt. Jessup to Soose to exchange some money. It was warm driving down and , aside from almost running down a couple of dogs, the trip was uneventful. Since the Banque D'Algerie was closed we went to the British field cashier's office. It was a gloomy place with a lieutenant and a lance corporal in the office. They were very quiet. It was a very different atmosphere with saluting and heel-clicking from that of our own office. The room was poorly lighted from two barred windows behind the officer's desk. I was glad to get out as it depressed me. The trip back was quite cool as the wind had begun to blow. Just outside of Soose there is an Arab town that is "Positively Out of Bounds to All Ranks". It is strictly Mohammedan and there are large areas of Mohammedan graves – white tombstones dotting the rocky, grassy fields. A few cattle graze in the middle of the cemetary and the watchers sit on the gravestones or loll in the grass. This would be a fascinating town to explore, but I'd carry a pistol if I started to go through it. There is that odor permeating the air – I think it's due to the lack of facilities for the disposal of sewage. That, coupled with the fact that the Arabs relieve themselves on the streets and are generally careless in that respect. We passed many olive groves where the Arabs were plowing the ground under the trees. They use camels or horses to pull their plows.

Tonight we saw Shadow of a Doubt with Teressa Wright. It was directed by Alfred Hitchcock and had his suspense. We all thought it good. After the show we stopped in at the Red Cross Club which is in the Hotel d'Enfidaville and had coffee and doughnuts (free). It is very nice and homelike there. There are three Red Cross girls (who are always occupied with a group of GI's) and a couple of Army boys who do the serving. I imagine that we will be spending a lot of our time there from now on. The doughnuts tasted good. Tomorrow I go for my final eye examination.

Sunday, November 7 – this has been a very busy day. The events leading up to it took place about three weeks ago. Wood, Johnson and Riccardi had gone to Soose to look the town over. They walked down one of the streets and from one of the houses heard music and laughter. The buildings in this particular block were apartments and there was a barber shop in the building. The boys all trouped into the apartment from which the sound of the music came, asked for a hair cut pretending that they thought it was a barber shop. The family invited them in, gave them wine and made them feel at home. They were invited to come again and did go down the next night. They met the friends and relatives of the family and when the Headquarters Squadron had a dance in Enfidaville, brought the family up here. There are four girls in this little coterie ranging in age from seventeen to twenty-one; the boys danced with them and gave cigarettes to the men and candy to the little ones. The family invited the Finance Detachment down for a picnic today – twelve of us went.

We left here at eight-thirty this morning in the weapons carrier and the jeep and got to Soose at ten o'clock. By the time we were ready to start it was eleven o'clock. We rode outside of Soose for about a half hour and turned off the road onto a side road. We stopped and walked through the cacti-fenced pastures to an olive grove and sat around and talked for a while. The head of the family, however, was not satisfied with this site for the picnic so – we piled into the two vehicles and drove to a nearby town, through the narrow streets of the Arab quarter to the beach. The beach was at the bottom of a rugged cliff and we didn't attempt to go down it but walked up a slight hill beyond some palms and spread our lunch inside of a three-walled roofless building (never completed because of the war, I suppose). We had bought the wine, five bottles, and the French had supplied the food. The lunch which they had prepared consisted of sandwiches made of a pudding of macaroni, eggs, chicken, green peppers and onions; other sandwiches were made of salmon, pickles and relish. All very delicious. The French people all had a sort of condiment made of red peppers on their pudding sandwiches and when I asked about it they said, "No good for English – too hot." I asked for some of it on my sandwich and one of the girls obliged. It was really hot and burned my throat and lungs, but I told them that it was good and washed it down with plenty of wine. The other boys and Lt.

Reynolds (classmate of Candy Johnson's at University of Texas) of Headquarters Squadron had to try it – they just looked at me and didn't say anything. After the sandwiches we had pastry confections for dessert. It was very good – made with citron, dates, nuts and a kind of syrup. The only flour available to these people is black flour and their bread and pastries are all coarse, but they taste all right. After we had eaten and finished the wine we felt pretty good. Lt. Reynolds got his saxaphone and played while some of the boys danced with the girls on the sand. We sang everything from "Mary" to "Mademoiselle from Armentiers". One of the Frenchmen was a lawyer – he had two small glasses of wine and was drunk. Later, he wanted to drive one of the cars and got on our nerves.

It started to sprinkle a little and we all headed for the cars. We got in the cars and rode back through the little town to another town called Monastir, a popular summer resort. There is a balustrade along the road which borders the seashore. We walked down some stone steps and along a stone walk which extends out to huge coral rock formations. We climbed up to the top of one of the rocks; there was a brisk wind blowing and the salt spray whipped our faces. There are caves in the rocks which seem to have been chiseled out by hand. From the rock we looked across the short stretch of water to the Kasbah which was built by the Romans – there are high walls with rounded merlons and crenels at the top of the parapet – high buildings beyond the walls. The walls look gray and worn and serried. This was the original town of Monastir and is now the habitat of the Arabs, called the Kasbah. Wish I could go through it sometime. We walked back to the cars, piled in and rode to a little town called Maknine, parked the vehicles just off the highway and got out of the cars. One of the Frenchmen stayed to watch the car while the others led us through the maze of streets in the Arab quarter. Finally, I asked the head of the family where we were going, thinking that we might not be able to find our way out so easily. He said, "We go to visit Arabic friend of ours." We went through a narrow passageway and came into a courtyard paved with red and white tiles in checkerboard pattern. The house was built around the court like the old Roman villas and the walls of smooth stucco were painted a pale blue. The contrast of this cheery, light interior to the dingy unpromising exterior was amazing. I had always wanted to see how the Arab lived behind his high walls and high barred (actually filigreed grill) windows. As we entered the court, to our right were two niches in the wall near the floor. At the top of the niches, which extended to a height of five feet from the floor, were rope pulleys for drawing water from the deep wells that furnished water for the household. One of the wells was salt water and the other fresh water. The house was very old, one of the French girls informed us. The Arab said that he was sorry we hadn't come to see him in the morning as they had had dancing and a party.

The part of the building which fronted on the street was a second-story structure with a balcony facing the court and steps running down to the court. There were no windows on this side of the building and the only windows in the house were those opening into the court – thus the Arab had complete privacy for his family. We soldiers wee ushered into one of the rooms directly across the court from the balcony or street side of the building. We sat down and from time to time one of the members of the French family would come in with one of the members of the Arab family who would shake hands with us. The ladies of the French family kept to that part of the house where the Arab women lived and visited with them. We did not see the female members of the household – they are the Arab's private property. By and by we were served black sweetened coffee (very hot) and various kinds of sweet pastries which tasted good. We started to leave at 4:30, but it was 5:30 before we left the house. We were told that there had been forty people living in the house while the Germans had occupied Soose and the town was being bombed regularly. The

Arab must have been a good fellow to take in so many refugees
– they lived there for five months. We took some pictures of the
children (about twenty of them) who kept asking us for "chew
gum". Finally, we left after shaking hands with all and I carried
little Gigi (the little French boy who was "cinq ans") through
the narrow streets back to the automobiles.

As we climbed into the truck a crowd of Arab boys, filthy,
stained deformed teeth, with casts in their eyes (one had an
eye that was turned in so that the iris was just visible) gathered around, shouting and begging. They followed the truck as
we turned around and were almost run down. Someone threw
some cigarettes to them and they fought like wolves over them;
then they ran with that wild fanatic look in their eyes after the
truck. One kept running for two blocks after the other had giv-
en up and straggled away

In the dusk we started back to Soose traveling over the dirt
road back to Monastir and then on the asphalt road again. The
moon came up and the French sang and sang – some songs
strange to us and some familiar. We arrived in Soose at seven
o'clock and they insisted that we come up and visit for a while.
One of the French women played the piano; soon, an English
sergeant came in and played . Then they led us to the back
of the house where there was a very large open porch with a
composition floor for dancing. Soon they had a drummer, ac-
cordianist, trumpet player and there was dancing. We left at
nine-thirty and were given a pastry as we left. It was a cool
ride back to Enfidaville. At the edge of Soose the British MP's
stopped us and asked us to take a couple of colored boys back
to Enfidaville. They had had quite a lot of wine. They got into
the back of the truck and one of them told us that his wife was
divorcing him for a sailor. He had sent her $1,600 since he had
been in the Army and had a little girl whom he had never seen.
He opened up a bottle of wine and passed it around. We sang
on the way home. The colored boys would supply the patter,
"You hip now boy – you really diggin' – now you solid." We

got home at eleven-thirty and we all had mail. It has been an interesting day.

Monday, November 8 – Tonight Dagwood is in charge of quarters and as we sat around the embers of the fire in our grate, he told us about some of his experiences while on guard duty in the states at a camp in Texas near the Mexican border. Dagwood's Christian name is Robert A. Palmer. He is blond and blue-eyed, just like a little cherub and he talks very slowly. When he is telling us something we all want to help him along. "The first time that I was on exterior guard duty", began Dagwood, "I was a super numeral" – laughter here because the word is 'supernumerary' and we pointed this out to him. "Well, goddammit you know what I meant", said Dagwood. "Well, there was a guy who had been AWOL (that's Absent Without Leave) and was brought into the guard house and I had to guard him. The Officer of the Day told me to take him to get his blankets and clothes because he was going to sleep there for the night. Well, it was the first time I had ever done guard duty and jeez I didn't know what to do. I followed him all around the camp and we came to his barracks. He talks to a lot of the guys and I'm standing right behind him and he says,

"That's all right, guard. I won't give you any trouble, I gave myself up."

"After that, I kind of relaxed. The next day I had to take him over to his C.O. and I didn't know what to do there, so I just stood at the door, but the major was a hell of a nice guy and he said,

"That's all right, guard, just sit down, I trust this boy."

"Come to fine out", continued Dagwood, "the guy had been a corporal and was up for sergeant. His CO was a good guy and, as the guy had been drunk and woke up in Albuquerque and had given himself up as soon as he realized he was AWOL, he got company punishment and that was sweeping out the orderly room for a week. The guy made sergeant the next month so he didn't loose anything by it."

"That afternoon I had three of the toughest prisoners in the camp, and I had to take them out to dig a ditch. These three guys were always fighting and the Officer of the Day said that he wanted them to work together, because they might get along better. They had three fights that day. The OD told me that if they started to fight I was to shoot in the air once and he would have all the soldiers I needed in a couple of minutes. Well, the first time they started to fight, the big red-head swung his pick at the other guy. I think he was trying to kill him. I got my gun between them – I don't know how I did it, but I did – and they stopped. The next time another guard stopped them, and the last time two of us stopped them. That same afternoon one of the guys who came into the camp at the same time I did, a new guy, was on the gate. His orders were to stop all cars and then call up the OD to check. Well, a girl drives up to the gate and he asked her who she wanted to see. She didn't know who she wanted to see at first and then she gave a colonel's name. The boy called up the OD and while he was on the telephone the girl drives away – fast, right into the camp. This guy who was on guard there was scared shitless – he could hardly talk, but finally he stammered out to the OD what had happened. A couple of guards got out in front of the guard house to stop her when she came by, but she drove right past them and turned around the corner going thirty-five miles an hour. They had every guy in camp trying to stop her and finally when whe went to drive out the gate, there were four guards with rifles pointing right at her. She would have had to kill a couple of them to get past – she stopped, and she was as drunk as a loon and , come to find out, she was just a common, ordinary town whore."

'What was she, Dagwood?" we asked.

"She was just a common, ordinary whore", he enunciated, and looked at us to see the effect, "and she was fined a hundred dollars and had her driver's license taken away from her."

"The next time I was on guard duty there, I had to guard the one airplane that was on the field. It was a trainer and I was miles from the camp with nothing but prairie around me. I was sitting on the step that comes down from the pilot's cabin, in the dark, there with my feet on the ground when all of a sudden a jack rabbit and a dog ran right between my legs and Jesus Christ, I jumped about three feet and my gun went off and I fell on the ground. The next thing I knew the O.D. and Sergeant-of-the-Guard were there in a jeep. The bullet went right through the wing of the plane. The O.D. had been on his way out to my post and they had passed the dog chasing the jack rabbit on the way. I told them what had happened and they got a hell of a laugh out of it."

"When I was in Casablanca I had guard duty once and had to guard one of the warehouses that was in the Arab quarter of town. Some Arabs went into one of the buildings and I shut the door. The door had a kind of catch on it, and it locked. The Arabs pounded on the door and made a hell of a racket and the Corporal who was around there came running up. He didn't have a key and he called the O.D. They had to chase all over town to get the key from the civilian guard that works there in the day time."

"You really have a tough time on guard, don't you, Dagwood." we said.

"You ain't a shittin, buddy. Everything happens to me." said Dagwood.

A lot of packages came from home today and a couple of the boys had received new pipes. Somebody asked "Chum" Karmelowitz why he never smoked a pipe and Chum told us all about it.

"When I came overseas I had my pipe with me and one night I got out of a taxi and dropped it and by Jeez, the cab ran right over it. The cab ran right over it. (Chum makes his point by repeating things over and over). "I know a girl at home", he continued, "and one time I went to see her and left my pipe there. I always forgot to pick it up and now every time I get a letter form her, she tells me she still has my pipe. She's married and has about four kids and she still keeps my pipe."

Laughter, and somebody said, "Hell, her kids are probably smoking the pipe now. She must love you to keep a pipe that long."

"Boy", said Chum, "If you knew this babe you'd know that , four kids or six kids or ten kids, she is plenty okay. No matter how many kids she has, she is okay. She's some babe, no matter how many kids."

"Just like Margurette", said somebody, "the more she took on, the better she got." Margurette is a prostitute who worked in Tripoli servicing about half of the British Eighth Army. The boys lined up in a double line all around a block with M.P.'s needed to handle the traffic. The boys were waiting for Margurette and three of her friends.

"You ain't a-shitten." said Chum.

We sat around the fire and talked some more. Some of the boys helped Harry Willner put up his pin-up pictures that he received from a friend who works for Warner Brothers Studios. They were pretty good. We talked about moving and rumors that Turkey has declared war on Germany – unverified. We didn't have our radio as something happened to our condenser. We'll have it fixed tomorrow and then we can catch up on the news. Pretty tired and so to bed.

Thursday, November 11 – For the past few days I have been "cheesed off" or "browned off" as the British say. I have felt pretty low, but today I had two letters from Barbara and two from Mary Louise and I'm feeling better. We're sitting in the office tonight, there's a fire in the grate, a poker game on, and two Italian prisoners have come in to visit with Rick; one of them is a corporal who puffs cigarettes in a holder. They are docile fellows who like Rick. We like them as we have learned that they don't care for Fascism, war and empire-building any more than we do.

Tonight the boys were talking about how they used to play jokes on the officer who used to be the Group Chaplain. He is probably home now. He was a hayseedy sort of a duck of about forty. When the group was in Palestine some of the boys got together and filled up the colonel's fox-hole; then, with a shoe which they had "borrowed" from the Chaplain's tent they put footprints all over the dirt. The colonel came back and roared, "Somebody filled up my fox-hole and here's a footprint. I'm going to try everybody's shoe until I get the right guy." Some of the boys got the Chaplain's shoe and fitted it into the imprint. The Chaplain was bewildered. He said,

"All right, I'll dig it out, but I didn't fill it." When he was almost finished with the job the boys came over and offered to help him dig out the fox-hole. The Chaplain certainly has a tough time in the service. He is an officer but he walks alone – not close to the officers or the enlisted men. Our new Chaplain has been with us about two months. He is a very nice guy, says "Hello" to everyone and always has a kind word for the boys. He goes out of his way to do favors for the men and is well liked by all.

Today is Armistice Day and for the French, who have suffered through long years of war, it is a day of prayer. We stood up by the little church opposite the monument to the men who died in the last war, and watched the French, British and American officers file into the church. Next, the civilians of the town came, then the Italians prisoners with their guard in the red turban (they had asked to attend). Finally, two young mothers came wheeling baby carriages. Two native policeman lift the carriages up the stairs – the first matron waits at the top of the steps while the policemen carry the second carriage up – then they walk into the church, the choir of young boys sings and the church services begin. At the end of the service the military files out and across the street to the obelisk with the cock on top. There are flowers and wreathes and palm fronds at the base of the monument. The flags of Tunisia and France are on the monument and the British and American flags are carried by their color guards. There are short speeches by an Arab, and by French, British and American officers. That's all.

Friday, November 12 – Tim Benitz told me a tragic story today. Tim is a homosexual, a fact that I have not mentioned before. Everyone in the office knows this and accepts it as a fact of life. As long as he does his job (which he does well in officers' pay) there's no problem. Anyway, this is the story as he told it to me: When he was working in New York he met a girl at one of the parties he used to attend. She was charming. She invited him to one of her parties. The young lady was a perfect hostess and her parties were always well attended by the smart set. Tim and the girl fell in love (Tim said), but by this time he knew that she had a large amount of money in her own name and that he could never keep her on what he was earning. They talked it over and decided to remain friends and did. Tim continued to go to her parties. The girl had few close friends – she had a complex that seemed to prevent her from forming close friendships – she shunned them. Her mother had murdered her father when the girl was quite young – there had been headlines and publicity. The mother had been adjudged insane and had been confined to an institution since the time of the tragedy. The girl had strange fears that she might one day become insane herself. Her father had been an executive in a large corporation and she had inherited a fortune which included stock in the concern. The young lady spent her time traveling from city to city living a few months in each in smart apartments.

Some time after Tim and the girl had decided to give up the idea of marriage, she became engaged and subsequently married another young man. At the reception after the ceremony the groom and all of the guests were present and waited and waited for the bride – she had disappeared. No one heard from the lady for three months and then Tim had a letter from her – postmarked from a country in South America. She told him

that she had become afraid and had run away. She was fear-
ful that the strain of insanity would be passed on to her children and couldn't bear the idea. She had gone down to South
America – had obtained the money to finance the trip from an
executive of the corporation – a friend of her father's. She had
told him of her fears. During this time the marriage had been
annuled. Tim saw the lady just once more – a few days before
he entered the army. She seemed content, apparently she is still
traveling from one metropolis to another – running away from
her fears. Well, that's the story the way Tim told it to me.

Tonight, our cinema was "Tarzan's Revenge," but we enjoyed it as a comedy. I am in charge of quarters tonight. I had
a letter from Mary Louise today. She sent me a little clipping
about Martha Geibel's having a little boy. I am growing old.

Wood and Couch just got back from Soose with a story.
They left Soose for Enfidaville at about nine o'clock. At the outskirts of town they picked up a French sailor who was carrying two suitcases and said he was bound for Bizerte. They told
him to get in the back of the truck and set out again. In a little
while the Frenchman passed his bottle of wine up to Wood
and Couch through the window. They took a drink and passed
it back. When they arrived at Enfidaville they asked the sailor
where he wanted off. There was no answer. They looked back in
the truck and there were his two suitcases, but no sailor. Wood
and Couch were puzzled but decided to drive back over the
road toward Soose and see if he had jumped off or perhaps
fallen off. Couch spotted the sailor lying in the middle of the
road. They got out of the truck and walked over to him. They
thought he was dead – Wood shoved him with his foot – the
sailor moved and come to. They asked him again where he was
going and this time he said "Sfax". Wood and Couch gave him
his suitcases, moved him over to the side of the road and told
him that he should go in the other direction. He probably slept
by the side of the road in the cold. He had passed out while
riding in the back of the truck. It was just luck that another

car hadn't come over the road after Wood and Couch did. He must have been lying on the road for a half hour before they found him again. God certainly does protect the drunkards. The sailor may live to a ripe old age.

Saturday, November 13 – Today I had a long letter from Mother and Dad in which they enclosed two snapshots – also in the mail was a Christmas card from Gladys Scheer and one from Phyllis Flick – the best mail call I've had for a long time. Tonight the big excitement was that the boys from the Finance Office who were with us in Benghazi were in town. We were glad to see them all and celebrated a little with some wine. They are leaving again tomorrow. We heard the German propaganda broadcast tonight. There are two characters, Gladys and a man. Gladys always wants to tell the "truth about Frank Knox" and the man won't let her because "that would be getting personal". There is also a colored resume of the news and a lot of popular tunes. It is aimed at the American forces and calls itself "the voice of the A.E.F." Gladys is a pretty poor actress and reads her lines in a monotone – expressionless – so crude it was funny. Neither of the characters has much of an accent and when they sign off the man says "Good night and best of luck to you, you fighting yankees." We laugh loud and long when we hear this.

Sunday, November 14 – This morning we left early to go to a large salvage yard on the road to Tunis, about twenty miles from Enfidaville. It was cold riding in the jeep and I regretted not bringing my overcoat as Candy Johnson had done. He had a GI face towel around his neck, using it as an ascot. We arrived at the salvage dump, drove past the British red-capped MP and rode over the winding, bumpy dirt road up a hill past an Arab house with strings of red peppers hanging against the light-colored walls – drying in the sun. We came to that part of the yard where the generator, which we had come for, lay. It was a huge heavy thing, much too large to get into the weapons carrier and much too heavy for us to lift. We decided not to take it. As far as we could see were wrecks of trucks, automobiles, half-tracks, motor cycles, armored cars, tanks and mobile guns; these were of all kinds, German, English, Italian, French and American. We were careful not to pry too closely as there are usually mines and booby-traps around abandoned equipment. We went to another section of the area to get a windshield for the jeep (broken when it had turned over one rainy day while Lt. Jessup was returning from Soose – miraculous escape there, too). An armed French guard came running up and shouted, "Forbidden" – it was the only word of English he knew. In French, he told us that that this section was reserved for the French forces. We left for another section; here, I saw a German light tractor – the kind used for hauling field pieces – named "Hildegard" painted in German script. I wish I had had a camera as Mother would have appreciated seeing German equipment named after her. It's a strange custom of the English (copied, I think, by the Germans) to name their trucks, tanks, motor cycles and jeeps after their wives or sweethearts – the Americans have now begun to do the same. I read someplace (I think in Cecil Brown's "Suez to Singapore") that the British think of war as a game, the Germans are all "Jerry". Jerry is smart – appearing in unexpected places, therefore not underestimated. That's the reason I think the British will come through this war and return to England with as little trouble to their government as possible. The common English soldier wants to finish the war so that he can get back to his pub – it's a job to do and he trys to make it as pleasant as possible. This results in his accepting the army as a way of life; he doesn't keep wondering when the hell the thing's going to end, he does his work from day to day. It's his job. Americans, on the other hand, are the most serious of all the armies. The American soldier chaffs under regimentation. He listens to the news – the whole thing is a temporary set –up to him – he wants to get the thing over in a hell of a hurry and get back to civilization – everything is ersatz to him – he gets mad when things are at a stalemate.

We left the salvage depot at eleven o'clock, stopped to buy oranges from an Arab, had a flat tire, and got back to Enfifda-ville in time for the noon meal.

In the afternoon I took a shower – it was very cold – the wind was blowing and the water was like ice. I felt much cleaner afterwards. Went to bed to keep from getting a chill.

Monday, November 15 – This afternoon Tim Benitz, Lt. Jessup and I went to Zaghuan to another salvage dump. We got some glass. The idea is to make a window for our accounting room. Tonight we went to a show – saw Barbara Stanwyck in "Lady of Burlesque" which was based on Gypsy Rose Lee's story "The G-String Murders". It wasn't too bad.

Monday, November 22 – I'm writing this by candle-light tonight –sitting on Harry Willner's bed since he has a K-ration packing case which is just the right height for a table. We are all packed, ready to move again. Every time we move I think I'll never be able to get everything in my barracks bags, but I always seem to manage. The other boys have three and four bags each, having accumulated them through all of their "special deals". I didn't' know what a special deal was until I got in finance, but we have a radio, ping-pong table, jeep, weapons carrier and generator – all acquired through special deals. These deals are made between the boys of our outfit and the non-coms of other outfits. Our boys are careful to be on the good side of everybody who is anybody in the other outfits. Candy Johnson and Harry Willner just got us three day's issue of K-ration. This K-ration is made up of compact little packages, one for breakfast, one for dinner and one for supper.

Last night Tew, Dagwood and Slonim were gathered around the fire in their room talking when suddenly there was a report like a pistol shot – something flew out of the fire – they all ducked behind anything handy when there was another report. It seems somebody had put a couple of shells – English shells, the size of our 30 caliber rifle shells, into one of the waste baskets. They went off when the fire got hot enough. The shell casing was what flew out of the fire.

Our Arab boy, Fayed, has been hanging around for the last couple of days, even though he is finished working for us. He is seventeen. When he is eighteen next October he will be drafted into the French Army in Africa. He will be paid three and a half francs a day (seven cents in our money). He has a scar very close to his left eye from his temple to half-way down his cheek – from a bomb fragment. I think it was when the Americans were bombing this area. He has told us much about the Arab customs. An Arab marries when his father can buy him a wife for five thousand francs (a hundred dollars). The bride's father does not keep the money himself. He buys the bride anklets, bracelets, a necklace and a new dress. This is so that she will have something in her own name. The jewelry is quite expensive. The five thousand francs comes from what a father saves out of the money his boy gives him. An Arab's son is dutiful in handing over his earnings to his father. Fayed says the Germans eat black bread, that their food is very poor; that Italian food is good, French food is no good. When the Germans were here they printed money like newspapers and the price of a liter of wine was two hundred fifty francs. It is now twelve francs.

I'll always remember the almonds, dates, and red peppers that are so plentiful around Enfidaville. This is a quaint little town. I almost forgot the wine – it's not too good – I've had my share. Guess I'll go into the next room and eat. The boys are celebrating. We are guarding our trucks tonight as they are all loaded. My shift is from twelve to two o'clock.

November 23 – Last night I stayed up until ten o'clock since I intended to take Candy Johnson's ten-to-twelve shift, if he shouldn't get back from visiting his little French girl friend. As it turned out he did get back in time, but while I was waiting, talking to the two Italian prisoners who had come to bid Rick goodbye, I drank a cup of wine which Wood had given to me.

He had gotten it from the two negro boys who were driving our truck. The wine seemed to have a terrific kick and by the time I had finished the cup I felt high. I went to bed and slept like a log for two hours when Candy woke me up for my shift. This morning we found out that when the colored boys bought the wine, it was poured into a water can which had some gasoline in it – no wonder it had a kick.

We got an early start – packed like sardines in the truck. We used my quiz book to pass away the time – arrived in the rolling hills outside Bizerte. Nothing but mud and rain, cold and windy – we eat spam, cheese, peaches, coffee, bread and apple-butter – later more coffee. Three of us did make our beds on top of the boxes in the truck, the rest improvise shelters over their cots. We are certain that it will rain during the night. Mud clings to our shoes, feet feel like lead – the day is gray and cheerless – it is dark at six o'clock and we go to bed. I write cramped up at the end of the truck using my flashlight. All of us have colds. A letter from Mrs. K would help now.

Directions from Enfidaville

Riccardi and Klahn opposite the Hotel d,Envidaville

Finance Office, Weapons Carrier and Leo Zabowa at Enfidaville.

Duino, Zabowa, Wood, Lt. Jessup and Johnson
Our Tennis Court

ITALY

BIZERTE – We wait in the mud to board the LST

NAPLES – We disembark, move to a camp site have
a four hour visit to the city.

CAROSINO – Nov. 29 – Jan 17, 1944

November 24 – Last night was terrible for the boys who slept outside the truck. It rained off and on all night. We have a good breakfast of hot cakes, syrup and coffee and go back to our truck. The mud is worse. We borrow a tent from the QM boys and put it up. We're prepared for anything now. We hear that we won't be leaving the staging area for a week and we're glad because we'll have a good Thanksgiving dinner. The QM has turkeys, frozen vegetables and butter (fresh) for tomorrow. We talk and read by candle light. When almost everyone is asleep one of the boys comes in and says, "We go on board tomorrow at nine".

November 25 – Dreary day – packing everything in the trucks – tearing down the big tent – slogging through the mud – waiting and waiting. We finally leave our area and drive to another just up the hill from our former area. We wait for two hours – eat C-rations and oranges, finally leave for the docks – more waiting – we eat K-rations and read. Finally, we drive onto the LST barge, climb over trucks to find our bunks in the upper deck. We bring up our bed rolls and musette bags and then take our canteen cups and scurry out on the docks. The Red Cross is giving out hot chocolate and doughnuts. We stand in line in the rain. The doughnuts are very good. We go back to the ship and are detailed to help chain down the trucks. We eat – no Thanksgiving dinner this – we talk to the infantry casuals who are traveling with us. They have been up here once, wounded, and sent back to the hospital, are now recovered and ready to go back. I listen to them tell about what they've seen. One man is on an anti-tank gun, another on a heavy field artillery gun. We go to sleep early and rest well.

Friday, November 26 – This morning we had a breakfast of hot cakes and syrup (two hot cakes per man), but we had to wait in line for an hour. We are up on deck as we pull out of the harbor of Bizerte. It looks like a nice town, but those who have seen it say it is almost totally demolished. It was bombed unmercifully by our planes when the Germans occupied it. The streets look to be lined with palms and the buildings are white. On the west side of the harbor is a barren, yellow-brown mountain. We go below as the ship is rocking and rolling. It's going to be a tough, rough, voyage, we think. We are told that we're going to have abandon ship drill. Somebody says, "Where are we going to abandon the bastard at?" We are assigned to our life rafts and told to wear our mae-wests at all times.

Saturday, November 27 – The ship has begun to roll continually and many of the boys are sea-sick. It seems that we are headed for Naples. This morning we passed by the coast of Sicily and could see the rugged mountains. We had a light Thanksgiving Dinner – cold by the time I got to it. Most of the time is spent in our bunks – reading, talking and listening. We have a lot of infantry men and tank men with us – they have been wounded and are returning to the front. Tonight, we listened to them tell of their experiences. Hill 609 seems to have been a tough grind in the Tunisian campaign. One boy was carrying a heavy machine gun tripod across an open field when a shell exploded over his head – the force of the explosion lifted the tripod off his shoulders and picked him up and set him down twenty yards away. Another boy told about a deal that two GI's worked on the Arabs. One of the boys got some bars for his shoulders and collars and the other boy would sell an article of clothing to an Arab. As the Arab was walking away, the boy with the bars would step out from behind a bush and take the clothing away from the Arab. They made quite a bit of money. The Arabs will pay $10.00 for mattress covers ($20.00 when the GI's first arrived). We had a good time talking.

Sunday, November 28 – During the night the ship rolled something terrible. For a while I thought I was going to be sea-sick for the first time, but I finally went to sleep. We got up early, made our bed rolls and collected our equipment and stood in the mess line on the open deck waiting for breakfast. As the day was breaking we saw that we were coming into the harbor at Naples. On our left we could see the mountainous shore of the Isle of Capri; in the distance and slightly to our right we could see the smoke of Vesuvius pouring over the side of the mountain, and blown by the wind toward the city of Naples – looking like fog in the distance. We ate and crawled down into the hold with our bed rolls and equipment, climbing over the trucks and trailers to put everything in our truck. After we dock, there will be no delay in the unloading. When the trucks were loaded we unshakled them and then watched from the deck while we docked.

Our first impression of Italy was of the umbrella-like cyprus trees against the skyline on top of the range of mountains near the shore. After the boat was tied up we got into our trucks and rode off the boat and to an open field beside a wrecked factory – about five miles from the dock. People crowded around the trucks selling oranges, apples, peanuts, souvenirs, wine – asking for biscuits ("biskwee") and cigarettes. They seemed so hungry and the children looked at us with such pleading eyes that we gave them most of our lunch (which was only C-rations) and bought oranges, apples and cakes. We talked to a boy who had been in Italy for two months and he told us that the people had enough to eat, but there was no bread or meat, except fish; . Later, we drove on to a camp site and after we had set up our cots under the hickory trees we were told that we could go in to see Naples.

Three of us started at four o'clock. In five minutes we had thumbed a ride with a GI who told us what he knew of the town. It was nine miles form our camp site into the heart of the city. The buildings are beautiful and modern. We went through a tunnel about a mile long (through the heart of a mountain) where drivers must use their lights even at high noon – this was because the electrical wiring inside the tunnel has been damaged by the bombing—and came into the center of Naples. We passed University Square, the Grande Hotel, drove along the beautiful avenue that borders the harbor and overlooks the bay. To our left we saw a once-beautiful park occupied by

American troops and made ugly with barbed-wire entanglements and tents – to our right, the bay. Further on the road
turned to the left and into the city again. The driver of the
truck told us that the way to find a place to eat was to go up one
of the many little side streets and we would have no trouble.
We took his advice and had walked about ten steps when two
boys of about ten years ran to us and asked us if we wanted a
woman (they used an obscene, half-American, half-Italian expression). We told them that we wanted spaghetti and they said
"come". They led us deeper into the maze of little side streets –
walls unbroken except for the double-doors at intervals – and
stopped and knocked at one of the doors. They had a conversation in Italian with someone on the other side of the door and
finally the door was opened. We entered what was apparently
the dining room of an old Italian couple – they had been eating, but when we entered they cleared the table and when we
had agreed to take steak instead of spaghetti, indicated that we
were to sit down. The old woman cooked in a small kitchen that
opened off the dining room. We ordered a bottle of wine and
sipped it while the old woman cooked. All of our conversation
with the old couple was carried on through the two boys who
acted as our interpreters. Soon the old woman finished cooking and we ate steak and french-fries, white bread and wine.
The meal was delicious – we found out later that all food sold
in Naples is through the black market and this is the reason for
all of the intrigue and middlemen (or boys) involved. While we
ate we listened to music on the radio which was coming from
the American station in the city. An American soldier knocked
and was admitted – he wanted wine and was served. When we
had eaten, Candy and Tim wanted female (and probably male
in the case of Tim) companionship – and we agreed to meet in
the same house at six-thirty (it was now five). Tim went with a
third boy and I went with Candy and the other two. Outside,
it was completely dark and we followed the boys closely. After
being refused at two of the doors in the dark narrow streets we

were admitted at the third. It was a dingy room furnished with
broken-down chairs and stools – the muddy-yellow wall paper
was peeling off the wall and the plaster on the ceiling in one
corner had fallen down so that the lath boards hung like the
ribs of a skeleton threatening with their weight to pull down
the plaster still remaining on the ceiling. A bright unshaded
electric light hung down from the ceiling accentuating the ug-
liness of the room. To the left of the door that led into the bed
room , hung a large colored picture of the Madonna and Child.
Two madams and an old man seemed to be in charge – the
boys acted as pimps, though I suppose they didn't realize what
they were doing. There were about six soldiers waiting for either of the two girls who worked there. As I had come only to
accompany Candy and not to buy anything, I would have been
willing to wait as it was warm in the room; however, an argument developed between the madame and the two whores over
a five hundred lire shortage. The girls came out into the waiting
room and counted their money over and over again, and then a
loud argument in Italian developed. Candy grew impatient and
asked the boys to show him another place, so we left. The boys
led us into the streets again and ran around a corner and lost us
before we realized what had happened. We walked in the direction of the building (doorway, I should say) where we had eaten
and bumped into Solomon, the soldier who had come in while
we were eating. He took us back to the house and we went in
and order more wine. Candy asked a young Italian man about
women and he offered to take him to some. I agreed to wait
with Solomon in the house. Solomon and I drank and talked.
He was staying at the Replacement Depot – had been wounded
and hospitalized. His crew was up with the field artillery and
had been straffed regularly.

Suddenly, the young Italian ran in, breathless, and told us
in broken English that the MP's had caught Candy and kicked
him. I thought that he was lying – that he wanted us to leave the
house (it was out-of-bounds after six o'clock), but I decided to

wait until six-thirty until Tim showed up. Meantime, a couple of British tank men drifted in and talked of the battles they had been in – both had been with the 8th Army in the Libyan desert. They couldn't praise highly enough our American equipment, but didn't think much of the Yanks as fighters. Solomon didn't like this a bit and began to get hot. The British corporal soothed him a little by saying "You haven't fought enough – the only thing that makes a soldier is action". They are a cocky lot, these Tommies, but they have paid in blood and for my part, they have earned the right to be cocky.

Soon Tim returned at six-thirty and Candy came back with his story : As he and the young Italian man were entering a brothel an MP came upon them and kicked both in the rump. This made Candy mad and he clipped the MP on the jaw – the MP fell down and his flashlight clattered on the cobblestones. He was up and cursing in a few seconds, but Candy was running through the dark narrow streets. He turned a corner and someone caught his arm and pulled him through a doorway and into a room – closing the door. He saw that it was an old woman. She asked him "Police?" and he nodded. They listened as the MP walked by, paused, then kept on walking. The old woman poured him a glass of wine and asked, "You like woman?". Candy thought she meant herself and he said,

"You too old".

"No me, no me." said the woman, so Candy told the old woman to bring in a girl. She went out and was back in a few minutes with a lady of pleasure. Candy used her bedroom, paid and found his way back to our agreed meeting place. We all thought it remarkable that three of us could be come separated and meet again in such a hidden hole-in-the-wall place. We left the old couple after shaking hands with them. They like Americans better than the English. We literally felt our way through the crooked little side streets down to one of the main streets. We walked for a half-hour then thumbed a jeep. There were eight of us beside the driver on the car. We had one other ride and walked about a half mile to our camp area. As we crawled into our cots, it was eight o' clock. The four hours from four to eight were as full as any other four-hour period in my life. We decided that Naples was the most wide-open city we had ever been in and that this was because of its proximity to the front. War has certainly done things to the women of Naples. I suppose it's that they are hungry for nice clothes and food and maybe a little for the companship of men – their men have been in the army for eight years and that's a hell of a long time.

I thought about these things as I lay in my cot, looking up at the stars and the mountains and the bare limbs on the hickory nut trees.

Monday, November 29 – We got up early this morning, packed, breakfasted, and had roll call. Major Summers, who is in charge of our convoy, spoke: "First", he said, "I've been told that Jerry strafed a convoy just twenty miles north of Naples, so let's remember that it's a possibility and keep our helmets handy. If we're unlucky enough to get strafed, let's keep calm and pull off to the side of the road, as we've been taught. When we go through Naples this morning I don't want anybody sightseeing. We have enough to do without having to chase any stragglers. Now, our route will be through Salerno to Portenza – we'll stay overnight at Portenza, if we make it. The trucks with the Italian trailers will go first. Now, the roads are mountainous and the connections on these trailers aren't too good, so take it easy and let's see if we can't reach our destination without any casualties."

From our camp area we drove through the city to the petrol dump, near the docks. The city was beautiful in the morning sun. The traffic was heavy – army trucks, jeeps, civilian trucks, a few civilian automobiles, amphibious trucks, a few buses, and many, many two-wheeled horse carts plodding along. The docks and harbor area of Naples have been bombed terribly and at intervals, along the coast road we saw the green cans called "smudge pots" which are lit during an air raid. These smudge pots give off a thick, black smoke that is quickly dispersed providing a smoke screen over the city. Naples is in a singularly vulnerable position for bombing, since the old volcano on Vesuvious emits a red glow at night – lighting up the sky and providing Jerry (as it did the allies) with a landmark from which military objectives of the city can be plotted.

As we were waiting in a street along the waterfront after getting our petrol, we hear two explosions close by and a piece of gravel landed near out truck. We decided that it was time bombs in one of the wrecked buildings nearby. The civilians paid no attention to the explosions – it's an old story to them. Finally, our convoy got underway – we passed the Anjou Citadel, an old huge Roman castle near the bay (wish I could have gone through it), and came into the old residential area of the city where business had begun to encroach on the purely residential. This would be called the slums in an American city – the streets are paved with huge cobblestones and are very narrow. Vendors have set up stands where they sell oranges, apples, nuts and a few sundries. The buildings are old. Here and there are little wall shrines – niches about five feet above the street with colored holy pictures – even Muscolinni couldn't change that. We passed several beautiful churches and many public buildings bearing the year in both the A.D. date and the E.F. (Era Facisti) date. Along the street we noticed Franciscan Monks with the odd hair cuts, close-cropped in the center with a fringe of hair in a circle. Soon we came into the suburbs where the rich live – here, we saw beautiful modern homes with gardens of olive and orange trees. We came into the country which is very intensely cultivated. The crops are grapes, olives, oranges, apples and mangoes. It's the first time I can remember of having seen oranges on the trees. To our left we could see the mountains and at every stop the children came and begged for a biscuit, some meat, or a cigarette – all of the little boys seem to smoke.

213

About noon we came into Salerno – it's a town of large buildings, wide streets, on a height overlooking the sea. The rocky coastline has a rugged beauty. We ate here and talked to an Italian business man and his secretary – they seemed interested in everything about America and had relatives in New York. The girl was a typist and I told her that my sister was a typist in Washington. We gave them cigarettes and shared our spam sandwiches with them. From salerno the country became more mountainous and the turns were so abrupt that our trucks had trouble negotiating them. We came through a little town called Battepaglia which had been almost completely destroyed. As we were coming up a mountain, to our left at the edge of an olive grove a family watched us. The Italian mother, soft brown eyes, black hair parted in the middle and drawn severely back to the knot – watching with arms folded. I waved and she smiled and made the sign of the cross – blessing us, I suppose. As the afternoon wore on, we realized that we would not reach Potenza. The mountains were becoming higher and the villages were walled and built at the top of the peaks. We didn't pass through any of these, but they were old and dated from Roman times. Every time that we came to a town, the streets would be almost lined with the citizenry – the children waving, shouting and begging for caramels, biscuits and cigarettes. We bivouacked for the night in a broad valley between two mountain peaks. On the top of each mountain was a village and as darkness suddenly came, tiny pin-points of light appeared high up in the mountain villages. As we waited for the cooks to finish our evening meal in the darkness, with the mud clinging to our feet, we listened to a news commentator and later to music – coming from the radio in the signal truck. Here in central Italy the war seemed far away. As a few of us stood around the gasoline fire which the negro truck drivers were using to cook their evening meal, listening to their laughter and jokes and negro talk, one could almost forget the war – almost, but not quite.

Tuesday, November 30 – Today was long and tiresome – it rained off and on and the only scenery was mountains. The roads were very difficult for the trucks to take and we had to stop at several places while each truck with a trailer backed, and backed again to get around a curve. We passed many more of the mountain-top villages and, something that I haven't mentioned before, at every fifty miles (a guess) in the mountain roads we passed brick buildings painted red, all built in the same style. These were called S. S. Canton Carbonieri and I guess were Fascist-sponsored hotels for travelers. We stopped outside of Potenza and ate our noon meal – through more mountains. The steep slopes are all either cultivated or used for sheep grazing. We ride down ten sinuous curves over a gorge and up into the very high-walled city of Tolve – through narrow, cobble-stoned streets – people cheering and waving – trucks roaring swiftly by – the black asphalt roads are not as curving and the convoy moves faster – into Isernia, a pleasant village on a lower mountain – through Isernia – more people cheering – we camp at a farm outside of Isernia. We learn from Italians who talk to Ric that the land is share-cropped by the farmers in the area – the owner lives in a distant village.

Wednesday, December 1 -- Today the trip was interesting. This morning we came to Gravina – all about this area we could see Roman ruins of what appeared to be an aqueduct – the walls on either side of the road looked very old and some of the arches were Romanesque. Many of the buildings were ancient. The Appian Way ran through this area to Brindisi and after we came through Gravina we saw more ruins. I wish I could have seen the ruins of Pompeii while we were in Naples. We passed through Altamura, Toritto, Bitetto and Modugno, all small villages with narrow streets and then came to Bari, a large modern Adriatic seaport and resort town. There is a huge refinery here guarded by the green-uniformed Italian troops. There were many Italian soldiers and officers in this city. We stopped for petrol and bought little custard-filled pastries (five lire a piece) which were delicious.

Outside of Bari we head for Brindisi on a road which follows the shoreline. We passed many beautiful villas – all bearing names like Villa Marie, Villa Pina – further on we were held up because of an accident – one-way traffic. As we pass we see a little group of British soldiers around a young Italian girl who lies on the road, her leg is bent at a queer angle and blood flows from an ugly wound. One of the British soldiers strokes her hair – she was hit and knocked from her bicycle by the British truck – one of the civilian casualties of the war. They happen daily in Italy now where the struggling civilians try to continue living with convoys thundering up and down the Italian peninsula. We drive through a country of olive groves and vineyards where the fields are bordered by stone fences, grass growing in the earth-filled crevices of the fences. We pass through Torre A Mare, Mola, Monopoli, Fasano, Ostuni, Brindisi and bivouac outside of Mesagne. As we came into Mesagne, we waved to a family riding on one of the two-wheeled horse carts. One of the girls grins and boldly winks at us – we laugh.

After we had set up our bunks we walked into Mesagne. It is dark and the town is completely blacked out. We walk down and around the main square, then seeing a group of people in a building, we go in. It is an olive factory, a small one. There are several negro GI's and some Italians – watching the rolls and the presses operating. A charming young Italian girl who is with her father says "Hello". We ask her if she speaks English and she says, "A little. I have studied it in school in Naples". We talk for about ten minutes and the negro problem becomes embarassing. She asked who the negroes were and we told her that they were Americans. She could not understand it. "Why have you these , ah, black and you are so fine?" All we could say what that we had all races in America. She said, "I do not understand – they are like Africans."

216

The colored boys were within hearing distance and we changed the subject by asking her if she lived in Mesagne. She said, "No, I do not live (she said it with a long i), is it live or live?"

"Live", we said.

"I do not live here". She was curious to know where we were going and when we told her that we didn't know, she wanted to know if our officers knew. We told her "No" and left her a little confused. We came back to our camp area and had the evening chow, then went to bed. Tim and Candy came in later as they have been visiting an Italian family – a little Italian boy watched them while they were making up their cots – Candy asked him if he knew where they could buy eggs and he invited them to come to his house for eggs – they gave them wine and beer and hard-boiled the eggs for them – the family was well-to-do – the father a beer distiller – a little girl played an accordion and they had an enjoyable evening.

Thursday, December 2 – An early breakfast of hominy and coffee – the coffee was good. We rode for a couple of hours until we came to our temporary destination – an airfield between two towns. We are quartered in Italian barracks – our cots are quite crowded, but somebody has a portable radio and Wood sets up our generator, so we have lights. The latrines are odd – the lavatory is set flush (no pun intended) with the floor with two foot rests. Most of them don't work and the place is pretty messy. We spent the time playing casino after we have washed – the water is ice cold – a few of the men take sponge baths. I spend most of my time getting my diary up to date.

Friday, December 3 – Today we had mail call. I had one letter from Barbara which is better than any number of other letters. It was written November 11 so I'll have a lot of mail when it catches up to me. In the afternoon, we have a picture in our barracks (Grogan, the projecture man is in our barracks). The picture was good, "Meet John Doe". In the evening the MP's from a nearby town came in. It seems that one of the boys tried to punch a colonel when the colonel reprimanded him in town. The MP's never found the GI to arrest him. Lt. Seitzer came in this afternoon and told us that we would be moving tomorrow. When we get to our destination we will have our office in a school building and be quartered in other Italian barracks. We're glad to hear about the barracks as this will probably be our quarters for the winter.

Saturday, December 4 – After breakfast we pack and load our trucks – it's going to be a short run as it isn't far to our station. We learn about one of the other ship convoys from Africa – they were attacked by German dive bombers the night before last and suffered losses. Many of the boys from our group are in the hospital, but all are expected to live. We were lucky to have made the trip without mishap. We passed several small villages and many Roman ruins and finally came to the village where we were to be stationed. As we pulled into the town a German reconnaisance plane soared above us – it was very high up and made a stream of vapor. We unloaded our equipment and got set up in our barracks, then unloaded our office equipment. We can't set up the office until the Italian medical supplies are moved from the building.

Some of the boys went into the village today – it has a population of about thirty-five hundred. There are two movie theaters in the town. The chief industry seems to be wine-making. Some of the boys bought vermouth and champagne – both were excellent, at least they tasted good to me. The boys also bought oranges and figs stuffed with almonds. We play casino tonight. Guess I'll listen to the radio a while and then go to bed.

Sunday, December 5 – Today has been a pretty full day. This morning seven of us went in the jeep to Taranto which is about ten miles from Carosino, where we are stationed. We went in to take a hot shower; we hadn't had a bath in about two weeks and were sorely in need of one. Taranto, we found, was a beautiful city of about four hundred thousand people. The only stores which were open were the bakeries, confectionaries and sundries (souvenir) stores. Five of us went to an Italian bath unit (ten lire per person) and Slonim and Duino managed to find the free U.S. showers. While Slonim and Duino were having their shower, I drove the five of us around town. We bought little chocolate fig cookies at a bakery (the cashier tried to short-change me by fifty lire) and Tim Benitz bought a dictionary (Italian-English). While we were parked, two American boys from our merchant-marine came over and asked us if we knew where they could get American cigarettes. They had been in the convoy that had been bombed at Bari last Friday night when thirteen ships were sunk. We told them that some of our boys were on their boats and that if they would come out to Carosino we would fix them up with cigarettes. Incidentally, they said that seventy GI's had been killed outright and that several others were missing.

In the afternoon Duino, Dagwood and I walked downtown in Carosino to get some almond candy. We walked down one of the side streets and an Italian man came up to us and asked if we would like some vino – we hesitated, but decided to go with him. He and his friend brought us to a shop (he was a harness maker), spread a cloth on the table, brought out chairs, glasses and wine. They brought out figs and toasted almonds and we ate. I don't know how much wine we had, but we started with vermouth, then had some Fernet China (an herb-like drink tasting slightly of anise and creme-de-menthe) which was apparently tasteless until it is drunk. It makes one feel cold inside. After the eating was finished the leather-maker's bambinos came out – Estellina, eleven, Dora, six, and Carolina, a boy of three. They were all nice looking, quiet and liked chewing gum. The man's name was Vinci Donato and he had been discharged from the Italian army a month previous because he was thirty-eight. He had been a sergeant in the anti-aircraft – had been in Greece and in Taranto. In Taranto the Italians had six ack-ack batteries and the Allied bombers had just missed knocking them out. When we had finished Signor Donato accompanied us through the town – he seemed to think it a privilege to entertain American soldiers. As we walked through the town people who had relatives in America would ask him if we knew them – they would bring out photographs and letters. They are a warm, friendly people. We walked down one street and a woman came out of one of the houses with a picture of her son; he had been taken a prisoner at Tobruk and she hadn't had a letter in four months. She was crying a little and looked so sorrowful when she spoke of her son. We told her that prisoners had good food, good barracks and were looked after, but that the mail situation was bad – that her son was probably safe and well. She thanked us and insisted that we come in for some wine, which we did. While we were in her home her two younger daughters came in. They were pretty girls but when another woman went to introduce them to Dagwood and Duino (I had told Signor Donato that I was married), the mother said "No". Signor Donato had teased the woman by saying that Duino and Dagwood might marry the girls and take them to America. The woman said that there were enough people from Carosino in America and she didn't want to lose her family. Donato told us that the woman was afraid of the English, but that Americans were warm and good. We came home after promising to return to see Vinci Donato in the evening. We went back and talked and listened to the gramaphone and had more wine. I've got to go to bed as I'm on guard from twelve to three and I suspect that I'm feeling the wine – just a little.

Tuesday, December 7 – I've just come back from visiting an Italian family. At noon today Rick, Chum and I went to Vinci Donato, the leathermaker's and got our bracelets. We had to have some vino, of course. The bracelets are simple leather wrist bands with "Italia 1943" scratched on them. I am having V. Donato make a belt for my money belt with his name on it.

This evening Rick, Duino and I went to the piazza (public square) to buy some nuts. An Italian came up to us to ask if we would come to his home for vino – we did and had a good time. Two of the old Italians had been to the states thirty-six years ago and could remember a few words of English. They tried to show off for the other members of the family; we could understand them a little but Rick took care of most of the conversation in Italian. There was a young man, the son-in-law, who was a little fascistic – Duino and I thought so, at any rate, He was polite enough, but not as warm as the others. We had vino and talked for a couple of hours, then started up the dirty muddy streets back to the barracks. I've found out that Carosino is a wine town. Their wine is sold to the merchants in the large Italian cities and shipped all over the world. They take pride in good wine and have won prizes in expositions – what a haven for a group of soldiers!!!

Today I had two letters, one from Barbara and one from Don; also a birthday card with a two-dollar money order from Oster Manufacturing Co. I was pleasantly surprised to get it. Guess I'll get to bed as I'm sleepy. Wine does that, apparently. I've felt awfully lonesome lately, for Barbara. It may be seeing the Italian families that makes me long for home life. This day two years ago Barbara and I were spending a pleasant Sunday when the news of Pearl Harbor came through. We knew that it would mix things up for a lot of people then. It did.

Wednesday, December 8 – At noon Rick, Duino and I walked up to the piazza and down one of the streets to an Italian home to arrange for a macaroni dinner in the evening. Afterwards, we stopped in to see one of Rick's friends who gave us some white wine. It was sweet and smoothe – delicious. It was a festa day – the day of the Immaculate Conception, and vendors around the piazza were selling toasted almonds, almond candy and a celery-like plant called "fenoikie" or something like that. It tastes sweet and like anise. Italians eat it as we eat celery.

At six o'clock seven of us trooped down to the Italian's for macaroni, meat, walnuts, oranges and wine – lots of wine. We had a good time – eleven of us at a long table – the seven in our party, Zabowa, Tim and two boys from QM. There were two Italian soldiers there who told us that a German had cut Mussolini's throat and that Il Duce had been dead for three months. Later, we asked some of the civilians who had heard nothing about it. We didn't believe it. After the meal was finished we went to an Italian movie. The star of the show was an opera singer, a short plump little man with a wonderful tenor voice. The sound was good, the settings fair and the acting good. I had left the others after dinner as Vinci Donato had asked me to come to see him, but his house was closed when I got there. I guess he expected me earlier. I walked into the show alone and as I wore my blouse I think the usher mistook me for an officer. The little movie house was crowded and he carried a stool and placed it beside one of the row of seats – for me. A little boy who was standing near came over to me and said "Hello". He spoke a little English. I gave him a stick of chewing gum and he stuck by me for the rest of the show. Near the end of each reel a buzzer sounds and at the end of the reel, the lights go on and the people come in or leave. After the last show people gathered around us outside of the cinema and we talked for a half hour. They want the Americans to take over Italy, if they are not to be free. They say we are more like them and not as hard as the British. I don't know how they figure the British as being hard.

Friday, December 10 – Last night I went down to see Vince Donato – Dagwood went with me and we struggled for a couple of hours trying to make ourselves understood. I had a good time and came back in time to do guard duty from nine to twelve. While I was on guard four of the boys from the signal company in the next barracks got full of wine and took a portable record player down to the town piazza – with several extra bottles of wine. They sang at the top of their lungs while they played the song on the record player. I could hear them roaring out "I'll beee a round" and then "Ai Yai Yai Yai" without a record.

Today at noon Lt. Seitzer told me that I was to work in the accounting section. I hope I can do the work as it will be a break for me. It rained off and on today and the ground around our barracks is a slew of mud – slippery as grease on glass. A couple of the boys went to Taranto today. They had a good meal, shower and explored the old section of the city. I hope I can get in to buy a couple of cameos soon. The Italians are reputedly the true shell artists. Guess I'll go to bed as I'm charge of quarters tomorrow.

Monday, December 13 – This little town of Carosino is very conscious of its religious significance, which is another way of saying "of its past history". It is supposed to have been founded by a shepherd. This shepherd was deaf and dumb and he prayed to the Holy Virgin to restore his speech and hearing. One night while he was watching his flocks and praying, a vision of the Holy Virgin and Child appeared to him and he was able to speak and to hear. He built an alter on the spot and later a church was erected there. This happened a thousand years ago and parts of this first church have been made a part of the present church. The town of Carosino grew about the first church. It became and is to this day a place where deaf mutes come to pray for healing at the shrine of the Holy Virgin and Child.

At noon today Tim Benitz and I went into the church. Outside, it looks old and run down, but inside it is beautiful. There are two alters from an older church and these have many oil paintings – very old works of art and glass-encased statues. The fifteen mysteries are represented in fifteen small paintings. These surround the central statue of Jesus on the Cross in the center of one of these old alters. Of the two newer alters one is used by the Bishop when he visits Carosino and is enclosed with a gate of bars. The regular alter is a work of art with marble, marble statues (beautifully decorated, some clothed in silk) of angels and Madonna and Child. The outstanding shrine in the church is, of course that statue (life size) of the Holy Virgin and Child. This is reputed to be the vision seen by the shepherd. It is in the old part of the church and is set in a niche covered with glass. The Madonna and Child are dressed in real clothes (silk) and the Child wears a large crown (of gold, I suppose). There are flowers about these figures and in front of the shrine a flame burns always. The vision and the statues representing the vision are known far and wide as the Madonna of Carosino. The Roman Catholics, through the art in their churches certainly inspire in me a feeling closer to reverence than do the members of any other sect. It seems to me that they are trying desperately to impress upon people that these things all have meaning and that their prayers will be answered. Tim told me that he has shown his crucifix to a few people in Carosino and when they take it from him, they must kiss it before he puts it back in his pocket. In all of the homes about here one is conscious of how deeply these people feel their religion. Every room has several holy pictures in it – no matter how humble the dwelling. I have respect for faith and though I have a very different sort myself, I always stand in awe of their faith, because reason can't shake it. I may change when I grow older.

Thursday, December 23 – Life has almost settled down to a routine in this little town now. We have moved out of the wooden barracks behind the school into the upper floor of what is, I suppose, an Italian apartment house. The moving took place last Tuesday while I was in Taranto with Dagwood. We have three large rooms and a smaller room which served as a kitchen for the Italians who lived here; our boys use it to cook snacks. We have a balcony in the rear of the building and we wash here in the morning while the little Italian boys peak out from their back doors to say timidly "Buon giorno" (Good day or hello). Some of our boys, there are fifteen of us in the finance section of Headquarters Squadron, wash while they are in their winter underwear – enough to frighten an American, let alone an Italian. We have a "sort-of" outside toilet on the balcony – only good for urinating – if one feels that his bowels are about to move, he must hike through the town to the latrine across the street from the school.

The rooms in our apartment have dome-like ceilings, arch and pendentives style. The walls are of smooth stucco and have had many layers of whitewash. We have one running water tap and electricity, but no Italian bulbs, so our light comes from lanterns and candles. Most of our evenings are spent visiting an Italian family or seeing an Italian movie.

Last Tuesday we had spaghetti at the home of Anna, Rossita, Pepina, Leonardo and Flora. After the spaghetti they brought out spam, which we declined, then a salad of olive oil, vinegar, egg plant, green pepper and olives flavored with garlic. It was very strong and I could imagine how my breath must smell. We had oranges, almonds and figs for dessert – wine throughout the meal. When we had finished we sang. We were all feeling quite happy by then. The boy Pepina says that the Germans have almost the same clothes that we have, but that we are better fed. They think that the reason for America's greatness is that most of the people of America are Italians. We laugh because they won't believe what we tell them. They think that we had something to do with the bombing of the Italian towns.

The Italian movies are funny little affairs: the buzzer rings and the lights go on after every reel – people crowd to get in – the Italians haven't learned that the quickest way to get in a show is to stand in line and wait your turn – everyone wants to be first. The theme of their movies seems to be that a man has a child by a woman, learns about it, then marries her when the child is two or three. The picture ends happily with the papa singing and the baby bouncing on his knee; everybody goes home, satisfied that justice has been done.

I've had several letters recently and in one learned that Chuck Watson had died. I thought a lot of him and more than once, planned how I would entertain him with stories of World War II – just as he had amused me with his stories of the AEF in France in World War I. I wrote Mid and Charlan a letter of condolence.

William M. Kennedy

When Dagwood and I were in Taranto we went into a store to buy a note book. When I found what I wanted, I asked the girl how much. She said "fif uh tee lire" and I laughed as it was not worth fifty lire. She looked at me queerly and then said something to the owner who said, "Fif-teen lire" and I bought it. They aren't quite straight on their English yet. At another shop where I went to look at some paintings, they didn't seem interested in trading with Americans; as we walked out, the janitor swept the floor after us. There are many unfriendly elements still in Italy.

We ate in a restaurant – soup and white wine – we didn't like the fish and the spaghetti and meat balls was finished so we didn't have a main course. We took a shower, got a haircut and came home.

Funny things have happened in the short time that we have been in Carosino. A couple of over-zealous, over-wined GI's wondered into one Italian's house one night, crawled into a bed and fell asleep. The Italian was excited and came to the barracks. The Officer of the Day got a couple of boys and went to the Italian's house, routed out the sleeping soldiers and brought them home.

It seems to be always raining here. The mud is slippery and sticky. We can't keep our shoes clean and we're lucky if we can manage to keep our pants from becoming muddy. It is not exactly the season for Christmas. I hope we have a good dinner. Lieutenant Seitzer is now Captain Seitzer. He found out the day before yesterday and gave each of us a shot of Seagram's V.O. It went down smoothly and served as an appetizer. He had his ladder-rungs handy and wore them the same afternoon. We laughed about it, but we knew and he knew that he would be a captain when he took over our office. Rumors are flying thick and fast about moving again etc., etc. It won't be a long move this time, anyway. Guess I'll be moving along to our casa now as it is nine-thirty and I'm a little sleepy.

Friday, December 24 – This afternoon the Special Service boys down the hall from our office, put the loud speaker in the hall and played records all afternoon – to get us in the holiday spirit. Tonight we had a GI movie "This is the Army". It's the first color film that we've seen overseas and was very good. After the show Duino, Riccardi and I went to visit the Italian family. They wanted to know if we would come for dinner and we told them that we were to have a turkey dinner at the "Scuola". They seemed hurt and we decided to eat with them. We told them that we would pick up our dinner there and then come to eat with them. They offered to have their dinner whenever it was convenient for us, so we made it 2:30. They were in the Holiday Spirit and we ate fritters, very good but cold, and a sort of pie made with figs and almonds, and drank wine. We stayed until it was time for mass. I went to mass with Riccaardi, Duino and Antonio who is a cousin of the girls – he is about fifteen. There were quite a few civilians at mass which was given by the chaplain. We laughed about Chum passing out song books – he had quite a bit on his conscience and was preparing himself for confession. I enjoyed the services.

Saturday, December 25 – Christmas – This morning, even before we woke up the people who are our neighbors were knocking on the door – bringing us bottles of wine. We had four before ten o'clock. After breakfast, we came back to our apartment, washed and dressed in our best uniforms. I went down to Vinci Donato, the harness-maker who had come to the apartment asking for me while I was in the office. I got my money belt which he had repaired for me, putting on a new leather belt – strong as a harness. I gave him a carton of cigarettes for a Christmas present. He came with me to our apartment and stayed until it was time for us to go to the office to pick up our dinner. We told him that we would see him at four o'clock.

A few packages came in – I got my birthday package from Mother and Dad Flick – a tie and three Arrow handkerchiefs.

We went over to the pharmacist's and had a dinner of spaghetti, meat patties, olive-oil salad (made with green peppers, olives and egg plant), almond-brittle, wine cookies, tangerines and oranges. We had wine throughout the meal – strong wine. Before the meal, I forgot to mention, Papa had to read his Christmas Card from little Flora. She wrote that she knew the meal wouldn't be too good because of rationing and that she didn't want presents, but she hoped that peace would soon come to the world. We were full after the first course and bursting when we had finished. We had a demi-tasse served in Japanese china-ware – imported from the U.S.A. We left at five o'clock and came back to our casa.

We all decided to go to the harness-maker's and then back to visit our landlord on the first floor. He had asked us to come down at seven. He is a stately old gent with a mustache like Von Hindenburg's and dubbed "Handlebars" by Wood and Johnson. We went down to Vinci Donato's and visited with the family and drank much wine. At six-thirty we came back to Handlebar's and learned that he had planned a full meal for us. We ate meat balls and sauce, muscles with olive-oil paste (good), fenoichi (the celery that tastes like sweet licorice), tangerines, oranges, figs and cookies with fig-jam filling. The old man's son and a soldier-friend of his ate with us. The son had been in the army fighting the Germans in Italy. An American general had asked the Italian general if the men were all volunteers. The Eyetie general said "Yes", but when the American general asked the men, they said they weren't so the army was dissolved.

From this house we went to the home of some friends of Handlebar's. They led us into a back room. All of the rooms of the houses around here have a dome –arch and pendentives style. Handlebar's son played the mandolin and blew through a reed-humming device while another Italian played the accordian. There were two women who danced with Bull Klahn and Rick and the Italian corporal who was a good dancer. They gave us two shots of cherry brandy (good) and we were feeling high. I remember that I was singing too loud, thinking everything was funny and laughing at everything and having a hell of a good time in general.

We left that house and Handlebars took us to another nearby house where there were more people and more wine. I didn't dance but watched a little boy stretching out his chewing gum. I'd say "buono" and he would put it back in his mouth, chew it a while, then stretch it out again. Chum was having a wonderful time whirling the girls around, Handlebars was having a good time singing at the top of his lungs and I was helping him. Our boys began to cut in and the dances became tag dances. They played Italian songs and finally, after much wine had been consumed, it was ten o' clock and we decided that it was time to go. We shook hands with everybody and wished them all "Buona note" and "Buon Natale", sang "Oh Marie" and "The Woodpecker Song" and left.

We walked through the dark, muddy streets, splashing in the mud puddles, singing loudly and feeling happy – with Handlebars quietly leading us. We came to our casa and thanked him and wished him goodnight. He told Rick that he wanted us to be his friends, that Americans are good – "Nothing matters in the world but friendship – Americans and Italians should be friends forever". We piled into bed, thinking that old Handlebars was a prince and that we had had a wonderful Christmas. Sunday, December 26 – We woke up late this morning and felt a little the worse for wine – it was raining and we were glad that it was Sunday which meant that we worked only a half-day. In the afternoon I wrote a letter and Vinci Donato met me while I was on my way back to our casa – he wanted Rick and me to come down to see him. At four o'clock Rick came back and we went down to Donato's shop. He was at the piazza, so we walked up there. A lawyer was giving a speech and the piazza was full of umbrellas – rain falling silently. The speaker was the Mayor of Taranto; he spoke for the Four Freedoms and at the end of his speech said, "Vive Inglise" (cheers), "Vive Americane" (roaring cheers), and "Vive Italia" (loudest cheers).

After supper Rick and I went down to visit V. Donato – we had wine, figs, and almonds and talked long. Donato says my Italian is coming along better and gave me a novel to read. Came back to the casa and wrote this. Time to go to bed.

1944

January 1, 1944 – This evening the seventeen of us from Finance had arranged a dinner to be held at Handlebar's house. Fifteen enlisted men from the detachment were present along with Captain Seitzer and Lt. Reynolds (Commanding Officer of Headquarters Squadron) who took Lt. Jessup's place. Lt. Jessup was away. We had spaghetti mixed with raviola that was delicious. It had been made with white flour which we supplied. Course followed course for a period of three hours. The last course was cake, cakes rather, as there were five of them. They were yellow cakes with a cream filling and chocolate icing with "Happy New Year" written on them in green icing. We drank a lot of wine and toasted everybody. Harry Willner's toast to Dagwood Palmer: "Here's to Dagwood, that Finance Dapper, Sentinel of the 323re crapper". Everyone was in a jovial mood. Captain Seitzer thanked us for our work and said that he wouldn't be wearing Captain's bars if it weren't for us, etc. etc. .. Went to bed and slept soundly.

January 2 – Tonight, Riccardi and I went down to the harness maker's and had rabbit. It was delicious and didn't have the wild taste that our American rabbits do. It is considered a delicacy as is the cream cheese which came next. Finally, finoichi and tangerines and a demi-tasse of hot chocolate. We enjoyed the meal.

January 5 -- Tonight Rick, Duino, Chum and I were invited to dine with Signore Tanese and family. The occasion was the eve before Befana, the day when all Italian children receive their gifts. They don't give presents at Christmas as we do. January 6, Befana, is the date when the three wise men, the Magi, are reputed to have arrived at Bethlehem bringing gifts to the Christ Child. The Italians thus follow history more closely in this tradition than we do. The bambini of Italy think that at midnight on January 5 an old woman with a funny hat and old worn shoes comes into their homes and fills the stockings of good children with gifts, and those of the bad ones with charcoal. There's an old, old rhyme that even the tiniest child knows:

> La Befana vien di note,
>   Con la scarpa touti rote
> Col capella a la Romana
>   Vive! Vive! La Befana.

Here's the translation:

> The Befana comes in the night
>   With the shoes very tattered
> With a hat like a Roman
>   Hurrah! Hurrah! for the Befana.

We had a good dinner of cauliflour (traditional main course on Befana eve), muscles, olives, fritters, sweetmeats, wine, demi-tasse of coffee – danced until midnight with the three girls. They are learning to dance a la American, but prefer their own music. A young friend of the girls, Antonio owns the record player.

At twelve o'clock we sat down at the table again and were served a kind of pie made with apples, figs, and nuts. First, we drank some anisette, since it was an occasion, and after we had eaten, had coffee flavored with anisette. This was very good. The girls brought out the present for little Flora, who had long since been put to bed. It was a doll in a cradle filled with candies. Most of the candy was what we had brought at various times. The cradle was put under Flora's bed and we left for home. We told them that it was the best Befana that we had ever celebrated.

Sunday, January 9 – This morning we worked in the office until dinner time. This afternoon Ric, Candy and I took some lumber to the carpenter who has his shop near Donato's. We are having foot lockers made. We walked next door to Donato's and visited for a while. We came back in time for chow – ice cream for dessert. After chow I went home and shaved, then went to Tanese's where Riccardi, Chum and Duino joined me. We sang, drank a little wine and talked – most of the time we listened while Riccardi talks. At ten o'clock we came back to our billet and crawled into bed.

Wednesday, January 12 – Two things happened today: First, we had an inspection of our rifles by the Group Ordnance Officer – it was a very different thing from the inspections I stood at the MP company when we had to be in uniform, shaved, neat hair-cut, and presenting spotless rifles. We brought our rifles or pistols or machine-guns into the main office and Sergeant Outlaw (First Sergeant of Headquarters Squadron) and the Ordnance Officer casually examined the various arms. I passed. The second thing that happened was the return of Dagwood from the hospital. His stomach had been out of order and he was worried about appendicitis, but it was something that he had eaten and he is in good health and spirits again. Received a letter from Jean and Al – they know that I am in Italy. Al has been classified 2-B until March 19 again. I'm glad to learn that he won't be called for a while. He is working hard on his machinist job and is an auxiliary fireman. Wrote Es and Sam, Jean and Al and Barbara tonight. Last night I finished Nora Waln's story "The House of Exile". It is an arresting true account of her life in China, first as a member of a very old family-household in North China and later as the wife of a British official stationed in China. It covers the time from 1922 to 1931 during the years when the Chinese Nationalists came into power. She writes without prejudice and I like her style. She went to Germany with her husband in 1934 and wrote a book, "Reaching for the Stars" based on her experience there. I want to read that book.

At eight-thirty last night Tew and I left the office, stopped at a little fruit store on the piazza to buy tangerines, olives, and eggs. Eggs are twenty cents a piece. We came home and fried ourselves a couple of eggs with an onion for flavoring and had egg sandwiches. The frying was done in olive oil which I can truthfully say is as good as butter for frying. It's been a long time since we have had fresh eggs. Guess I'll listen to the news and go to bed. Captain Seitzer told us that some of the boys in Area Command Headquarters are saying in rhyme:

Singapore in forty-four
Golden gate in forty-eight
Bread line in forty-nine.
The future doesn't look too rosey, as far as a short war is concerned. Ho Hum.

Friday, January 14 – Yesterday Johnson and I went down to the carpenters and waited until our foot-lockers were finished. We had taken wood for the lockers to him last Sunday. When I went down to see about the lockers yesterday at noon, the little shop looked like an assembly plant with seven or eight men working busily at various jobs. The carpenter is busier than he has been in ages. We paid $2.50 a piece for our lockers and they are worth all of the price. As a rough estimate I would guess that he has made lockers for about 250 soldiers.

Today, at noon we went down to paint the lockers (olive-drab). When we got to our house we found that no one had the key. We worked for about a half-hour trying to figure out a way to get in. We knew the simplest way was to unscrew the hasp on the front door but didn't want to do that as many of the little kids hanging around would see and get ideas; finally, we had to do it and about fifteen minutes after we were in, Slonim came back bringing the key – it seems that Tew had it in his pocket.

This morning Tew, Zabowa had Dagwood were told that they are going to Manduria to work on D.S. (detached service) with the finance office there. It is only a temporary set up; they'll leave tomorrow.

This afternoon I went into Taranto and had a shower. The government showers were crowded with British troops so we went to the Italian showers – "bagni", we call them. It used to cost ten lire, but the price has gone up to fifteen lire. Had a wonderful shower. The truck driver who took us in is one of the new boys to join the group. He is a good driver, but takes too many chances. The road from St. George to Taranto is as straight as a die but narrow, with slow-moving wagons, and bicycle traffic on either side of the road – with an occasional Fiat or motorcycle to make things interesting. The driver missed all of the bicycle traffic by at least a foot and coming back to St. George from Taranto, he had to put on the brakes and skid to avoid hitting an Italian soldier on a bicycle. The Eyetie looked up and waved at us as we moved past him. Some of these people will be hit sometime unless there is some provision made to clear the highway. Tonight, at the theater in the Carosino piazza we saw a GI movie, "Palm Beach Story" with Claudette Colbert and Joel McCrea – it was funny. After the show I came over to the office and wrote Barbara, enclosing the poem about Italy. Rick had received it from a friend and Chum had cut a stencil and run off several hundred mimeographed sheets.

Went back to the apartment and found that Tew had had a foot locker made, painted and with a lock. He had gone down to the carpenter at five o'clock and worked a fast deal. Everyone who is having a locker made waits from three to five days for it, but listen to what the wiley Tew did, when he knew that he was leaving on DS in the morning: with the help of Riccardi as interpreter he told the carpenter that he was leaving in the morning to distribute cigarettes (American) to the Italian troops fighting at the front. Tears came into the little carpenter's eyes – he finished the locker in a few hours and wanted to give it to Tew. Big-hearted Tew insisted on paying for the locker and gave the carpenter some extra packs of cigarettes. American ingenuity. Tew is from Chicago, but he operates like a New Yorker.

Saturday, January 15 – Dagwood, Zabowa and Tew left for Manduria this morning. We expect to see them in a couple of weeks, but this DS business is uncertain. The Chaplain came into our office (the accounting office) this morning, looked at our Esquire pin-ups very long and said, "Why don't you take these things down, they aren't even funny". We laughed at him. Once before he rebuked Duino for having a picture of Betty Grable in a bathing suit under the glass-top of his desk. Duino just laughed, but the boys got an idea: Wood had a little snapshot of a native girl in the nude – he had bought it at some dive in Cairo. They put this picture under the glass-top on Duino's desk and hope that Duino doesn't notice it until they call the Chaplain's attention to it. The Chaplain leads a hard life. From what I've seen of Army chaplains they aren't very intelligent, but they are good enough.

At noon I put handles and a hasp on my foot locker and put my clothes in it. I think I'll still need two barracks bags after the Christmas rush.

In the evening I went with Duino and Couch to the Tanese family. They welcomed me like a prodigal son and made me feel at home. I hadn't been there for three or four nights. We played dominoes, ate a kind of pudding and drank wine. Went home feeling a little high. Slept soundly.

Sunday, January 16 – This morning Wood, Klahn and Johnson felt pretty bad – they all had hangovers. Klahn and Wood drank in the apartment last night until ten o'clock when Johnson returned from visiting; then all three of them drank. They were hungry so they decided to fry some eggs over the gasoline in our kitchen stove. When it was Candy Johnson's turn to fry his eggs, he had difficulty breaking one of them. Finally, he banged it down on the floor and he swears there was a chicken in it with feathers on it. It was dead of course – he dumped it in the garbage and went on cooking. You can't always be sure that you are getting fresh eggs here in Italy, even at twenty lire (20 cents) a piece; however, that's cheap for chicken.

Today we worked all day packing machines and equipment, getting ready to move. In the evening we went to the Tanese family's and danced, ate and drank wine. They have been very nice to us and it will be just like leaving home. They hate to see us leave too. They say that we are the first soldiers to be admitted to their home and they won't ever forget us. The mother cried, the girls looked sad and all invited us to come back to visit them. Anna Tanese was almost in love with Couch when we left. She was kind to me – gave me three Quaderno books to use for my diary. She is studying Pharmacy, thinks American girls are quite loose and American men are funny, but attractive. Little Rosita gave Hank Duino a lock of her hair in a blue bow. He hated to leave her – she is a charming little miss.

Monday, January 17 -- This morning we got up at six o'clock and hurriedly packed our barracks bags and foot lockers in the trailers of our two trucks. I picked up my laundry at Handlebars, which wasn't quite dry, and we went over to chow. There are to be just ten enlisted men from finance and nine others from Headquarters Squadron in our convoy of twelve trucks. After breakfast we climbed into our trucks – Duino and I were in the back of the fullest truck. Just before we pulled out, Vinci Donato, the harness maker, came up to us, shook hands with me and kissed me on both cheeks. I like him and his family. Pepini Tanese and Leonardo shook hands and waved and as we passed through the streets of Carosino (perhaps for the last time) we stood on the tailgate of our truck and waved at the Tanese's who were on their front steps.

We passed through Taranto across the bridge that spans the channel into the inner harbor, and into the old city. The streets are narrow and paved with huge cobble-stones. Near the docks several of the buildings have been destroyed by bombs. We passed through the old city and then began to ascend the mountains. We passed through several small towns – some we by-passed (these were the towns on the tops of mountains). We arrived at our destination, Spinazzola, at about one o'clock – rode down to a building where a group quartermaster company was set up and ate. It was a very good meal.

Slonim and Vesey by our Christmas Tree, Carosino, Italy 1943

Town Hall, Carosino, Italy 1943

SPINAZZOLA

January 17, 1944

To

May 16, 1945

We came back and unloaded our trucks. We are going to be in a huge school building which was built in 1936 and was previously used by the Italian and British armies. It was cold in the city when we arrived and as we are high in the Apennines, we don't expect to be any warmer until Spring comes. We set up our cots in a room on the first floor.

In the evening four of us walked down through the town – our building is in almost the exact center of town. We went into a large modern Italian barber shop and had a shampoo, washed our faces – I had brilliantine put on my hair. We were covered with white, fine dirt from the truck ride and felt much better after washing. The barbers and their little-boy helpers were anxious to please and seemed happy to serve us. We have heard that the people here are not friendly as they have had bitter experiences at the hands of the Germans (here for three months) and the English who were here until a short time before we arrived.

After having our hair washed we walked down the Corso Umberti, the main street, to a cinema where American movies with Italian sub-titles are shown three nights a week. We saw "Across the Pacific" for the third time and walked up to the school where we are quartered. I found that I was on guard from four to seven in the morning. It was only nine o'clock so I thought that I would get plenty of sleep. I climbed into bed and fell asleep, but not for long.

Tuesday, January 18 – Woke up at 2:30 this morning as I could tell by the ringing of the big town clock across the street from the school. I couldn't get to sleep from then on, and at four o'clock the guard on duty, Conrad of the medics, came up and woke me, or rather reminded me that it was my turn. I climbed out of my bed in the bitter cold, and walked down through the long corridors and out the door. The main entrance is actually at the right side of the building as one faces the front of the building, and is on a side street. The side street curves outward from the entrance to the building and is narrow and cobbled. From time to time I could hear the clatter and echo of a person walking up or down the street, or down on the Corso Umberti. A tiny pin-point of light shone through the shutters of a first-floor window in the house across the street from the school. I could hear the murmer of voices; at four-thirty the light went out. I heard the footsteps of Italian black-caped men who walked out through the front entrance of the building onto the Corso Umberti. This was probably a meeting of the Fascists, still powerful in Italy in some sections. In this town there is also a Communist Party – one is reminded of this by the hammer and sickle insignia painted on the facade of many buildings (crudely drawn and daubed on with red paint). Other reminders are the paper symbols glued on the windows of several shops, and finally by the Communist Headquarters across from the cinema. It looks as if there will be a bloody time in Italy when the war is over, unless she is occupied by a strong military force.

At five-thirty a town crier walked through the streets shouting something which I couldn't understand. He did this again at six o 'clock and by this time it was light enough for him to see me: "Buon Guirno" he called.

"Buon Guirno", I answered him.

People began to walk the streets, going about their morning tasks, carts rattled over the cobblestones, and a boy walked by the school on the Corso Umberti singing an air from some opera in a very good voice. At seven o'clock my relief came out. I was glad as I was very cold.

After breakfast several of us walked down through the town – we went into a little shop and bought post cards, visited a carpenter shop where the men were glad to see us, then a jewelry store where we bought chains for the keys to our foot lockers and where a couple of the boys had their watches fixed. We went to the Municipia to the post office. A couple Italian soldiers were on guard here and when we turned away because the little office was crowded with civilians, they wanted to take us in ahead of the civilians. We had a hard time telling him that we did not want him to take us in ahead of them as we could come in any day for stamps. After the noon meal I helped a little in the kitchen which was set up temporarily in the room next to the one in which we had the boxes of our equipment. Some of the officers got some Italian soldiers to clean up the building – they are doing this for their meals. They are rather self-effacing and take orders from any of us – we like them. In the afternoon we set up our stove and had a big gasoline fire blazing when suddenly the elbow of the pipe fell down – it had been soldered – and the black smoke came out of the short stack into our room. We couldn't bend the pipe out the window, so somebody put the can with the burning gasoline on the window ledge. The captain smothered the fire with an empty mail sack but not before the room was filled with thick, black smoke. In the evening we read by candle light in front of the stove. Went to bed at nine-thirty, listening to Chum talk about his visit to an Italian family with Rick and the little Italian sailor who works for the cooks. He came up with them from Carosino. Chum said, "It's the language that does it, that's what it is, it's the language." He was talking about the mis-understanding and the reason for the Italian's dislike of armies. Rick said that the Eyetie had gone with them dressed in British battle-dress which the cooks had given him. The papa of the family that they were visiting kept saying "He speaks good Italian", and Rick kept explaining that the little Italian was Italian – papa kept saying "He speaks very good Italian". I suppose he still thinks that the little boy in British battle-dress was an American who spoke very good Italian.

Wood changed the subject by explaining to us the sex life of porcupines; it seems the female hangs upside down from a limb of a tree and the male approaches from above. We derived one important conclusion: the female porcupine cannot be raped. "It's the god-damned language that does it", I heard Chum say as I fell asleep.

Wednesday, January 19 – Relieved Berglund at seven this morning – was relieved by Klahn and went to breakfast. The Italian soldiers are going to do all of the daytime guarding – they will eat here and be allowed to buy our cigarettes. We moved all of our personal goods down to one of the basement rooms – it doesn't look very promising. In the afternoon we moved all of our equipment into the two rooms which are to be our office. The rest of Headquarters Squadron came in at three-thirty. In the evening we found to our surprise that the electricity was on in our "dormatory" – there are twenty-two of us in the one room. We of Finance are with the provisional QM. A couple of the boys put in a stove and Chum got our radio working. The stove is beside my cot and the radio is on the other side of the room from my cot – it's just like home, almost. A wood fire, electricity and a radio. The surprise that I had today was getting my G.I. glasses. They seem to be all right. I'm certainly glad to get them. The English boys who were here before had written on the walls of one of the rooms, "Sicily, Rome, Berlin, Home!!" Guess I'll get to bed.

Sunday, January 23 – We've spent the past few days getting settled – a business which involves uncrating typewriters, adding machines, tables, cabinets, files and wiring for electricity, then arranging everything in the space available for an office. We have a stove set up in our office and another in our room in the basement and we keep warm enough – except when we eat in the large room which was built for a gymnasium; we don't linger there after we have eaten.

A couple of afternoon's ago, before we were unpacked, we were sitting around the stove when our Medical Officer, Major Grogan came in. Couch began to talk to him about some articles on medical research which he (Couch) had read in Collier's, Readers' Digest, etc. The Major listened politely as Couch went on to tell about the 48 hour cure for syphilis. "There's an article in the December Readers' Digest on it, "said Couch, "Here, let's see it, Klahn."

"What's that," said Klahn, looking at the table of contents, "Out of Bed – Into Action?"

We had a good laugh about it – the article Couch was referring to was entitled "Stamping Out Syphilis with the One-Day Treatment" by Paul de Kruif. It probably wouldn't have seemed funny out of the army. I have finished "The Way of All Flesh". Enjoyed it. I suppose my next one will be a detective story.

Riccardi talked to an old shop-keeper in the town who told him about a German soldier who used to come to visit him. The German told the Italian that he was tired of the war and didn't want to fight the Americans – wished it would end soon. The old Italian told Riccardi that he thought there were good and bad in every army.

Duino looked up a family whose name had been given to him by Rosita and Anna Tanese back in Carosino. He said they seemed to be quite rich and ardent non-Fascists. There are supposed to be three political parties in Spinazzola, equally powerful – Fascists, Communists and Liberals. I must write to Barbara soon.

After the noon meal Johnson, Duino and I had planned to go to Vinosa, a town about twenty miles from here where Hank Duino's parents lived before they came to America. It turned out that a couple of majors had asked to borrow the weapons carrier to move from one house to another. We offered to help them move so that we could get the truck sooner, but the job turned out to be pretty tough. The major had more personal equipment than our whole finance detachment. The building that they left was an apartment building and we thought it was nice until we saw the rooms they moved to. It was a mansion. The house was built flush with the narrow street – you enter through heavy steel double-doors (large enough for an automobile to enter) into a paved court; looking straight up you see the sky; further down you see a second-story balcony – like the mezzanine in a department store. On either side of the mezzanine on the ground floor, stairways ascended to that part of the house where the family lived. I saw only four of the rooms. They were large, beautifully furnished (period furniture) with crystal chandeliers, paintings and etchings. The marble floors were waxed. This was some contrast to the ordinary houses in which we had visited and it made me homesick.

We left at about two o'clock for Vinosa. We thought we had enough gas as it was only a matter of twenty miles. About three miles outside of Spinazzola we asked an Italian on a bicycle if we were on the right road. He said "Si" and we asked him if he wanted a lift; "Si" again, so we hauled his bicycle into the back and we were off. The country was beautiful, the grass green, and we passed several two-wheeled wagons and a couple of herds of sheep which were driven to the side of the road as we approached. We came to Palazzo, a town about the size of Spinazzola, and crept slowly through the narrow cobbled streets in the car as the streets were filled with people. They seemed friendly. Outside of Palazzo the country became mountainous and as our gas became lower we almost decided to turn back. The Italian in the back of the car said that his home was in Palazzo but he would accompany us to Vinosa if we were coming back the same evening – we said we were. When we arrived in Vinosa our gas tank was just about empty. We stopped in the piazza, cobblestoned – to our right was a huge castle, quite well preserved with crenelated walls, two huge towers and a moat, very deep in which there was no longer any water. Our Italian hitch-hiker had told us that he knew a family of the same name as Hank's mother and as we got out of the car he went over to an old man and said something to him. Soon, several men had gathered around and before we knew it the entire piazza was crowded with men and boys shouting and crowding to see the Italian who had come back to his parents' birthplace. One of the men was a fourth cousin whose name was the same as Hank's – Duino. He took us to some other cousins. Johnson decided to go with our hitch-hiker and another Italian to get some petrol. The fourth cousin took Hank and me in town with, I should say, fifty boys hanging on to us and a crowd following through a maze of winding narrow streets to the home of Duino's second cousin. We sat down and there must have been a hundred people in the small room, counting the bambini. We drank wine and ate nuts and people dragged out photographs. One old lady who was a first cousin on his mother's side brought a picture of his mother. Hank showed them the picture he had and everyone crowded around to see it. Finally, we left and went to anothe house – more cousins. We visited four places. At one, an old woman dug deep into her bureau drawer for eggs We refused as we knew they were at a premium here. We had to take a bottle of wine and some dried figs – arranged in a slab. They were held in place by a sort of fork-like affair – except that the tines were straight. At the last house we had vino bianca, white wine which was very good and tasted almost like champagne. We were feeling pretty good by this time, especially me as I never refuse wine. We promised to come back at the first opportunity. Got into the truck and drove through the town with kids shouting on all sides of us and hanging on the truck. We began to sing and Hank kissed the last of his relatives as we stopped at the edge of town. They insisted on seeing us as far as the edge of town. It was a pretty glorious homecoming for Hank and we enjoyed it too. Johnson had a tank-full of gasoline and we felt happy. We sang all the way home. It was very cold and dark when we got to Palazzo where we bid our hitch-hiker goodbye. He told us that he had a good time. We got home (i.e. to Spinazzola) at six o'clock and had pineapple, bread and tomato juice for supper – missed a chicken dinner, but I think it was worth it. Got to bed by nine o 'clock and slept soundly.

Friday, January 28 – Today and tonight Spinazzola is off-limits for American soldiers. The reason for the order: "a demonstration by a minority party of the town against the party in power in Italy". It seems that on the occasion of a similar demonstration in a near-by town a British soldier was killed, so our officers are being careful. I imagine the minority party referred to is the Communist – although it may be the Fascist. In Spinazzola the Fascists, Communists and Liberals are all equally powerful.

Tonight we saw "Jane Eyre" with Orson Wells and Joan Fontaine – it was a wonderful picture – almost as good as the book.

Saturday, January 29 – Well, nothing happened in the demonstration; in fact, it was so quiet that we don't know if there was a demonstration. Today we received a lot of our back mail. I must have received fifteen letters. It made us all feel pretty good. Duino, Johnson and Matis took the day off to visit Vinosa and had a wonderful time. They want to go back again on Monday as there is a wedding and that means a big celebration.

Monday, January 31 – After work today Duino, Wood, Johnson, Bice and I left for Vinosa. Bice is from Provisional QM and, since he is in charge of transportation and we had to have transportation, we took him along. We rode in an open jeep. It was cold but we were comfortable in our overcoats. The country was beautiful in the twilight, mountains in the distance, rolling farmland on either side of the narrow half-paved road. At intervals we slow down to pass a farmer riding high on the stack of wood piled in his little two-wheeled cart drawn by his horse. Both the farmer and horse look tired as they plod on to the village for the evening meal of probably black bread and beans for one and straw for the other. From Palazzo to Vinosa we traveled the narrow dirt road on the edge of the mountain in darkness.

We arrived at six o'clock and met one of Duino's cousins who guided us to the first house we were to visit. We went in and had several glasses of wine, then to another place where we ate a wonderful meal. We had a salad of greens (I think they were dandelion greens), spaghetti and sauce, huge portions of rabbit, chicken, french-fried potatoes, and almonds, apples and oranges for dessert – wine throughout the meal. Much wine was spilt on the white table cloth and much was drunk – plenty of wine but not enough glasses – one glass for every three persons – kind of like common-cup communion. After the meal the table was pulled to one side next to the bed – these people live in one room which serves as kitchen, dining room and bed room – and we danced to an accordian. Later, we went to another house which was larger and danced to a larger orchestra. The people were all friendly but not quite as genteel as the people of Carosino. Candy Johnson and I danced most with the little girl who is twelve, pretty, and a good dancer. She is young enough not to be sure of herself and is therefore not as noisy as the others. We drank a little more wine and left at eleven o'clock. Candy Johnson told us that one of the girls asked him to be her "fidanzata" (fiance) until her husband got back from being a prisoner in Germany. I don't know how she managed to ask him a personal question like that with the many chaperones all around. She certainly is practical. We were cold riding back. We got in at mid-night and the warm bed felt wonderful, even if it was only a cot. I don't know if I enjoyed the trip or not – something happened and we didn't get to go to the wedding celebration, but we saw how these people eat (sometimes) and it was another experience.

Friday, February 4 – Today Riccardi, Couch and Karmilawicz left for Bari where they will work on detached service for a while. They were pretty happy about the deal as there are several WAC's in Bari and we haven't seen a WAC yet. Couch won't lose any time there – he never does. I worked all day today. Felt pretty low this evening. There was a show but I couldn't go as I'm Charge of Quarters. Last night and the night before we had "Italian Unit No. 1", a stage troup made up of Italian performers, ten girls and twenty-two men. We all enjoyed it – some of the acts were strictly burlesque, but the show as a whole was very good. Received one letter from Barbara today, a V-mail of January 10, the latest that I've had, also a post card from John

Caputo who is in a tank-destroyer battalion in Oklahoma – said he is married to Thelma, his old flame and is expecting to go overseas soon. I don't envy him. I hope he doesn't have to leave the states. For the past few days we've been receiving replacements, corporals and sergeants who had been in Italy two days and less than a month out of the U.S. They look at us when we tell them how long we've been overseas.

Just finished reading "Toward a Durable Society" by Robert M. Hutchins. It was in the June '43 issue of Fortune which I found lying on the Captain's desk. It is well-written, represents a whale of a lot of pellucid thinking and is exactly what I've been searching for all these months that I've been reading every panacea for post-war dream worlds that come into print. Hutchins is realistic, philosophical and yet not pessimistic. Who am I to criticize what he writes? One advantage in writing a diary. I like his thinking and when I read his article I knew that I was reading what he believes and always has believed and not some trumped-up rationalization written to sell during wartime.

Wednesday, February 18 – Today Candy Johnson and I moved our accounting section into the next room after connecting our stove and starting a fire. We needed the fire as the weather has been very cold and we have had snow for the last two weeks. It hasn't covered the ground, just floats down and melts. The puddles are frozen in the morning. We have had just enough work to spend the time in our office, but the bomb groups are beginning to come in and we'll soon have plenty of work. The four boys who were in Manduria on D.S. have returned – Dagwood, Zabowa, Willner and Tew. We were glad to see them. Chum, Riccardi and Couch are still in Bari, so we are not yet up to strength. We have had a couple of good mail calls and I'm still behind in answering my mail. We have the radio in our accounting office now – it's almost like home.

Last night Berglund and I went to the cinema in town to see "Tails of Manhattan" – it was a good picture with an ingenious plot. In the evening we went into the theater in our building and saw "Powers Girl" – it wasn't too good. The boys from Manduria told us about their detached service life: They lived in a private home because the building in which the other men lived was crowded. They ate their evening meal at their home; every evening the landlady would have a vat of hot water for them to wash and there was always a jug full of wine on their table. A young girl who lived in the house, a distant cousin of the landlady, was very friendly to the boys and they had everything they wanted. They kept the young lady in cigarettes. All-in-all, they said, they were sorry to leave Manduria.

After the show I went down to our living quarters and listened to Fox, who is in charge of Officers Mess, talk about everything – from the menu, to his experiences with his Italian waiters. One day, coming out of the building that houses the officers mess, Fox saw a woman with a baby, both crying loudly, the baby was burned terribly about the face and eyes. The woman begged him to do something, so Fox took them in the jeep to the building where the medics were. The woman told Fox that the baby had fallen into a charcoal brazier when she left the room for a few minutes. The baby's eyes were burned and Fox thought it was dying when he first saw it. Later, Major Grogan (the doctor) said he expected it to die in three days. The mother had been to Italian doctors and to the Italian civilian hospital and they had sent her away. However, miracles do happen, the baby is recovering.

Jaegli, Master sergeant of Provisional QM contributed this story about the Italians: Two Italians came to see him about a dead horse. It seems that the horse had fallen dead out near one of the airfields. The owner of the horse agreed to sell it to another Italian (whom I'll call Joe for convenience) for three thousand lire. Joe wanted the horse meat. Meantime, the commander of the field ordered a GI to haul the carcass away as it was interfering with progress and, as he knew nothing of the value of the dead horse as meat, he thought he was doing Italy a favor in removing it. The GI tied a chain around the horse and onto his truck and began to drag it down the road. Our Italian friend, Joe, on his way to pay three thousand lire for the horse, meets the GI on the road and asks him if he can have the horse. "Hell, yeah", said the GI, glad to get out of a job and he leaves the horse with Joe and returns to the airfield. Meantime, the owner of the horse hears that Joe has his dead horse and goes to Joe and demands his three thousand lire. Joe says "No", that an American soldier gave him the horse. They both come up to see the executive officer in our building to try to get it settled. Joe says he won't pay because the American soldier gave him the horse and ""Anyway", he said, "when the soldier dragged the horse down the road some of the meat scraped off and it got all dirty – it isn't worth three thousand lire". Nobody knows what the final settlement was, but there will be plenty of meat around Spinazzola for the next week.

Saturday, February 18 – Today we had rain and the motor pool that we walk through on the way to the mess hall was a slew of mud. It was cold too. One letter in the mail, from Rev. Mac. He tried to write an interesting letter. Captain Seitzer bought a new pipe for me at the Officers' PX – for forty-eight cents. I certainly needed one.

Wednesday, February 23 – I've just come back from seeing Humphry Bogart in "Sahara". It was a good picture and we enjoyed it much more since we have been around Tobruk where the action in the picture took place. It took us back and reminded us of the dust storms and life-less desert strewn with the wrecked engines of war.

This afternoon Harry Willner and I went down town to one of the local barber shops to get haircuts and shampoos. It's an ordeal to get a haircut with the ubiquitous little apprentices trying to help, let alone a shampoo. For the shampooing a machine (actually a portable wash stand which can be raised or lowered) is wheeled in back of the barber chair. The water is heated on a small portable electric heating element. There isn't much water used in the operation. After the barber has finished the rinsing he soaks up the excess water, combs the hair, puts on a pink hairnet and wheels out the dryer which is complete with a hood and hot air dryer. It's a funny looking sight to see a soldier sitting in the chair, trying not to look self-conscious, while the hood is on his head. It is reminiscent of feminine beauty parlors back home. While we were waiting our turn one of the boys was having his hair dried. The hood was over his ears and it seems that the air was too hot to stand. "Hey, Tony", he said, "this god-damn thing's burning my ears off. Get the god-damn thing off my ears", and so Tony hurried up and pulled his ears out of the hood and folded them along the outer side of the hood.

Thursday, February 24 – Today Irv Slonim received orders to return to the states. They have been pending for a long time, ever since he first heard that his father had a heart attack and we were glad that they had been approved. He will leave tomorrow by plane for Algiers and Casablanca. Tonight we had a celebration, beer and peanuts. Italian beer, but still beer, the first in five months. Dagwood, who was transferred out of finance into Special Service, joined the party. Dagwood was not able to do the work in finance and he felt badly about leaving, but he did get a nice break. He helps Grogan Adamson run the motion picture projector and takes care of the Special Service lounge. Slonim promised to write to all of our families and tell them that we are fine. It would be a happier occasion for him if he weren't going home to a dying father. We felt pretty good on the one quart of beer alloted to us and then played a little small-stake poker at which I dropped a dollar.

Friday, February 24 – Irv told us all goodbye and left this morning. He is the second from our outfit to leave; Major Olson was the first back in Benghazi. The question now becomes: Who will get the Tech Sergeant rating. It will be either Chicken Zabowa or Tim Benitz. Either is a good man and it won't much matter which one gets it. There will be a new Staff Sergeant too, but no new sergeants or corporals. This is because headquarters is over-rated due to a colonel's blunder back in Cairo. This has cost Duino and me our corporal's rating for six months. I still like finance.

This afternoon Wood and I walked through the town and up to the civilian hospital at the edge of town. The 323rd has taken over the bath unit, consisting of three bath tubs. We couldn't take a bath however as the electricity had been shut off, which meant that the pressure had been shut off. It began to rain as we left the school to go up to the hospital. When we got to the hospital which was on higher ground, we could look across the valley to the mountain range – the view was beautiful, the same on either side since Spinazzola is built on a hill. We went up to the hospital door and when we found it locked, asked some Italian soldiers where the American bath was. One of them came with us. He knocked on the door of the hospital – a sister came to the door and unlocked it. The soldier asked her a question, addressing her as "Sorella". She replied and then motioned for us to follow her. It seems that the baths are in a separate building behind the hospital and the rear entrance is used. Anyway, we didn't get a bath.

As a surprise, I won the extra quart of beer in the lottery today – drank it tonight.

Saturday, February 25 – Today has been an easy day. This morning Wood, Duino and I went up to the hospital and had our baths. It is the first bath in a bathtub that I've had in five months and I felt wonderfully clean.

In the afternoon Wood, Duino, Johnson and Tew left in a jeep to go to Vinosa where they planned to spend the night. After an hour they came walking into the office. They had turned over the jeep and were all bruised and scratched. It happened while they were passing a big Italian truck. The Italians swerved just as the jeep was alongside it and they went into the ditch. The jeep turned over as they were coming out of the ditch onto the road which was slippery. The steel braces in the top kept them from being crushed, but the jeep was smashed so badly that they were barely able to drive it back into town. In three hours they had another jeep and were on their way again. Such is the resiliency of youth. Slept upstairs tonight as I am taking Duino's place as C.Q.

Another thing, we have just received two new replacements – for Dagwood and Slonim. They are PFC's fresh from the states – one from Virginia and one from Syracuse, New York. They seem to be nice chaps and are impressed with our office, radio, library, etc. I remember how impressed I was when I first came into the office.

Sunday, February 26 – The tattered little kids who stand outside the barbed wire fence which encloses the area used for our motor pool at the front of our building, have a little rhyme that they chant now. They all carry cans which they hope we will fill with coffee that we don't drink. We almost had a riot when we first came – there were too many kids and they don't know how to share anything, so we empty our mess-kits inside now. The rhyme goes thus:

Cigarette per papa,
Saponete per mama,
Ciocolotte per signorini,
Caramelli per bambini.
Translation:
Cigarettes for papa,
Soap for mama,
Chocolate for the girls,
Candy for the babies.

There have been a lot of funerals lately. I've heard rumors about it being the flu. They are dreary processions led by professional mourners in their Ku Klux Klan uniforms, followed by the ugly-looking glass-enclosed wagon hearse, drawn by two black horses dressed in black blankets with white edging. The heads of the horses are swathed in masks. The priests follow the professional mourners and the true mourners straggle behind the carriage. It certainly makes for a gloomy exit from this world.

Monday, February 28 – Tonight I went with Duino and Johnson to visit some friends whom Duino had met through Rosita Tanese. When we left Carosino she had given him the name of a girl whom Anna knew in college in Naples. Hank Duino looked up the family and called on them. They are one of the wealthiest families in Spinazzola. There is an uncle who has money (a landowner), a mother and three grown children, a boy, twenty-three is studying medicine, a girl, twenty-one has two more years to study for her Ph.D. in languages, and a young boy of sixteen. We enjoyed talking to them. Their house was beautiful with much silverware, crystalware and marble in evidence. They had to show us the family jewels, huge diamond rings, pearls and broaches. We admired them as they seemed to be trying to impress us. They had a large cabinet radio-phonograph and played records on it. They tried to make us understand that they were not ordinary Italian people – reminded us of the nouveau riche in America. We had cookies and creme-de-menthe then went in to see their Louis XIV room. It was done in blue and gold. The furniture, rug, drapes and tapestry wall paper were in a matching blue pattern. There were many mirrors, the furniture was done in gold gilt; there was a cupboard of china and crystalware, a huge chandelier of crystal and a marble-topped table. It was a beautiful room. We danced with the girl whose name was Rosa Marie and who was quite plain. She didn't seem to be able to follow us and decided that Americans weren't such good dancers. We ate some cookies and left for home.

Tuesday, February 29 – Tonight we saw a movie called "Street of Chance" with Burgess Meredith and Claire Trevor. Enjoyed it a lot. There were many poker games and much money won and lost. I didn't play. Harry Willner won $100 and Wood lost over a hundred.

Talked to some British boys who have been overseas three years – ack-ack men who have really seen action. Their latest was up at the Volturno, but they've been around Tobruk and Benghazi. They said they had heard rumors about their going home, but didn't put much stock in them.

Wednesday, March 1 – Busy all day today getting out reports. In the evening we had a little snack. Chicken Zabowa went down to the mess hall and stole a loaf of bread. We heated boned chicken on the stove in our accounting room and had chicken sandwiches. Went to bed and couldn't sleep. I'm getting a stye in my left eye and it bothered me. Guess I'm reading too much.

Sunday, March 5 – This afternoon the Red Cross Club opened in Spinazzola. It is the best club that any of us have seen outside of the large cities. They have a music room with a phonograph. I saw an album of Scherzade in there and intend to go down and play it some afternoon. They served cake and coffee (free, this time); the coffee was the best we've had in Italy.

In the evening we went to the local cinema where Sun Valley Serenade was showing. I think I've seen it three times now. Afterwards, we came back and played small-stake poker; I lost three dollars, but had a small straight flush one time and four jacks another. I was ahead but played unwisely.

Monday, March 6 – The sun is shining brightly and it begins to look like a beautiful day – time will tell. It did and it rained. The lights were off tonight and as we sat around in the candle light feeling blue and homesick, we groused about the war and made ourselves feel worse.

Wednesday, March 8 – Today a British hospital unit came to Spinazzola and took a pint of blood from all type-O volunteer donors. Johnson, Klahn, Lt. Jessup and I gave a pint. We were given a pint of ale (Canadian) after the ordeal and will receive $10.00. We felt a little weak afterwards and I could sympathize with Barbara for giving two pints – she's a little trooper. Tonight we saw a U.S.O. show – one girl and three men. It was the first time we have seen an American girl since last October in Enfidaville when we saw the girls at the Red Cross. She looked whiter than the Italian girls around here.

Friday, March 10 – This is a song that was written by a German and sung by the Africa Corps in Libya and Tunisia. When we were in Enfidaville someone found a record with the music to Lili Marlen, but not the words. We used to hear this record played over the PA system while we were waiting for the show to begin. It has become popular in Italy now and some Italian translated the song into English. I think it will become popular in the states. Here are the words:

> Outside the barracks, by the corner light,
> I'll always stand and wait for you at night,
> We will create a world for two,
> I'd wait for you, the whole night through,
> For you, Lili Marlen, for you, Lili Marlen
>
> Bugler, tonight don't play the call to arms,
> I want another evening with her charms,
> Then we must say goodbye and part,
> I'll always keep you in my heart,
> With me, Lili Marlen, with me Lili Marlen.
>
> Give me a rose to show how much you care,
> Tie to the stem a lock of golden hair,
> Surely tomorrow you'll feel blue,
> But then will come a love that's new,
> For you, Lili Marlen, for you, Lili Marlen.
>
> When we are marching in the mud and cold,
> And when my pack seems more than I can hold,
> My love for you renews my might,
> I'm warm again, my pack is light.
> It's you, Lili Marlen, it's you, Lili Marlen.

Sunday, March 12 – Today was a dreary cold day. Worked a little in the afternoon. Read a little.

Monday, March 13 – This afternoon Candy and I sneaked off to the Red Cross Club for a cup of coffee and a game of billiards with Harry Willner and Milton Jaegli of Provisional QM. They beat us 21 to 3 in the hole. Guess billiards is not my game. In the evening we saw "Claudia". It was an excellent picture.

Thursday, March 16 – Candy and Wood came back at noon and I left at one o'clock to go to Bari. Wood and Candy had been at Gravina since yesterday afternoon. They hired an orchestra and had a party for their Italian friends – took turns directing the orchestra, drank much wine and both passed out at different stages of the evening. They said they had a good time. I thought I wasn't going to be able to go to Bari, but Candy got back in time to take over the accounting department.

We left Spinazzola at two o'clock and got to Bari at four fifteen. In Spinazzola we had a lot of snow; in Bari it was warm and dusty. It was nice to see the city again. We went to the Red Cross, a huge building, and listened to a string quartet playing "Music, Maestro, Please" with the vocal by an Italian girl. We envied the boys in Headquarters who don't even know that there's a war on. Guess we can't really complain, though. We ate at the Red Cross snack bar – two sandwiches and hot chocolate for five lire, then went to the opera.

We saw some WACs, the first I have ever seen. They were dressed nicely, but weren't so nice looking. We were in the theater at five-thirty when the doors opened and got good seats. The opera began at six-thirty. I don't know how good that performance of Rigoletto was as grand opera goes, but to me it was wonderful. I would like to see all of the operas, but it is hard for us to get away. The opera was sponsored by Special Service of U.S.A. and was put on by the members of the San Carlo and La Scala opera companies. The prima donna was young and good (I thought) as Gilda and Rigoletto was excellent as was the orchestra. All in all, it was worth the cold ride to Bari and the cold ride back. We got to Spinazzola at midnight – didn't have any trouble falling asleep.

Sunday, March 19 – This afternoon Johnson, Duino, Wood and I went to Vinoso. I didn't intend to go, but was feeling low and thought a little wine might help. We went in a command car and, according to the latest directive from Headquarters, had a chauffeur, Walters. He drove pretty fast and Duino and Johnson were nervous (having had one previous wreck and another close call) so that finally they asked Walters to take it easy. He cheerfully complied. When we got to Vinoso Wood and I went to a little shop to drink wine and Johnson and Duino went to the home of Duino's relatives. Wood, Walters and I had two bottles of wine. Walters was drunk on the first glass of the white wine and then confessed to us that he had had quite a bit of wine earlier in the day. We drank the wine and ate almonds and talked to Tony, the proprietor. After we had finished the wine we went out and walked in the sun. It was a beautiful day and everyone seemed to be "passaging" as the Italians say. We met Duino and Johnson walking with some Italian friends, drove the car back to the home of Duino's relatives and walked some more. It was a festa day and on every street corner, whether near the piazza or in the maze of narrow streets extending off the piazza, a huge bonfire of pine wood was burning in honor of St. Giussepe. Around each fire were gangs of children of all ages. We stopped in two bars and had some rum. I felt pretty wonderful. Then we walked down the main street again. The huge smooth worn cobblestones shone gold from the rays of the setting sun. The old castle across the deep wide moat was golden – like something from a fairy tale. I thought how wonderful life was and how much more of it there was to live.

Wood kept saying, "Look at them legs, Kennedy. Look at them legs", referring to the legs of the Italian girls who were walking up and down the street. I would say to Wood,

"It's a beautiful day", the while, inhaling deeply. We went back to Duino's relatives and danced. We danced the tarantella and one of the men called the directions for a sort of group dance. I danced mostly with the little girl who is a distant cousin of Duino's. She is twelve years old, but a good little dancer. She seemed to want to learn the American style of dancing, but it is hard to dance our steps to Italian music. We danced until about eleven o'clock and then when all of the neighbors had left, ate a sour olive-oil salad and meat balls, and had more wine. We left for home at eleven-thirty. The ride back was cold, but when we got to bed at one o'clock we slept soundly.

STILL IN SPINAZZOLA

I make corporal April 12, 1944

Life in the office

Candy's friend's story about

his escape after 15 months

as a prisoner of war

Monday, March 20 – Didn't feel so good physically today, but felt wonderful mentally. I seem to have shaken off my lethargy for a while. There are rumors of our T.O. (Table of Organization) being straightened out. When it is, Duino and I have a good chance of becoming corporals. Dagwood has been transferred out of Finance into Special Service where he helps Grogan Adamson to run the movie projector, delivers Stars and Stripes and helps at the Red Cross Club. He seems to like the work. We have two other boys, Gary and Griswold, transferred in; they replace Slonim and Dagwood. They have been out of the states about a month and a half. Gary is twenty-five and married. Griswold is twenty-one which makes him the baby of the outfit. I don't think I've mentioned that since we have been in Spinazzola we in Headquarters Squadron have formation in the open court in the center of the building. When we are dismissed from the formation there is a mad pushing, shoving rush to get down to the mess hall and into the chow line. One morning Bull Klahn fell on the gravel at the foot of the front steps and cut his knees and hands. He had his hands all bandaged for a while. I threatened to beat him up while he was incapacitated. He never runs to chow now. The one morning that we don't have formation is Sunday and we sleep in until 7:30.

Friday, March 31 – Today, with our ration we drew our first bottle of coca-cola – the first we have seen in our army life overseas – except for the one that Captain Seitzer keeps in the safe to remind him of what it looks like. Eight of us put in fifty cents to buy a quart of rum. In the evening after the show (cowboy picture) I had my canteen cup filled with rum and coke. Drank it in two hours and felt very good. Went to bed and slept soundly. I fear I am becoming a bit of a toper. It must look bad in my letters home. Barbara is afraid that the wine will make me fat. I told her that I didn't drink as much as it would appear from my letters. I do drink comparatively little, but actually there is more drinking in the army than out of it.

Saturday, April 1 – A busy day today getting our monthly reports in. I intended to take a bath this morning, but was too busy. This afternoon I had three V-mail letters from Barbara, written on March 18th. Made me feel good to hear from her. She said that Mr. Mac, the preacher, quoted one of my letters in a sermon without mentioning my name. Barbara thinks that I should examine my personal philosophy – that the cause of my personal dissatisfaction (the lost and looking for something feeling) lies in my failure to discover what other people are like. I think if I were living with her and doing something to earn a living that I wouldn't have that feeling. Time will tell. The news sounds pretty good – the Russians are pushing steadily forward and it is possible that the war with Germany will end sometime this year. Certainly hope so.

Wednesday, April 12 – Today has been a red letter day in my army career – just made corporal. Duino, Couch and I have been made corporals and Berglund got his sergeant's stripes. It has been a long wait for us and I hope the next stripe doesn't take as long. Monday, I got my good conduct ribbon. It came through on a separate order. Last July when I came into the 323rd, a mimeographed list of all of the members in Headquarters Squadron was sent in. As I had just come into the outfit my name was not included in the list. Since then, Woodie has put in three different letters trying to get it for me; however, we have a new Group Commander and he maintained that the ribbon should be awarded to only a certain percentage of the Group. Captain Seitzer knew that I wanted it, even if it didn't mean anything, so he fixed it up with Major Carey, Group Adjutant. The Captain wanted to give it to me at the same time he showed me the order making me a corporal. Wood happened to be in the orderly room and heard that it had been approved – then told me. The Captain was a little provoked, but when I thanked him profusely, he changed and said that he hoped to have me made a corporal.

After the show tonight we went to a hole-in-the-wall sort of place and had wine (bad, tasted like vinegar) and eggs. There was a fat old Italian hag whose English vocabulary was limited to the most obscene words used in the army. Had a letter from Barbara today, a good one. She talked of a lot of little things that we used to do and of what we would do after the thing is over. I wrote an answer before we left for the eggs and wine. It has been a pretty good day.

Sunday, April 30 – Last night while we were sitting around the office, Group Ordnance called up and told us we were invited down to their office for a send-off party, the occasion being Wally Basse's departure for the states. "Bring your own cup", they said. We went down and congrutaed Wally Bass and had a drink that Vesy called a Louisiana something or other. He took liquor out of six different bottles and then added a tablespoon of lemon juice. It was good, but powerful. One of them made us feel high and the boys who had two were singing and higher than a kite. The ones who had three were weaving on their feet. Wally Bass is leaving by plane today. He is going home to join a B-29 outfit, but he'll have a short furlough first. Then, it's overseas again.

The picture tonight was called "No Time for Love", a light comedy which we enjoyed. I finished reading A Tree Grows in Brooklyn, a wonderful book. I wonder if Betty Smith's next book will be as good. I also read an anthology, "The Jewish Caravan" by Leo W. Schwarz. From Hayyim Nahman Bialik's story "The Legend of Three and of Four", this poem is attributed to Agur, son of Yakeh:

There are three too wonderful for me,
Four and I know them not.
The way of an eagle in the heavens,
The way of a serpent along the rock,
The way of a ship in the heart of the sea,
And the way of a man with a maid.

Another story that I liked was one from the Apocrypha, Susanna and the Elders. It is said to be the first detective story. There is a cross-examination in it that proves Susanna's innocence. It is an old, old story, written about 90 B.C. and hasn't been widely distributed because of the suggestion of immorality among the upper classes. Another story tenderly written (almost) is "Bontche Shiveig" by Isaac Leob Perez. It's about what happened when a timid little begger went to heaven. Ludwig Lewisohn's "The Romantic" is very well done. Many of these stories were published in this book for the first time in English. It's a wonderful book.

Our assistant finance officer, Lt. Jessup is leaving us this Tuesday to go to Naples where he will be on the Chief Finance Officer's staff. He is being replaced by Lt. O'Brien, an Irishman from Georgia. He is quite old, in his 40's I'd guess – a second lieutenant. Tomorrow night we are having a going-away party for Lt. Jessup. Wood and Johnson went to Vinoso last night and brought back a hundred quarts of wine. It should be a good party.

Monday, May 1 – Today was May Day and also marked the end of my first eighteen months overseas. We had a hard day in the office since we've disbursed more the past month than at any time since last October. After work we had a dinner at the Spinazzola Albergo (hotel) where Wood and Johnson have a room. Before we ate we stood out on the roof-porch overlooking the piazza and watched the people standing, moving and walking. We had plenty of wine since Wood had bought a hundred quarts from an Italian in Vinoso. At seven we went into the dining room and ate. The occasion was Lt. Jessup's leaving for Naples. Besides Lt. Jessup, Capt. Seitzer and Lt. O'Brien, we had Lt. Reynolds, Lt. Alexander of the Post Office, and Capt. Bentley of Chemical Warfare. We had macaroni and sauce, egg omlets and wine. We toasted everyone and everything and felt pretty good. Lt. Jessup had been drinking all day and he was feeling good – even before dinner. In order to get our bread

Wood had invited Trapper Arnweine, the Mess Sergeant, and Gordon Johnson, the cook. It seems that they had a good time. I left at nine o'clock with Hank Duino to go to the second show. When I got back I heard about the rest of the party. A crap game was started and a few of the boys cleaned up – Wood, $300, Griswold, $50. The officers did most of the donating. Lt. Reynolds lost $150, the Captain lost only $10. Even so, everyone had a good time.

Friday, May 5, 1944 – Last night I finished "The Robe", a good book. I am reading a translation of The Koran now, according to Muhammad who wrote the Koran. It is supposed to have been given to him by the Angel Gabriel at various times after Muhammed's 40th year, on Mount Hira near Mecca. His description of Heaven is inviting:

"These are they who shall be brought nigh to God. In gardens of delight . . . . . On inwrought couches, Reclining on them face to face, Aye-blooming youths go round about to them, With goblets and ewers and a cup of flowing wine; Their brows ache not from it, nor fails the senses: And with such fruits as shall please them best, and with flesh of such birds, as they shall long for: And theirs shall be the Houris, with large dark eyes, like pearls hidden in their shells. In recompense of their labours past . . . . And on lofty couches, of a rare creation have we created the Houris, And we have made them ever virgins, Dear to their spouses, of equal age with them (Like them grow not old)." Sounds much more inviting than the Christian Heaven.

Interesting Little Story: The Sidrah tree marks the boundry beyond which neither men nor angels can pass. It is the loftiest spot in Paradise, in the seventh heaven, on the right hand of the throne of God. Its leaves are fabled to be as numerous as the members of the whole human family, and each leaf to bear the name of an individual. This tree is shaken on the night of the 15th of Ramadan every year, a little after sunset, when the leaves on which are inscribed the names of those who are to die in the ensuing year fall – either wholly withered, or with more or less green remaining, according to the months or weeks the person has yet to live. The Sidrah is a prickly plumb which is called Ber in India. A decoction of the leaves is used in India to wash the dead, on account of the sacredness of the tree.

Sidelight: The Arabians worship Sirius, the Dog-star. Quote:

"Which then of the bounties of your Lord will ye twain deny? He created man of clay like that of the potter; and He created the djinn (angels) of pure fire".

Something I just read in Readers' Digest, along the same line as the Korans' Paradise:

Letter to Saint Peter

by Elma Dean

Let them in, Peter, they are very tired;
Give them the couches where the angels sleep.
Let them wake whole again to new dreams fired
With sun, not war. And may their peace be deep.
Remember where the broken bodies lie. . .
And give them things they like. Let them make noise.
God knows how young they were to die!
Give swing bands, not gold harps, to these our boys.
Let them love, Peter – they have had no time –
Girls sweet as meadow wind, with flowering hair . . .
They should have trees and bird song, hills to climb –
The taste of summer in a ripened pear.
Tell them how they are missed. Say not to fear;
It's going to be all right with us down here.

The past few days have been beautiful – warm and sun-shiney. The little Italian children are comfortable now in their thin clothes and their bare legs are no longer blue with cold – although they are probably dirtier than in winter.

Saturday, May 6 -- Today was beautiful. After the evening meal four of us went for a walk in the country. Duino, Klahn, Johnson and I walked through Spinazzola and down one of the narrow little side streets until it became an unpaved lane extending along a ridge between two valleys. On either side of the road were high grassy meadows. About a half mile from Spinazzola the lane divided forming a Y and at this point was a ruined stone Roman arch. We took the road to the right which led down into the valley, then we left the road and followed a path that hung on the edge of a hill. Duino and Johnson were trying to find the little hut of an old man whom they had met the other day. From the path we could look through the trees and see valley after valley stretching out into the sky, little plots of ploughed ground, scattered groves of olive trees and little stone shelters perched on the edge of every hill. These shelters have grape arbors over the front porch for shade in the summer. In the nearest valley a little stream (it would be called a ditch in America) ran and near it the grass was very green – bamboo shoots, apparently cultivated, grew near the ditch. In a level spot in the floor of the valley grew four tall popular trees – the highest trees in the area.

We walked along the path – the fields directly below us were planted with grape vines. Each vine had four bamboo sticks formed in a pyramid above it (so that's the reason for the bamboo). The plants looked very small, but an old farmer told us that they would bear this year. We walked up to one of the shelters and admired the view from the porch – roses and lilacs grew near the shelter. We saw two men working in a field far below and decided to walk to them. When we got there the old man and his son told us about their crops – tomatoes, potatoes, and beans. They live in Spinazzola and come out to the fields every day to work. The shelters are used when it rains and during the harvest season when they live there. We walked back and talked about the absence of cows in Italy – from there, to ice cream and milk shakes. Felt sorry for ourselves by the time we got back to town.

Sunday, May 14 – This afternoon we went for another long hike. It was a warm day and we took off our shirts to get the sun. We took several pictures – one of us with scyths and sickles which we borrowed from a farmer. We walked to a distant hill where we saw some rocks jutting out of the ground. When we came to the rocks we found a deep rocky gorge with grottoes in the sides and a stream running through the gorge. We walked along the sides of the canyon until the sides became lower and the gorge became a valley. We walked back through the canyon, exploring some of the caves. We took off everything but our shorts, waded in the water, then lay in the sun. We took pictures, talked, saw some frogs and snakes. Soon an old Italian came down the canyon. He told us that he had lived in Brooklyn from 1912 to 1914. He came back to Italy to fight in the World War, said that he knew "a leetle bit of eenglish". He told us that the canyon had been used as a stone quarry at one time.

We got back to town at five o' clock, took a shower and had chow. I felt pleasantly tired and relaxed.

Wednesday, May 17, 1944 – Tonight we saw John Garfield and Maureen O'Hara in "The Fallen Angel". It was a good picture with a surprise ending. The girl was true to the Fatherland, but she loved him; the Fatherland won, but she was caught. Afterwards, I came back to the office and talked to Frank Evanhuse of the Medics. He had read just about everything. Dagwood came in to write a letter and told me about his girl who was married recently to a marine. He found out from his mother. The girl didn't want to tell him because he was overseas. Poor Dagwood – he has his troubles. Rotation appears to be working now. Three of the cooks in Headquarters Squadron left last week – they had two days notice. I hate to think of going home and saying goodbye all over again, but it looks as if it's going to be a long war.

Monday, May 22 – Tonight we saw The Song of Bernadette. It was more than a picture to me – it was a religious experience. I think her character was beautifully portrayed by Jennifer Jones. When there are among us men and women who can conceive of such a beautiful character, produce such a perfect cinema record of such a life – even if Bernadette were not as perfect in real life – it restores my faith in man – there must be a better world tomorrow. The Song of Bernadette is the most moving, profound and beautiful picture that I have ever seen.

Tuesday, May 23 – Today I had a letter from Walter Butler who is in Sardinia with the old 981st. He said that Ray Young and Bob Yorkston (My former tent-mates) together with Bill Hamman, Brannan, the Mess Sergeant, and Bargaran had left for the states via rotation, and that he had moved in with Zilk and Peterson. They seem to have a pretty good set-up although they suffer from boredom too. I miss the boys in my old outfit. There's some thing about your original outfit that stays with you. There is a bond, a feeling of camaraderie with the boys that you learned to soldier with. When I think of the 981st and the trials and initial experiences in the desert behind the British Eighth Army – I'm sure that those memories will be with me always.

We are set up in Spinazzola just as if we were in the states – prescribed uniform, passes to leave the town, Red Cross Club where they serve ice cream three times a week, movies three times a week, racks for our mosquito nets over our bunks, racks to hang our clothes behind our bunks. The Italian soldiers and sailors working with us take care of all that as well as all cleaning and K.P. work. We have no duty roster in Headquarters Squadron. The only work we do is when we are Charge of Quarters. At that time we sweep the office. I should say, that's the only labor that we do. We are busier in the office than we have ever been before, but the days go fast. Everyone is talking and thinking about rotation. I hate to think about going home and then returning overseas. If I stay here until October,

I'll have two years overseas and a good chance (I think) of being permanently assigned in the states.

The other day I had a letter from Bob Szuba, Butch Kroft's boy friend who is around Naples. Barbara had written him asking exactly what a star on a campaign ribbon meant. She thought I was holding something from her when I told her that it didn't necessarily mean action in a major battle. I told him to tell Barbara about the WAC's who were wearing them – that should convince her. I owe so many letters and I can't seem to find the ambition to sit down and write them. I've been reading a lot of books. At present am reading Franz Werfel's "The Forty Days of Musa Dagh". He is a great writer.

Barbara sent me a pipe and tobacco for our second wedding anniversary. I wrote her last night congratulating us on not having a single fight in two years of married life – a joke as we've had just two months of life together and lived for those two months with the Flicks. Keep thinking that the war can't last forever and that we'll soon be able to resume our normal life. It looks like three more years of war. Time will tell.

Wednesday, May 31 – In the last week we've had two days off and this morning I had a half-day off: this is the result of our new policy established a week from yesterday. At a meeting of the heads of our different sections the captain decided that we would be able to do as much work if we had a little more time off. We were getting "office nerves". Last Friday Moe Gary, Hi Feinstein and I had off. We walked up to the town cemetery which is on a hill on the western edge of Spinazzola. It is surrounded by a high stone wall. We walked through the imposing entrance, opened half of the iron-barred gate and went in. There are many shade trees, tall cyprus trees, flowers of every color, poppies, blood-red, roses, lilacs and vines growing on the wall of the cemetery. The wall serves as a burial vault and the marble or stone plaques arranged in neat rows bear the names of the dead – from the beginning of the nineteenth century. This graveyard is comparatively modern, however, for

Spinazzola was a town two thousand years ago. There are many beautiful private mausoleums in the cemetery, some of marble with mosaic figures of the holy virgin and child, some with reproductions of great paintings. We looked at the graves of six young Germans who had been killed last September when our fighter planes strafed them. From the cemetery we walked down the valley to the north, through fields and up a hill to the ruins of an old house. It was over grown with weeds and grain. We climbed to the top of the hill and admired the view. We walked off of the top of the hill where it was very windy. We sat down and talked about home life. The three of us are married and we talked about other married men and their apparent indifference to the faith their wives had in them. We decided that they would never know what a real marriage was because they would never know what real love is. Since they don't know what they are missing, they won't understand if you try to explain it to them. We walked home. I got a hair cut, ate chow and then went up on the roof and took a sun bath.

Today we played horse shoes and went up on the roof where we tossed the softball around.

Thursday, June 8 – The invasion of France was begun on the sixth, the day after the fall of Rome. We have listened attentively to the bulletins every hour. Things seem to be moving as well as might be expected. I hope the thing is a success because the sooner we get to Germany, the sooner the war will end. I'm sick and tired of the whole mess. I haven't existed since I came in the army and I won't begin to live again until I'm out of it. If I don't get out of it soon, I'm afraid I'll lose my love for my fellow men. I've certainly seen some of the poorest examples of civilized men since I've been in the army. I've met one or two angels and remembering these good men – that is what keeps me clinging to my ideals. I've become pretty crude myself. I think about myself first and act accordingly. I swear and use the foulest language – it has become a habit. It doesn't help to remind myself that swearing and cursing are simply substitutes for correct words and therefore ought to be primarily the language of the uneducated. I'm going to try to cure myself, beginning tomorrow – no, tonight, I mean.

Saturday, June 10 – It's 8:30 in the morning and I'm lying in the hot sun on the roof taking a sun bath. This is my day off; tomorrow will be Candy's. Last night we saw "Phantom Lady" with Ella Raines and Franchot Tone. It was produced by Joan Harrison, Alfred Hitchcock's protege. I thought it was very well done.

Back to this morning. From the roof of this school building one can see over the town – the fields surrounding Spinazzola, valleys, hills of olive orchards and in the beyond, the mountains, slate-colored, enveloped in a murky haze. The fields in this panorama are brown (ploughed), rich green or straw-colored. Scattered over the hills beyond the town are isolated buildings, some red, some dun-colored and some white. All are of concrete – not enough wood in Italy, I guess.

Last Wednesday Candy went to Bari to visit a friend of his who had been a prisoner of the Germans for fifteen months. The story he told is fantastic. In February of 1943 the Liberator in which Fred (I'll call him that) was a tail gunner, left Benghazi to bomb Naples. The ack-ack ws heavy and two of the four engines of their Liberator were knocked out. The navigator lost his bearing on the way home and, as their ship was limping along, the pilot decided to land on what he thought was the island of Malta. As soon as they landed they felt instinctively that something was wrong. Fred crawled out of the plane and made a suggestion: "I'll walk until I find somebody. If I sing 'Blues in the Night', you guys destroy the bombsight and all secret equipment. If I sing 'Deep in the Heart of Texas' you'll know everything is all right." He walked to the edge of the field and saw some Italian soldiers with guns pointing at him. He sang 'Blues in the Night' and then heard the reports of five forty-fives being fired in the plane. The Italian soldiers, thinking the Americans were shooting at them, began shooting. Fred dropped to the ground in one of the deep ruts made in the past when a heavy bomber had landed in a soft field. Miraculously, he was not hit. They surrendered when the Italians had finished shooting and were escorted to headquarters and from there to a train.

While they were in the city waiting for the train, a mob of civilians armed with pitch forks and knives attempted to get them from their guards. If their guards hadn't stood off the mob with guns, they might have been killed. They were taken to an ancient castle, the officers and enlisted men separated, and the six enlisted men were put in a little stone-walled room in the castle. The room was just large enough for the six of them. They were in this castle for two months. Their food was soup three times a day with one piece of black bread a week. About once a week they were permitted to be outside in a courtyard for an hour. Their bodies were filthy and covered with lice.

After two months they were shipped to a camp in northern Italy. This camp was run by the Germans and was better managed. In the old castle their Italian guards were actually afraid of the Americans. This amused Fred and his companions as they were too weak to subsist outside the camp let alone overpower their guards. In the German camp in northern Italy things were better. The camp was an old one. They had their first shower in over two months and felt better. Most of the other prisoners (there were twelve hundred of them) in the camp were English who had been taken prisoner in the earlier stages of the African war. Many had been in the camp for three years and for some, the long confinement with no benefit of female companionship (they never saw a woman from one month to the next) had affected their minds and perverted their emotions. They formed attachments to one another, caressed one another, and would become violently jealous if the partner seemed to be interested in another man. This horrible state that these poor imprisoned former "desert rats" had fallen into was a warning to Fred and Bob, a technical sergeant, and their other companions. They knew that they must escape. Anything, even being shot while attempting to escape, was better than a life that ended in one becoming a mental wreck – like the drooling soldiers. In a few weeks Fred was made sergeant major for the entire camp. He had red hair, a magnetic personality, a jovial disposition and was soon a favorite of both the guards and the other prisoners. He organized baseball games, cricket matches, football games and anything to get the men interested in living again. All of the time he and his five companions were whispering and planning to escape. It seemed impossible – the walls were high and guarded with barbed wire on the top. They concentrated on learning Italian for the day when their escape would be come a reality. For seven months Fred and Bob and their companions were kept in the camp. They heard rumors of the invasion of Sicily, then Italy and their hopes went up. They received Red Cross packages via Switzerland. The Germans saw to it that these were distributed regularly. The men were grateful In the week before Christmas 1943, the prisoners were told that they were going to Rome for the holidays because their behavior had been good; . They were loaded onto a train, under guard, and detrained in Rome. As they came off the train there were German women photographers and newsreel women taking pictures of the prisoners. Fred said he was scratching himself all the while the pictures were taken – he couldn't help it since he hadn't had a bath from the first day he arrived in the German camp. He didn't care what the German women thought – he scratched. They were given an excellent meal in a barracks near the city, then driven through the city. Fred, as the sergeant –major was taken to General Kesselring's headquarters to be interviewed by the general. The General asked him how the food was and Fred told him it was good – better than the Italian food. The general was accompanied by the Japanese ambassador and several SS men, those super semi-Gestapo men. These men talked to him about the war. The general was convinced that Germany would win. He knew that Fred's mother had been an Austrian and he told Fred, "You are German. If you will agree to work on our bombsights in Berlin we will pay you seven hundred dollars a month". From the day they had been captured, the Italians and Germans had assumed for some reason that Fred was the bombardier (actually, he was the tail gunner) and, as this assumption seemed to carry a more respectable treatment with it, Fred had allowed them to believe it. Fred told the general that he did not want the job, that the money wouldn't do him any good after Germany had lost the war and that he and his mother were both Americans. Up spoke the Japanese ambassador in faultless English, "Do you know, sergeant, that Los Angeles, San Francisco and every large city on your western coast has been leveled to the ground and that New York has been bombed?"

"Do you know about the thousand-plane raids we're sending over Berlin?", Fred asked him.

"Yes", said the ambassador.

"Well", said Fred, "In a little while we're going to fly over Tokyo and all of Japan with thousands of planes." The ambassador turned and walked away. Fred was dismissed by the general and talked to several S.S. men – all of these were either English or American and Fred was surprised by the hatred they felt for their native country – called them "capitalists" with hate in their voices. One had been born in Chicago, was of German descent and had come to Germany in 1933 to join the Nazis. When Fred asked him why he had done that he explained that it was during the depression and he had no job and things looked better in Germany. He told Fred that he realized that he had made a mistake but that it was too late, now.

They were herded back on the train on the day after Christmas. On the floor of one of the cars Fred saw a wire cutters. He picked it up and hid it inside the lining of his coat. When they arrived in camp their guards searched each man but did not find the wire cutters in his coat. In January all of the prisoners in the camp heard rumors about being moved to a camp in Germany. Meanwhile Bob had escaped – he had disguised himself so that he was able to slip through the guards at the gate. Fred and he planned to meet in one of the towns along the coast whenever Fred could escape. Meanwhile, Fred covered up for bob by shouting "hospital" at every morning formation during the roll call.

In the middle of January they were loaded onto box cars – destination, Germany. Fred and his four companions decided to try to get through the small window in the car which was barely large enough for a man to crawl through. It was dark when the train began to move. As soon as it started Fred took his wire cutters and began the slow process of cutting through the heavy mesh wire that covered the window. They drew lots to see who would go first. The train was moving about thirty miles an hour now, through mountainous country. The first boy got halfway through the window and was momentarily wedged. "I'm stuck", he said from outside the window in a voice loud enough for those inside the car to hear but so loud that the guards on the roof of the train heard. The guards began shooting and one of the bullets went through his head. The boys in the car pushed his body out. When the second boy met the same fate, the others decided that it was useless to make the attempt. Fred said,

"I'm going, I'd rather be dead than a prisoner in Germany". He crawled through the window, bullets singing past his head, and jumped from the moving train. He landed on his feet on a steep bank and rolled down the hill. He sat up and examined himself. He had some cuts and bruises form the leap but the bullets had not touched him. He was on his way to freedom, but he knew that the chances were slim and that the going would be hard. He kept to the hill country, avoiding the cities. He spoke Italian, almost like a native, if he didn't say too much. He walked several miles after the jump from the train and slept all night in some bushes near an olive orchard. It was cold but there was no snow. He stopped at a farmer's house and asked for food. The farmer suspected nothing since he appeared like many of the other peasants – his clothing, a hodgepodge of German and Italian uniforms, discarded by or stolen from soldiers. He asked the directions to the city where he was to meet Bob. After traveling overland for several days – he was not afraid to travel by day, now – he arrived in the city and down near the waterfront he met Bob. Bob was staying with an Italian family who lived in one of the dirty little winding streets in the old part of the city. They went there and spent the night. They decided that their best chance to reach their own troops would be to go through the German lines. They walked and hitched rides from native vehicles, avoiding the army trucks. When they wanted cigarettes they asked the Germans who thought them Italians. They were walking on the road leading from a small town, relaxed and talking in English when two Italian civilians stepped into the road. They had overheard them while sitting in their car nearby. One questioned them shrewdly. The Italians wore black leather putees of the Fascist home guard and carried rifles. They knew that Fred and Bob were not Italians and thought they were spies. They loaded their guns and decided to shoot them on the spot. Two girls were walking towards them and they decided that this was to be their last impression on earth. Then a miracle happened: the girls seemed to sense what was happening. They walked by the party of four, then hesitated; they seemed not to see the two who were about to be shot, but they smiled at the Fascists, walked up to them, joking with them, very close to them, they opened their blouses exposing their breasts, seized the Fascists' hands and moved them over their breasts, down their hips and thighs. The Fascists were young and human and the girls led them into the town on foot. Fred and Bob couldn't believe their luck. The girls had never by a gesture or even a glance in their direction indicated that they saw the boys.

They proceded toward the front. It was cold and it began to snow. They slept with peasants, ate black bread and somehow managed to exist. Everything was confusion among the civilians who were near the front and everything was wreckage and suffering. One night they decided to make a dash for the Allied lines. The snow was waist-deep and the going was rough. They got through the German lines and promptly lost themselves floundering in the deep snow between the two lines in no-man's land. They were fired on by both German and Allied patrols. Pinned to the ground by machine gun fire from both sides, they decided that they were going to die, either by gunfire or by being frozen. In the dawn a German patrol suddenly appeared. "Achtung", said the German officer. He marched them back to the German lines, then back to the cook tent a half mile from the front line positions. They talked to the commandant telling him that they were escaped prisoners of war – they were afraid of being shot for spies. The Germans fed them well – fresh meat, fresh vegetables and fresh milk. The Germans wanted to know if the Americans ate that well. Fred told them "No". Fred and Bob were held at this outpost for about a week. During this time they observed the behavior of the Germans. The veterans were bitter toward Hitler; some of the very young replacements who had just come were Nazis to the core, but the veterans laughed at them. When it came time for them to go into the line some of the boys lay down on the ground and cried. Some of them were fifteen years old. From this outpost Fred and Bob were driven by truck to another city and put in a prison. They were not questioned after they had given their names and serial numbers. While they were being driven from the prison to a train which was to take them further north (this was about March), they escaped from the truck and quickly made their way to the old quarter of the city. They went into one of the dirty little hovels, ordered wine and thought about their plight. They decided to try to get to one of the towns on the coast to see if they could get to allied territory by way of the sea. They sat drinking their wine and suddenly realized that there was a constant movement of Italians coming and going –

a middle-aged man came up to them and quietly said, "You are Americans?". They decided that he could be trusted and told him that they were Americans. He took a slip of paper from his pocket and, all the while talking to them, drew a diagram showing them how to reach a certain building near a city about twenty miles distant. He told them that they could be helped there. They studied the crude map, then burned it and thanked the Italian for his help.

They slept that night in the same hovel where they had been drinking and early the next morning left for the distant city. They walked until mid-afternoon to the building which the Italian had described to them. It was a mansion with a coat of arms over a great doorway – built on a rise of ground surrounded by poplars and cyprus trees.

They went up to the door and knocked, wondering if they were falling into a trap. The door was opened by a middle-aged woman. They asked for the person whose name the Italian had given them. The woman told them to wait. She returned with a beautiful blonde woman of about thirty. She told them to come in. They followed her to an exquisitely-furnished drawing room where she asked them who they were. They told her that they were Americans who were trying to escape. She said that they could tell their story to the Count when he returned.

They were shown to their room which had a private bath and a huge bed; they bathed and went to sleep. When they awoke it was dark. They dressed and walked downstairs. The blonde – looking even more beautiful in the evening – met them at the foot of the stairs. She took them in to meet the count who was about forty, intelligent, and strong of character. They told him their entire story and asked if he would help them to get to a seaport. He said that they would have to remain with him for a while but he would arrange for their escape. The Count was a leader in the underground movement. During the month and a half that they stayed there they learned that the blonde was the Count's mistress. Fred got along wonderfully with the blonde and perhaps this inspired the Count to greater effort. At any rate, one day the Count told them that all arrangements were made: that they would be driven to a city on the coast to another link in the underground; there, after a boat was built, they would sail down to an allied port. As they were leaving the blonde asked Fred if he wouldn't reconsider and stay with them longer while she squeezed his hand.

From the next city (on the coast) they left one June day – they had to wait until a boat was fitted for them and for an Italian to guide them to an allied port. They had been fifteen months away from allied territory. They told their story to a British officer. He sent them to Bari where they were taken to see General Twining. When they had finished, they were sworn to secrecy (that is the reason for the many gaps), were given some medals, some dinners, and asked what they wanted. Fred wanted to be a pilot and so he was given a letter from the general and told that he would go to Cadet Training. Bob said he wanted to fly reconnaissance over the Mississippi River for the duration. The general said that he could arrange that too.

STILL IN SPINAZZOLA

Visit with Dale Byers

I make sergeant August 20, 1944

Candy leaves for the states

and I take over the accounting department

July 23 – Sunday. I've just come back from Foggia where I was visiting Dale Byers. He stopped in our office two weeks ago and surprised me. It was the first time that I knew that he was in Italy. We had a good time visiting in the captain's apartment. We couldn't do much in public as Dale is a captain and everything around here is either Enlisted Men Only or Officers Only. The day after he arrived here we went to Bari in his jeep – looked around the shops – he bought me an officer's cap at the PX (which I'll convert to an EM cap by substituting finance braid for officer's) and on the way back we stopped at Castel del Monte, a castle about halfway between here and the first town. We walked through the old castle after obtaining permission from the sergeant of a radar outfit which is stationed on the hill on which the castle stands. The castle was built by Frederick II in the year 1212 (or thereabouts). The walls are bare and there are no furnishings in the building, but in some of the rooms much of the marble art work remains – clusters of columns, parts of the stone fireplaces with their conical chimneys narrowing up to the very high ceilings. We walked out on the top of the building. We could see Bari in the far distance and the sea. This hill is the highest in the area. There was no moat surrounding the castle. We decided that Old King Frederick thought that this was unnecessary as the castle was at the very top of a high hill and was probably unassailable by any enemy, or could be taken only at great cost – since the enemy would be continually exposed to the fire of the defenders. One of the sections of the castle was boarded up and we were told that Italian art treasures had been stored there from the time that the bombings had begun. The castle is octagonal in shape and is built around an inner court. It didn't have many windows and must have been gloomy when it was inhabited. I wish I had had a camera (It's about the fiftieth time I've wished that since I've been overseas). The three of us, Dale, Bill Koslov, a first lieutenant in the Canadian Army whom we had picked up in Bari, and I walked down the hill and drove on, taking a last look at the old castle.

After we arrived in Spinazzola we went to the captain's apartment and drank some wine, listening to Bill Koslov tell us about his experiences. He was going back to the front – had been in the hospital in Bari for a week recovering from yellow jaundice. He has been overseas almost five years, in action for the last year and a half. Before that, he had been in England for a long time. He told us that Jerry was definitely using the abbey at Casino for an observation post and that after we bombed the abbey, he moved in and fortified the mountain. He had had some narrow escapes; one time Jerry artillery hit one of the gasoline trucks in his outfit and a man was burned to death – he said he'll never forget the smell of burning flesh. He is twenty-six, seemed like a pretty nice chap. Dale drove him up to Foggia.

I had a good time yesterday and today visiting Dale. He lives in a tent but it isn't a bad set-up. We went through a flying fortress and in the evening went in to see a stage show, an Italian USO unit; finally, a movie with Charles Laughton, Robert Young and Margaret O'Brien (she's wonderful) in "the Canterville Ghost". It was a good picture. I had a good night's sleep after eating eggs at Dale's mess. It was a nice change sleeping in a tent. The next morning, after breakfast, I left for Spinazzola. Dale drove me in a civilian car into Bari and left me out on the road to Cerignola. Had good luck on my rides and got home in time for noon chow.

Wednesday, August 2, 1944 – Today was a bad day for Candy Johnson. At three o'clock this afternoon he received a letter from his sister informing him that Maxine had died. She felt ill the evening of Candy's grandfather's funeral – that was a Wednesday – that night she was taken to the hospital with severe sinus trouble. It pained her terribly all day Thursday and she was unconscious all day Friday. At 3 o'clock Saturday morning she died. The doctors tried an oxygen tent, penicillin and every other known cure to help her breathing, but nothing helped. They could only guess at the cause of her death; either an infection resulting from her sinus settled in the brain or the poison from the infected sinus drained into her system. It was so sudden that her family was stupified and Candy, who had had a letter from her just two days ago, was heartbroken. When his grandfather had died, affairs at home had been so unsettled that his mother wanted him to see about an emorgency furlough. He had been placed on rotation by Red Cross recommendation and was looking forward to going home within the next two months. He and Maxine were going to be married then. They had planned the type of house they would build and, with the end of the war almost in sight, things seemed to be going along nicely. Maxine was a school teacher in a little town in Texas. Candy met her the year that he taught there.

This morning Tom Quinlan stopped in the office to tell me that he was going home this Saturday. He and I used to patrol the desert back in Benghazi when we were in the 981st together. He transferred out of Headquarters, 323rd last March and was a mechanic in a bomb group. He made corporal a month after I did and just made sergeant two week sago. He was happy about going home (he's to be sent to school to learn B-29 engines) and said he would be married when he gets to Cincinnati. He asked for Barbara's address and said he would write. I hope this thing is soon over – 21 months is a hell of a long time to be away from your wife. I hope the whole damn thing is over before we are too old to have kids.

Saturday, August 5. Tonight we had a USO show. It was a little better than the average, but the reason that I'll remember it is that the magician was "Patty, the Miss Who Mystifies" – Patty Krisco from Butler. Her act was pretty good. I went back stage to see her after the show. I knew her just from what Mother had said – she and Mrs. Krisco are in the same bridge club. She knew of me from her mother. I told her that I remembered her sister Rhea as a little girl. Patty is younger than

Rhea – she certainly is healthy looking now. I talked to her for about ten minutes. Her father worked in a bank and was an amateur magician. He came to our Boy Scout troop with his two daughters. One of his props was a long, narrow, canvas roll about six feet long. On this was printed a long string of numbers designating pi, the ratio of the circumference of a circle to its diameter. The girls were blindfolded and he had each of them recite the numbers from memory. I reminded her of this. She said she would write Mother telling her that she had seen me. She seemed like a nice girl, very poised. I felt gauche while I was talking to her, reminding me of the adjustment that will have to be made when I get back to the U.S.A.

Tuesday, August 7, 1944 – In the last couple of days I've had a lot of mail from Barbara – all of the letters that I didn't get two weeks ago – anyway, I'm feeling pretty good now. It always puts me in a good mood when I get a nice letter from my wife who is pretty okay by me. That is not malarkey, Mrs. K. I read a good book too, The Just and the Unjust by James Gould Cozzens. It's the first work of his that I've read – very well done – the characters are solid and the author knows his subject. I hope to read other works of Mr. Cozzens.

Tonight I went down to the Red Cross and while we were in the music room several colored boys from one of the squadrons came in and started a jam session, playing the piano and singing one of the songs that goes on and on. Different persons each sing a verse and everyone joins in the chorus after each verse. The rhythm is the thing and these boys really feel it – they shuffle and dance with each other, imitate instruments with their hands. A huge black boy came in the room.

"Hello Bull", they shouted. He was the biggest man I've ever seen. He had on first sergeant chevrons and the lozenge in the middle of his chevrons was tinseled shiny silver. These negroes have their own fashions, even in the army. They have pants that are much too long, then roll them up so that they have a "pegged" cuff; hats are worn with the length across the head from ear to ear, that is, exactly perpendicular (at right angles) to the correct way. The negroes had such a good time that their mood was caught by those of us watching (there were a lot of us, soon) and I wondered what the secret of their race could be. The quality that enabled them to enjoy themselves fully under present conditions.

The news has been good, but we are on edge waiting for Germany's downfall. Things look good and I feel that I'll be going home this year. That's probably the reason that I feel a little more expansive inside myself.

Thursday, August 10, 1944 – All day we were thinking about Lt. O'Brien's farewell party. The lieutenant had received a large Virginia-baked ham from a friend of his who is a captain on a Liberty ship. We had plenty of beer, ice and bread and after the USO show in the evening, we had our party. Lt. Pickle (of Officer's PX) and Lt. Alexander (of APO) were the only officers beside Lt. O'Brien since the captain had a light touch of the grippe. We had the party in the office – baked ham sandwiches and beer. We ate and drank and drank – and there were speeches by everyone. Some of the boys had too much to make a coherent speech, but they tried and we laughed. The long table was loaded with empty beer bottles and we had the group photographer in to take a picture. Somebody went over to the gym where the colored boys from the USO show were staying and brought back a guitar player. He was good — sang "Whispering Grass" (reminded me of when Zilk and I used to mimic Ed Lenzen in the 981st), "So Long" and all of the Ink Spot favorites.

Lt. O' Brien, Candy and I went into the next room. He wanted to tell us goodbye alone. Lane (S/Sgt on DS) followed us in; he's usually a quiet fool, but he was pretty far gone with beer and couldn't take a hint, so the lieutenant told him to go into the other room as he wanted to tell Candy and me something. He started to and said enough that I knew that he knew what the score was in our office. He said, "I know that I'm talking to a couple of boys who know what I'm talking about". Then Wood came busting in. I could have pasted him, but the others came in and we realized that we couldn't say goodbye alone. The party broke up then and I went to bed in the office as I was C.Q.

Friday, August 11 – Tonight we saw Charles Boyer and Ingrid Bergman in "Gaslight" – it was very good. I finished reading Laughing Boy by Oliver LaFarge, a very good novel about a Navajo Indian and his wife who is making money from a white man by being nice to him. In the end she is killed by another Indian as she and her husband, reconciled after he discovers about her double life, are riding back to his country (away from all white men) to make their home. Beautifully done.

Today, I had a letter from Bob Thomas who said that he had been visiting Dale for three days. He has been overseas 26 months. I don't know where he is located, but Dale can tell me the next time I see him. It would be nice if the three of us could have a reunion.

Tuesday, August 15 –Today, we heard the news of the invasion of southern France. It didn't make any great impression on us – we are learning to take the news of invasions in our stride. Yesterday, when our bombers went out to bomb a target in southern France they saw the invasion fleet. When they returned the crews were told not to mention it, but there's always a leak and we knew about it on the 14th. I hope they don't encounter much opposition. Couch's brother and Candy's brother-in-law are in it.

Thursday, August 17 – Today was very hot – it was my day off and Harry Wilner, Moe Gary and I had planned to go swimming at Trani – if we could get the jeep, but as it happened we could not – the captain said the steering wheel was in no condition for a long trip. Couch and Wood had used the jeep last night and went on a mission to Potenza, I guess; anyway, more of that later.

I spent the morning in the Red Cross Club reading and in the afternoon took a sun bath on the roof. Later I played shuffleboard with an Eyetie soldier on the roof. He beat me and enjoyed it. Came down, took a shower, and got into some clean clothes. Came in the office and had a letter from mother and dad waiting for me. The captain called me over to his desk and told me that something had come up in a hurry and that he was submitting my name for sergeant. It was quite a blow – Candy and Berglund came over the started to call me "sergeant". I told them it was bad luck and that I would believe it when I had seen the order – then there was the problem of Duino and Tew, both of whom have more seniority than I. Tew was in three months before I came into finance, but he hasn't done any work and I think I deserve it over him, but Duino expected to be the next sergeant and he felt badly about it. We were talking together the other night, Duino and I, and he told me that the captain "as much as" promised it to him. He works hard (but I think I work harder). The captain said that since I would be the accountant when Candy left for the states that he felt I should have the rating. Anyway, I'm not a sergeant yet and I'll believe it when I see it on the Group Order.

To get back to Couch and Wood – it seems that while they were returning from their mission at about six this morning, they had a flat tire – just outside of town. While they were fixing it an MP sergeant drove up in a jeep, and at the same time three girls came walking down the road – the MP sergeant asked the girls if they would accomodate him and his buddies (Wood and Couch). "OK", said the babes, but only one of them looked good to the boys, so they took turns going into the bushes with her. She wouldn't accept a cent for her services and when the girls had left Wood and Couch finished repairing the flat tire and came home. In the early afternoon an MP came in the office and wanted Wood and Couch to come over to the station with him. It seems that the girl had forty dollars taken from her brassiere and she said one of the GI's took it – I

guess she blamed it on the sergeant of the MP's. It seems that
the MP sergeant has been on some pretty shady deals with the
girls in town and they're gunning for him. By evening rumors
had it that the MP sergeant was held for rape and robbery, but
I think it's only a case of robbery since it' s only a prostitute's
word against a soldier's. There is something funny in the whole
deal, but at any rate Wood and Couch are out of it.

Friday, August 18 – We saw a good show tonight – Charles
Laughton, Binnie Barnes, Donna Ried, Richard Carlson in
"The Man from Down Under". I thought it was a swell show
– not entirely escapist. Have heard no more about my prospective rating – haven't mentioned it to Barbara as I don't want her
to build on what may be false hopes. I know the army too well
to feel sure of anything.

Saturday, August 19 – The news is very good from all
fronts. American forces are reported in bulletins as being 23
miles from Paris. Unofficial reports have them fighting on the
outskirts of Paris – time will tell. I'm homesick for Barbara,
more these last few weeks, I think, because the war is moving
swiftly and yet I'm not as optimistic as the new boys or the people at home seem to be. I have a lot of letters that I must write.
I don't feel like writing and I've put it off for so long. Still no
news of my promotion. Moe Gary, who is to get my corporal's
rating says he's afraid that it's another false alarm. If anything
happens to obstruct it, it will be from the higher-ups – like my
good-conduct ribbon which I was so proud to get – it had to go
through on a separate order.

Candy had off today and I finished our work in the morning and spent the rest of the day reading Lt. O'Brien's text
books which he left with us. Our last news of him through Lt.
Alexander of A.P.O. is that he is in Naples yet. Lt. Alexander is
a very nice person. He thinks the world of his wife and when
Lt. O'Brien was here he used to kid him about "going out tom-
cattin' with the local signorinas". We always have a good time
at our finance parties when "Alex" is there. He is a veritable

"Poo Bah" in Headquarters Squadron. When he answers the phone he says "Lt. Alexander, Postal Officer, Statistical Officer, War Bond Officer, Intelligence Officer speaking". He is from Kentucky, sleepy-looking, slow moving – speaks with a drawl. He must be around thirty-five, but he looks as if he were fifty. Guess I'll sign off for tonight as I want to get back to my book "The Ministry of Fear". Hope I hear from Mrs. K tomorrow.

Sunday, August 20 – Tonight we saw several short films of what the army designates "Orientation", which covers a multitude of subjects from news (not very current, but colored) to "Snafu", the sad sack of army films whose trouble comes from not listening to army doctors and his army teachers – he gets blown up by a booby trap, stung by an anaphles mosquito, etc. There was an excellent British Army film entitled "Kill or Be Killed" in which a British sergeant sets out to get a Jerry sniper who has potted at him – the thoughts of each is spoken and it actually keeps you on the edge of your seat, wondering which one is to be killed. They stalk each other in the woods – the Tommy wins and he then mops up a five-man patrol with his bolt action rifle.

No word of my promotion yet.

Monday, August 21 – As of yesterday I've been a sergeant – the orders came out today. I don't feel any differently than I did as a Pfc, but I'll be able to send home $50 a month now and that will give Barbara a hundred to budget. The news is pretty good, but I think it's going to be a long war.

Wednesday, August 23 – Paris fell today – we heard the news this morning, but it wasn't as momentous to us as we thought it would be back in the pre-invasion days, when it was a vision. Free-French forces freed the city. I hope the war doesn't last long enough for it to become the Mecca for officers (and a few enlisted men) that it was during World War I. For us it represents another milestone on the road home. Candy's name has been submitted to higher headquarters for approval; practically no one whose name is submitted is refused so it is virtually a certainty that he will be leaving for the USA soon. I'll have my hands full as an accountant, but I'm glad that I'll have a section of my own. Duino feels badly about my getting the sergeant's rating, but it seems to me that he's a poor sport. I know I would have congratulated him if he were promoted. He has ignored me since the captain submitted my name – talked loudly about a transfer, but did nothing. The captain has made it up to him by bonding him as cashier (he'll help Berglund part of the month, taking him out of enlisted pay, putting him in accounting for the first ten days of the month). He will thus be able to learn how the entire office functions. I can see that the promotion has been a pretty lucky thing for me, but it certainly hasn't made me popular.

Tonight, we saw Frederick March in "The Adventures of Mark Twain_ --it was interesting and March's interpretation of Mark Twain was excellent. He was a great man and tonight I remember how I felt when I first read "Tom Sawyer" and "Huckleberry Finn".

Tuesday, August 29 – Today has been one of the happiest that I've spent overseas. I had the day off and Harry Wilner, Orville Jensen and I went with the boys from the Wing down to Trani. The truck left from here at 9:30 AM – the ride down to Trani was pleasant. The countryside in Italy is beautiful in the early part of the morning. We passed through Corati where American soldiers seem to be very popular. On every block little boys shout, "Hey Joe, want a woman?" Only, they use language a trifle more earthy. Trani is an Italian resort town – the padrones with money had summer homes here. There is a bay that is fine for sail boating and the beach is sandy, the water shallow – the country is picturesque enough to make an ideal vacation spot. The town itself is much larger than Spinazzola. There are nice shops and the main thoroughfares are wide for an Italian city. There are attractively-dressed ladies and other women. There is a parkway extending down the main street and dividing the street. The parkway has a wide sidewalk, a strip of grass on either side and tall shade trees, uniformly planted down the length of the parkway. In the middle of the parkway is the traditional Italian fountain. We drove down to the beach and walked down the road to the entrance. The road is along the edge of a low cliff which marks the beginning of the sandy beach. The Major from the Wing who was with us paid our fee (10 lire per person) and we went into the bath house (four people to each of the little huts) and got into our swimming suits. I had Hyman Feinstein's suit, Harry wore his British shorts and Orville had Duino's trunks. We swam for a while then lay in the sand.

I struck up a conversation with a British corporal – he was very intelligent – we talked about the post-war world. He had been overseas just two years – his wife was in a London hospital. She had been hurt by one of the flying bombs which exploded near the bus on which she was the fare-taker. The bus driver was killed. He said his wife had been in the hospital two weeks ("a fortnight" he said) and was suffering from shock brought on by the concussion. I told him about my wife. He said we had more democracy in the U.S. than they have in England. He was with an ordnance outfit near Trani.

We opened our can of fruit cocktail and some cookies that Jensen had received from home and had a noon snack. Afterwards, we swam and talked while the little Italians hung around and begged for cigarettes. At about two o'clock the Major decided that he would like to go for a sailboat ride and invited us along. We sailed up the bay just outside the swimming area, then back and out to the point. Just above the point on top of a high cliff, a monastary (or a convent) stood. It was of rough field stone and the long, many-arched cloister faced the sea. It was a perfect location for the secluded life. I learned that the Major was from Mexico, Pa. around Harrisburg – went to Albright College in Reading. His friend who had come to visit him from Bari, was a corporal in headquarters of an Air Depot group. They had known each other from the time they were boys. Both are from Mexico, Pa.

It was wonderful sailing under the blue sky, the wind blowing spray in our faces. We went far out into the bay and jumped out of the boat, swam for a while, then sailed back. I'll never forget the panorama – the cliffs jutting out from the sea, summer homes of green, pink, blue and yellow along the top of the cliff – palm trees, olive orchards, Trani looking like a miniature city in the distance. We came in at three o'clock, dressed and rode through the city. We saw a number of British soldiers on crutches, some with one leg, some with one arm. There is a British convalescent hospital in Trani. We stopped at the "Toc-H Club" just opposite the market place in Trani. It is an organization for South Africans – like our Red Cross Clubs. We walked in and the little Italian girl who sold tickets said "Allo Joe". All over the world an American GI is "Joe". We had tea and cakes, very good. The Toc-H Club was formed in Flanders during the last war. I don't know the significance of the name. Got back in time for chow in the evening – ate and took a shower. It has been a wonderful day.

Sunday, September 24 -- Well, Candy has left for the states, last Wednesday. Tuesday night we had a farewell party for him. I drank quite a bit and ate a lot of fried eggs and fried potatoes – made a bit of an ass of myself reciting poetry (not classic).

I am the accountant in the office now. Things have been running the same – work, work, work – boredom. The war news has settled down to a waiting – as far as we're concerned. I miss Barbara more and more – the news is such that I think the war will end any day and then I get the jitters, and can't write or read, so I just work like hell. It's the best way to pass the time. Last night several of the boys from the 43rd who had been with us in Benghazi came down – they are stationed in Cerignola – and we had a party at the boys' apartment. Drank a lot of rum and ate a lot of eggs and recited a lot of poems and sang. We had a good time reminiscing about Benghazi – the time when the MP's came up and asked us to keep quiet so the Wogs could sleep, and Berglund almost fell off the roof. Felt surprisingly well when I got up this morning. Another thing, I haven't smoked a cigarette or a pipe or a cigar for about two weeks, since the tenth of September. I gave all of my pipes away and I hope to quit for good. Aunt Alm and Unk are sending me the Washington Star. Barbara sent me Tom Jones and Disraeli.

Thursday, September 28 – It's about ten o'clock – I'm very tired as I've been playing basket ball. Last night we of the finance office played the men of the orderly room and lost 20 to 18. We practiced at noon today and again tonight. I'm physically tired and I ache all over. At this stage I usually feel sinking into my thick skull the realization that I make as ass of myself running around chasing a ball so seriously when I could be writing some of the letters that I've put off answering, or reading some of the Readers' Digests that I've accumulated for the past five months, or reading some of the books that I've intended to read. It's always that way – I just don't have enough time for everything and I don't have the sense to concentrate on the finer things of the mind. I haven't written Barbara for a long time. We have a birthday coming up. I never think of how wonderful our life together was – unless I get so very melancholy that I begin to pity myself. Then I tell myself that I must be tough and come through the thing and believe that things will be the same and soon.

Most of the time I keep grinding from day to day – going to movies, reading, one day is just like another. The only thing I have to look forward to is the movie on nights when we have movies. It's pretty dull for the most part – the monotony is varied by those significant moments – those revelations that we all have – they last for only an instant – someone does something, makes a gesture or expresses an opinion and you are suddenly gifted with rare insight that enables you to see what mean creatures we are – how selfish, assine, egotistical, we are, and you wonder if the whole business of life is worth the trouble; and then there are other moments – golden ones – when for a matter of seconds your soul wells up within you and you feel pity for all men, and you would help all men – your soul is calm and at peace. These little infrequent moments – these rare treasures are touched off in the mind by varied stimuli – sometimes a sunrise on a fresh spring morning – sometimes a sunset – sometimes a moon on a clear night – or the stars; then again the face of a child or the face of a mother when she holds her baby. The feeling doesn't come often and that's the reason we recall its effect. You can never recall the feeling, it's a subtle thing. The effect is what makes life a thing of beauty and a joy forever.

Sunday, October 1 – Today is Barbara's birthday. Wrote her a V-mail. Tonight we played the cooks in basketball and lost. We're not in condition. Worked all day getting our reports.

ROME

October 18th to October 23, 1944

Frank Evenhuis' knowledge of Roman

history made for a most enjoyable visit.

Wednesday, October 18 – Today at one o'clock I left with Frank Evanhuis, Bill Maytis, Dave Barnum and Bob Haddock for Rome. It was a tiresome and rough trip up in the GMC truck. We were about fifteen miles south of Rome when the driver stopped to pick up two hitch-hikers. From a distance they looked like two British soldiers – they were in British battle-dress and carried their rifles with them. It seemed odd though as most of the British troops were in their summer khakis. They crawled into the back of the truck with us – then we realized that they were women – very young women. They were members of the organized freedom fighters from occupied Yugoslavia. They had to carry their weapons with them when they had leave. It was not too clear how they got to Italy for their week's furlough. They had their shirt sleeves rolled up above their elboes – revealing large muscular biceps. They sat on the bench in the back of the truck and grinned at us. One of them said to Vito Ciprini, a corporal who spoke Croatian, "You and me companions in Rome?"

"No", said Vito, "Must work in Rome." Vita said later that the lady Yugoslav freedom fighter was not his idea of an ideal companion for a furlough.

We got to the AAF rest camp at 3:30 in the morning, slept until 8:00 AM, then left for downtown Rome. Frank and I got a room in an apartment (rented from a family). It is fairly centrally located – costs us two dollars per night.

Thursday, October 19-- After we had washed, Frank and I went by Gherry to the Vatican City – this cost us one dollar. I'm mentioning prices because Rome is typical of a continental wartime city – inflation has caused prices to rise beyond reason. We had an old man guide us through St. Peters. The church is huge and rich and the mosaic is beautiful – grandeur is the word, I think.

The Vatican Museum has more true works of art. The old man took us through the museum where we saw these beautiful statues:

Laocoon of Apolidor – this is a representation of Laocoon, a Greek priest and his family being destroyed by Minerva.

Perseus – holding the head of Medusa by Canova – beautiful.

Appolo of Belvedere by Leo Cares – the cape on his left arm is like cloth – the niche that frames Appolo is painted sky-blue – the effect is striking.

Niobide – Wingless Victory by Scopas – commissioned by the Athenians to build a model masthead for ships of Greece. He built one with wings, but the Athenians were superstitious and thought it might fly out of Greece (Victory, i.e.) so he made this Wingless Victory. The Winged Victory is in the Louvre.

As the museum closed at 2 o'clock we had to rush, but decided to go through it again tomorrow. We walked down the Via Della Conciliazione to Vittorio Emanuel Bridge and rode back to the Red Cross Club with an officer who picked us up. We ate cookies and coffee and rested a while, sitting at the tables under the trees, listening to an Italian orchestra play American songs. This was formerly the Cassino della Rose – it is now the enlisted men's Red Cross Club. We left and walked through the city to the Pantheon. It is as awe-inspiring as St. Peters when one realizes that it was erected in 27 BC – it seemed to me that it was like St. Peters also in that it is impressive for its hugeness, primarily and not for its beauty. We saw the tomb of Raphael and those of some of the nobility which are in the Pantheon; incidentally, the Pantheon is now a church and no longer a temple for Jupiter, Appolo and Co.

A student took us into some rooms at the rear of the Pantheon and showed us some paintings – they were originals, he said, but we couldn't understand him very well. We saw the Coliseum in the early evening – I learned that the structures in the arena weren't part of the original building, but were added during medieval times when the Coleseum was turned into a fortress. It was dark when we came out of the Coliseum and we walked toward Victor Emmanuel Monument – it began to rain. We walked and walked and finally found a GI restaurant where we ate. Walked to our rooms which were at 33 Via Cernaia, Apt 9. We had Maria (whom I suspect is a retired prostitute) get us a bottle of Marsala and after we drank that I slept soundly – tired – comfortably tired.

Friday, October 20 – We got started at 8:30 this morning – had breakfast of hot chestnuts which taste like sweet potatoes. We (Frank Evenhuis and I) had our picture taken in front of the Baths of Dioclitian and I had my shoes shined. We got to St. Peters at ten o'clock and went through the church again. We decided to go through the Vatican Museum – we were to meet our guide at nine o'clock in the piazza, but we were late. We met him inside the museum. It's difficult to write about art without being self-conscious, so this is not for public consumption. From the moment you come into the Sala Rotonda to the time you leave the museum, it is an amazing experience. It's tiring when you try to do it all at once – the best way would be to come each day and see a portion of it. As we were rushed there are only certain highlights of feeling that I can recall – a lot of it comes back to me now that it's over, so I guess I'll enjoy it for a long time as bits of experience are remembered – with a "warm glow of pleasure" to be trite. These are taken from notes that I made on the back of pamphlets and odd pieces of paper. In the Sala Rotonda – all Greek. Juno Barbarini – beautiful. Bronze statue of Augustus, Ceres, Hadrian, Jupiter (striking) and busts of the following: Pericles, Solon, Alcibiades, Socrates (ugly, looks like a barbarian), Zeno, founder of the Stoics, Sophocles, Plato, Homer and Aristides. There they were – the originals of the busts, the pictures of which every student has seen in his Latin, Greek and history books. I enjoyed the time spent here and I wish I could have spent a whole day here. Another room of the museum had the busts of all of the Roman Emperors.

This list is not complete: Augustus, Claudius, Nero, Otho, Titus, Domitian (he was the last of the Romans to be emperor). Nerva, Trajan and Hadrian were the Spanish emperors. Antonius, Marcus Aurelius, L. Veros and A. Veros were the French emperors.

From here we went to see the other sculptures – in the courtyard was one called Niobide or Wingless Victory by Scopas – I guess I mentioned seeing it yesterday – the lines of the gown of the figure are so very carefully done – it might almost move – no head or arms, though.

Torso of Belvedere – MichaelAngelo found it in a shop where the proprietor had smashed it to a size that would fit his scales.

Laocoon Group – Laocoon was a Greek priest whom Minerva destroyed. He and his two sons are being devoured by snakes.

Perseus with the Head of Medusa – holds head in his left hand, cape over his left arm – supposed to be by Canova.

Apollo of Belvedere – very good – he holds the apple (signifying beauty) in his left hand, cape over his left arm – by Leo Cares, 4th Century BC.

Apoxyomenos – by Lysippoo – a runner – he scrapes the dust and perspiration from his right arm.

Sleeping Ariadne – she was abandoned on an island by Theus, her husband. She later married a god of some kind. Her cloak or "skenti" clings to her body so naturally – it is Greek of course – it is almost unbelievable that such a figure is stone, it is done so delicately.

Something I forgot to mention is MichaelAngelo's "Pieta" which is in St. Peters itself. Mary is holding the body of Jesus. The striking thing is the feeling expressed in the face of Mary.

From the museum we went to the Vatican Art Gallery building nearby. We hurried through it and I have a vague impression of some of the masterpieces – Raphael's "Transfiguration" – "Madonna of Foligno" – Domenichinon's "Communion of St. Jerome".

Next we walked through room after room of the Vatican Library and finally down to a lower level through a narrow winding passage to the Sistine Chapel where MichaelAngelo lay on his back for four years to do his masterpiece. "The Creation" and "The Last Judgment" are great; so are the paintings of Botticelli and Perugino, but we didn't have time to study them. I was disappointed in the colors, for they are quite dull – partly through age and partly through smoke from the many candles which have been burnt in the Sistine Chapel.

We had to leave the Vatican as it was two o'clock – we paid our guide and got on a streetcar going toward Porta San Paolo. We rode hanging on to the back of the trolley (customary in Rome these days), transferred a couple of times, and got out at St. Pauls Outside the Walls. The basilica is huge. I was interested in the cloisters and in the great mosaic on the facade of the basilica which I remembered from my art course. There is a lot of marble in and about this church. The windows are of alabaster and the light which filters through them is yellow – an odd effect. We stopped at a little bar near here and had a little benedictine. Evenhuis tells me that this liqueur was first brewed by the monks from Monte Cassino

We stopped at the Protestant Cemetery and looked at the graves of Keats and Shelley. It's a quiet shady spot. The pyramid of Caius Cestuis (30 BC) is on the edge of the cemetery. We rode the trolley back to the center of the city and walked until we found a restaurant. After we had eaten we decided to find the operahouse to buy tickets. We asked several people how to get there but nobody knew; finally, an old, old man offered to take us to the opera house. He spoke French, his wife was English – took us to the Teatro Opera and when we couldn't buy tickets, was careful to explain to us that tickets went on sale tomorrow morning between nine and nine-thirty. We walked home and ate fried potatoes and a little meat and drank marsala which Maria and Gina had gotten for us. It has been a very full day.

Saturday, October 21 – This morning we stopped first at the Opera House to get our tickets for tonight. It's the "Barber of Seville" – tickets $2.00 each. Then we walked down to the Corso Umberto to the Eliseo theater to get tickets to the ballet tomorrow night. Next we walked to the Piazza Venezia, then to the Capitoline Hill, up many steps. We wanted to see the Capitoline Museum. We walked up the steps to the top of the Capitol and stood there thinking of how Julius Caesar once went up to the Temple of Jupiter between two lines of elephants holding lighted torches in their trunks. I don't suppose it was morning then. We went into the museum. The three main attractions were three statues in a very large room: Capitoline Venus, beautifully and tenderly she has been formed just as Pygmalion's Galatea. Dying Gaul, portrays a young warrior dying on his shield. The third statue is of a young girl. Frank and I decided that it was Diana, goddess of the moon and of hunting. We saw, in another room, the original (reputedly) bronze wolf – the little boys were added later. The bust of Brutus was also here. In another room were four paintings by Michelangelo – small, but very well preserved. Of the other statues which we saw, I thought the best was a bronze about 18 inches high of a young boy pulling a splinter from his foot. It was called "Spinario" – would like to have a good copy of this.

We came out of the Capitoline Museum at 11:30 and walked down the Piazza Venezia. We heard about an exhibition of masterpieces at the Palazzo Venezia and after we found the entrance we decided to eat and then go to the exhibition. After we had eaten at the Air Corps Restaurant we came back along the Corso Vittorio Emanuele, stopped at an art shop where I paid $20.00 for a little bronze of "Fortuna". We went to the exhibit which consisted of masterpieces of the 15th and 17th centuries. I had seen many of these in magazines and books. These were the ones which impressed me: "Virgin Annunciate" by Antonello da Messina. Her shawl is dark blue, a wonderful face. Your attention is held by the eyes. I liked this. There were many other famous ones like Holbein's "Henry VIII", Georgioni's "Tempest", Correggio's "Danae", Raphael's "Marriage of the Virgin", "Deposition of Christ", "Portrait of the Fornarina", Dosso Dossi's "The Magician Circe", Titian's "Sacred and Profane Love", a fine Velasquez, "Portrait of Pope Innocent X", the face is strong, the colors bright.

Two large paintings of Caravaggio impressed me, "The Calling of Matthew", these figures are true to life, they aren't stylized or idealized – the light coming from the doorway gives a theatrical effect. The clothes on the boy in the center of the picture and the boy's face are very good. "The Martyrdom of St. Matthew" represents the slaying of St. Matthew while he was saying Mass.

We left the Palazzo Venezia, walked to a GI restaurant, ate, and then took a gherry to the Teatro Deli Opera. We enjoyed the Barber of Seville, went home and slept soundly. I almost forgot, after we came out of the Palazzo Venezia we walked to the Villa Medeci and that is a long walk to the Piazza di Spagna with the flower vendors at the foot of a long flight of steps. We walked up the steps to the Villa Medeci which is not open to the public – so we couldn't get in. We had a photographer come back to the Spanish steps with us because Frank wanted a picture taken in front of the house where Keats lived; we got the wrong house at first. Then we walked up and down the steps until we were ready to drop – I felt sorry for the poor Italian with his tripod and camera. Finally, we found the house which is pretty hard to miss since it is a museum. Well, we found the house and had our picture taken, then went inside and through the museum, came out – it seems the picture didn't turn out because the day was too dark. When we had asked him if there was enough light he said "Si, si". Well, we accepted the pictures which were not good and gave him forty lire for his work.

Sunday, October 22 – This morning we first went to St. Maria Maggiore, a basilica – it is huge and rich inside, a very old monument that has never been rebuilt. The interior is an example of how Byzantine architecture was fused into early Christian western churches.

Next, we walked to the Church of San Piertro in Vincoli – expressly to see Michelangelo's "Moses". The narrow street and steps which we ascended to get to the church reminded me of those in Jerusalem. Moses was completely covered with bricks to prevent damage from bombs (c'est la guerre), but we saw the chains of St. Peter which the Empress Eudoxia brought from Jerusalem. The little boys who guided us to the church were amazed that we did not give the priest who showed us the chains any money.

We walked down to the Coloseum and walked through it. We met a guide who volunteered to take us through the Roman Forum and the Palatine Hill. We hurried through and only a few things stand out in my mind – one is the view looking west from the Palatine – you can see the huge area that once was the Circus Maximus, the Temple of Sibyl with its umbrella-like roof, and the Arch of Janus; another is the view of the Forum from the Palatine – it was morning and beautiful – looking down on the ruins of temples. We walked through the Forum. Our guide pointed out to us what was once the College of the Vestal Virgins, Temple of Vesta, Temple of Castor and Pollux. We saw the Arch of Titus and the Arch of Septimius Severus. We had to leave as we had to check out at the rest camp. We checked out and rode back to the city, walked to the Basilica of St. John Lateran and were guided through by a boy of fifteen who spoke English, French and Italian. We saw the statues of the twelve apostles and the cloister, the "colonnaded court of the ancient monastry founded by Benedictines from Monte Cassino". It was peaceful in the cloister – green grass and a clean blue sky overhead. We walked back through the church and down toward the Eliseo theater. We stopped in a shop and had marsala and cakes and walked to the Eliseo. The ballet was wonderful. The theater was a modern one as beautiful as many in New York. We saw Delibes "Coppelia" and Stravinsky's "Petrouchka". It was the second ballet that I had ever seen and I enjoyed it. The prima ballerina was a girl named Attilia Radice – very beautiful, lithe, graceful, poetry in motion. I liked her best in Coppelia. We walked back from the Eliseo in the dark and I thought, "I wonder when I'll be seeing Rome next". We found our apartment at 33 Via Cernia – going through the same ritual of slowly walking down the dark streets – pausing at intervals to wait for the lights of passing cars to light up the street numbers – finally finding our doorway – up the dark steps (five flights of them) until we came to our floor. We had a bottle of sweet vermouth waiting for us. We drank it, talked a while and then went to bed. Had a wonderful, soothing, cool dreamless sleep.

Monday, Oct. 23 – Up early and walked to the Cassino delle Rose, the American Red Cross Club, where we were all to meet for our trip back. We finally left at about ten o'clock. First we had to go back to the rest camp to pick up my blouse which Bob Haddock had left there. The day was cloudy, but we were in pretty good spirits. Bill Holland of Texas had come late. He had been knocked out and rolled last night – lost his jacket and sweater. Some of the boys talked about their girls in Rome. One boy had a girl who sang "Shoe, shoe, shoe baby" all night. He told her he was going up to the front. "No front, Giorgo, al campo", she cried, he said.

The truck sputtered several times on the road and we had to stop for water; luckily, it was raining and there were plenty of puddles. We got to Naples at about 6:30, stopped the truck in front of the Red Cross and couldn't start it again. We pushed it down hill. It ran around the block and we had to park it. We were looking for the transient mess as we hadn't eaten all day – not since breakfast. We walked down the road to the transient mess which was in an apartment-house section of the city. We flashed our orders (they were supposed to read "Capri" – ours read " Rome") and were able to eat a good meal. We decided to look for a place to sleep. We went to the MP guard house, just around the block from the rest camp mess and left our barracks bags there. We looked for a place to sleep but couldn't get accomodations at any of the rest camp hotels. The MP's took us to a place where we got our room for a dollar-and-a-half a night. The woman who ran the hotel was very well educated, spoke good English and was helpful. We called up Major Carey and told him about the truck which the driver said needed a new radiator. The major said he would send another driver up with a new radiator, so we'll be here tomorrow. Drank several glasses of anisette and slept soundly.

Tuesday, October 24 – Today Barnum, a Pfc whose name I forget, and I walked down town after breakfast. We wanted to see Pompeii – we had all decided to meet at our quarters at 1:30 so we didn't have much time to see it. We climbed on the bus, rode with our party down to the train station, got on the train and were in Pompeii in about an hour. We saw Capri from the train window. Pompeii impressed me because it is so well preserved, but there is not the grandeur about it that there is about Rome. We left our party when we saw that we wouldn't have time enough to see everything, and walked through the ancient city to the far gate (gate of Nola) to ask about train connections. We were told that the train left from the other gate, Porta Marina. We walked through the city to the Porta Marina. We had a rush trip, but we saw the highlights of Pompeii – Temples of Apollo and Jupiter, Arch of Nero, Faun's House, house of Vettie with its wicked pictures painted on the walls, House of the Silver Wedding, House of the Golden Cupids. The houses are really huge mansions, homes of the rich of the ancient city. They have been restored, I understood the guide to say, and were not actually in their present state when first uncovered. Pompeii was destroyed in 79 AD by the eruption of a volcano – our guide said that it was not Vesuvius, but another volcano.

It is interesting to think of yourself walking on the very same streets where Nero rode in his chariot. The streets have ruts in them worn by chariot wheels. To be realistic, the odor of the place must have been foul – no sewers and horses all about the place. Even today, one can smell the towns of southern Italy as he approaches them. What must it have been like 1900 years ago in Pompeii.

We waited at the station – felt hungry for some peanuts, so we had a little boy get some for us – ten lire for a small bag. When the train finally came we squeezed on. It was crowded, which is an understatement. It was called an express but it stopped at approximately ten stations on the way into Naples. At every station some people would get off and a lot more would get on – huge oxen-like Italians, both men and women reeking of garlic – carrying suitcases, bundles of clothes, large boxes and boards. When an Italian gets on a crowded train he doesn't stay in one place, he heads for the middle of the car and gets there, not by crowding and shoving between the people in front of him or running into the man who happens to be in front of him, but by either pushing his suitcase or bundle directly into the back of the man in front of him or running into the man who happens to be in front of him. He is a psychologist – the man in front pushes his neighbor aside and the man in the rear goes through. We had a pretty rough ride back. Barnum got excited one time when a woman got his tie and jacket caught in her hand bag and started to walk to the rear of the car.

"Madame, my Jack-ketta", he said in a high-pitched voice. We laughed. When we got to Naples at about 2:30, we called the MP guardhouse from another MP station and learned that the boys didn't have the truck fixed. We walked back and ate a good meal in an apartment house near the one where we slept. Cost us $2.50 for wine, salad, eggs and chips. We had good conversation over our meal, then went for a walk. We decided to go to the show tonight as we weren't leaving until the morning; first, we stopped in a bar for a couple shots of anisette, felt good, ate again at the rest-camp mess. I lent my khakis to the truck driver – went to see Eleanor Powell in "Follies of 1942" or some such picture. It wasn't good, but it was a movie. Went to bed early.

Wednesday, October 25 – After breakfast we piled into the truck and were on our way about eight o'clock. Around noon the engine began to miss and finally stopped entirely. As we stood at the side of the road a soldier driving a "carry-all" – one of those extended touring cars with three seats in them – stopped. He was from our group and picked up those of us who were from headquarters squadron – Barnum, Maytis, Evenhuis, Haddock and I. We said goodbye to the boys in the truck and climbed into the carryall – it was a much smoother ride than the truck; Cohen, the driver, was to pick up Corporal Zitterman in Avalina, a clean little town, a little larger than Spinazzola. He left us off at Zitterman's hotel and said he was going to have the engine of the carryall checked over. We walked around the town, bought some postcards and Frank Evenhuis and I decided to have a look at a nice-looking bar across the street. We went in and saw some Canadian soldiers drinking and got into a conversation with them. We had some excellent marsalla, just the thing to rejuvenate us. We had several drinks, then went outside, then came back in as Cohen still hadn't shown up. The Canadians had been overseas for five years – they were an MP outfit. One was an old boy of thirty-nine years – most of them were nearly forty. One was named Fred, another one, Bill. Fred hadn't many teeth – when he would call "Frank", he would say ""Whooo ank", blowing between his lips to make an eff. The more he had to drink, the worse his eff's became. We felt pretty good and by this time quite hungry so we went to a nearby restaurant and had eggs and chips and wine. There was an accordion player and everyone was gay. Fred kept asking Frank about his sweater – he wanted it and when Frank wouldn't give it to him he called him "chicken-shit". We went back and drank some more marsalla after the meal. Eventually, Cohen showed up with the car – by this time we were very close friends with the Canadians. I almost forgot, we met a Czech who was in the intelligence unit of the Canadian Army. He talked to us for a long time and told us things which I suppose I should forget. His name was Bill and he was a chemical engineer in Czechoslovakia, had married a French girl and was just starting life when the war came. He was a prisoner for a while and then escaped to liberated Italy. He didn't like the Italians, said they were no good and were just waiting to get rid of him. He had been shot at several times at night. His wife was with him. He said she was a good wife, "Ah, they know how to live, these French", he said, "These girls here, all of them practically virgins, poof!" His wife must have taught him the "poof".

He said over and over, "Jeez Christ, I hope dees ting ends – I am so tired – Christ, I am so tired – you don't know how tired I am. There is no good German." He spoke several languages fluently, was very well educated and I knew that he was one of the few honest idealists who were fighting for a better world. A lot of them talk about it, but a fighter and an idealist together in one man – most of them have been killed. That leaves the practical men to take charge of the war. Maybe that's a lot of mumbo-jumbo. Who knows. We finally left Avalina and after a long, tedius, rough ride up and down hill, through dirty little villages perched on the top of mountains – smelling terrible because of their crude methods of sewage disposal – we arrived in Foggia. We went to the Red Cross for a bite to eat. Got to Spinazzola at about 8:30. Everyone wanted to know where we had been so long

Group public relations took this picture of me when I made corporal. It was sent to my hometown newspaper (the Butler Eagle) together with an article about my overseas service. They published this.

Corporal Kennedy

Here are the three members of the accounting section of the finance detachment, Candy Johnson, Andy Augena, and Bill Kennedy.

Candy Johnson, Andy Augena and Bill Kennedy
Accounting Section

Bill Kennedy and Andy Augena in the courtyard of the school in Spinazzola, Italy.

Bill Kennedy and Andy Augena, Spinazzola

This finance detachment picture in Spinazzola looks more military than the one taken fourteen months ago in Benghazi, Libya. Front row (LtoR) Lane, Duino, Johnson, Maj. Seitzer, Wood, Griswold, Gary. Second Row (LtoR) Zabowa, Willner, Kennedy, Berglund, Jensen, Feinstein. Third Row (LtoR) Benitz, Couch, Karmilowitz, Tew, Klahn, Agena.

Finance Detachment, Sept. 15, 1944

The six day visit to Rome was something to remember. I was very fortunate to have Frank Evanhuis as a companion. His knowledge off the city's history meant that we were able to see much of Rome, even in the short time that we had. The picture of us was taken in front of the Baths of Diocletian on October 20, 1944.

Bill Kennedy and Frank Evanhuis

Berglund had worked in a bank as a civilian. He could count a stack of money in no time – didn't make any mistakes. He was able to pick out the counterfeit currency which the major kept under the glass top of his desk and took credit for finding it when he showed it to the other officers. This bothered Berglund.

Berglund, Our Cashier

Regardless of the relationship of my Adjusted Service Rating Score to the present critical score and such changes as may be made herein prior to the defeat of Japan, I elect to remain in the Army. I understand that as a result of this choice I will not again be considered for separation under the Readjustment Regulations until after the defeat of Japan.

Waiver

In May 1945 the service group was leaving for a destination in the West Indies. The men with over two years overseas service had to sign a waiver to stay with the group. Sergeant major said if I would sign I would be a tech-sergeant the next day.

Me and Candy Johnson – Spinazzola

This is a pictue of Candy and me in the courtyard of the school a short time before he left for the states.

When we had time off from work in the office, we used to hike in the hills around Spinazzola. This picture was one of the days in early spring when Duino and I hiked in the hills and tried to get a little sun.

Duino and Me in the hills outside of Spinazzola

SPINAZZOLA –
THE LAST MONTHS

I make staff sergeant March 19, 1945

We recover the radio from the 519th

Germany surrenders May 7th

Major Seitzer leaves

This, that I'm writing now will serve as an epilogue to the twelfth book of my journals. I'm writing this about five months after the last entry so that I can look back on that period of my life. I hope I never feel as spiritless as I have felt in the past – during the time when I was writing this journal. I finally got to the stage where I couldn't even read a book; the fact that I couldn't become interested in a newspaper hadn't bothered me. I always excused this by rationalizing that I couldn't do anything about the present plight of the world while I was in the Army – not while I was an enlisted man anyway. But when I found that I couldn't read a book, I knew that I had reached the nadir of my fortunes.

The one good book which I read was one called "Trelawny". This, I've copied down from my notes: Trelawny took charge of the cremation of Shelley near Viareggio where Shelley's body was washed up. He and Byron stood by as the body of Shelley was almost consumed by flame. Trelawny: "I restore to nature, through fire, the elements of which this man was composed, earth, air, and water; everything is changed, but not annihilated; he is now a portion of that which he worshiped." Then he sprinkled spices and wine as a libation on the pyre. Byron remarked,

"Why Trelawny, I knew you were a pagan, but not that you were a pagan priest. You do it very well!" I remember in the Protestant Cemetery in Rome, standing in the shade of the old Roman Wall under which the ashes of Shelley and of Trelawny were buried side by side. Shelley's stone reads:

"Nothing of him that doth fade

But doth suffer a sea-change

Into something rich and strange – Shakespeare". It is from The Tempest.

Sometimes when I reread parts of my journal I think Romanavich (of the 981st MP company) may have been right when he said that a diary, if kept properly, would be worth a thousand dollars to anyone. When I think back to the many things that have happened in the last two-and-a-half years, I can see that If I had written something every day, this record would have been valuable in later years – when the significant events of the past two-and-a-half years have assumed their place in history. It would be a written record of the impact of contemporary events on the life and thinking of a soldier. I can't imagine who would buy it.

The only consolation for me is that Barbara will read it, no matter how long or boring it is. I think it's served a useful purpose for me, this journal record of mine, as an emotional outlet. When you write something down the paper doesn't talk back or point out the fallacy and specious reasoning. It enables me to close my notebook with a smug, complacent feeling that having a secret induces.

I'm sitting in our tent as I write this. There are five of us in the tent – Duino, Klahn,Gary, Jensen and myself. Our life isn't too bad. We have a stove built out of a third of a 55 gallon drum with a carburetor attachment; a hose runs from the carburetor to the gasoline supply (a 5 gallon can of gasoline outside the tent). Each morning Orville Jensen wakes up at 5:30 and lights the fire. When we wake up at seven, the water in the 5 gallon can on top of the stove is hot. We fill our helmets from the little faucet at the bottom of the 5 gallon can and place them in one of the three holders on the wash stand. The wash stand is an old arm chair with the back sawed off down to the height of the arm rests and a board nailed on top to hold soap, shaving lotion etc. It's rather hard on the rest of us when Orville doesn't wake up.

Friday, November 24, 1944 – Well, yesterday was a pretty good Thanksgiving – better than a year ago when we were at Bizerte in the mud. The meal was excellent – turkey, dressing, gravy, potatoes, creamed peas, salad, cranberry sauce, olives, oranges, nuts, coffee and wine. For dessert, apple pie with cheese, and ice cream and cake. We all ate too much. Our dinner was served at 2:30 and no one worked after that. Harry Wilner and

I took a walk later. We walked out the road past the hospital down a slight hill and read our mail – I had received two letters from Barbara. We walked on a little further – sat on a concrete wall and watched a few Italians picking olives. It was dusk. We talked about how fast the past year has gone – a whole year in Italy. In some ways it was slow. There's always the everlasting, never-ending sameness, emptiness of life. I've become a sergeant and I still feel the same. I suppose when I'm a lieutenant, I'll feel the same. What a life. I feel pretty damn helpless about the whole affair, more like a slave every day. When I look at my life to date, in retrospect, probably I've been a damn fool at more times than I've been the victim of fate. I'm feeling pretty moody tonight. I've found myself arguing when I know I'm wrong or trying to argue with people whom I know are wrong and to whom I realize it is impossible to prove anything. Ordinarily (outside the Army) I would ignore people like that, but I seem to be under a compulsion to argue with them. When I realize what I've done, it disgusts me. I hope I can remember that one maxim: it is impossible to argue with someone unless you use his criterion of values. Any man who amounts to anything knows and practices that. Guess I'll never be a sage.

Tuesday, November 28 – Yesterday was my day off. Just loafed most of the day. In the evening we saw Dennis Morgan and Ann Sheridan in "Shine on Harvest Moon". It was entertaining. Read a little book by Donn Byrne called "Messer Marco Polo". It was delightful. The book was published in 1920 when he was thirty-one. He led a gay, reckless international life (denounced as a professional Irishman by some) and died when he was thirty-nine in an automobile accident. Was a small nervous man who made enemies everywhere, but he made one good work when he wrote Messer Marco Polo. The world would be better if every man who ever lived had contributed one good work – not necessarily a great work, but simply a good one.

Tonight, we saw orientation films at the theater. There were some very good documentary films on New Britain and on the battle for Rome. I haven't yet finished my account of the Rome trip for my diary.

A lot of the boys are going home on 30-day temporary duty. Evenhuis, Hill and Hyson of the medics are leaving in December some time. Harry Willner had a chance to go but turned it down. He thinks there is a chance at permanent rotation.

Monday, December 4, 1944 – It's ten o'clock in the evening and I'm sitting by the radio listening to the Philadelphia Symphony –it's a work of Beethoven. I'm also drinking beer. Just wrote Barbara a double V-mail letter. I'm feeling a little better mentally this evening for some reason. We had an average movie tonight – a Signal Corps short entitled "Pick Up", which dealt with social diseases and ways and means of obtaining the same. They are effective, I imagine, for the unenlightened of our Army. Incidentally, they are very well done, technically, I mean. The army films being shown now are very different from the crude amateurish films in 1942. The Army has gradually become a streamlined and wider-awake organization (especially since it made me a sergeant). The main picture was called "Gildersleeve's Ghost" with Herold Perry. I enjoyed it. It made me think back to when Barbara and I used to listen to "The Great Gildersleeve" on Sunday afternoons in Cleveland. I'm a sentamentalist – I guess I'll never outgrow that. Probably I'll never outgrow the thought that I'll write a book someday either. I know that I'm too lazy to take the time and make the necessary effort and that if I did ever write one, it would be very, very bad – disconnected and garbled and syrupy and crude – that it would take years to write it. I'll probably never get over the idea and go through life thinking of what I might have done. What a deal!! I ought to force myself to sit down for a certain number of hours each week (or day) and convince myself that I can't write and that the reason I haven't written before is not that I just didn't have the time, but that I just do not have the ability. Oh well, someday I'll write it (I'm really laughing at myself).

In the accounting section we have three extra men, Duino, whom we always have for the first ten days of the month and Jimmy Rhodes and Orville Jensen whom the major intends to have for his accountants when the big breakup comes. The big breakup being when our finance office is split up into smaller units to be attached to the bomb groups. There are (it is rumored) several ratings open under the new setup, since each bomb group will have a ten-man office; but, there are also rumors that there are 150 finance men on their way over here from the states – time will tell. We don't know if the big split-up is coming before or after we go to the Pacific. It begins to look now as if we shall spend another spring in Italy. Will it be Spinazzola?

Saturday, December 9 – This morning in formation we were told the grand opening of our enlisted men's club was scheduled for tonight – that the girls who were hired for the entertainment were nice girls and couldn't be "pawed". We turned out to a man to see if he was right – he was. There was a magician who was pretty good and the main attraction – a girl who stripped – she had her "father" with her for protection – wasn't too good. I suppose she was too aloof, her figure was too roly-poly. The act went off without a hitch, the boys were very well behaved; afterwards, the little lady went over to the officers' club and did a repeat performance.

Sunday, December 10 – It rained and rained today. I went with the boys down to Bari to see Il Trovatore. It was very good and worth the uncomfortable, wet ride down and back. The settings were beautiful, the anvil chorus scene very effective. The gypsy, Azucena, was a contralto who was very good. Leonora was beautiful (her name is Tina Savona). I enjoyed this opera much more since I sat beside Chester Pearson and Hyman Feinstein who had a pair of field glasses. It brought the performance much nearer. At the conclusion of the opera we went over to the Red Cross snack bar and had coffee and cookies. Tim Benitz and I talked about other operas all the way home. He went regularly to the Met in New York City. Some day Barbara and I will take in an American production.

Sunday, Dec. 17 – Today I moved in with Maytis, Zabowa, Klahn and Harrod in a room in the Municipal Building. It's private and away from the office – also is on the second floor where the ventilation is better. Frank Evanhuis left today to go home for a 30 day furlough. I'll miss him. Yesterday, he and I had off. We went for a walk in the country through the local cemetery – mud on our feet. We walked through a field on a hillside to a place where we could see hills in the distance. The sun made huge patterns of light on the mountainside. We decided that the sky had "character" – full of clouds, rain clouds. We talked of unimportant things. I told him that I'd miss him. Frank told me that I was "conventional". I regarded that as a compliment. He is a good boy, Frank Evanhuis.

1945

Monday, January 1, 1945 – This is the third New Year's Day which I have celebrated overseas. We worked until two o'clock in the afternoon, then ate a big meal. In the evening we saw Bette Davis and Claude Raines in Mr. Skeffington. It was very good and I enjoyed it.

Tuesday, March 19 – Today I was made a Staff –Sergeant. Bull Klahn was made a Technical Sergeant. Don't feel any smarter.

Thursday, March 29 – I've just returned from a visit to Foggia where I saw Dale Byers. Had a good time. Dale was surprised that I was a Staff-Sergeant. Kemble (Captain Kemble), his room mate, informed me that it was the first time he had ever seen a corporal (my rank last summer when I visited them) become a Staff-Sergeant. I like Kemble, he's my friend

– very intelligent, brusque, calls a spade a spade, stimulating; a former architect, interior decorator, photographer, and accountant. He is in Intelligence, the group intelligence officer to be exact. He thinks the war will be over soon. What bothers me most about the whole trip was something that happened on the way home.

Moe Gary had come up to Foggia with me to see a friend of his. We got a ride from Foggia to Cerignola in a jeep driven by a Red Cross girl. She had been overseas 27 months. I asked her what induced a girl to come overseas and why she had stayed so long. "You tell me", she said. She said that she didn't know but that she wanted to go to CBI (China-Burma-India) when this was finished. I asked her what she had done before she came into the army. "Not very much", she said in her best rendition of the enigmatic smile of the Mona Lisa, "I did advertising copy and radio script". She was from New York City. I told her that if she wanted to write about her experiences that she had stayed too long. She said that she knew that now. I never found what her name was; I didn't ask her as good little Red Cross girls are expected to be pleasant without being familiar. I had been cross-examining her from the time I got into the jeep. She was an intelligent girl and I'll always wonder why she stayed overseas. She was (or seemed to be) attractive physically and obviously wasn't interested in marriage since she could have found herself a husband in less than 27 months. Something must have happened that bothers her. I guess it will bother me for some time. Wondered about catharsis by abreaction here. She was a very attractive intelligent girl. Incidentally, Moe Gary was in the back seat of the jeep too, so it was actually a three-way conversation. Moe laughed now and then.

From Cerignola to Spinazzola we rode on a bomb truck. The back of the truck was loaded with them and every time we hit a bump (which happened about every ten yards) Moe and I would hold our breath. We're just a little leary after the accident a while back. Some of the boys in another ordnance outfit were unloading bombs from a truck; they do this by rolling the bombs one at a time off of the back-end of a moving truck in a big field. Something happened and a lot of the men were blown to smithereens. That's the reason Moe and I worried.

While I was with Dale we talked about where all of the boys were – had a couple of drinks of Haig and Haig before dinner – just enough to make us mellow. Ate in officers' mess – very good food. Afterwards we talked and drank beer and went to the show.

We slept in late and went over to the officers' mess at nine o'clock for toast and coffee. While we were eating, in walked the wing major and a second lieutenant on an inspection tour. The lieutenant looked down his nose at me. The major had flat shallow blue eyes – strictly GI – ignored the enlisted man (me) in the dining room and wanted to get on with the inspection tour. Dale said, "Do you have any objection to having coffee and toast at this time?" He said "No" and sat down. I left after breakfast.

I caught a ride to Foggia with a truck driver who shouted at the top of his lungs and almost leaned out of the truck cab when he recognized a stream-lined blonde signorina who "wanted thirty bucks last year when I asked her 'quanta costa'". Met Moe and his brother Irvin at the Red Cross where we ate cinnamon rolls and coffee. Moe and I bid Irvin goodbye – on the way out we saw two WAAC Lt. Colonels and one full Colonel whom we did not salute. We thought that it probably was Ovetta Culp Hobby. Then we met the Red Cross girl in the jeep with a complex!! Tomorrow, I resolve to catch up on my diary which I have neglected for almost a year.

Sunday, April 9, 1945 – Among other things that I didn't do was to keep my resolution of the last entry. Incidentally, the lady colonel was not Hobby, but a nurse named Beachwood or Beachcraft, I think. It's my day off and I'm in the tent shivering. The wind is blowing and it's cool, though the sun is out. Last night we saw "Rhapsody in Blue" with Joan Leslie and I forget the name of the chap who played George Gershwin – an excellent picture, but long. Oscar Levant was very good. The night before last Moe Gary, Duino, Jensen and I went in to Spinazzola to see "The Woman at the Window" with Edward G Robinson and Joan Bennett. It was thrilling, the direction was tops. I've seen enough movies that I'm beginning to feel that I could be a movie critic. All you have to do is write as if you were holding your nose and when a good picture comes along, look for something wrong (the costumes were not strictly period or miss so-and-so's gowns were a trifle flamboyant or mr. so-and-so, it seems to me could have used a little more restraint in such-and-such a scene). What good is a critic who writes like that? They pay them for writing that way. As I started out to prove, if I weren't so deeply involved in numbers and their relation to money, I might seriously consider becoming a movie critic for a newspaper.

Wednesday, April 11 – Had a letter from my best girl today. She got two orchids for Easter Morning – delivered at 6:30. They looked nice on her yellow coat and she had a hat with flowers over one eye. Guess I'll have to wait until next Easter to take her to church.

Wednesday, April 25 – Well, a lot has happened in recent weeks: first, a letter from Mother telling me that Pa is recovering nicely from an appendectomy. It's amazing at his age – I don't remember what it is, but I think it's seventy-two. Next, we've moved to the new area, near the bomb group. The office is better than the wine cellar. We have electricity throughout the day and two windows in the accounting section. The camp area is level. We can see Castle Grande up on the mountain. This is supposed to be the oldest castle in Italy. Orville Jensen and I climbed it Sunday the 15th, the day after we heard about Roosevelt's death. There is little remaining except the lower walls and two of the lower rooms. It is admirably situated for defense. The view is beautiful. Under other circumstances, I could dream up there. Orville and I followed the rocky mountain ridge from the old camp area down to the castle. We were chased by three sheep dogs who came barking and running over the rocky barren plateau. We heard them when they were a quarter of a mile away as the wind was blowing from their direction. We walked just under the ridge and they lost us. We found parts of a wrecked airplane scattered all over the mountain. Worried about some shooting in one of the ravines – soldiers go there for skeet practice. We went over to the bomb group, took a shower and came home. Walked more that day than any for a long time.

Our latest rumor, confirmed by Major Seitzer is that the 519th is going home (it may be to the South Pacific). The payoff is that Major Seitzer and our office was originally slated to be with the 519th, but we wanted to stay in Spinazzola. What a deal! Tim Benitz, Al Tew, Griswold (Karmilowitz has already gone home) will be going either home or to the Pacific. They think it's home, probably before going to the Pacific theater. Lt. Smith is a pretty good officer. I forgot, he just made Captain as did Larry Trupo. I'm glad that Trupo made it. I always liked him.

Thursday, April 26 – More rumors about going home – this time we're supposed to be leaving soon. I certainly hope so – the news is good on all fronts and I'm more optomistic than I've been for a long time. I can't conceive of going back to Barbara again. It seems that it would be too much like heaven. I had a letter from her today. She chided me a little for not telling her how I voted when I had told Mother and Dad. It was purely unintensional. I thought that I wrote her that I was thinking of voting for Dewey and giving my reasons (all negative). I assumed that she assumed that I had voted for Dewey, or rather against Roosevelt. I'll learn someday – the one thing I shall never do is to keep secrets from my wife. But one think I want to keep from doing is crying on my wife's shoulder. What a problem. It won't seem so difficult when I'm with Barbara. The weather is cool yet, especially in the evenings. I wish I had more time to read and write in the evenings.

Friday, April 27 – Tonight, Major Seitzer, Klahn, "Zeek" Lane, Jimmy Rhodes and I hopped in the jeep and headed for Monte Malone where the 519th is located. Our main purpose: to bring back the radio which Karmilowitz had filched for them during the split-up. "Chum" Karmilowitz had come into the office in Spinazzola just at noon when no one was there except a few of the boys on detached service. He pulled off the connecting wires, threw the radio in a box and ran out to the truck which moved him to Monte Malone. Because of the peculiar circumstances surrounding the acquisition of the radio, nothing had been done about it. When the finance detachment of the 323rd Service Group was in Alexandria, Egypt, the radio had been obtained from a Special Service Officer. Major Olson's signature was affixed to a miscellaneous receipt (in Army parlance known as an "MR") by Chum and someone else, since transferred. It has been in the office ever since. When Major Seitzer took over the office from Lt. Jessup, he signed an MR to Jessup – the radio and all other office equipment was listed on it. The Major said that it should have gone to the office with the largest number of "old" men and he said he intended to draw lots for it. Nothing was done about it and Griswold and Tew felt quite smug about having the radio. They had goaded Karmilowitz into taking the radio in the first place. Chum Karmilowitz left for the states shortly after the break-up.

We enjoyed the scenery on the way to Monte Malone, known as the dirtiest city in Italy – even dirtier than Minervina which is the filthiest hole I had ever been in. The country is mountainous and green. It reminded me just a little of the country in the Hudson Valley in New York. We arrived there at 4:30 and talked. They are all ready to go home – most of them can't believe it yet. As we went into the mess hall a clerk was checking the towns where each man planned to spend his 21-day furlough. We didn't mention the radio in accordance with the Major's instructions. We sat down and talked after supper. I went out for a few minutes and when I came back the radio was gone. The major came in and Lane told us what had happened: the telephone rang and Lane answered it; it was Lt. Christopher Smith, the finance officer asking for Griswold; when he learned that Griswold was absent, he asked for his accountant who talked for a while and then hung up; immediately, the accountant began to disconnect the radio saying "Well, it's not playing, I guess I might as well take it up to the quarters". Then, Griswold walked in and the accountant said, "Hey, Lt. Smith wants you to take the radio up to your quarters." Griswold took the radio and walked out. A few minutes later I came in and then the Major appeared on the scene.

"Where's the radio?", he asked. No one was in the room except the four of us and a new boy from the 519th. Lane then told him that Griswold had taken it to his quarters. We went up and searched and found nothing. The major went into the Special Service Office and called up the colonel who is the commanding officer of the group. While he was talking to him he saw the radio underneath a table in the room. He ended his talk with the colonel abruptly, mused loudly for the ears of the corporal in the room, "Well, here's the finance radio that I've been looking for", and when the corporal (who had undoubtedly been instructed by Griswold to thwart any attempt to carry off the radio) made as if to interfere, said firmly, "Why, those sons of bitches, I'll court martial the whole office." The corporal shut up like a clam and the Major hurried out the door struggling to hold up the big radio. We were in the hall of the school building and carried the radio out to the jeep. We hopped in the car, covered the radio with my blanket (carried along expressly for that purpose) and drove madly down the bumpy dirt road. We felt exhilarated – an old score had been settled. Anti-climax: the Major had forgotten his jacket. When he called the next day (by telephone) they informed him that the supply sergeant had picked up all loose clothing. He didn't expect to get it back anyway.

Tuesday, May 1, 1945 – It would seem that we are entering the last month of the war. On April 28th a rumor that Germany had surrendered unconditionally spread all over the U.S. Most of the newspapers put out extras and many people were disappointed when President Truman squelched the rumor. Mussolini was executed by the partisans; all we know about it is what we read in Stars and Stripes which reported its information as largely based on rumor – that Mussolini and his mistress, Clara Petacci were both shot in the back as were a number of his henchmen. They were then displayed in the Piazza Loreto in Milan. One radio announcer spoke of them hanging by the heels. They were captured near Lake Como on their way to the Swiss border. Mussolini had his pockets stuffed with gold and English pounds. His final words were apparently not recorded for posterity.

Wednesday, May 2 -- This morning the first thing I heard over the loud speaker was someone reading a list of names of men in the squadron who were to report to Personnel immediately. They are being transferred to the 62nd and will go home very soon. The second thing that I heard was the announcer saying that the German radio had announced the death of Hitler and that Admiral Doenitz was the new head of the German state. At noon it was announced that Von Runstedt had been captured.

I have talked to some of the boys who are being transferred to the outfits going home. They say they will sign a waiver giving up all of their points which they have accumulated in this theater. I don't know what I would do if it came to that – would I go to a Replacement Depot and take my chances? I'll have to decide in a hurry because I think I'll be called on to sign such a paper soon.

Sunday, May 6 – This has been an eventful week. Thursday, May 3rd it was announced that all of the axis troops in Italy and northern Austria under General von Vietinghoff had surrendered unconditionally. Documents were signed at the Royal Palace in Caserta. Yesterday, all German troops facing Field Marshal Montgomery surrendered unconditionally. This means that the troops in Holland and Demark are finished. Friday, the Russians announced that Berlin had fallen. Hitler was said by the Germans to have died at his command post in the Reich Chancellery – the Russians say his body is not to be found. Time will tell what really happened. Things are moving so swiftly that the surrender of Germany is imminent. Now that it is upon us, I can't believe it. Is this what we have waited, hoped and prayed for? Is it really and truly happening? And yet everyone is calm. The denouement has been well-planned so that every soldier realizes that there is yet a job to be done in the Pacific. Had a wonderful letter from Barbara today. She realizes that the course of events in Europe has played havoc with our plans for a furlough this summer. I miss her so very much.

Monday, May 7 – This afternoon the news commentator announced that the German radio had broadcast a statement purporting to be from Grand Admiral Doenitz. The text: "Men and women of Germany, the fighting forces of our nation have surrendered unconditionally to the overwhelming superiority of our enemies." That is paraphrased somewhat. Of course, what the Allied Nations await are the statements of Truman, Churchill and Stalin – that will mean that V-E day is here.

Tonight, Bull Klahn and I went over to the bar at the bomb group and had a couple of rum-cokes and brought back a demijohn of Yugoslavian port wine. We drank a little and then went to the show. We saw Ann Baxter and John Hodiac in "Sunday Dinner for a Soldier". It was so poignant – the little girl and boy were excellent. Went to bed after the show.

Tuesday, May 8 – Today is V-E, Victory in Europe Day. It was announced this morning that the Big Three, Churchill, Stalin and Truman would make the announcement. Today is almost a holiday, except that we worked. There were many speeches – the gist of most of them is that some of us will go directly to the Pacific and those of us who will go home will not go home for some time – it was no surprise to most of us. All units have been restricted; this we assumed is to keep soldiers from going berserk – a wise move. I suppose, but it also prevented us from going in to Spinazzola to see "The Night of January 16th", a USO play. It is playing a one-night stand. We have formation at seven o'clock.

I have been thinking – I have been looking forward to this day for years and now that it is here, it should be very different. When I looked forward to the day I could imagine that my emotion would be one of relief and profound relief, I mean tempered of course with the realization that Japan is still at war with us. Now that it is here I have no feeling, just emptiness – maybe I have been here too long – my feelings have been dulled and jaded since the time I left the states. I suppose that the important thing is that we have been so far behind the lines and our life has been so normal in the last eighteen months that the war was something we read about – not with the detachment (i.e. freedom from military control) of the civilian population, but with the feeling that, good or bad, the news wouldn't vary our lives much from the norm. Now the question becomes, how soon do we move and where do we move. Thoughts of home are uppermost in our minds, but not many of us will see the states this year.

At the formation at 7:00 PM Major Keeler, our group executive officer (husband of Jane, the Red Cross girl), called together all of us with more than two year's service and told us that we would be given a choice if we had a G classification of going to a "Repple Depple and thence home or of staying with the group. The group is going – well, I won't write it down for a while, but it's with ATC and it's in the American theater. Reason I won't write it down is that I don't know any more about it. The salient point to us in finance is that we are critical – that means that we don't have any chance of getting out of the army until after the fall of Japan. It looks as if I won't get home for some time, but I intend to take TD at the first opportunity. The major has been gone for two days – he is going up to Rome. Our officer is Lt. C. M. Anderson from Hymen Feinstein's outfit where he is assistant finance officer. He is not deputized so he can't do anything except sign correspondence. Most of the time he draws pictures. He has been overseas almost a month – lives in Mississippi – was stationed in Texas for the last two years. He must have led a rough life.

Today, my name was drawn for a Benrus, shock-proof, pink, gold, fifteen-jewel wrist watch – cost $14.98. It's a very nice looking watch. Gary and I both won watches.

Sunday, May 13 – Well, a lot has happened in the last five days. I think it was Wednesday that Dave Barnum, our sergeant-major, asked Duino, Klahn and me if we wanted to stay with the outfit or go to a replacement depot and wait for a ride home. Klahn and I said "Yes" to the replacement depot and it looked good, but Wednesday evening there was a meeting of the group and we were told that the deal of the afternoon was off. We could not go to a replacement depot; instead, those of us with over two year's service must sign a waiver or be transferred to another group. The waiver reads: "Regardless of the relationship of my Adjustment Service Rating score to the present critical score and such changes as may be made herein prior to the defeat of Japan, I elect to remain in the Army. I understand that as a result of this choice I will not again be considered for separation under Readjustment Regulations until after the defeat of Japan." Klahn, Duino and I refused to sign the waiver.

Tuesday, May 15 – Dave Barnum, sergeant-major, came in to The office and wanted to talk to me. He said, "If you will sign the waiver to go with the group to Trinidad, you will be a tech sergeant tomorrow morning". It would be a lot easier staying with the group and it would be nice to be a tech sergeant, but it looks to me that I would be signing up for another two years overseas until Japan surrenders. I told Dave Barnum that I could not sign the waiver.

Klahn is being transferred to the 525th Air Service Group which is being formed from the 324th Service Group in Foggia. Duino and I are going to the 527th. We don't know who our finance officer will be, but rumor has it that Major Seitzer is not going with the group. He may be going with us. Time will tell. I don't know which way to turn. It seems that those of us who have over two year's service are being punished for not signing the waiver. How I envy those individuals who can accept what fate has in store for them and who never condemn themselves because it isn't them, it's fate. What I mean, of course, is that I wish I were clairvoyant.

We had an "overseas physical examination" the other day – received a typhus and a small pox shot. The vaccination is really taking this time – right below the one I had before I started to school.

Everything is torn up. I've sent two boxes of stuff home (one was a German helmet) in an attempt to make myself mobile. Comes now the old skin game. With three of us and the major being transferred out of the office, the other boys are watching us closely to see that we don't take too much with us. There is always some item of equipment that becomes a bone of contention.

We saw a good movie tonight – Mary Astor, Phillip Dorn and a blonde who looks like Ann Southern in "Blonde Fever". The dialogue was smart.

Wednesday, May 16 – I finished closing out Major Seitzer's accounts. I worked day and night for three days. Tonight, the major brought us up a quart of Philadelphia blended whiskey. Klahn, Rhodes and I had the major part of it and we felt pretty good. Later, the major came up to the office and we had a pretty good time. Klahn sang "Give my love to Nellie, Jack". Moe Gary and I sang our duet, "Swanee", and I recited two poems. Tomorrow we go up to our own outfits – Klahn to the 525th and Duino and I to the 527th. Klahn is going home. We don't know where we're going.

CERIGNOLA, ITALY

I am in the 527th group on detached service to the 43rd

I take a 9 hour flight in a Liberator described as an

"Aerial Tour of Northern Italy, Austria and Southern Germany"

Thursday, May 17 – This morning at nine o'clock Duino, Klahn, Newton (Supply sergeant) and I got into the truck with our equipment and set off for our new outfits. We took off our shirts and got a lot of sun. We went into Foggia, ate at the transient mess, dropped Newton off at the 60th Service Group Headquarters, went to the 18th Air Depot Group Finance Office to find out if they knew anything about our outfits. They had a good office – just like a bank. We arrived at our destination at 1:30 and Duino and I got all set up. This outfit is just being formed. The old 37th Service Group is being split up like the 323rd. First, all men with over two year's service were transferred to the 525th Service Group – they are going home – there are only a few of us with more than two year's service. The first sergeant told Duino and me that we would probably be leaving tomorrow for Cerignola to be on detached service with the 43rd Service Group. This is the group from Benghazi with Ray Gedair, Irucci, Vernon, "Pappy" – old friends. The other finance men assigned to the 527th haven't shown up yet.

Friday, May 18 – We waited around from noon, but no transportation. Finally, after the evening meal the truck came. It had been a hot day, but driving into Cerignola was cool and wonderful in the early evening. We rode in the back of the truck, standing so that the wind blew against us. The sun was low, the scent of the new-mown hay was perfume. The country is rolling, almost flat and one can see mountains in the distance on either side of the black top. I felt as if it were a good thing to be alive – even if one had no talent except the enjoyment of life.

Saturday, May 19 – Today has been a long day. First we moved our barracks bags and bed rolls from the hall of the school (where we slept last night) to an apartment on the second floor of an imposing building on Strada. We have three rooms, a bath and a kitchen; only, the kitchen is finito. The boys from the 18th Air Depot Group lived here and they had an explosion in the kitchen last winter.

We worked. I'm in officers' pay section until the end of the month. After the day's work Duino, Lane (also here on DS) and I went to see a movie – "The Animal Kingdom" with Ann Sheridan, Dennis Morgan, Alexis Smith and Jack Carson – good. Then we played a little ping-pong and went to a party given by the 43rd medics. There was a lot of extra liquor which they were trying to get rid of since they are going to break up. I drank too much for the second night in a row, this time champagne. I ought to be sent home to my wife so I won't want to drink. Saw a book last night in the medics' day room – Nora Waln, "Reaching for the Stars". I read her book on China (what was the name of that?). This is about Germany where she went with her husband in the British foreign office in 1934 and stayed until the war in Europe began.

Tuesday, May 22 – Tonight was a big night in the 43rd Headquarters bar. Ever since we came drinks and sandwiches have been free, but tonight was the biggest night of all. The reason that everything is free is the huge surplus in the squadron fund. When the 43rd is broken up any balance in the fund must go to the Veteran's Administration. Tonight they had an orchestra and a girl, name of Maria. She sang and danced with anyone who asked her. Later she did a solo. The boys say that she is the squadron whore. She doesn't sing very well, but she doesn't look too bad. She sang "Lilli Marlene", "Anapola" and a couple of Italian numbers and danced a sort of Italian rumba by herself. One of the boys who was at our table remarked that he had "shacked-up" with her for three weeks when they first got into town. He said that he had gone with her into a lot of houses and that she had given money to the people in every house. He said, "She may be an old you-know-what, but she's good-hearted". After all of the talent of the squadron had been utilized, Duino sang. I left the party at eleven o'clock before it got too rough.

Wednesday, May 23 – There's an Italian girl, a civilian employee, who works in the finance office. She is a typist, a one-finger artist, but fast. She types bond schedules and does routine office work. Her name is Anna. She has been working in the office about six months, speaks less English than she understands. She's a large girl, but charming. Somehow she heard about the girl Maria being at the party last night and said that Maria had plenty of money. "She must be a good typist", we said with tongue in cheek.

"No", Anna said. "No typist".

"What", we said. "How else could a girl get so much money?"

"Americans like", said Anna simply.

"Americans like, what?" we asked.

"Sing", said Anna.

"Yes, what else?" we said.

"Dance", said Anna.

"Yes", we said, "What else?"

"And Amore", said Anna, and giggled.

We all laughed with her. She's a good girl. When she checks over the bond schedules with Ed Haven, Ed reads and she checks. When they come to a name of Italian origin Ed will mispronounce it and Anna will correct his pronunciation and say, "He's a dago". I get a kick out of that. When she's tired she'll say, "I'm pooped". She was talking to Duino in Italian and he told me what she told him. She lived with her mother, father and sisters in Foggia. Came the war, the father was killed in a bombing, by American bombers. Anne, her mother and family moved to Cerignola to get away from the bombings. Anna had to work to support the family. The only place where she could work and get enough money was for the British – later for the Americans. Her friends and neighbors look down on her because she works for the Americans. They shun her. It isn't too bad now, but it will be bad after the Americans leave. She told Hank that sometimes she cries at night when she thinks how terrible their life is. I feel sorry for Anna and I can't help thinking of those pictures of the "collaborationists" – women who had their hair shaved off by the partisans of the different countries because they consorted with the Nazis. They were probably doing just what Anna has done and most certainly for the same reason – because they had to exist. I don't think that those who lived luxuriously were captured by the partisans. They were too rich for their blood. War is a very complex thing – little people suffer. What does the whole thing mean, this smashing out a way of life. Will it be good for those of the race who survive. Who can say that it will be better this way? I'm glad that I'm not an Italian – I wouldn't face the future with very much hope.

Saturday, June 2, 1945 – Well, we are now living on the third floor of the school building. We moved here about a week ago. I hated to leave the apartment, but it isn't so bad up here as there aren't many soldiers around. The 43rd has been broken up, the finance office is still here but the rest of Headquarters Squadron is out in the field.

We hear persistent rumors about our outfit, the 527th being moved to the states, thence to the Pacific. We have been told to get rid of our excess baggage, given a shipping number, and expect to be in Naples on the 5th. The latest is that the shipping date has been moved back slightly. I had three letters from Barbara, wonderful letters, boosted my morale. She tells me that I have 83 points, exactly what I figured. I may be able to get 84 out of it.

Before we left the apartment an amusing thing happened. I think it was the last night that the 43rd was here. They celebrated at their bar and Lane, Bellvage, Gillen and Lidia drank their share of liquor. Duino and I came home (to the apartment, then) early and went to bed. Anderson had been in bed for some time (incidentally, he has an M.A. in Agricultural Economics from Univ. of Minnesota), and I was just about asleep when the boys all reeled in. It was about 12:30 and they began banging doors and slamming lids and shouting. Then they left and I lay in bed trying to sleep; periodically, the door would slam with an ear-splitting noise. I lay there and quietly fumed.

Finally, I got up and Lane was in his room getting something out of his barracks bag. I asked him why they were slamming the door so often.

"We're getting these people next door to cook us sumpin' to eat. I think maybe they'll like this candy". I realized that he was drunk, but I was mad.

"God dammit, Sam, where's the key to the door?" I said. He was gone in a whiff and the door slammed again. They had opened the door and pulled the key out without turning it completely around. Result: the catch was not out and the door banged in the wind. They had the key with them and I couldn't release the catch without the key. I closed the door and slipped the safety latch over. I knew I would have to get up again when they came home. Some time later I heard the commotion outside the door. They were taking turns trying the key in the lock and couldn't understand why it didn't work. The people from across the hall were trying to make helpful suggestions in Italian. I slid back the safety latch and they finally came in after saying "Buono note" and "Gratzie". Then they talked so much that I couldn't get to sleep and finally, listening to Lidia, I had to laugh. They were talking to Andy, telling him what a wonderful evening they had had.

Zeke: "Well, we took the spam over and they mixed it with some onions and a little old vino – man was that good."

Lidia: "You should have been with us, Andy. Those people are just as nice", he said this in his southern drawl, "We said", he continued, "maybe, you'll think it's funny, us comin' in like this an' askin' you to fry us up a spread – maybe you'll think we're imposin'". I laughed so much to myself that I had to get up and go into their room to enjoy the joke with Anderson. He laughed too. The other guys couldn't see anything funny about it. I never did find out just what the Italians had said to Lidia when he demurred about breaking in on them at 12:30 and asking them to "fry up a spread". Funny world.

Sometimes I think of some of the things that happened when we were with Frankie Seitzer. Frankie decided back in November 1944 that he would stay in the Army of Occupation if he could. His girl works for the state department in Caserta so he has everything he needs here. We decided that he would be foolish not to. When the break-up took place and the various outfits and men were being transferred, he was in the office one day and, out of a clear blue sky made the statement, "Well, I'm afraid I'm going to get stuck in the Army of Occupation".

"I thought you wanted to get in the AOC," I said, "Would you get out of it if you had an opportunity?"

"Well, I won't fight it" he said.

Duino and I had our private little joke about that statement. About the current rumor that we are going home, I told Duino, "The way I feel about it, if they send me, I won't fight it." Not much – I'm so lonesome for Barbara that I have a heartache. I'm just tired of wondering and sick of being always in someone else's country – as a soldier. How I hope that Barbara and I will be together soon. I've been smoking again – had a relapse that started when I visited Dale Byers. Hope to call a halt again soon. I've been trying, but not very hard, I'm afraid. Well, I'm tired and I guess I'll go to sleep.

June 6, 1945 – Well, on this anniversary of D-Day I put in a full day. Duino and I have been on an "Aerial Tour of Northern Italy, Austria and Southern Germany", beginning for us at 4:30 this morning when we arose and ending at six o'clock this evening when we returned. It was long and grueling, but I'm glad that I went. I'm sitting on my bed now. I've had a cold shower and I'm drinking a coke (mixed with some very good cognac – Cognac Folonari) and thinking over everything that happened today. I feel very, very good after spending nine hours in the air today.

We rode out in the command car in the very early morning. Dawn was just breaking – the morning smelled cool and damp and earthy. The high two-wheeled carts had been moving since before dawn – carrying loads of hay, sacks of grain, a pig, wood. As we passed them the people looked at us with dull eyes – none of us spoke. It was the magic hour when the day was being born – a new, clean day. Duino and I got there too late to eat breakfast. We piled onto the truck which took us to Operations, thence to a place where we were given parachutes and life-preservers, called Mae Wests. We rode out to our Liberator and had our parachutes strapped on. The parachute is worn over the Mae West – part of the equipment of the Mae West is a little bag of dye which colors the water around the distressed airman an orange color. It's visible for miles, they say.

We took off at 7:30. It was the first time I had been in an airplane since September 1943 and I felt alive as soon as we were air-borne. Little toy towns, toy fields, tiny people, animals, trees, buildings, fences and railroads – and the sun just coming up to paint everything rosey gold. The first town we came to was Ancona. It looked interesting, a beautiful harbor, blue water, rugged gray cliffs rising abruptly out of the water and a sandy beach. I hope Mrs. K and I can visit it sometime. She should see it just as I did in the early morning.

We crossed the Adriatic for about thirty minutes, then came to Pola, a Yugoslavian city that is built around several islands. It is quite large – in one part of the city are the ruins of a great colosseum – it looks to be larger than the Roman Colosseum. We flew quite low every time we came to a city. I was in the waist, with a set of ear phones and a throat microphone – "Just like a real mission", I thought, "only without the flak and fighters". Next we flew over Trieste. It's quite large and seemed to be damaged by many bombings. I couldn't see any soldiers around. This city is at present a bone of contention between Yugoslavia and the United Nations.

From Trieste we flew over the Alps, or rather threaded our way through the passes. It became cold – we could see the snowy peaks above and below us. The mountains came to knife-like peaks that were not peaks, but ridges – they looked wicked. The first town we came to was Villach, Austria. We flew low. We could see that the character of the buildings was different; these buildings were German. Churches had steeples instead of domes. Houses had two and three stories. In the mountains they were chalets, very wide, high-pitched sloping roofs. The town had been heavily bombed. There were a few vehicles in the streets – several columns of soldiers marched down the road – I wonder what kind. This country was very green, heavily wooded, and there were many lakes, Klagenfurt lies on the tip of Worther Lake. It had been bombed mercilessly. Steyr was another badly-bombed town, but Linz, on the Danube had been hit very hard. It is on the main rail line between Munich and Vienna, home of the Reichwerke Hermann Goering Steel Works – largest of its kind in southern Europe. There were 165 ack-ack guns around Linz. The pilot and bombardier talked about combat missions they had made there – it had been a hot flak area.

We flew over Welc and then came down over Salzburg. We couldn't get over how beautiful the country was – this Austria – green velvet fields, thick forests, prosperous-looking farms, neat fences. It reminded me of central Pennsylvania, land of the Pennsey Dutch. I wondered why these people went to war. We flew directly over what was once Hitler's retreat on a mountain near the little town of Berchesgaden. His retreat has been completely obliterated – the earth is scorched brown and nothing remains of the buildings but crumpled walls and twisted melted girders. It was called the Eagles Nest and was in the Ober Kehl Alps.

We flew low over Munich and Oberwessenfeld, the airport south of the city. Munich has been damaged beyond repair. Huge buildings are shells – cathedral, factories, apartment houses, private homes – only the walls remain. There is nothing there, and yet, the streetcars are running. I actually felt sorry for the people of Munich.

We flew over the Alps from Munich. It was high and cold over Innsbruck, but we couldn't go down because of the mountains. On to Bolzano and Trento – we flew low here, it is the Brenner Pass. On the mountains around Trento, eight thousand feet in the air, the Germans had installed ack-ack batteries. How they managed to get those guns on top of the mountains, I can't imagine. The combat crew said they were very effective – we flew low to examine them, so low that we could smell the aroma of the pine trees and see the guns in the pits – now silenced.

Verona, of Shakespearean fame has been hit hard. It is a railroad terminus and manufacturing center. We could see ruins, coliseums and castles; in fact, throughout the trip we saw many castles, just as you would imagine them, surrounded by moats, on the top of high mountains.

Venice looked more modern than many towns of southern Italy from the air. We could see the Grand Canal, St. Marks, gondolas and motor launches. Venice is on the Lake of Venice. I wish I could see it from the ground. We flew over Bologna and then headed for home. By the time we started home my parachute had begun to feel very heavy and I felt that the men who flew certainly earned their flying pay.

Duino and I got back into town at six o'clock. Had a letter from Barbara waiting. It's a wonderful world. I'll certainly sleep tonight.

June 7, 1945 – Today has been another full day. Walter Butler of the old 981st MP Co. walked into the office this morning with the authorization for the Tunisian battle participation star for me. That gives me 89 points and now I'm wondering what happens. First, I'll have to get them on my service record.

We ate here and I went back with Butler to the company. They are in charge of the stockade on the Foggia-Manfredonia road. There are 276 prisoners. They are as isolated as we were in the African desert. They have a complete new set of officers, all good ones – there are 45 of the original hundred men still in the company. I visited with everyone. Saw Gillardi whose girl is still waiting for him; Hale, Sellars, Ford, now First Sergeant, Bennett, Duggan, Zilk, VanDuyne, Salzer, LuBair, Wolensky, Lembo, Cave, Homsey, Hoeffling (Willie owes about everyone in the company, Walter says), Calvin (Clemens, his very good buddy, has gone home). A lot of the boys are up at Capri where Koester has charge of them. VanDuyne drove me in to Manfredonia to see Zilk who is a sergeant and is the provost marshall of Manfredonia. They brought in a couple of Italians, a violinist and a guitarist who played for a while. Zilk rode me back to the stockade on his motorcycle – scared to death, I was. I ate with the boys, then Butler, Sellars and Hale rode back to Cerignola with me. It was a wonderful day, just as I thought it would be. They haven't changed any. They have all gone up in rank, not much, but some, and they don't think they'll ever get home. Yorkston is home, married to Leona, Young is home, Blossom is home married and expecting a baby. Sergeant Shaw is home. Kremin went out of his mind and is in a hospital. Phelps was sent home. We talked and reminisced about Ripley. Lockbourne, Deolali, Tobruk, and Benghazi. It was a very full day.

June 15, Friday – Last night I was CQ. I spent the time reading from the "Pocket Book of Modern American Short Stories" which Barbara sent me several months ago. I reread Ernest Hemingway's "The Snows of Kilimanjaro" for about the fifth or sixth time in the past five years. I think it's the best short story ever written to date.

June 16, Saturday – It's 10:30 PM and I've just heard an orchestra play Grieg's "Concert in A Minor", first movement. I hope I can remember to get it when I get back. We must have it in our musical library.

Tomorrow, Duino leaves for Pisa – he's going to be in the army of occupation. We've been together for two years, he and I – a lot has happened in that time. We've come across Africa and up Italy. Sometime when Barbara and I go to California we'll have a get-together. Meanwhile, those of us still in the

527th don't know what is going to happen to us. Rumor is that we'll go back with the 527th in July, unless we're pulled out and sent to a repple-depple before that time.

Sunday, June 17 – The reason I'm making an entry on this date is that I went to church with Anderson this morning. Services were in a tiny chapel – one room in a building across from the Officers' Red Cross Club. Judging from the size of it, there can't be many Protestants in Cerignola. As I came out a little Italian pointed to the chapel and said, "Buono, Sergeante?" and I said,

"Si, buono". He said,

"No buono for me, me Cattolica".

As we walked into the chapel, three little Italian children were dusting the benches. They were dressed in very worn, but spotless clothes and talked very softly, in whispers to be exact. They looked very pious. There was a little girl, about eight and her two brothers, younger.

Tuesday, June 19 – Today, Bellvage, Gillen, Anderson and I were transferred to the 455th Bomb Group which we assume is preliminary to a trip home. Duino is now in Pisa with the 533rd Air Servie Group in the Army of Occupation. Lidia is the only one left in the 527th with Lt. Anderson. Actually, we are still with the 536th on DS from the 455th. The question now is, how long do we wait for the boat home – I hope it is home.

Wednesday, June 20 – A letter from Barbara today. She writes that she will have her M. A. in American Culture in October. She's going the second semester at Western Reserve University. I don't guess there will be any conflict in our plans as things are moving at present. I'll be lucky to get home for Christmas. I wish I could get home to see her awarded her hood. We should have some pretty intelligent offspring with a mother who is an M.A. – even if their father is a scatter-brained romantic with an inferiority complex.

Thursday, June 21 – It wasn't a bad first day of summer – hot all day – it looked like rain, but it didn't. I took off this afternoon and took a sun bath on the roof. I'm getting quite brown, but I wish I could get in a little swimming. In one of the bomb groups they were shooting off defective bombs – some that were too sensitive to move to the Pacific. Rumor has it that one lot of bombs were made in which the inside of the casings had been coated with shellac or perhaps some secret substance, which after a time formed a gas which reacted to detonate the bombs. There were several instances of bomb dumps exploding for no apparent reason and one case at the 517th where a bomb exploded when the ordnance men were kicking them off of the truck – blew everything to smithereens. The explosion at Bari was, according to rumor, caused by these sensitive bombs. Today there were 13 separate explosions, about ten or twelve miles away – the windows in Cerignola that weren't closed, were broken. I can imagine what the Japanese must be going through.

Tonight was very clear. From the roof we could see the mountain range in the distance, about twenty-five miles. After dark we could see the lights out at the bomb groups.

Today was a holiday in Cerignola, St. Luigi Day. A band played this morning as it marched past the office. Tonight there was a procession, semi-religious as the band followed playing a little too sprightly a tune for a strictly religious celebration. The procession was led by the priests, according to hierarchical rank, dressed in their vestments, wearing miters, crimson chasubles, white dalmatics. Some of these must have been assistants or perhaps students. It was a colorful scene. We watched from the roof, six men carried a canopy of gold cloth – behind the men who carried the canopy the people followed in an orderly rank; they were followed by the band. Andy Anderson, our Master Sergeant, decided that the people in the parade were the wives, mothers, sisters and cousins of the Luigis of the town. The Luigis he maintained, were all of those dressed in the red chasubles. We had watched the people on the roofs of the houses near the building threshing wheat by flailing it with sticks. "We ought to get some of that wheat up here", said the agronomist, "and beat it like they do".

"It would be more fun to sow some oats", said I, getting doity. Martel bought some lemons, oranges, soda water, ice, sugar and gin and we've been drinking Tom Collins tonight. Martel taught us how to mix them "just like a bartender". I should have written to Barbara tonight. I wonder just what address I should use, the Bomb Group or the 536th Finance Office.

According to the latest rumor, we're to be about the last ones to leave Italy – those of us with over 85 points. This sounds logical to me as all of those units headed for the Pacific via the states should be moved first. I hope I'm home this fall.

Well, this is the end of another notebook. I don't imagine that anyone, even myself, will ever read all thirteen. Heaven knows how many more there will be before I get home, but they have been an outlet. Maybe Barbara will wade through all of them.

It has been hot for the past several days and the wind that blows almost continuously is dust-laden and so hot that it offers little relief.

Dorn Martell is an empiricist if there ever was one, and a Philistine to boot. He never reads books, he explains, because he's more interested in life as it really is – "I don't have to read any book to find out what life is". The night before last he got out his bottle of genuine Scotch whiskey and sold scotch and sodas for fifty cents a glass. The Italian soda water wasn't too bad and there was plenty of ice. I drank five and felt pretty good – not a trace of a hangover the next morning – that's good whiskey.

I've been reading "Mission to Moscow" and have read the last two issues of Time – am regaining my lost interest in current events. That, I think, is a healthy sign. I hope I'll be able to make enough money when I get back to give Barbara some of the nice things that she deserves.

Saturday, June 30 – Another hot day, pay day. Russ Kindig has been at Capri for the last six days and I've taken over civilian pay – it's a head ache. Planned to go swimming this afternoon and just as we were starting out in the weapons carrier, Crosby, chief clerk, called me back. There was a rush job on a payroll because the outfit was moving out, so I didn't go swimming.

I've been reading the Somerset Maugham Pocket Book – a novel, "Cakes and Ale". It reminded me somewhat of H. G. Wells' "Tono Bungay". I thought it very well done. Also reread "The Circle". I must read "Of Human Bondage".

Today, in the mail I received a long letter from Moe Gary from Natal. He writes that it is almost like the states – ice cream, hamburgers, coca cola, beer – everything seems plentiful. They went by boat to Trinidad and then flew to Natal. The plane flew low so that they could see the jungle country and the Amazon river. The office was all split up. Orville Jensen is no longer in finance; neither is Jimmy Rhodes. Moe, Orville, Rhodes and Tribble got promotions. They are near the beach but are working six and a half days a week and have little time for swimming.

I also got two letters from Barbara dated May 12 and 15 – she had just heard that some service units in Italy were on their way to the Pacific and thought of the possibilities – she was pretty down in the dumps. She feels better now, I think. The latest rumor is that those of us with over 85 points who are in the 455th Bomb Group will be on DS to Lt. Anderson in the 535th Service Group. We'll be moving out to the country and the dust again. I don't know why I feel so terribly down in the dumps. It's hard waiting. I have more overseas time than anyone around here except Bellvage (who has been home on TD) and Gillen, who has the same amount of time as I, and I can't get excited about anything in finance – I'm just burned out. I need my wife.

Monday, July 9, 1945 – Well, today has been the first breathing spell that I've had for fifteen days. I've set up Lt. Anderson's books and filing system, and finished the civilian pay department. For a while it was terrible: I worked from 7:30 in the morning to twelve every night and tried to run both departments. The lieutenant doesn't know much about finance overseas. Bellvage, Gillen and I still don't know where we stand – we're still in the 455th as far as we know. About a week ago all of the men who had been transferred into the 455th were sent back to their own outfits, except those of us in the 527th – because the 527th had left. We don't know where we are. We aren't in the 535th yet, we're still on detached service. I think Lt. Anderson is trying to keep us (I know he's trying to keep us and I think he doesn't care if it means we can't go home). I'm going to try to call Captain Fried at Fifteenth A.F. Headquarters and see if I can get home as soon as I get Ed Haven broken in as an accountant. God, how I want to go home. Lt. Anderson has been overseas only three months and he doesn't care. I don't blame him. If I had someone who was my eyes and ears and general flunky, I wouldn't want to release him. Anderson (Arthur Anderson, our master sergeant) was transferred out of the 455th because he had only 84 points (because enlisted reserve time doesn't count) into the 537th and went home with them. I thought a lot of him and I hated to see him go. He was a fine clean boy (or man since he is 37). I hope I see him at home. He left me his mattress and some stationery "to write to Barbara", he said.

Sunday, July 15 – Well, I've had another tough time of it. Just finished closing out Lt. Anderson's accounts. Yesterday at noon, 15th Air Force called up and informed him that he had to be closed out and in Naples this morning. Result: I worked from noon yesterday until 2:30 last night closing out everything. I must be a patriot. He went upstairs and drank with the boys and came down occasionally to sign what I had ready.

Monday, July 16 – Rested today and took a sun bath. In the afternoon Wing called up and told us that we could send two men from the office to Capri. We drew lots and Martel and I won. I couldn't believe it.

CAPRI

July 17th to July 21st

An enjoyable visit with my good friends

In the 981st MP Company

Tuesday, July 17 – Today, early, Lidia, Gillen, Martel and I set out in the weapons carrier for Naples. We drove through Caserta. The wide highway that runs directly from the palace toward Naples is very impressive. It is bounded on either side by a double row of tall and large maple trees. We ate at the rest camp mess (where I had eaten on the return trip from Rome) and at one o'clock were driven down to the boat that would take us to Capri.

On the boat I met Butler, Lembo, Hale, Moody, Eagen, Captain Baer and some of the other boys from the 981st MP company who were going over for a rest. We ought to have a real reunion with the boys who are the permanent party on Capri. We came to the island at about 4:30. It looked like something out of a story book – a little island with a rugged shore that rises up sheerly out of the sea and tapers off high up into a plateau. Villas are perched on the rugged cliffs and hills. I walked down the gangplank and I heard someone say, "I'm sorry, sergeant, you can't stay on this island", and there was Paul Koester. He told me to get in one of the jeeps at the end of the dock and he'd see me later. Martel and I got in one that was going to the Ercelano Hotel (ours) and we rode up the narrow asphalt switchback road bounded on either side by a high wall on which were morning glory vines, blue and pink, and beautiful, reddish-purple bougainvillea vines. On the terraces were rhodendron, pink and white, and oleanders, pink and red. We went to the Ercelano Hotel which we reached by taking a very narrow paved sidewalk that wound between and under buildings – outward from the square. At the Ercelano we were assigned to a small hotel called the "Splendide". We were in a large room with a view of the sea and a balcony – a bathroom across the hall. The beds were comfortable. Martel and I decided to go have a beer. We met John Dugan and went with him to the Tip-Top Bar where the whole 981st were drinking. We reminisced and after four beers I felt quite mellow. Martel and I went up and ate with

Dugan on the terrace of the Morgano Hotel. It was delightful – just below us a vine of bougainvillea grew on an arbor
that shaded the ground terrace of the hotel. In the distance
the hills of Capri and then the sea. I don't think I'll ever grow
tired of this place. I went down to get Walt Butler at the MP
station, but he was at the International Bar. I was persuaded
to stay with them, so I drank some rum-cokes and then we
walked over to the La Palma Hotel (that's the Wacs' hotel)
where a dance was in progress. Watched a couple of dances,
then we rode by jeep down to the hotel where the MP's stay –
the Svizzero Hotel. They had a couple of cases of beer which
they put on ice. I drank beer until it was quite late – everyone
in the company was there. Then I slept in Tarahaj's bed as he
was CQ – woke up in a half hour with mosquitoes all over
me. I put the mosquito bar up and went back to sleep. Woke
up early, had some coffee and went up to the square in a jeep.
Went back to the Splendide. Martel thought I had passed out
somewhere. We had breakfast at the Morgano and I went
swimming at the Piccola Marina. You wait in the square until
the jeep bus arrives – the road down to the beach is winding
and twisting and narrow. Swam awhile, then hired a kyak.
Went back for dinner at the Morgano – then went on the tour
to San Michele. We rode by jeep from the square up the narrow winding asphalt road that is cut out of the rocky mountainside to Anacapri, a smaller town on the central western
part of the island. First, we went through San Michele church.
It is famed for its majolica tile floor – representing the creation. This covered the entire floor of the little church. The
guide showed us the two tiles which had been replaced –
pointing out that the colors could not be matched with the
original. A lot of work must have gone into the floor. From
the church we walked up a narrow asphalt sidewalk, shaded
in places by pine trees (there are many on the island) to the
Villa San Michele. It was built by Dr. Axel Munthe, a Swedish
physician, about forty years ago. He wrote "The Story of San

Michele" which I must read someday. He certainly had an eye
for a view – he built one villa right on the edge of the high
cliff that forms the shoreline and from the balcony of this one
can see the ships in the sea far below. The architecture of the
villa is an amalgamation of ancient Roman, Greek and Italian
Renaissance. He wanted to use all of the relics that he found.
A woman of about fifty took us through the villa and told us
its history. We contribute a little something to the poor or
the association for the blind or something on the way out
the door. We stopped at a souvenir shop where the prices are
too high, then went down to the main part of Anacapri and
waited for the jeep. After we got to Capri, I went into the Air
Force Gift Shop on the Piazza and bought Barbara a bracelet with three bells. Walked back to the Splendide Hotel and
woke up Martel and Jess. Martel says the only smart thing the
Italians do is sleep in the afternoon – that he came here for a
rest so he intends to sleep.

We walked down to the Morgano – actually, it's right in
front of the Splendide, separated by a small garden; however,
the path (or sidewalk) is winding and that makes it about a
block from the Splendide to the Morgano. As you eat at tables
with white tablecloths, a Red Cross girl with a dog named Bismarck (she's always calling "Here Bizzey" in a whining voice)
comes around and briefs the men on the entertainment for the
evening. I walked down to the show. I forget what it was.

July 19, 1945 – This morning I went swimming and in the
afternoon took the Red Cross tour to Monte Tiberia and the
Villa Jovis ruins. Four of us (three lieutenants and I) and the
guide went on the tour. We decided to walk for the exercise. A
donkey cost two dollars, but I should have spent the money to
ride – it was a mistake for me to walk. It's a long steep grueling
climb to the top – it's on the highest point of the eastern half
of the island (1100 feet). When we got to the top we stopped
in a little two-room tufa building, bought some bad red wine.
We sat in the cooler room and looked at some pictures that an

old crone dressed like a gypsy brought out. She showed us a picture of her as a girl of twenty. One of the lieutenants had to show her the picture of his baby and a little one of his wife, so I exhibited mine.

Somehow or other, the old lady brought up the subject of lovers of different nations and it went something like this: "Spanish – Don Juan, Italian – Don Giovanni, English – Henry VIII, American – George Washington". The lieutenants tried to straighten her out. She said that a soldier had told her that George Washington fitted, but the lieutenants told her that it should be Tommy Manville. Just before we left she sang or rather chanted a song and drummed on her tambourine.

The guide took us to the cliff where Tiberius is reputed to have disposed of his women after they became pregnant. Then the guide threw a rock over the cliff and we waited several seconds before we heard it hit. The ruins of the Villa Jovis are quite extensive – it was built about 27-28 AD – must have been a beautiful palace. There are three huge cisterns for rain water; there were beautiful terraces, some have been restored, I guess. The view from the terrace is beautiful. I don't think you can look out of any window on Capri without seeing a beautiful view. Old Tiberius spent the last ten years of his life here. Lloyd C. Douglas mentions Capri in "The Robe", but I associate "South Wind" by Norman Douglas with Capri.

We walked down and I could tell that I was getting a blister on my little toe, left foot. The lieutenants were all from the same outfit, I don't know which one now, but I liked them. Got back to the Splendide and went to dinner after washing up. In the evening I went to the show.

Friday, July 20 – This morning I went swimming at the Piccola Marina. I haven't mentioned it, but this is one of the beauty spots on the island. Paul Koester of the 981st drove us down and he invited us to eat at the Albergo Svizzero tomorrow night. There will be steak, french fries and beaucoup beer. We accepted, Martel and I, since it wouldn't conflict with Martel's sleep. Koester took us through Gracie Field's villa. It must have cost a fortune – I forget how many terraces there were – all seaside villas must be built on terraces which provide a gradual descent to the sea or bay on this side of the island. We walked down to the Piccola Marina from the villa. From this beach you can see the sirens' rocks where Ulysses heard their fatal songs with impunity (I think). To the east within kyak distance are the Faraglioni, or lighthouse rocks – three famous rocks – they are about 325 feet high and on top of them, the guide book says, lives a species of blue lizard found no place else in the world. Incidentally, on the top of one of them is also an American flag waving in the breeze. It was put there by a GI from the 10th Mountain Division – one of the college boys, a medic told me. All around the beach the mountain juts directly out of the sea. The side of the mountain is rough and there is little vegetation. Several villas are built near the top – as you float on your back in the water you can look up at the white, yellow, pink and gray villas, and splotches of color that are bougainvillas, rhodedendrons, oleanders and morning glories. You can see olive trees and pine trees further up. They shade the winding road for a part of the way.

Martel left the beach early as he wanted to drink some beer. The bars open at eleven and serve beer until two o'clock. I went back to the piazza at noon and went to the dispensary which is just off the square. Felt a little self-conscious as the huge sign in front of the entrance indicated that it was primarily a "PRO" station and secondarily a dispensary. After you walk inside the building those whose destination is the dispensary turn right up a narrow turning flight of stairs while those who had been sinning turn left. The enlisted man on duty had me sit for a half hour with my left foot in a basin of epsom salts and water. He told me to come back the next day at the same time unless my toe bothered me in the interim, in which case I was to report on sick call in the morning.

From the dispensary I walked directly to the MP office as we were to leave on the trip around the island at 1:30 in a small motor boat which belonged to a friend of Koester's. Since Paul is in charge of the MP's on Capri, he has many friends among the civilian population of the island. I ate at the Albergo Svizzero and we rode down to the Piccola Marina and climbed into the motor launch. It was a delightful trip – from the Piccola Marina west to the Green Grotto – we backed out of this and went around the southwest tip, around the northwest tip to the entrance of the Blue Grotto.

We had to get into rowboats in order to ride through the narrow entrance of the grotto. We had to lie down in the boat – the oarsman can't use his oars as the entrance is not only low, but narrow. He pulls the rowboat through by hand – there is a chain overhead for this purpose. The sea at the entrance to the grotto is very blue, but inside it is light blue. The sunlight passes through a great opening in the rock under the level of the sea and it gave me the feeling that I sometimes get when I enter a cathedral. Everything is suffused in a blue light. If you put your hand in the water it looks silverish. We all got out of the boat and swam inside the grotto. We looked like so many fish – odd-looking fish. The water is supposed to be sixty feet deep, but you can see the bottom as it is very clear. It's about fifty yards long (I'm guessing) and not quite as wide. We came through the entrance and back to the motor launch and renewed our trip. Our next stop was the White Grotto – this is a cave halfway up the mountainous shore from sea level. We left the boat and climbed up a flight of steps cut in the rock to see the White Grotto. There were a few stalactites and stalagmites, but it was not very impressive. Back in the boat we rode through an arch in the Faraglioni, back to the Piccola Marina where I swam for a while – then on to the hotel for dinner and the show.

Saturday, July 21st – This morning I went on sick call – the doctor said I'd have to go to the hospital and there I went.

My little toe was no better and inflammation had spread to my foot, so I felt relieved. The hospital is in the Villa Sirene near the Quisisana Hotel. There were just two of us in the ward – an English soldier named Ernest Owers, and me. The beds are very comfortable and the meals are good. My foot is kept in wet packs and on a pillow. I put on pajamas of baby-blue flannel. It's the first time I've worn pajamas since I was on an overnight pass to Cleveland in 1942 – what a luxury! I didn't know how long I was going to be in, but I had a suspicion by this time that I was going to miss the steak, french fries and beer this evening. I talked to Ernie and slept a while.

In the evening Ernie and I had another patient to keep us company, a boy of 20, Bob somebody – he had a light case of flue – a little later an old man named Lyter came in. Ernie had a bad case of athletes foot – sometimes on his hands. He had been there seven days, there being no English hospital on the island. He said that he expected to be out of the army by Christmas since he was 36 and had been in four and a half years. During the time that I spent in the Villa Sirene he and I became close friends and talked a lot about England during the blitz. I thought at the time that the three days I spent in the hospital were wasted days, but now as I look back, I realize that they will be a part of my memories of Capri – largely because I became acquainted with that little emaciated, scrawny bloke, Ernie Owers. In the night the packs were taken off my foot and sulfadiazine salve put on my toe.

Sunday, July 22 – My foot is better this morning, but it is still red. Today, I finished "Mission to Moscow" – that's something accomplished. I started it just about a year ago. The hospital is just off the Via Camerelle on high enough ground that the sea is visible. It's beautiful at night. The balcony of our room is just over the Via Camerelle on the side of the villa facing the sea. I spent most of this day in bed and my view was toward the Mounts Capello and Cetrella. I could just see the rugged cliffs between the trunks of a palm tree and the ivey-covered trunk of a pine tree that grew in a plot of ground next to the Villa Sirene. I thought, "How shall I describe this, the way the sun filters through the dust in the evening just before it goes down, when it seems to me that the view that is framed by the trees is only a vision, ethereal and dreamlike, for just that time while the sun is sinking behind the mountains into the west – so that I look through gold dust, to the rugged hills – then quite suddenly the hills are in the shade.

I talked to Frank who is our ward boy in the evening. He wants to get the "Beach Job"; the boy who has this duty stays at the beach all day to be on hand for emergency first aid. Frank says, "All they do is take splinters out of signorinas and you get a free feel".

Ernie Owers is married, has no kids, owns a home (half of a duplex) in south-eastern England. I asked him about the bombs. They have fallen all around his house but not on it. Something I didn't know, the British government paid for individual air raid shelters and would install them if the owner agreed to put them where the workmen wanted. If the owner wanted to choose his own site, he installed the shelter himself. Also, the bomb damage to private homes was born by the government – actually, by all owners as they paid an extra tax for that. Ernie worked for the Bank of England in the printing office – printing five pound notes, one pound notes, and other bank paper. While he is in the service the bank makes up the difference between his salary as a private and what he used to get with the bank. His wife gets a check every two weeks for the difference.

Lyter came to the hospital in a blanket. He had sent his khakis to be laundered the night before, so he had no clothes with him. He had a temperature. Today, the soldier who had been rooming with him (Lyter never saw him before) came in and Lyter asked him to get his khakis for him. The soldier who was in od's (olive-drabs) (ground forces don't get khakis overseas) came in and sat down.

Lyter: "Did my laundry come back?"

Soldier in o d's: "Yeah, it came back."

Lyter: "Will you bring my khakis down?"

Soldier in o d's "Yeah, I'll bring them down. I just don't remember of seeing your khakis. I'll look again. I don't know, but I'll look again."

I thought, "There's a crooked s.o.b. if I ever saw one. He wants Lyter's khakis."

Lyter: "I can't understand that – I had only my khakis, a pair of socks and a pair of shorts in my laundry."

Soldier in o d's: "Yeah, well I'll look again, if I don't see you again, goodbye."

Lyter: "Look and see if you can find those khakis and send them down with somebody. I don't have any clothes."

Soldier in o d's: "Yeah, I'll do all right by you. I'll send down your laundry, but I just don't remember if your khakis came back or not, but I'll look again."

Naturally, Lyter's khakis never were seen by Lyter again. I talked to him afterwards and told him that I thought the soldier in od's had his khakis. He said, "I wouldn't be surprised." When I left the hospital Lyter was wearing a large one-piece fatigue suit, too big for him. The hospital boys had found it someplace.

Monday, July 23 – My foot is much better today. The doctor said it would not be necessary to use wet packs. Paul Koester came in and we talked for a while. He said he didn't know what had happened to me. I had told Walter Butler that I was going to the hospital, but apparently he forgot to tell both Koester and Martel as Martel came in later after Koester told him. Koester said, "Well, I looked in all the whore houses to see if you were there; then, as a last resort I came here." – making a joke. Martel came in later and brought down my barracks bag.

In the evening, I asked the doctor if I could go to the show and was given an okay. Young Bob wanted very much to go to the dance, but didn't see the doctor as he was out on the balcony when the doctor made his rounds. He was heart-broken as he had made arrangements to meet one of the signorinas at the dance. Later, at 10:30 when the doctor came around (Ernie told me) young Bob asked him if he could go to the dance as he had a date – "No", the doctor said, "but tell me who your girl is and I'll fix things up for you."

After the show I came back and told Ernie about it, then we talked until 1:30, mostly about the London blitz. His wife is an air raid warden. He showed me a picture of her – a large woman with a homely but pleasing face. He told me about their experiences in the first blitz. He and his wife and his mother and father lived together. Every evening the four of them would go down in the shelter and spend the night there. They could tell by the sound of the bombs falling just how close they were going to land. He said it is impossible to imagine how unnerving those screaming bombs can be. Some of them sound like a baby crying – some of the noise-makers don't explode and some of them do. He rode to work on the train every day. Several times there would be an unexploded bomb along the railroad track. Often, the tracks were hit and it took him three hours to get to work. He smoked endlessly as he talked and I could see him reliving that period, wondering how he had stood up and kept living, amazed, and then when it was over, emerging with a new confidence in himself and in all men. He said they were about ready to crack. "In the beginning we would see two Spitfires or Warhawks go up and break up a formation of Jerry bombers and make them turn tail". The tile on his house was stripped off one side of the roof from the force of a bomb that blew up his neighbor's house. Later, when he was in the army down at Plymouth walking with a nurse in the local lovers' retreat ("Ah", I thought, "so he wasn't always the faithful husband", but I made amends considering that those were parlous times) an air raid warden came up to him and made him put out his cigarette.

"You wouldn't do that if you were ever in a raid", the warden said. Ernie put out his cigarette and said nothing. He hadn't seen any action since he had been overseas two-and-a-half years, but in England he had had a bomb explode just behind him as he ran for a shelter. It threw him up against a wall, but he was unhurt. On another occasion he saw a line of men (a bucket brigade) who were fighting a fire beside a stone wall, blown right into the wall and mashed and mangled. One danger that I hadn't realized was that of falling ack-ack. He said that a great portion of the casualties were caused by this. London had a "terrific" ack-ack barrage, Ernie said. He saw a girl standing with her face upturned looking at the homeward bound Jerries. One minute she was standing there and the next minute she had no head to speak of – falling ack-ack. "You wouldn't believe it", he said, "but I've seen a girl, lying stark naked, not a stitch on her and not a mark on her body, dead after a bomb went off nearby. Bloody queer things, bombs. "I wish I could describe some of the dialect that Ernie Ower used – to me it was funny. I like him. I think his kind were the backbone of England. I know that it's their war and they feel that it is – they know they had to fight. I wonder how it is to feel like that? I went to bed feeling very tired – didn't dream about bombings as I thought I might.

July 24, Tuesday – This morning the doctor said I would probably leave tomorrow. I guess he'll give me my release tonight, but as my time has run out at the Splendide I'll have to make other arrangements. Paul Koester eased my mind on that when he came in at noon bringing my shoes which Martel had forgotten when he brought my barracks bag. Paul asked me to the Albergo Svizzero to spend the three days that I missed by being in the hospital. After dinner (the noon meal), I went swimming at the Piccolo Marina, came back, ate supper and went to the movie. Slept in the hospital

July 25, Wednesday – We, young Bob and I, were given our release this morning in time to get the boat, but I got off at the

MP station. Bill Evans went to one of the little shops near the MP station and bargained for a silk blouse for me (for Mrs. K) for $12 – supposed to be a $20 one, but of course it isn't. At eleven o'clock I went with the boys to drink beer, but before that I went for a walk to the Natural Arch. It's on the eastern part of the island. To get there you must walk for twenty minutes up and down a narrow path; then, when you can see the sea (or Gulf of Salerno, actually) the path winds down to a small built-up balcony. Standing on the balcony you can look through the arch. The country is ruggedly beautiful and there are several stone benches around, for twosomes. I would like to come here at sunset and in the moonlight. At one point in the path that leads to the Natural Arch, the trail divides and one path leads to the valley which you can see from the arch. Looking at the valley, I thought "I don't have enough time to really see this island."

When I came back I walked down to the right of the Hotel Quisisana along the Via Augusto to the Parco Augusto. From the terraces of this park you can see all of the southern part of Capri. There are pine trees trimmed right up to the top so that the view is unobstructed. This makes the pine trees look like umbrellas or mushrooms from a distance. There are stone shelters, now used for lovemaking but once used by picnickers, with stone seats, bridges, asphalt paths, benches and a large balcony with a view of the Faraglioni and the Piccola Marina At night from this balcony or from the balcony on top of the Roxy Theater you can see the lights of the many fishing boats. The men leave at sunset and come back at 3:30 or 4:00 AM. They catch many sharks, some weighing 200 pounds, but they are not man-eaters, they say.

The view from on top of the Roxy at night is something that can't be described. It's what you dream of and what you think of when you think of "Capri in the moonlight" or "A sea bathed in moonlight" – just beautiful.

Well, to get back to the MP station, I drank a few beers at eleven o'clock with Ed Turner, Redfield (new man), Andy Anderson, Paul Koester, and Harrison. Afterwards, we went down to the Albergo Svizzero and ate lunch – a very good lunch. The owner of the Albergo Svizzero is a German who has lived here on Capri for some time. He and his family live in one part of the hotel. They are friendly and intelligent – his sister is a wonderful cook. He said when the Germans occupied the island, he was drinking with them one night and a German colonel said to him, "Johnny (everybody calls him Johnny), tonight you drink with us, but one year from tonight you will drink with the Americans". Johnny couldn't get over this bit of truthful prophecy.

I am to sleep in Frank Martin's bed tonight as he is CQ. Stanley Slaskey and Ellsworth sleep in the same room. After lunch Redfield, Harrison, Moody and I rode up on the funicular railway from the Marina Grande to the Piazza – cost 5 lire – it was an experience. Moody spent the time making arrangements with a fisherman to go shark fishing some night. Moody is permanent party and can go anyplace.

Earlier, I had gone to Moody's and Koester's room and he had shown me the fishing rod that he made by hand while the company was in Sardinia. He made the reel too – caught some large trout with it using minnows for bait. He was proud of it. We talked, sitting on the balcony facing the sea – just below us a lemon grove and on a hill to the left, above the Grotto Azure Hotel, the pink villa that reputedly belongs to Williams, of the shaving cream Williams. We talked of the desert, of Captain Hinote and Lieutenant Svella, of men who had left the company, of the contrast between life with the 981st on Capri and life with the 981st in Gambut and Benghazi. I like Moody and Koester – I hope to see them again sometime.

Well, from the Piazza, Redfield, Harrison and I went down to the Piccola Marina to swim while Moody went to work. We came back at 4:30 and went down to the Albergo Svizzero to eat. Afterwards, I came back to the MP station and was sitting on the front step when Jinx Falkenburg walked by; she said "Hello". She has a nice figure – tall and tan. Moody and I walked down to the Tip-Top and had a rum and coke – then walked down to the Parco Augusto and watched the sea from one of the balconies – then we went to the show. Afterwards, we walked back to the MP station through the narrow, dark, tree-enclosed walks. The trees form an arcade – high walls on either side of the walks shut out the moonlight except for those places where there are no trees overhead. You can think as you walk home from the Roxy.

Outside of the MP station I met Frank Martin. He talked about Willie Hoeffling who has been drinking very heavily all of the time. He told me about one instance when Hoeffling had been drinking and went to bed. He was asleep when Phelps came in drunk, sat on Hoeffling's bed (or cot) and woke him up:

Willie: "What do you want?"

Phelps: "Hey Bill, Hey Bill, where's your bottle, huh?"

Willie: "Don't have no bottle".

Phelps: "Hey, listen to duh guy, my old pal, Bill. He's gonna do awright by me. How about a drink?"

Willie: "Go away Phelps. I don't have any bottle. Get off my bed and let me sleep".

Phelps: "What, you wouldn't treat your old pal Phelps that way. Where did you hide your bottle?"

Willie: "If you don't get off my bed I'm gonna throw you out."

Phelps: "Ha, Ha, Ha."

Willie got up and pushed Phelps out of the tent. Phelps came roaring back, took off his hat and handed it to Frank Martin who was also in the tent.

Phelps: "Here, hold my hat while I show dis guy."

Frank acted as moderator, stepped between them and then Phelps said: "Awright, I don't want to hit my old pal Bill."

Willie: "Hell, you're my friend, Phelps".

Frank left the tent for a while and when he came back they were both sitting on Hoeffling's bed drinking the bottle of whiskey that Hoeffling had in his barracks bag.

At about midnight we all rode down to the Albergo Svizzero and had beaucoup beer. I had a couple of rum-cokes and was feeling pretty good. Koester was high himself. He talked about when we were back in the desert and told me something that I never knew: that he used to help Lt. Svella censor the letters that we wrote. He said, "I know how it is with you and your wife, you always signed your letters, Mr. K. Did you ever get over that country-club complex?"

"What's that?" I said, "It's been so long and so much has happened."

Koester said, "You wrote 'Sometimes I think that after some of the things I've seen that I can never go to the places we used to go and do the things we used to do. I used to think that I could go anywhere with you." I felt a little flattered by his remembering that, but a little outraged at having my personal mail quoted. We wound it up at about 1:30 and I climbed into bed – after taking a last look by moonlight at the view from the balcony. Just after I got into bed I heard Frank's little dog bouncing around under the bed where he sleeps. I had put all of my clothes on top of my barracks bag so he couldn't drag them around. I slept fitfully since I had a mixture of rum and coke and beer in my stomach. Couldn't lie on my back as I would get sick, I knew; so, I lay on my side with my head high. It's a matter of foolish pride – not to get sick. I always made it a practice not to mix my drinks, but I was easily persuaded to drink beer with the boys after I had the rum and cokes. C'est la guerre.

July 26, Thursday – Woke up early as I usually do after I've been drinking and the first thing I saw when I got up was that my shirt was all wet. It was draped over the barracks bag and Frank's little mutt had used my barracks bag for a tree. Shaved and had breakfast with Claude Carroll – rode up to the MP station with Koester, Carroll, the lieutenant and a couple other boys. Went down to the store and bought the blouse which the girl there had cleared – bought a couple of silver bells. Got into the jeep and rode back to the Albergo Svizzero to pick up my barracks bag. Rode down to the boat with Koester and Gilbert, the MP who is on the boat trip from Capri to Naples and back every day. He is middle-aged, runs a tavern – his wife runs it now. I was the last person to board the boat as I talked with Koester at the gangplank – the MP's check everyone's pass – I had the feeling of being an insider as I didn't have to worry about a pass or anything. The Red Cross girl who owns Bismarck was going over to Naples, so she had to put Bismarck off the boat. "Goodbye Busy", she kept saying. Boy, did that get on my nerves. Busy finally stayed ashore and we took off. I rode in the cabin on the upper deck with Gilbert. We were later joined by a Red Cross girl (not the one with Busy) who had Kurt von Schussnig, Jr. with her. He was a nice-looking boy, blond and tanned, going to Rome. He had a lot of luggage and a tiny white dog on a leash. the Red Cross lady wanted to know if I would be able to get him a ride, but I told her that I didn't know Naples channels – that she should be able to get one through the Red Cross there. He talked to us, mostly to her, for some time about the underground movement in wartime Germany.

When I got to the rest camp hotel in Naples I went down to eat. While I was waiting I asked the guard how I would go a bout getting a ride to Foggia. The soldier behind me spoke up and said he was going to Foggia, in fact, to Cerignola. We got started at one-thirty. I rode in the cab of a six-by-six truck – it was very hot. It turned out that the driver was a chap named Teeter, 30 years old, from some place in Ohio. He had a wife and three kids and had been overseas 14 months – was homesick for his family. He was a reclassified infantryman. It was a hot ride, but better in the cab than out on the back of the truck. We got to Cerignola at about 6:30 – ate coffee and cookies at the Red Cross, then had steak sandwiches which Martel had thoughtfully brought back from the mess hall. Teeter drank ice cold beer and talked about his experiences in the infantry – 43 days at the front. A shell went off near him – blew him out of his fox hole. He regained consciousness three days later in a hospital. The left side of his body sometimes feels as if it were asleep. He can touch objects with his fingers and hand, but can't feel them. The nerves on his left side were torn and the doctor told him that except for this occasional loss of feeling in the left side of his body, he would have no trouble. He was reclassified and sent to an Air Service Group – the 535th.

The boys in the office had no new rumors. They asked me why I hadn't stayed longer. Captain J. Vaughan of the 531st Air Service Group in Foggia (he was formerly the Asst. Finance Officer of the 43rd) is disbursing from our office with our personnel except for Meyn, his chief clerk, whom he brought with him. There is a little friction because Meyn has taken over everything and the boys feel that it is still the 535th and not the 531st. They told me that Gillen and I almost went home – the C.O. of the group called up and asked what two men could be spared, so they held a meeting and decided that George and I should be the ones to go. Then Vaughan called up the 15th Air Force. Captain Fried said that we were essential and that we would be going home anyway in a few weeks. I knew that Fried wouldn't allow us to go home.

July 27, Friday – Back in accounting again. Captain Vaughan had a call from the CO again asking for one finance man. I could tell from this end of the line; then I heard Vaughan talking to Fried and just from the way he talked I knew that Vaughan didn't want to let me go. Later, Vaughan called me in and said, "Kennedy, do you want to go home by yourself or do you want to stay with the fellows in the office?" What an assinine question.

"I want to go home, whichever way is the quicker". I said.

"Well, take a case like this," said Capt. Vaughan looking hard at his pencil, poised on a sheet of blank paper, "If you knew that you were going home in three weeks, would you rather wait and go home with the office?"

"Captain, if I had a chance to go home alone tomorrow and I knew the office were leaving the day after, I'd want to go home tomorrow by myself. You've been in the army long enough to know that nothing is certain in the army.", I said, trying to clarify my position.

"Well, I don't know", he said and I thought afterwards that this conversation should have told me that it was Vaughan and not Fried that was keeping me from going home; he continued, "There's still a possibility. I have to talk to Captain Fried. It's not finished yet."

I was almost as furious with him as I was with Anderson when he had us transferred into the 535th. Vaughan has been over six months too. They don't think of anyone but themselves. Afterwards I heard Vaughan talk to Fried and then to some other officer. I heard him say, "Well, I thought at first I might lose some of them, but I don't think I'm going to lose anyone now". Bad cess to all finance officers!

Tonight we took the weapons carrier to Marguerita and went swimming and drank a lot of beer that we brought along in Martel's ice box. We all got quite drunk and sang all the way home. I forgot to mention that I had eighteen letters from Barbara when I got home from Capri. I felt good about it too.

Saturday, July 28 – Today we learn that we're to have two guards from the squadron to guard the money until pay day. It's amusing to us. We used to work in offices that paid out over a million dollars on payday. Captain Vaughan is very cautious. Meyn came in as we were going to chow in the evening and said, "Before I tell somebody to go, does anyone want to go to Foggia tomorrow to get the money. I need three men."

"What! Three men!" said everybody. Then, "It's the god damndest thing I ever heard. Three men to guard a hundred and fifty thousand dollars," etc.

Meyn said, "I want you to go to help count money, Al.", but Bellvage said,

"I'm gonna go to church tomorrow morning, and you and the U.S. Government ain't gonna stop me."

We silently filed out of the room and got in the weapons carrier and rode to chow. When we came back Vaughan wanted to see us all in the office. I thought he would ask us to air our troubles, but he avoided all of that and seemed to plead with us. He's very weak but I think he's like Seitzer: after he has his office organized, his word is law. Well, it ended up that Vernon Maines and I were the only ones not going to church, so we go to Foggia. Captain Vaughan talked about going to the beach after we come back.

Sunday, July 29 – We went to Foggia, got the money, and came back at 12:00 noon – ate and went to the beach. Took along plenty of beer – swam, sunbathed and drank beer – sang all the way home. We drank three cases and some odd bottles of beer. In the evening we drank some more. It was so hot that I couldn't sleep. At 2:30 Gillen and I went out looking for a pump, but the water was turned off. It's turned off in the building at 11:00 PM. We came back and put our cots up on the roof where we had a little breeze. The only drawback is that the sun comes up right in your eyes – and early too.

535th SERVICE GROUP
SURRENDER OF JAPAN

August 15, 1945

Tuesday, July 31 – Payday – I hope my last one overseas. I hope Captain Jessup comes back soon. He is our regular finance officer, though he hasn't joined us yet. He is somewhere in France at a rest camp. He was our assistant finance officer at the 323rd for a long time and came over with the 43rd. He's a prince of a fellow and I hope he gets here soon as I really want to see him. I kept his books back in the 323rd.

Wednesday, August 1, 1945 – Up to date at last. Had a nice letter from Mrs. K today. I forgot to mention that she sent my new pair of rimless glasses and "The Leaning Tower" by Katherine Ann Porter. Enjoyed it – would that I wrote like that. Barbara sent me a picture of her in her new coat (new to me) with a funny hat (ah, but attractive, but attractive!) and a picture of Judy trying on my cap with the visor. She looks sweet.

As we were riding back from chow (pork chops, corn, mashed potatoes and gravy, apple pie a la mode) we had just passed that section of the railroad siding where the track runs perpendicular up to the road and ends in a large bumper of earth and timber piles; actually, the track can't be seen from the road as there is a high brick wall running parallel to the road for the length of the block. We heard the engine steaming up the siding and just as we passed that place where the bumper was, we heard the rumble as the engine plowed right through the bumper. We stopped the car and all turned around to see two little boys scurrying out from the wall, as the engine forged ahead relentlessly crunching earth and bricks underneath its wheels and poking its nose halfway out into the road. It had gone through the brick wall as if it were a straw mat. Anything can happen in Italy today.

Friday, August 3 – Today Captain Jessup arrived. He walked into the office just as I thought he would – all tired out. He had just returned from Paris where he delivered a lot of French francs and had several days per diem and rest. He said prices were very high. He was the same old Jess that I remembered back in the 323rd when he was our assistant finance officer. He asked me how long I had been overseas and I told him that this was my34th month. He said, "You'll be better off going back with the group, then you'll stay there (in the states)". I told him I wasn't worrying about leaving the states once I got there as I had 89 points. He said, "Can Haven take over in accounting?" I told him "Yes" and he said,

"We'll see what we can do". Time will tell.

The boys had a drinking party lat night and A.B. Lidie (called Abie) and George Gillen were full of beer when they finally went up to bed. They have slept on the roof since the heat wave. This morning someone discovered that the chimney had been knocked down last night. Abie was the first one to make the office this morning and his story was full of holes. His story:

"I's makin my bed (Abie has an Oklahoma accent), rangin mah blankits and thot I heerd George say, 'I wonder if we could knowck over the chimney' and after ah finished my blankits I's thinkin' of comin' over to hepp him when I hear the thing go crashin' down. I think George jest leaned against it – I don't think he done it a-purpose". Abie is that way.

We were all worried about what Cosimo, the custodian of the building would do. Cosimo is a wiley Italian and when anything is not according to the book he goes up to the Town Mayor's office and tells tales.

George came down to the office at eleven o'clock and made his statement:

"I had my mattress hung on the wire clothes line to dry and as I went to pull it off, the chimney came down. I think it was a good thing it happened then – it might have fell down while I was sleeping and crushed me. I had my cot right beside the chimney."

It is my personal opinion that George caught hold of both ends of his mattress as it was on the wire and pulled. Abie and George claim that the strong wind which was blowing last night would have blown over the concrete and brick chimney anyway. It could only happen in Italy.

Saturday, August 4, 1945 – Today I got Capt. Vaughan's accounts in order and opened up Captain Jessup's account. In the evening John Meyn, chief clerk of the 531st (Vaughan brought him down here) and I went to the 304th Wing movie. Saw "It's In The Bag" with Fred Allen, Jack Benny and Robert Benchley – funny in places. Came back and drank beer and ate a cheese sandwich with George Miller of Lakewood and Meyn. We talked about Cleveland and then Meyn and I talked about literature. He says Sholem Asch's books are good. I must read them. Went up to the room and found the boys in a party mood again. Sometimes I'm sorry that Martel put his bar in our room. The boys stay up till all hours of the night drinking and throwing beer cans out the window. While Martel and I were at Capri they threw all of the chairs out the window – boys will be boys. Finally got to sleep to the lullaby of beer cans bouncing on the street below the windows. What a life.

Sunday, August 5, 1945 – Got up in time for breakfast this morning. Drove Capt. Vaughan and John Meyn up to Foggia. In the afternoon Capt. Jessup, Haven, Mains, Lidie, Iarussi, Tony and I went swimming at Margherita – this town is about as filthy as any that I have seen in Italy. The streets are gutted and full of stagnant water and filth of every description – they are the sewers of the town. The principal industries are the extracting of salt (by evaporation) from sea water and fishing. The town is out of bounds to allied troops and, as in most towns that are out of bounds, the natives are hostile to allied personnel. I have often wondered if this hostility is the cause for the place being out of bounds or the result. The hostility is evidenced by the filthy little street urchins who make obscene gestures and shout obscenities at passing vehicles. Margheriti di Savoia, to call it by its complete name, is not as hostile as many other towns that are branded with the cross in a circle because of the troops who use the beach on the far side of the town. They leave empty beer bottles for the tatterdemalions to carry home to sell. Glass bottles are at a premium in Italy today.

We drove through the town which is about three miles off the main highway by a very dusty, rough road – stopped to let off an Italian sailor whom we had given a lift – and down the road to the beach. On our left were the salt beds, large rectangular tracts of land bounded by dikes to hold the sea water until it evaporated, leaving the salts. Further to the left were many pentahedrons of salt – huge piles that looked the color of unmixed concrete, grayish. We came to the beach and, though there was a fisherman and his wife taking a siesta in the shade of a tilted two-wheeled cart, some of the boys stripped down and went in – later, the woman left. I was glad that I wore my trunks. The trip back was uneventful.

Monday, August 6, 1945 -- Two letters from Barbara today. She said that the 537th Air Service Group had landed on the 29th of July. That is Bill Forrest's outfit. He wrote that he had 30 days at home, 30 gallons of gas, and was ordered to report to Kerns, Utah after his furlough and expected to go to California from there.

Libero, the Italian who works in our office, came to me today and asked me if I would help him write a letter to the Regional Allied Control Commissioner of Venice. Libero, who is a Ph. D., University of Siena, explained to me that his step-brother, a man of 60, had been jailed by the authorities of Venice. He had been denounced as a collaborationist by his father-in-law. After he was in jail the father-in-law died. Libero knows that his step-brother is not a Fascist and has never been one. His mother wrote him from Venice begging him to do what he could to secure his step-brother's release. Aventino, the step-brother, was formerly a Captain in the Royal Venician Guards which is something of an achievement. He was working for the Soil Conservation (as a director, Libero says) at the time the Allies came to Venice.

In 1937 Aventino married a girl and later had a daughter by her. From the date of the marriage the father-in-law bore Aventino ill-will. When Aventino's wife died of typhus, the father-in-law went to Aventino and said, "Give me back the furniture which I gave my daughter when she was married to you."

"No", said Aventino, "that shall be our daughter's dowry when she comes of age."

The father-in-law bided his time and when the allies arrived and began to clean out the Fascists, he went to the authorities and accused Aventino of being a collaborationist. Aventino was arrested and imprisoned – not told upon what charge he was held. Neither was his 80-year-old mother, nor his sister told. He had lived with both of them in Venice.

Libero founded the Action Party section in Cerignola in 1943. The Action Party is an anti-Fascist party to which Count Sforza and Alberto Tarchiani, Italian envoy to the U.S.A. belong. He said that he was having influencial members of the Venician section of the Action Party intercede for his stepbrother. I told Libero that I understand how many people of a vindictive nature denounce their enemies as collaborationists. Libero said that the partisans were founded by good men, but many of the partisans were opportionists from the gutter who took malicious joy in seeing the suffering of men above their own status. He says that in northern Italy it is just like the French Revolution when sans-culottism ran rampant and men in liberty caps roamed the streets in mobs. I talk like a patrician. Well, I wrote the letter from Libero's rough draft. He has a little trouble in composing a letter in English, but he knows when something is correct. His wife is going to present him with a second child in about a month. I must remember to get some powder for him. A baby needs talcum powder – that I know

Tuesday, August 7, 1945 – This morning when Libero Salme came to work he invited me to dinner this evening because, he said, he was able to procure a good piece of meat at the market.

His wife is charming and intelligent and his little son is the same. His wife is going to have a baby in less than a month, but I think, normally she must be beautiful. She knows about as much English as I know Italian. Little Dante goes around asking everyone if they love him ("Tu bene?") – the answer to that is "Eo voglia bene", Liberto told me. We had a kind of noodles which the Italians call "little ears" because each one resembles the ear, somewhat. The tomato sauce was excellent and the wine just right. After the noodles and sauce and meat balls came the meat course – the meat was cooked with onions and peppers and was tender, which is an achievement in Italy today. I was beginning to feel the wine and could have kept drinking well into the night. After dinner we sat on the small balcony that overlooks the main street and Signora Salme served the demi-tasse, Italian coffee made of burnt wheat, barley grain and a blend of real coffee. It tasted faintly of popcorn to me. I enjoyed the evening very much. They showed me pictures of them when they were on their honeymoon in Rome, pictures of Dante (taken by an American soldier who befriended them up north and was later killed), pictures taken in 1908 of Aventino, pictures of Libero's brother, Dante who was a Captain in the Italian infantry in Greece. I left early and came home and went to a show at the 21st Engineers. Latest rumor is that we leave on the 29th of August. We hear that the brass in finance in the states is taking care of all finance men who have been overseas. I hope it's true.

Wednesday, August 8, 1945 – Something I've been meaning to write about is the absence of commercials on the AAF Expeditionary Stations in Foggia and Bari. We don't have commercials but:

"Drive carefully through town – better to have them wave at you than to shake their fist at you". Little GI shop-talks like this patterned after the spot commercial come over the air every day. Here are some others:

"Men, the post-war period that everyone has been talking about is here. Do you have money saved for that home you've always wanted? Start today – put your money in U. S. Savings Bonds or Soldiers' Deposits."

"Want to get 4% on your money? Invest your money in Soldiers' Deposits – see your personnel clerk today."

Another one is a monologue by a frog-voiced individual called "Dead-line Dan". His truck is always dead-lined, you see. Dead-line Dan says something to the effect that his truck doesn't need oil or gas or water, it just runs. Again, in a drunken voice he says that he knows he's sober enough to drive.

Another announcement urges soldiers to take the course offered by the Armed Forces Institute or to see their supply sergeant today if their shoes are wearing out.

Word has sifted down through the upper ranks that there is an increasing hostility toward the military by the civilians in Cerignola. We have been warned not to aggravate the situation by arguing with the civilians and not to travel about alone after dark. I wondered when things were coming to a climax. I hope I'm out of Italy when the riots start.

Friday, August 10, 1945 – I have a terrible cold that I caught the night before last when I played ping-pong and got overheated, then went to the movie at the signal company. It was on the roof and there was a cold breeze so --.

The big news today is the announcement by Radio Tokyo that Japan was willing to surrender unconditionally, provide she were allowed to keep Hirochito as ruler.

Russia had declared war on Japan on August 9th (yesterday) and on August 5th the first atom bomb was dropped on Hiroshima, Japan –

60% of the city was destructed we read. The Japanese called the bomb "inhumane". Tokyo radio reported that all living things in Hiroshima, human and animal, were literally seared to death. It probably hastened the end of the war.

One thing is all that concerns me – when do I get home. I'm tired.

Sunday, August 12, 1945 – I've just finished Mary Johnston's "To Have and To Hold", published in 1899. I should have read it when I was fourteen. It's full of romance, chivalry and deeds of derring-do as would gladden the heart of an old maid. The hero, Capt. Ralph Percy of the early Jamestown settlement does everything from capturing a pirate ship to dueling with the villain, a black-hearted nobleman named Lord Carnal who wants Jocelyn Leigh. Jocelyn ran off from the English court and joined a shipment of girls sent to Jamestown to be bought for tobacco. The girls were to serve as wives to the bachelors of the colony. Percy gets to keep his wife who learns to love him and everything is just too devine.

We hear no more news about when we move. Japan has not announced her acceptance of the terms of surrender yet, but it is certain to come. I'm very tired.

Tuesday, August 14, 1945 – I've been talking to Libero Salme, about world politics. Our discussion began when I asked him what happened to Virginio Guida, the former editor of the "Journale de'Italia. Libero said that Guida, together with his family, was wiped out in one of the raids on Rome in 1943. Libero thinks that our aircraft spotted his house and carefully blew it up – it's possible. I said that I thought that the only solution to the problem of war was for everyone to be employed, to have enough to eat, to be clothed adequately and to have enough leisure for enjoyment. Libero said that the people in Italy had a normal standard of living with leisure time (of course, his ideas of a "normal standard" are different from mine) but that the people of Italy thought when Mussolini told them of the huge amount of the materiel of war that they had, "If he is not telling us the truth, the King would tell us." The people still believed that the King was the supreme ruler. Libero said,

"If you had been living in Europe in 1940 when Hitler had control of the continent you could not see how he could lose."

He says the mistake that the Italian people made was under-estimating America. He does not think that they were morally wrong when they began their wars of aggression. A lot of the people in the United States think that the people of these conquered countries should believe that they were wrong to start wars. The people of Italy are realists – as long as there are obstacles to free trade, as long as the people in any section of this universe are kept from sharing the riches of the world, there will be wars. Of course, it's possible to go to extremes; some historian (Rousseau?) once said that the first man to put up a fence was the man who brought on wars – could be.

Libero feels that Italy should be allowed to retain those colonies which she acquired before Mussolini's Fascist aggression, because they should have some place to migrate, overcrowded as they are. I think he is right.

For my part, I'm satisfied that the German Army and the Japanese Army have been crushed. That is what we went to war for and that has been accomplished. The rest is so much fudge.

At 7:30 PM the program on the radio was interrupted for the following announcement: "The White House in Washington has announced that the Japanese reply to Allied terms of surrender is not acceptable." The announcer in the seven o'clock broadcast had stated that the international situation was all muddled, London had one statement, Bern, Switzerland, another, Tokyo, another, U.S. Information Service another, and the secretary at the White House yet another. What a dilemma! Tokyo radio speaks of surrender constantly, yet our air raids went out today on a grand scale. On the eleven o'clock newscast the announcer stated that it was "announced officially" that the Japanese reply has been received in Washington and "That's the situation as it is officially, until the next bulletin". I hope the thing ends soon. I wonder how many people are being killed because of the delay. Certainly is ironic.

Wrote a long letter to Mother apologizing for the belated birthday letter which I should have mailed on August 7th. Wrote one to Barbara to tell her that we had no later rumors. Forgot to tell her that the Fifteenth Air Force called up today to get our point totals again.

August 15, Wednesday. Headline from the Mediterranean Edition of Stars and Stripes: PEACE AT LAST. It seems that it actually is true; the Japanese have surrendered, agreed to cease hostilities, and to have Emperor Hirohito take orders from the supreme allied commander. The announcement was broadcast simultaneously from the four major Allied capitals at 1:00 AM Rome time. Pearl Harbor was forty-four months ago and all but ten months of that time was spent overseas for me. This is the day I've been waiting for, the day I thought at times that I'd never live to see. I would be more excited if I were home where I could enjoy it with Barbara. For most of us here, the most exciting thing that can happen is to go home. We've been waiting to go home for a long time and the waiting has us on edge. The surrender of Japan hasn't even phased us, and that's the truth.

Last night I thought about what it was like in basic training at Camp Croft. There was Lt. Nichols, small in stature, refined with a soft southern drawl, Sgt. Rice, a good man, Corporal Joe, tough – all likeable. Bill Barrett slept next to me. We used to talk about glazed doughnuts and his girl, Dot Lehman sent us some. Barbara sent me a clipping from the Cleveland Press that told of their marriage after Bill was transferred to a camp near Boston. Dick Doty, whom I met at the induction center had lost the index finger of his right hand and wanted to be a glider pilot. We were separated after we left Camp Perry and I never heard from him again. I wonder about all of the boys in basic. I forget their names, but we were very close as we made that first step from civilians to soldiers together. Will I ever see them again? It won't be the same if I do. Continuing the intro-spection I wonder if I am still a pacifist and what the posture of a pacifist is now. I know that when I see violence it is revolting to me. I'm glad that I never had to shoot my gun at the enemy, but I know that I would shoot someone who was going to shoot me or my loved ones. I don't think I'm a coward because I'm not afraid of dying. I keep asking myself why I didn't do something in this war since the Germans and the Japanese were shooting free peoples in the beginning. They didn't come to the United States but we were told that they intended to invade us. It seems that I was too shortsighted to forsee an invasion of the U. S.

We now have a great imperialistic nation and, like Great Britain, must expect to fight to keep it. We will have a wonderful luxurious existence. Is that good and will I enjoy living in luxury even though I didn't fight for it? Answer: "yes". What does that make me? Answer: "Tired as hell, that's what". I only know that I don't like the army and at times feel a real kinship to George Bernard Shaw who said during World War I, "The soldiers on both sides should shoot their officers and go home". Trouble is that I really liked almost all of the officers that I have known. Conclusion: We are still a lot of asses on this planet but we may be able to blow ourselves up with the new atomic bomb.

August 16, Thursday. After Al Bellvage and I returned from the movie, I talked to Toni, an Italian friend of Ralph Iarussi. Toni is twenty and is going to the university this fall. He is intelligent, of a good family – one of the young men who will build the new Italy. He is very concerned with the political situation. Coming from an upper middle-class family, he detests the communists, fears Russia, hates the English, and is very bitter about the future of Italy. He thinks the communists will ruin Italy. I told him that when the Italian people have food, clothing and work, they will be sound politically; until then, no party could expect the support of any great number of people.

Toni then told me about a ship that put in to a northern port with coal. It seems that it had to be unloaded by hand and the workers refused to unload the ship (he said the "communists refused"), so the captain sailed his ship full of coal out of the Italian port over to Marseilles. I told him that when the people had food and clothing the communists would lose their following. Toni said, "Yes in fifteen or twenty years". I said I thought the Italian nation would be economically normal in five years, but I knew that those who could help Italy would not be moved by any motives except their own profit. I realized that here the seeds of the next war are sowed, unless we put Italy on her feet again. Toni said.

"In your country, election is a good thing but here," and he named the five major parties, some of which want the king, some want democracy, some want communisms, "they can't get together". What he tried to tell me was that the lower classes in Italy have risen to the top. I didn't tell Toni but it seems to me that it is the only hope for the poor in Italy. If they could wipe out the landed gentry, a new Italy might emerge. I say "might" because it would happen only if the U.S.A. and Britain did not interfere. Obviously Russia is the big factor in the problem.

After we were no longer talking about Italy's present, Toni talked about Italy's past when the Americans were bombing their cities. He was on the train that ran from Bari to Foggia when Foggia had a big raid. When he arrived in Foggia the streets were strewn with the dead, children and babies, some horribly mangled. He said during the war 27,000 people were killed in air raids on Foggia.

"If the Italian people are sometimes angry with you, it is because of this", said Toni. He is an Idealist and cannot understand why the U.S. helped Russia when Stalin is a dictator just as is Franco and as were Mussolini and Hitler.

"Why you do this? Stalin kill many people too. Why do you help him?" What could I say?

August 18, Saturday. This morning Bellvage and I went down to the Red Cross for coffee where we met the civilian pay roll clerk of the 455th and his friend. The friend had been to Greece for three weeks to see his people there. I asked him what it was like there. He said there is enough food but the people need clothing. They do not like the British who have an army division camped outside of Athens. The people want to elect their own government, but will not go communistic as they distrust Russia. British propaganda has been planted there and the people resent it. There is a political right and left. The reason for the violence is that the British have armed the natives. It is a beautiful country. He said he had talked to an FBI man there who said the British were playing one party against the other so that the British could foist the king on the people "to preserve law and order." What is one to think? I've read that the British do this in Palestine to further their own ends.

There is a rumor around that the 304th Wing is sending home all men with over 85 points next Tuesday. I wonder. The latest is that men with 95 to 100 points in the 535th leave next Tuesday. Acting First Sergeant Greenblatt says he has a hot tip that all men with 85 points and over will be leaving very soon after Tuesday.

I talked with Libero this afternoon. He says that he hopes someday to come to America to live because only in America can a man say and write what he thinks.

Aug. 20, Monday. Spent the afternoon on the roof taking a sun bath. This evening at eight o'clock I went to Libero's apartment to have cake and wine and nuts. The cake is called cocolo, quite dry, unsweetened, made with olive oil and tomatoes with a hard crust on top. Libero says that farmers eat this cake in the evening with their wine. Libero's wife says that I remind her of Robert, an American soldier friend of theirs from Manfredonia. He was killed in an airplane crash – lived in St. Louis. He got toys for their little boy Dante. They showed me a picture of Robert and I showed Signora Salme the picture of Barbara.

"Very nice, very beautiful", she said, "Is she jealous?" This just about bowled me over. I told her that neither one of us is jealous, thinking that you had to be seeing each other to experience jealousy. Then, I thought you could say that after being separated for three years because of the war Barbara is probably as jealous of her rights as a wife as I am jealous of my rights as a husband.

Libero and I talked politics. He says the Socialists are in favor of a coalition with the Communists to procure a majority in Italy. If the Christian-Democrats and Action Party unite to fight such a coalition, it is probable that neither will have a majority. The British have informed the Italians that they would frown on such a Socialist-Communist alliance. I told Libero that I thought the first concern of UNRRA should be to get factories working in these countries, responding to his statement that the workers followed the communist banner because they were promised more by the communists. I hope things are built up again in Italy soon. It is very depressing.

We had a clothing inspection by the supply sergeant today. We turned in our extra items as we are supposed to be moving soon. Barbara wrote that she had her green taffeta housecoat cleaned in honor of my homecoming. Said she would let me work the zipper.

Aug. 23, Thursday. Spent some time this afternoon talking to Libero about Italy before the war. For 10,000 lire you could buy a small automobile $100 at the current rate of exchange, $500 then). He earned 2000 lire ($100) a month as a white-collar worker. Obviously, only the richest people could afford an automobile. Libero was with his battery north of the Volturno at the time of the armistice. The German troops nearby were forced to man their guns even though according to Libero they did not want to fire them. The situation was chaotic – no one knew what to expect – the Badoglio government was new and they didn't know how permanent. Libero says they were waiting for some order from the Badoglio government and when it came it was disappointing – all units north of the fluid German line were to hide and escape to the allied lines. This was a grave mistake, Libero said. The Germans had few troops in southern Italy at that time and they moved cautiously not knowing what the reaction of the Italian civilian population or or the Italian Army would be. Libero claims that if they had resisted the Germans they could have routed them out of southern Italy as far north as Rome and saved a lot of lives. It's an error that was made because of a decision made in haste; however, no one thought that the Germans would fight for Italy as they did.

Libero's wife and baby were in a small town near where he was stationed. He went to see them while he was still in uniform before they had received orders to hide. When he returned to his unit, which he had left believing that they would resist the Germans, he found his captain on the floor of the officers' barracks gasping and clutching his throat – a bullet through his head and blood all over the floor. Earlier, Libero said that he had talked to his captain and persuaded him to fight the Germans instead of giving in to them. The captain had written a letter to his mother saying that he was taking his life because he could not bear the disgrace. At first, Libero thought that the captain had been murdered because he could find no gun, but he later realized that the Germans had taken the gun as they requisitioned all of the Italian firearms, cannon and ammunition. Libero said that he felt helpless, that this was the most tragic personal experience of his life.

Libero and some of his companions then hid in a barn near the town where his wife was staying. His wife brought the baby who was a few weeks old and they hid together. Often the Germans would pass close by. One time they were hidden under the straw when the Germans were passing and the baby began to cry. His wife gave the baby her breast and he became quiet. All day long they would scan the horizen hoping to see allied troops. There were many people hiding in the barn.

One day his wife asked him to go to a field near the town to get some melons. Libero and several of the other men walked to the field. Libero had thrown away his uniform as the Germans captured all soldiers, wore a huge hat, the clothing of a shepherd, had a beard and carried a staff. When they were returning from the field with the melons, they saw an automobile of the Wehrmacht approaching. The others ran away but Libero, knowing that the Germans often shot at those who fled, walked slowly. "What are you doing here?" asked the German officer.

"I just came to get these melons that I have in my bag." said Libero. "Don't you know that it is forbidden for anyone to go near a military post?" said the German who was from the Herman Goering Division. Libero knew that it was a German ack-ack post but said,

"I did not know that it was a military post but I'll not come here again."

"All right, go on your way." said the German officer.

When Libero returned to the barn his wife was crying because the men who had run away from the Wehrmacht car had returned before him and told his wife that he was a prisoner of the Germans.

One day as they were watching from the barn, the troops that they saw approaching were British. They came in with a portable radio, a walkie-talkie, and asked about German positions. Libero told them about the German ack-ack post and they relayed the information.

When more British troops came to the area Libero decided to go into the small town where he and his wife had their clothes. The town had been bombed and both the highway bridge and the railway bridge were demolished. As he walked into the town the odor of decaying flesh became overpowering. The stench of the dead bodies, the hogs rooting about the rubble and eating the corpses, was too much for his stomach. He could not go on into the town.

Libero was able to sell a gold chain, a gift from his father-in-law, and his wife's earings to obtain money for food and transportation to Foggia. He found employment immediately, but he had only one suit from that December until the next October when he was able to go back to the little town where his clothes were. This is Libero's story of his battle with the miseries of life in wartime Italy. I admire his courage.

The Stars and Stripes carried an article assuring 85 pointers that they would be out of Italy before the end of September. Hope so.

August 27, Monday. My new nickname is "Steve". The other night we saw "A Tree Grows in Brooklyn". The husband of Aunt Kate was christened Steve but Aunt Kate liked Bill for a name so she and everyone else called him Bill. Finally, after Katie had his baby and it lived (she had lost five others) she called him Steve and so did everyone else. Since my name is Bill, I'm now Steve to the boys.

Last night we saw an excellent picture, "The Clock" with Robert Walker and Judy Garland. The story is about what happens during the two-day pass of a corporal who is about to go overseas. He goes to New York and there in Grand Central Station meets a little office worker who is as lonesome as he is. They walk through the park, see the zoo – all of this time she has qualms about being picked up by a soldier – and finally she breaks her date for the evening. By the time they realize that they are in love, he has just one afternoon and a night left. They become separated in a subway and finally meet again and decide to get married; just at 4:30 as the office where marriages are performed is closing. The marriage ceremony is poignant. It's a good picture with so many little touches that make it believable.

I could have gone to Switzerland if Haven had been here. He's in Venice and won't be back until the night of the first. It's tough to be a "wheel". Hope we go home soon.

Libero asked me if New York City was a clean city. "Do they have municipal showers for the use of the people?" he wanted to know. He can't conceive of a civilization where everyone has access to a bathroom with three fixtures. Take me back to heaven.

I just finished reading Walter Lippman's U.S. Foreign Policy, a very realistic study of our foreign policy. Lippman examines our behavior from the time we became united and, by tracing our growth step-by-step from the acquisition of Louisiana to the occupation of the Philippines, shows that our foreign policy became inadequate after 1900. Our foreign commitments became so great that we must rely on allies. He concludes that after the present war (the one just ended) we must have Britain, Russia and China as our allies and that any organization on the order of the League of Nations must be built around these four powers. I like Lippman's way of getting at the heart of a problem. I used to read his column every day. He is a very intelligent man.

August 28, Tuesday. Major Berglund of MTOUSA called Captain Jessup tonight and asked him if he wanted to take the detachment up to Venice to disburse for a while. He talked as if the group wouldn't be leaving until January. Jess said that he did not want to move up there until he found out if the group was leaving. We are all keeping our fingers crossed. I would rather wait in Venice than in Cerignola, but I wouldn't want to go to Venice if it would delay my departure five minutes.

August 30, Thursday. Gillen heard a rumor this morning to the effect that 90 point men would be leaving Monday – 89 point men should be leaving shortly thereafter and that's where I come in. At the Red Cross this morning we talked to one of the cooks who said that they were told that they'd have to turn in their stoves sometime next week. Greenblatt, Acting First Sergeant, told me yesterday when I went out to get my shoes and pants that we should be moving by the 5th of September. Barbara sent me a long typewritten letter telling me that she is getting nervous and jumpy waiting. Vesta told her that what she needed was a good loving. "Hurry home" she said. I told her that I felt the same and that it was to be expected since we hadn't seen each other for almost three years. Certainly love that woman. Finished Earth and High Heaven by Gwethalyn

Graham. It reminded me of James Gould Cousins The Just and The Unjust. The characters are so well done and intelligent; the dialogue is smart.

September 2, 1945 Sunday. We have heard from several different sources that our alert orders came today and that we are to move before the 10th. It looks as if we may get home in September. All rest camp leaves have been stopped and several low-point men have been transferred to the 5th Wing. It looks promising.

September 4, Tuesday. This morning I drove Libero up to Foggia to see Captain Vaughan who wants him to work in his office. I had to talk to Captain Jessup for a little while to get him to agree to my taking Libero there in the jeep. We are not supposed to have civilians riding in army vehicles. Finally, he said "Okay, but if anything happens, it's your ass." Jess is really a good man, though.

Captain Vaughan wasn't in the office but John Meyn and Leo Kennedy (CPA), cashier for the 531st, fixed up Libero with a pass and told him to come back tomorrow. There is a regular truck run from Cerignola to Foggia as a lot of the laborers who work in Foggia live in Cerignola; the pass would make it possible for Libero to get to Foggia on the truck. Came back and worked into the night. We are going to close out on the 7th – that's official. We'll probably move soon after that.

September 5th, Wednesday. At about eleven o'clock Libero came into the office and said, "Kennedy, I could not go to see Captain Vaughan this morning as my wife had a baby boy this morning." I congratulated him. He wanted me to call Captain Vaughan and explain, which I did. Captain Vaughan was not back from Naples yet but I talked to Leo Kennedy. Libero wanted me to go with him to see his wife and baby in the evening. I said I thought I should wait until his wife was not so tired but he said, "No, it is quite proper to visit at this time", so I did. The baby weighs seven and a half pounds (three and a half kilos to Libero). He looked very small lying in the bed beside his mother. She smoked a cigarette after she drank some chicken broth – looked pretty well. She was in labor only a half hour, but she said it was just as hard as having a first baby because she was not as healthy. Yesterday I had asked Libero whether he wanted a boy or a girl. He shrugged his shoulders and said, "We did not want to have this baby because of the way conditions are, but there is a saying in Italian that the Lord will provide for unwanted children." Libero and his wife are strict Roman Catholics.

We drank some Marsalla wine "to the new life" and I left. I felt good inside from seeing the new baby and partly from the marsalla. I was glad that I went up to see the young Salme, called "Domenico".

Sept. 6, Thursday. Tonight Iarussi and I went down to the 21st Engineers to see National Velvet. It was in technicolor and starred Mickey Rooney and a sweet, petite brunette whose name I forget. It was a good picture, exciting at times.

Sept. 7, Friday. Today was the big day. I didn't have much to do in the afternoon so I took a catnap for about an hour and a half as I knew I would have to work at night. The accounting section has the rough work when an office is closed. In the evening, as luck would have it, the lights were off. Captain Jessup and I went out to the group to get a couple of Coleman lanterns. When we got back to the office it seemed that the electricity was on in the half of the office across the hall; the half that we haven't used since the 43rd was disbanded. We moved everything over there and worked. Most of the boys helped me. Jessup and Haven worked right with me until 5:30 AM when they went to bed. I worked right through, finished up, shaved and went to breakfast. Felt good about closing out everything and going home: or rather, getting ready to go home.

Sept. 8, Saturday. Captain Vaughan and Meyn were at the office when I woke up at ten thirty. I slept a little after breakfast then went down and sealed everything. Captain Jessup and I went out to the group to get the Form 3 signed by the

Commanding Officer, then came back and mailed all packages. Captain Gruenwald and Meyer came up in the afternoon and got some more equipment, our counters, etc. In the evening we burned up all of the forms, had the place swept out, then went to the show. Al Bellvage came down to the show. He got back from Switzerland at about ten minutes after we had finished cleaning up – couldn't have timed it better. He said that Switzerland was so wonderful that he would take a year of occupation there in preference to going back to the states (Dreamland).

Sept. 9, Sunday. This morning I took my mattress (the one that Andy gave me) up to Libero's house and he gave me a couple of glasses of cherry brandy. It was very, very good. I told them goodbye. We loaded our goods on the truck and waved and shook hands with the crowd of people who were gathered to see us off. They were glad to see us go, I'm sure. We arrived at the group area just before lunch, set up our cots in what had been the bomb group dispensary. I repacked my duffle bag. Vern Mains found the duffle bag in the clothes closet in our room. In the evening we saw Lauren Bacall and H. Bogart "Rick" in "The Big Sleep". It was a murder mystery and very good, but very hard to follow, unless you see it twice. William Faulkner had a hand in writing the script.

Sept. 10, Monday. It rained hard last night. Gillen had his cot right under the skylight and the rain forced him to move. This afternoon we saw Greer Garson and Gregory Peck in "Valley of Decision", a story about the Pittsburgh Steel Mills. Greer Garson is excellent. I would like to see "Random Harvest".

Tonight, all of us in finance went over to the orderly room to check the Adjusted Service Rating Point Scores. We worked there with Greenblatt, the company clerk until 8:30. While we were there two soldiers came in. One of them wanted his points checked again. Al Bellvage had his record and told him that his points came to 68. He had lost one point because he had seven days bad time. It seems that he went AWOL to get married and go on a honeymoon. As he walked out he said to his buddy,

"Wait till I tell her, that f – kn' pig of mine cost me a point." His pal laughed at him, thinking it was a good joke.

Greenblatt is from Pittsburgh where he had two years at the Ad Arts School there. He wants to be a commercial artist. He showed us a picture that he had done in pastels on a large green blotter. He had copied it from a small picture. I told him that I thought it was very good.

Sept. 14, Friday. We've been here almost a week waiting and waiting for our orders to procede to Naples to the staging area. We are all impatient and on edge. Those of us with 85 points have given up hope of going home as casuals. Because they are holding us here, I feel that we'll be moving soon and yet – about twenty men who are over 35 with two years in the army have left for the Replacement Depot. We hear a different rumor every day, some good, some bad. Up until today the rumor was that we were to move tomorrow, but now we hear that it will be the 29th. Ho hum, well, I will get home this year, I hope.

I've been doing laundry for the last three days and am all set for the boat trip. It has settled down to an existence very similar to life aboard ship with one exception; we have one movie a day, all first-run pictures. Except for the movies and the morale, it will be like this during the trip home Some of the boys play cribbage continuously, others play solitaire continuously: then there are the round-the-clock poker games in which the games are continuous, the personnel changing; the crap games which are relatively short-lived but in which more money changes hands in less time than any other game of chance. There are also the bull sessions and a certain number of men reading. I am tired of waiting. I have Walt Whitman's Leaves of Grass that I read from time to time.

Vito Ciprini is in the cot beside mine. He is from Bedford, Ohio, knows Uncle Floyd and Auntie Cleo. He is a friend of Ralph Iarucci. Vito showed me a letter that he had received from the Postmaster of Bedford offering him a job. Vito wrote and said that he was interested. He had lived in Italy until he was twelve years old. He is thirty-four now and speaks English without an accent. He is a good, sincere, clean-living, sociable, hard-working boy. He has many relatives living around Naples. He has visited them and has acted as a go-between for other people in Bedford with relatives in Italy. He has just returned from the G.I. University in Florence where he spent a month. On the way back he stopped to visit his relatives. There was a girl, just 22, who has had three years at a university. She is something of an artist. Vito showed me her picture. She is a pretty girl, very serious – "Penseroso", as the Italians say. Vito took her to a movie and his aunt tagged along. He resented it because he thought she didn't trust him and it did cramp his style.

Now Vito, who is thinking seriously of marriage for himself, but to no particular girl, has a problem: will the Bedford girl who hasn't written for a month be available when he returns home, or should he have an understanding with "La Penserosa". Since Vito had told the Bedford girl not to write since he was on his way home, I advised him to wait until he returns home before making a decision. Wrote my honey tonight – love that woman.

Sept. 15, Saturday. Jessup came in tonight and told us that:

1. We are definitely leaving San Giovanni on the 19th, next Wednesday, three movies from now according to my reckoning;
2. Mains and Iarussi are being transferred to either Casserta or Naples. We think that this is because Vaughan's insistence that he doesn't have enough men. He won't actually have Mains and Iarussi (they wouldn't work for him and he knows it) but probably two other men from Casserta or Naples will go to Vaughan's office. Jessup is going up to Foggia tomorrow to see what he can do. Personally, I don't think there's much hope.

Last night, I had just fallen asleep when all hell broke loose. A big rat scurried into the room and was chased by half the men in the room. Finally Baker, the big corporal who drove for one of the colonels in Service Command, hit the rat with the small end of a broom stick. Somebody else ran out and got the cat who picked up the rat by the scruff of the neck and ran out with it.

At noon today, right after chow Iarussi chased a baby rat and hit it with a broomstick. He broke its hind leg. Somebody brought the cat in. The cat picked it up by the neck, the rat squealed, the cat put the head of the baby rat in its mouth. We heard a sickening "crunch". Someone said, "Get that damn cat out of here before she gets blood all over the floor." Then we chased the cat around. Soon there was nothing left of the baby rat except the tail – hanging out of the cat's mouth. Finally, she swallowed that and scooted out the door. What a pasttime for adult men.

This afternoon we saw Lana Turner and Loraine Day in Keep Your Powder Dry. It was very good. I had seen it before on Capri. Wrote a letter to Barbara.

One of the boys who is with us here waiting to go home is Teeter. He is the boy from Ravenna, Ohio who drove me from Naples to Cerignola when I came back from Capri. He sleeps in the same room with Mains and Lidia (Abie) and is the only man around with tobacco. I go to him when I need a smoke. Teeter says, "One reason I know my old lady's true to me is she's bashful as hell. She's too bashful to run around." Funny, funny, funny world. I don't know if I would have it any different if I were Mr. Big.

Sept. 18, Tuesday. We are sitting around talking by candle light. It is eight o'clock and we will be going to bed soon as we get up at four o'clock tomorrow morning, eat breakfast at four-thirty, and leave for Naples at six-thirty. We spent today cleaning up the area. Haven has been transferred to Bari, Mains and Iarussi to Casserta to Seitzer's office, I think. We of the finance office have been selected for several details of late since Sunday when Bellvage, Gillen, Mains and Haven went to Foggia to visit the boys in the 529th. They had passes for Sunday only and stayed overnight. Monday morning at eight o'clock formation the first sergeant announced that they were AWOL and when they came back at ten-thirty they were given a lecture by the first sergeant, Major May, the squadron commander, and Captain Jessup, who told Bellvage that he was taking Goldberg (S/Sgt from another finance office) with him to Naples instead of Bellvage. I don't know why he took him instead of me or Lidia. The only thing I can think of is that he was mad at the whole office because of what the four of them did. He was very careful not to be so hypersensitive as to our comings and goings before his accounts were closed out. I guess I'll forgive him as I feel pretty good about where we're going. The boys brought me a lot of very fine pictures of Capri which they developed while they were in Foggia. I'll write Barbara when we get to Naples. It's going to be pretty wonderful. I hope I have some mail waiting for me at Naples.

This is a picture of our finance group which Art Anderson called the "Changeable, transferable 527th, 455th, 535th detached service bunch". Left to Right: Al Bellvage, George Gillen, Lt. C.M. Anderson, A.B. Lidea, Art Anderson, Bill Kennedy, June 1945, Cerignola, Italy.

Detached Service Finance Group

I think this picture was taken on the day that Art Anderson persuaded me to go to church with him. It was along Oleander Boulevard. Left to Right: Unidentified "Ragazzi", Art Anderson, Bill Kennedy.

Art Anderson and Bill Kennedy

William M. Kennedy

After the grain is harvested some of it is stored in deep concrete pits in this level area in Cerignola.

Italian Workers Stacking and Hauling Wheat from one of the Grain Pits

This is a beautiful cathedral along Main Street in Cerignola.

The Cathedral, Cerignola

404

STAGING AREA NO. 3 –
"THE CRATER"

September 19th to October 8th 1945

VOYAGE HOME ON THE
DANIEL H. LOWENSDALE

October 9 – October 27, 1945

Sept. 23, Sunday. We have been here at Staging Area No. 3, "The Crater" since last Wednesday. We know now that we are expected to sail on the Lownsdale on October 2nd. It's a very difficult business, this waiting for the boat.

Our area is situated in a crater which is about a mile in diameter. It's thickly wooded and quite cool even during the afternoon hours when the sun beats down. The sides of the crater rise abruptly and are also heavily wooded. I would guess that the top of the rim at its highest point is about nine hundred feet. When Major Mays talked to the squadron in formation he said, "I might as well tell you before you find out for yourselves, the woods in the hills are full of whores." Naturally, certain of the boys had to investigate that night. In our tent we warn each other soberly every time one of us goes to the latrine at the foot of the hills,

"Remember, the hills are full of whores." Mayor Mays is an elderly man and some of the boys call him "Fuddy-duddy Mays".

We sleep in tents on cots; when we were issued extra coverings, I got a sleeping bag instead of a quilt. It's very convenient; I keep my blankets folded on the cot as an insulation of the cold from the ground, and sleep in the sleeping bag. The area is covered with fine dust about three inches deep in some places and this blows all over when anyone stirs it up; that is, walks on it which is most of the time. There has been a full moon for the past few nights. It lights up the entire camp shining through the trees and making a fairyland of the crater.

There is a Red Cross Lounge, Snack Bar, Barber Shop, Tailor Shop, showers and a dispensary – everything to make life comfortable for men waiting for the boat home. During certain periods of the day recordings are played over the public address system. Eight men sleep in each tent. It is a little crowded, but we don't spend much time in the tent. In our tent we have Bellvage, Gillen and I from finance; Ed Zeisler and Vito Cipriani from the old 455th Bomb Group and Baker, Moon

Lazaro and Tom Papa from Air Force Service Command in Bari. Baker, who is from South Carolina, drove for a colonel in AFSC. He and Lazaro and Papa all had a pretty elegant set-up. They lived in the same apartment as the officers for whom they drove. They were responsible for seeing that the larder was always well stocked with steak and chicken and that there was plenty of good liquor in the refrigerator. This was available for their own use when the officers were away.

Lazaro is from Boston. He reminds me of Bill Sichak from Allegheny. He looks like Sichak, talks like Sichak, has the same mannerisms, is very intelligent, but uneducated. He is a good gambler and has won a thousand dollars in the last week. He is only 24 but has been around. He and Papa came into the army at the same time and have been together ever since. They are good boys. Tom Papa is also from Boston. He drove for General Mollison, head of XV Air Force Service Command. He knew his wife two years before they were married – seven days before he left for overseas. When he had been overseas a while they decided that their marriage had been a mistake and decided to separate. His wife has put all of his allotment checks in the bank since then and has put Papa's 41 Chrysler roadster in storage. I think Papa still likes his wife and that they will become reconciled after he returned. Lazaro does too.

At night when we are in bed not yet asleep we talk about experiences that we have had: Bellvage talked about a friend who was from the same finance office. He ran around quite a lot and wound up catching venereal disease. The finance officer demoted him from staff sergeant to private. He wrote his fiancee, told her about the venereal disease and said that he would not marry her. The way Bellvage tells the story his friend insisted on a court-martial and outwitted his commanding officer and his finance officer and was given back his staff sergeant's rating. His girl friend wouldn't let him break their engagement. They were married when he got home six months ago.

Another story of Al Bellvages: when he went home on TD there was a red-headed Irish soldier in his group. After their thirty days were up they all came back to camp. The Irishman brought his girl back to camp with him and she stayed in the town near the camp. Bellvage said that she had circles under her eyes and obviously hadn't had much sleep. She was a nice girl – pretty, but terribly run down. She and the Irishman had met at the beginning of his furlough and had been together constantly since then – staying up late every night. She wanted to be with him every waking hour and didn't want to let him go. They finally did get married before the Irishman was scheduled to leave. Bellvage said, "He had to so the poor girl could get some sleep." I laughed and asked Bellvage if they were still glad that they got married. "I guess so," said Bellvage, "something happened and he never had to come back overseas, so I guess they're happily married."

Got a two dollar money order from Oster Manufacturing for my birthday.

Sept. 24, Monday. It's nine o'clock and I'm sitting in the lounge of the Morgano Hotel on Capri. This is what happened: the names of the men who were chosen to go to Capri were posted at ten o'clock today. Al Bellvage asked the first sergeant to put me on the orders as I wanted to see the boys in my old company, a detachment of whom were on Capri. Roberts, the first sergeant said, "Let's see, you are the only finance man who didn't go AWOL aren't you?" He said it with a straight face but I think he was kidding. Anyway, Bellvage told him that they could get along without me. I was supposed to help compute the group payroll.

We left at 11:00 AM, ate at the AAF Rest Camp Center in Naples, boarded the boat at 2:00 PM and sailed a half hour later. It was a very rough trip and a lot of people were seasick. It was cloudy and windy and the few people who were on the fore-deck at the beginning of the trip, were soon driven by the spray to the cabin or the aft-deck. I was at the rail a few yards in front of the cabin when we hit a large wave. My jacket was soaked; I retired to the cabin.

After we got up to our hotel – we had to ride the Funiculare – I noticed that there weren't as many people around as there were last July. I should have realized that if we could get rooms in the Morgano it mustn't be crowded. I got a single room, number 84, with a private wash stand. I washed and went downstairs, bought a bar book, then walked down to the MP station with the two packs of cigarettes that I owed Tom Moody. When I got there I asked one of the boys if either Moody or Koester were around, "Hell no", he said, "all of the old boys have gone home. Butler left over a month ago. Moody and Koester left a couple of weeks ago. They all went to the Seventh Replacement Depot." It rained hard outside and I thought,

"Well, I'm going to be the last of the old men to leave Italy". And the rain that was coming down harder now, the rain that heralded the Italian monsoon season was a sort of symbol. It was the end of the summer on Capri, the end of that season when the sun shines every day, week after week and you make plans for swimming or picnicking a month ahead, knowing the constancy of the Italian summer – and the end of the 981st MP Company in its original form – the company consists entirely of replacements now. It was also the end of Italy as a military theater. I wasn't sorry for the ending of all of this, but I had the sort of empty feeling that you get when you pass through a summer resort town in November. The people who are still here are trying to hold on to the intangible essence that was a part of Capri in summer, but it's no good. We'll be in America next summer and Capri will never be as American as she was the last two years.

I walked back from the MP station, drank a rum and coke at the bar, then felt lonesome so I went over to a table where some of the boys from the 535th were drinking. I don't know any of them, but they don't know each other very well either. We've been gathered from many different outfits to form the

535th – a lot of us should have gone home before this. We had three rum and cokes and then ate. The food was good and the rum gave me an appetite. No movie tonight as I've already seen it. Guess I'll read a while and then go to bed.

Sept. 25, Tuesday. Slept soundly last night on a soft mattress and between sheets. It was raining when I awoke and it rained intermittently all day. After breakfast I went down to the hotel lobby and bought a booklet on Capri, read it and mailed it home. I wonder if it will ever get there. At eleven o'clock I went into the bar and drank beer with the boys. We talked about politics and felt pretty mellow after several beers. From the full-length windows in the bar we could look across the valley to Monte Solaris and the villas perched on the slope of the mountain. The castle at the peak of the mountain and the villas on its slopes were blurred through the diaphanous silver curtain of rain. I thought that if I hadn't seen Capri in the rain I wouldn't have known that it could be like this – so isolated and yet self-sufficient. I want to bring Barbara back here someday. After the beer drinking we went up to the dining room and ate.

In the afternoon I went down to the Piazza and bought four tablecloths, a necklace with a bell for Mary Louise and a woodcut of the Faragilioni. I bought these at the AAC Gift Shop. Came back to the Morgano and played casino with one of the boys. While I was waiting for dinner I talked with Ward Goodenough, a sergeant with whom I ate last night. He told me something about himself. He was graduated from Cornell, majored in Scandanavian Ethnology and was in graduate school at Yale when the draft caught him. He is 26, married and has two little girls. He is on detached service from the War Department in the statistics branch of MTOUSA – has been overseas six months. In 1939 when Germany marched into Poland he was in Denmark. He managed to get home by working his way on a freighter. He wants to teach after he gets his Ph. D. He told me a story about the Swede who operates the book store across from the LaPalma Hotel on Capri. The Swede was visiting Capri when war came. He met this Italian girl who was a native of Capri and did not want to leave. The girl's parents were against her marrying a foreigner, especially a Protestant. Finally, the Swede was taken to an internment camp in the vacinity of Naples and the Italian girl visited him frequently. After a year they were married and spent a short honeymoon in the internment camp. When she was about to leave to return to Capri to make peace with her family, she was told that she could not leave the camp as she was now a Swede. After another year the girl's father relented enough to go to the authorities and pave the way for their return to Capri where they were in effect interned. Actually, they were permitted to come and go as they pleased on the island. The couple told Ward that the only Americans they had known until the coming of the American soldiers were the very rich Americans who owned villas on Capri and were snobs. They liked American soldiers.

I went to the show with Ward Goodenough and then we shook hands, wished each other good luck and said we might possibly meet in civilian life. His home is in New Haven.

Sept. 26, Wednesday. Left Capri at nine o 'clock on the little steamer. We had a calm voyage – it took just two hours. Arrived back in the Crater in time for the noon meal. The boys all had colds. When it rained here the area turned into a slew of mud.

Sept. 27, Thursday. The four of us from the Finance Office went up to the Disbursing Section in Staging Area No. 1 and computed a few payrolls. We had a good dinner of pork chops, chocolate cake and ice cream. Saw Rita Hayworth in Tonight and Every Night – we had front row seats as we got there at six o'clock when the show begins at seven.

Sept. 29, 1945, Saturday. Today, Ed Zeisler and I went into Naples. We decided that it would be less monotonous to wonder around the city than to wonder around Crater Haven. We left at one o'clock, hitched a ride on a truck which stopped at the QM Laundry and Dry Cleaning Plant. A couple of officers got out and came back three-quarters of an hour later and announced that they had only one more stop to make before the Red Cross Club. The long wait made us mad and when the truck stopped at Air Force Headquarters, we got out and walked until we came to the Via Roma to the PX where I bought some overseas stripes and a lot of magazines for the boat trip. The PX is just like a department store with Italian girls clerking. Zeisler thinks they're all looking for GI sugar daddies; his theory: the GI's to whom they had attached themselves have been sent back to the states and they're worried about the source of cigarettes, candy, clothes and money. Met Captain Jessup in the PX. He said that he had talked with Major Seitzer who wanted me to come down down to see him and said that he would see that I got back. I don't think that I will have time.

We went down to the Red Cross Center, looked at the movie schedule, and then went to the snack bar. We decided to see Since You Went Away at the Ensa Garrison Cinema at three o'clock (according to the Red Cross schedule). We walked up the Via Roma to the theater and found that the show had begun at two o'clock and the next one started at five o'clock. We went to a theater where there were news reels and left at four-thirty and went back to the Garrison Cinema. The picture was excellent, the best I've seen this year. Claudette Colbert gets my vote for the Oscar this year – Ingrid Bergman gets second for Saratoga Trunk. It was a masterpiece for direction too.

After the picture we walked down the Via Roma in the rain The sidewalks are so narrow on this street that it is necessary for half of the pedestrians to walk on the street – something should be done about it.

We stopped in the snack bar again, then asked the MP at the entrance to the Red Cross Center if there was a good bar in the vacinity – it being Ed Zeisler's idea that a birthday should be celebrated with at least one drink; however, the bars were closed. We crossed the street to the car park and got in a truck which we were told was leaving for Crater Haven at nine. We waited for an hour in the crowded, hot, airless truck, then climbed into another truck which got to Crater Haven at ten-thirty.

When we came near our tent there was a sense of excitement. Baker, Lazaro and Papa had been at the dice table and had won $3,000. They were talking about forming a partnership to buy a race horse when they got back to the states.

This was a memorable twenty-eighth birthday and my heart went out to Ed Zeisler who tried to make it a happy one. My next one will be the best for a long time, I have a hunch.

Oct. 2, Tuesday. Today is the day that we were scheduled to leave Italy – it seems that our boat has been delayed. The latest schedule of shipments has the 535th listed as sailing on the Lownsdale with a question mark as to the date of departure and another question mark as to the port of debarkation (this was formerly listed as New York).

I wonder what Barbara must be thinking. I'll have to write her tomorrow and explain. I didn't want to tell her that our sailing had been delayed, but now that it may be a matter of a week, I'll have to write. I'm certainly having trouble getting home. I'm so tired of this business. I can't think how it will be to be with Barbara again. I wish I would get some mail. It worries me when I lose contact and yet I know it's just that she thinks I've already started. I messed up her summer school too. I shouldn't be complaining – I got through the war alive and uninjured. All I have to do now is make it back home.

Today I read James Hilton's So Well Remembered. It isn't in a class with his better books. Think I'll read A. J. Cronin's The Green Years – if I can get it at the library, a room at the rear of the snack bar. We've had rain quite often lately – Italy's monsoon season has set in. I'm sitting alone in the tent writing this. Just returned from a Class B movie, Caribbean Mystery. The other boys are up shooting crap or watching. The boys who built tables for the acie-ducie crap games have lights so that they are able to add to their income for the day. Some of the "house-men" have made over two thousand dollars during their stay here. The way it works is this: when a man throws an ace and a duce on his first roll for a point, the one who fades the shooter gets his money back and the house-man gets the shooter's bet. The house-man is the man who originally built the table or it could be someone who purchased the table from a builder. Some of the tables have several partners. All of the tables are thriving, although there is a post order forbidding organized gambling. Most of the men feel that this order was instigated by the permanent party men who formerly held a sort of monopoly on the acie-ducie tables. We've been here so long that our men know all the ropes. I hope we leave soon as I want to go home.

Oct. 3, 1945, Wednesday. Today four of us went into Naples. Gillen, Bellvage, Vito Cipriani and I arrived in Naples at eleven o'clock. We walked slowly up the Via Roma taking in the Italian atmosphere and deciding to eat at an Italian establishment if the opportunity presented itself. We walked up to the museum and one of the little street urchins asked us if we wanted to eat. We asked him if the place was clean and out-of-bounds (it was both). We followed him for several blocks through a maze of side streets, then into a ghetto where the stench of fish and old meat permeated the air. Next he led us up a flight of steps to a vacant lot, then into a building. One other soldier was there – a lone wolf type. We ate at a table on a balcony – spaghetti, fried potatoes, eggs and sweet vermouth. We felt a little lost there. Naples always depresses me. There are too many people with nothing to do, working so hard just to survive. I think they should be forgiven for their questionable business practices with allied soldiers. As an example of that, the lone wolf who was eating in an inside room came out on the balcony and said, "I'd like to let you fellows in on a little deal here. I can get you good American whisky, Four Roses at twelve dollars a quart". We told him that we weren't interested. At first, I thought that the soldier might have his own black market on genuine American whisky but this was not the case. Vito, who speaks Italian, talked to the boy who brought us in. He told Vito that another little urchin had gotten the whisky for the lone wolf, that it is Italian whisky in a Four Roses bottle. "No buono", he said. Then I remembered hearing stories of such dealings when I first came to Italy. We didn't say anything to the lone-wolf corporal. He may never know – may think that Four Roses is a terrible whisky for the rest of his life.

We left the house after paying three dollars a plate for the spaghetti and two-fifty for the vermouth. All of the Italians wished us "Bon voyage and bon fortuna". They know that almost everyone in Naples is waiting to go home. Vito and I went to the museum and Bellvage and Gillen went to the show. The museum has a fine collection of statuary and bronzes. The upper floors are not yet open to the public. I was sorry as I wanted to see the paintings. Our guide was an old man who wore a brown, olive-drab knit skull cap, shell-rimmed spectacles, dirty shirt with a frayed tie, baggy trousers. His mustache was untrimmed. He had a kindly look in his eyes that seemed to apologize for everything about the place. He soon convinced us that he knew what he was talking about; that of the ancient Greek sculptors Praxitiles was the master who specialized in female figures, even his male figures were rather effeminate; that Policlites was the master of the male figure, huge of muscle. The only think that I can remember is a bronze bust of Berenice by Miron. Berenice was the most beautiful woman in Greece, and I would say that she was beautiful. Of course, I enjoyed all of the busts of the famous Greeks and Romans – ugly, kindly old Socrates, Plato, Aristotle, Herodatus, Solon, Julius Caesar, Tiberius, Augustus, the Ptolemies, and Titus. Most of these were found around Naples, Pompeii, Herculaneum and Pozzuli.

We left the museum at about four and walked down the Via Roma to the Red Cross, noting that the store windows were

William M. Kennedy

full of merchandise – men's shirts $21.00, men's shoes $65.00. We decided to see And Now Tomorrow at the Red Cross Theatre on the third floor of the Red Cross Building. We ate at the G.I. Restaurant opposite PBS headquarters and then saw the movie. It was a good movie. We came back in a truck that left after the show was finished. I felt good as we were riding down the highway that skirts the Bay of Naples. It was cool and the red lights on the cars ahead of us, the lights scattered on the hills of Naples to our right made me feel good. It was not a bad day for a day overseas.

When we got back to the Crater everything was quiet in the tent: it seems that the race-horse investment trust sought to add to their holdings (envisioning a stable of race horses) and lost the entire $3,000 at the crap tables.

Oct. 4, Thursday. This morning I wrote Barbara that I would arrive around the first of November. I wish that I would get a letter from her, but of course she has been expecting me since September 5th. Our ship was in Trieste a couple of days ago (according to rumor) and was to put in at another port for a week and arrive in Naples about the 14th – all according to rumor.

In the afternoon Vito and I went on the group truck to see Pompeii. I saw much more than I did when we stopped on the way back from Rome. We saw the amphitheater which is very well preserved and a couple of houses of prostitution with their lewd pictures. Sometimes I think that is the main attraction at Pompeii for the service men. Our guide explained that the symbol of good fortune, fertility and happiness in ancient Pompeii was the penis and testicles. Representations of these are found above the entrances to shops and on many monuments. It may be as he says, but the religion of the people of Pompeii was Polytheism. It would seem that they became so degenerate that a sort of phallic worship existed apart from their regular religion.

As we were walking up the Via Veteii, a group of British sailors were in front of us. The last sailor had a girl with him. She looked like a lady of easy virtue. The fact that she had earth on the back of her green jacket in places where the earth would naturally cling while she was engaged in practicing the oldest profession, caused considerably comment and knowing laughter.

The House of the Veteii is one of the best preserved in Pompeii. It has been partially restored as it is one of the best examples of the style of the homes of the Roman aristocrats. There is one room with pictures showing the various positions of the sex act. To view these pictures the guide takes the gentlemen and ladies in separate groups; naturally, this is a difficult time for the ladies as they are obliged to look nonchalant and unknowing as they stand in one of the hallways while the soldiers carry on as soldiers do. The girl in the green jacket went in with the sailors and came out laughing. She was very composed. Next we saw the baths where two bodies were found in the excavations and covered with plaster of paris and enclosed in a glass case. I guess this was to show the general configuration of the people who lived in the first century (Pompeii was destroyed by the eruption of Mount Vesuvius in 79 AD).

We went to the modern town of Pompeii where we had muscatelle wine (very bad at $2.50 a bottle) and entertainment (a violinist and a guitarist who played the Pennsylvania Polka very badly). The sailors and the girl in the green jacket came in, went to the garden, then came back again. Someone had brushed off the mud on her jacket. She carried her toilet articles in a loose-knit (fish-net) bag after the fashion of the traveling whores in Italy today.

We rode on to Naples in the rain. We lost two of our party just before we went through the Holy Rosary Cathedral. This is said to be one of the richest in the world. There are diamonds inlaid in the picture above the alter (Our Lady of Pompeii) and gold leaf and silver on the walls at various places throughout the cathedral. We ate at the Oriente restaurant, opposite PBS headquarters in Naples and got back to Crater Haven at eight o'clock. The two lost men got back to the crator some time later-drunk. Another day has passed.

October 9, 1945 – Tuesday. Aboard the Daniel H. Lownsdale, fitted Liberty ship 10,000 tons. It's twenty minutes to ten in the evening and we are four hours out of Naples. It's a wonderful feeling to be going home. I am writing this in my bunk which is the third from the bottom. It is shaking up and down from the vibration of the ship. We are to stop at Oran for some cement for ballast ("balance", the sailor who gave us this inside information called it). They say we'll be about twenty days at sea to New York. Our meal tonight was wonderful – baked ham, yellow beans, salad, baked potato, fresh butter, pineapple and ice cream in dixie cups for dessert.

This whole business came up very suddenly yesterday at noon. I was going into Naples to see a movie and intended to leave at one in the afternoon. At noon all passes were canceled and we were told that we would be leaving the next day or the day after. We had our physical inspection, got our custom slips and were all set. This afternoon at one-thirty we got into trucks, left Crater Haven for the last time, came through Naples into the port area. We were lined up on the quay and waited for some time. The wait was made easier by the Red Cross girls who passed out doughnuts and coffee. The Red Cross has done a wonderful job for my money. They have made things a lot easier for us. Finally, we marched single file up the gangplank from the quay to the hull of an Italian vessel. This was either bombed or scuttled. It lies on its side and is used as a dock. We walked along the hull of this vessel onto the Daniel H. Lownsdale. My duffle bag felt like a ton of bricks – I'm out of condition. We ate dinner and went on deck in time for our embarkation at 5:30 PM. We watched the lights of Naples grow dimmer and dimmer, passed quite close to Capri off our starboard side. The only landmarks we could recognize in the dusk were the Faraglioni, those giant rocks that loom out of the sea. A few lights flickered on the island and several lighthouses were blinking. Guess I'll go to bed.

Oct. 10, 1945, Wednesday. The weather has been good as we continue smoothly on course toward Oran. We are to have three meals a day, not two as we thought. The noon meal is a light one. My appetite has been good, better than it was at Crater Haven. The meals have been delicious—fresh lettuce salad, fresh milk (frozen, then thawed), fresh meat, ice cream, oranges, cereal, milk and cookies – all delicacies that remind us of the deminishing miles to home. I can't believe it, not yet, not until I see the Statue of Liberty. And then not until I kiss Barbara.

We saw a movie tonight, Hudson Bay, an old picture but we enjoyed it. We have a radio speaker in our compartment and were able to hear the the final game of the World Series which the Tigers won handily nine to three. I spent most of the day reading "Yankee From Olympus", the story of the life of Oliver Wendell Holmes, Jr. He had such illustrious forbears that he couldn't help being a success. He seems to have been all mind – too cold for me.

Oct. 13, 1945, Saturday. It's one o'clock and we are docked at a small town west of Oran – taking on manganese ore. Yesterday at noon we pulled up outside the harbor at Oran. We could see the city sitting on top of the rugged cliffs that formed the shore. When the lights came on at night we wished that we could have gone ashore to see Oran. It looked quite modern with high stone buildings, much like Tunis. On the nearest shore the houses were of wood and could have been the homes of fishermen or summer homes of the more affluent. The ship's motor launch took off for the town with some of the ship's officers and high-ranking army officers. When they returned we learned that our destination had been changed from New York to Hampton Roads, Virginia. It's still home.

Last night we saw "Home in Indiana". It was the second time for most of us but still a good movie. During the night we lifted anchor, to use a hackneyed phrase, and as we awoke, were docking at this small town (Tafna, I think) to load manganese. We are quite close to the town and some of the boys are seeing their first Arab (pronounced Ay-rab by the GI's) and laugh as they watch the sheeted figures slowly climbing the switchback path that ascends the steep mountain to the Arab village at the top. There is a certain rugged beauty about this small harbor.

The manganese ore is mined close by and transported in tiny cars drawn by a midget steam engine to the pier. It is then dumped into a loading crane which pours the ore into the hold of our ship. The stone pier and nearby buildings are covered with the red manganese dust. I was reminded of one of the jobs that I had when I worked for Armco Steel during the year that I worked to earn money for my last year at college. My job was to lift the large pieces of manganese (called pyrolucite) into a grinder that made fine pieces to be used in the open hearth melt. The fine manganese dust got all through my system (just like the sand in a desert sand storm) and I tasted pyrolucite every time I burped for the next several days.

The Arabs row out to the ship to trade straw hats, straw shoes and wine for cigarettes and candy. They want clothing and soap, but no one has these articles, so they settle for cigarettes and candy. Early this morning we watched an Arab boy unload baskets of fish from a large row boat. He dumped the fish into several other baskets, distributing them so that each basket was about a quarter full. He took each basket in turn and held it in the sea, raising and lowering the basket, using it as a strainer to clean the fish – picking out the damaged ones and throwing them back into the sea. Some of the smaller boys swam out to the ship shouting "candy". Some of the soldiers threw coins to them. The little boys are naked and are almost black.

I finished William Faulkner's "Sanctuary". It was written to make money as Faulkner admits in the introduction. I agree with him. The story is crude, but the writing is even more crude. I wonder if he ever wrote for the pulps? He has done some fine short stories, but this is very bad.

Yesterday I wrote a letter to Barbara. It will be mailed from Oran and should reach her about a week before I get to the states. I am sitting on the number one hatch taking a sun bath from the waist up. The African sun is warm.

Oct. 14, Sunday. Today at 9:00 AM we passed Gibralter. It's a huge rock connected to the mainland by a sort of isthmus. To our left we could see the coast of Africa; to our right Gibralter and then Spain. The shore looked barren.

Oct. 15, Monday. The sea was rough all day, many of the men were sick. I ate every meal – felt queasy. After we passed Gibralter there were a lot of dolphins that seemed to be attracted to the ship. They jumped right out of the water, seemed to us to be about twelve feet long, were unbelievably fast as they swam round and round the ship. They were having a good time chasing one another.

Oct. 18, Thursday. Since Monday the Daniel H has been bucking and rolling like a rodeo steer. The sea has been rough, the sky cloudy and we have had several rainy spells. Today the ship is still rocking but the sun is out and the sky is blue in places. About half of us have been seasick and the rest of us have not felt too chipper. Vito Cipriani has had a bad time. He has eaten very little since Monday breakfast when he became sick in the middle of that meal.

The latest information is that we will dock in Boston, but there are rumors that the captain believes that we will yet dock in New York. Tonight at midnight we set our watches back another hour; that will be the third hour we have gained. We gain six altogether from Gibralter to the east coast.

I'm beginning to remember that first unpleasant voyage on the West Point – the difficulty of keeping clean by using salt water – regular soap won't dissolve and there doesn't appear to be enough saltwater soap. You feel greasy all the time, your hair feels thick and matted. In this ship we have hot water, but it's either so hot that you can't use it or it's cold. When I shave in the morning, I can't wash off the shaving cream. I use brushless as salt water doesn't make a lather. When I finish shaving I wipe off the excess cream with a towel. Do I mind all of this? Not much, I'm going home! I'm worrying about how Barbara is going to be; if she will think that I've changed; if she will have changed. Three years is a long time and so many things could happen. I could make a mental case of myself if I went on and on. I tell myself that our love is enough to bridge a three-year vacuum.

Economically, things in the states seem in an awful mess – strikes, strikes, strikes. I wonder how many of the strikers were overseas.

Oct. 22, 1945, Monday. According to the latest information via the mimeographed single-sheet newspaper which a couple of the boys put out, this will be our last Monday at sea – providing we have good weather. We are supposed to dock at Boston next Sunday, the 28th of October.

For the last three days the ship has been rolling from side to side, sometimes at a very acute angle. One time, just as we were about to go down to mess, the ship leaned to one side and all of the condiments in the racks at the ends of the tables fell to the floor. These items were anchored in little niches arranged like bottled milk cases or soda-pop cases, so the ship did list to quite a degree to dump them on the floor.

For the last two days I've been playing Hearts with Cherry, Hallsey, and Ed Zeisler. The time goes quickly; also, I've not had a cigarette since Saturday morning before breakfast – almost a record, I guess. This time, I've really quit. Must remember my sinuses.

It rained last night but today seems like another clear day. It has been warm enough that we can take off our shirts in the afternoon. I imagine that we are near Florida in the matter of latitude. We are going to sail over to the longitude of Boston (I hope I have this longitude and latitude business correct) and then straight up to Boston; thus, if we have a last-minute change in orders we can proceed to Hampton Roads or New York without any loss of time.

One of the boys in our ship is a cook named Adams. He is married to an Italian girl from Cerignola; she is waiting in Naples for transportation to the states. I wonder if it was impossible for him to wait there with her. It's a very trying time for the girls who are waiting shipment to the states.

I've been reading selections from the poems of Keats and Shelley – Armed Services Edition. I'll always remember them when I think of Rome. Finished some short stories of Damon Runyan. He drinks forty cups of coffee a day. One more week to go. I think it will be pretty wonderful getting back to the states. I hope Barbara and I can get a furnished apartment. I suppose everyone else is thinking of the same thing. It's pretty hard for us with me being the "first-in, last-out" category. What the hell do I want – egg in my beer? I've still got my life, limbs and my love. That's batting pretty close to a thousand in any wartime league. Guess I'll go on deck and play some hearts.

Oct. 23, 1945, Tuesday. The ship's newspaper came out with the very latest dope yesterday – that is that we are going directly to Boston and not west to the southern coast and north along the coast. This will enable us to dock next Saturday according to the Daniel H. Dogwatch (the name of the newspaper).

Yesterday the waves increased in size until in the evening they were larger than the ship itself and we were bobbing all over the ocean like a toy boat. The sea took on that slate color and the crests of the waves were white. The wind whips off the tops of the waves and lashes the spray on the ship. I went to the fantail last night about seven o'clock. The ship would ride over a big wave and the propeller screw would be lifted out of the water spraying water high in the air; the rear of the ship rides high up, very high and then when the wave passes, it goes down until the wave is higher than the ship itself. I stayed at the rear of the ship holding on to the rail and getting salt spray showered on me. When I tried to go to the front of the ship, there was a guard there who stopped everyone who tried to go up front. Four of us played hearts in the mess halls and then at eleven o'clock we all walked back to number four hatch and examined the night. The moon was out but there weren't many stars – too cloudy.

At this time the waves began to grow larger and this continued all night. Everyone was awake. I may have slept an hour all told during the night. It was quite an experience. There were times when I had to hold on to my bunk to keep from being thrown out. Mess kits, bottles, barracks bags, peanut cans and books flew down from shelves and tables and slid around on the floor of our hatch. The table with the books and cards fell over and something banged in the hold with such periodic concussion (in phase with the list of the ship) that we expected the side of the ship to give way and the water to pour in. It's been a very trying journey but what the hell do I want – I'm going home.

Oct. 24, 1945, Wednesday. Last night I heard a radio program from Philadelphia; it was long-wave and for the first time in three years I heard a radio advertisement. This one was for Ivory Soap. I didn't listen to any more of the program, but I think it was Vic and Sade. We saw Mary Martin, Herb Marshall and Sue Peters in "Young Ideas". It was pretty funny though I like a little more subtlety in my comedy.

Today I am dining room orderly. It isn't too much of a detail. I just keep two tables supplied in coffee, milk, sugar and clean off the tables after each serving. There are five servings per meal; that means I take care of eighty men. The only other detail I've had this trip to date was cleaning the latrine one day. It hasn't been bad. The weather has been wonderful since yesterday afternoon. The sea is blue again. It's going to be a wonderful homecoming. I'm beginning to feel like a spark of life remains in my worn-out old body.

Oct. 26, 1945, Friday. Tomorrow we expect to walk off of this ship and on to U.S. soil again. It has been foggy since early this morning. Around five o'clock the deep foghorn of the Daniel H. Lownsdale blew and has blown at three-minute intervals since then. I awoke at four-thirty and felt very cold. I put on my wool sweater over my T-shirt and went back to sleep. This winter will probably be a severe one for me. I've become a hothouse creature since I left the states.

Last night we saw a stage show presented by the soldiers aboard ship – the ones with talent. Most of us enjoyed it. One of the GI's in the band had a cello which he had made from plexi-glass. It was a beautiful piece of work and to my untutored ear sounded like any other cello.

After the "Veteran's Jamboree" we saw a movie, "Honeymoon Lodge". It wasn't very good, but served to pass the time. After the movie we went down to the mess hall and played hearts; then, up on deck to talk for a while about the army and how glad we would be when we're out of it. I wonder how long we'll have to wait for our discharge.

At a quarter to four this afternoon we saw land, low in the sky and above our native country. Terns had been following the ship since yesterday and today smaller birds flew about the ship. It is very cold tonight. It has been a very cold day. The fog has been so thick that it has been a drizzle on the ship. It would have been a cheerless day but for the fact that we are on the threshold of home. None of us minded the weather. We commented about it because it is habitual in the army to talk about anything that is different from one day to the next. Because there is so little to occupy the mind, we need to check each other's reaction to any change. We need to prove to ourselves that we are able to think and observe as individuals even though we are in the army. So today we said "It's cold today", and that's the end of it. Our thoughts are all of home.

Tonight we see the lights of the area in the vacinity of Boston. We hear the radio programs emanating from Boston. Tomorrow at 5:30 we get up, eat K rations at 6:00, and (rumor has it) leave the ship in the morning at 8:00. We are the first unit to leave the ship. I must shave tonight before I go to bed. Will continue when next I have the chance.

Oct. 29, 1945, Monday. I'm in the barracks at Camp Myles Standish at Taunton, Mass; it's about an hour's ride from Boston. I thought I ought to set down my first impressions of my native land while I remember them.

Saturday morning as our ship pulled into the harbor the sun was rising and on several piers were welcome home signs. We left the ship at about nine o'clock, marched to a train platform, were given a pint of milk and doughnuts by some Red Cross girls, got on the train and were on our way.

The train passed slowly through the city and at every crossing and from the windows of the houses, from automobiles, from the trains, from brakemen we were cheered; people waved and smiled at us. The children waved and smiled in welcome. As the train moved on the same thought kept running through my mind – a phrase from Sir Walter Scott's "The Lay of the Last Minstrel": "This is my own, my native land, this is my own, my native land"

People waved from those flimsy frame houses that border a railroad line – the war is a great leveler. We passed a large green lot where boys were playing football and the soldiers shouted at them. They felt good inside seeing those boys playing football with all their hearts. That's America to us. In Europe the kids don't play like that. It may be that the war has robbed them of their childhood. We passed through some beautiful forest land. The trees were dressed for autumn, the air was crisp and several hunters were out with their dogs – that's America too.

When we got off at Camp Myles Standish we marched to the theater where a band played and we heard some orientation talks. After a steak dinner I went up to the telephone building.

I knew that Barbara would know that I was in because I read in the Boston paper of our arrival. I placed my call and waited twenty-five minutes for it. Then I heard her voice and I knew that everything was all right. I forget what we talked about but I know that she has a furnished apartment for us. We move in on November 7th.

Sunday morning, yesterday, I called Mother and Dad. Told them that I would call again from Indiantown Gap where we are going this morning.

EPILOGUE

It has been more than 60 years since I was mustered out of the army at Indiantown Gap. My last entry on October 29, 1945 was written in the barracks at Camp Miles Standish at Taunton, Mass. At Indiantown Gap in Pennsylvanis we were given new army uniforms, received our final pay checks, and were encouraged to join the national guard.

I remember that Barbara met me at the train station in Cleveland on Friday morning November 2nd. We could not get a hotel room as that was the weekend of a very big football game so Barbara's father drove us to Oberlin where we spent the weekend at the Oberlin Inn.

Barbara and I lived in the furnished apartment of a woman who was spending the winter in Arizona. When she returned we moved in with Barbara's folks. The company that I worked for before the war hired me back as an accountant. I began taking night classes in accounting at Cleveland College.

Barbara completed her teaching contract in June and took over the work of running the home that had been her parents; this was necessary as the chemotherapy treatments which her mother needed made it difficult for her to do the housework.

Our son was born in 1947 and our daughter was born in 1949. I joined Barbara's church and have attended regularly.

After many years of night classes I received a Master of Business Administration degree in 1955 and eventually became a Certified Public Accountant in Ohio in 1961.

In 1961 I began my own public accounting practice. At the time I did not have any clients but Barbara was able to get a position as a full time teacher again. When I first set up an office to do accounting, I needed to keep the office girl busy until I had enough accounting work. I had the girl type copies of my diary from the fourteen notebooks that had been gathering dust in a cardboard box over the years.

Barbara and I have celebrated our sixty-seventh wedding anniversary – the first three anniversaries were during the war. We have had some health problems but consider ourselves fortunate to be wearing out at the same rate.

I often wonder what happened to the men that I lived with in the army. I have not seen any one of them in all of the years since we were discharged. It seems that I was too busy. I would like to tell them that I wished them all well.

William M. Kennedy